Orientation

Pity the traveler who strives to know Mexico in merely a few days or weeks. The country so blithely caricatured by outsiders as the land of mariachis and swaying palms encompasses 31 states, several mountain ranges and volcanoes, vast deserts and diminishing rain forests, and the second-largest city in the world. The languid **Caribbean Sea** slithers against her eastern shores on the white sands of the **Yucatán**, while 2,000 miles west the **Pacific Ocean** pounds the stalwart granite cliffs of the **Baja California Peninsula**. The volcanoes **Ixtaccíhuatl** and **Popocatépetl** slumber under caps of virgin snow over the smoggy skyline of **Mexico City**, a metropolis of some 20 million residents that's the site of world-class museums and restaurants. The capital city was built on the site of **Tenochtitlán**, the center of Aztec civilization, and you can explore the temples of this ancient city-state alongside archaeologists from around the globe.

Such contrasts of nature and culture attract hundreds of thousands of visitors to Mexico each year, much to the federal government's delight. The growth of tourism has been the goal of most presidential administrations since 1974, when an agency dubbed **FONATUR** (the National Foundation for Tourism Development) took on the task of creating megaresorts from huge swaths of jungle and sand. **Cancún** was the first offspring, followed by **Los Cabos** and **Ixtapa**. Their success begat the revivals of **Puerto Vallarta**, **Acapulco**, and **Mazatlán**, as well as **Loreto** and **Huatulco**, where competition from the newcomers sparked a frenzy of modernization.

The government wisely focused on the country's most desirable attributes along the shores of the Pacific Ocean and the Caribbean Sea. This guidebook follows that lead by offering an in-depth tour of Mexico's most popular locales, including the east and west coasts of mainland Mexico and the southern tip of the Baja California Peninsula. Mexico City is covered as a destination unto itself, a popular stopover on the way to both coasts.

Just about every coastline in Mexico has a culture and flavor of its own. The **Yucatán Peninsula**, which includes the states of **Yucatán**, **Campeche**, and **Quintana Roo**, is Caribbean in style and mood, with jungles wrapped around Maya ruins. Mexico's mainland Pacific coast, this country's version of the French Riviera, incorporates Mazatlán, Puerto Vallarta, **Manzanillo**, Ixtapa, **Zihuatanejo**, Acapulco, and miles of beaches both secluded and settled. Los Cabos, at the southern tip of the Baja Peninsula, bisects the merger of the Pacific Ocean and the **Mar de Cortés** (Sea of Cortez) with the desert foothills of the **Sierra Gigante.**

Travelers, primarily from the United States, Canada, Europe, and Japan, now swarm over Mexico's shores. Some bask in the Acapulco sun, sipping piña coladas by sapphire-blue pools, while others clamber about the temples of **Tulum,** puzzling over Maya mysteries as they gaze upon the sea. Naturalists gather sea-turtle eggs under midnight skies, guarding endangered leatherbacks from extinction during annual migrations to Quintana Roo's shores, and snorkelers and divers cruise silently along **Cozumel**'s coral reefs, captivated by eels, groupers, and millions of neon-colored fish.

Naturally, this influx has brought great change to the beaches where recluses once sought refuge. Four-lane highways have replaced dusty dirt roads, and rustic beach huts are dwarfed by big-name hotels. But hideaways do exist on Mexico's soft sand beaches and rugged clifftops. You can still stretch a hammock between two palms at the end of an unmarked trail and watch the sunset. You may have to wander away from the sybaritic zones of commerce and lavish consumption, but you can find simplicity, solitude, and a sense of undeveloped space in this vast country. After all, variety is one of Mexico's greatest appeals.

Maya jaguar bas-relief

MEXICO ACCESS® is arranged by city so you can see at a glance where you are and what is around you. The numbers next to the entries in the chapters correspond to the numbers on the maps. The type is color-coded according to the kind of place described:

Restaurants/Clubs: Red   **Hotels:** Blue

Shops/ Outdoors: Green   **Sights/Culture:** Black

Rating the Restaurants and Hotels

The restaurant ratings take into account the quality, service, atmosphere, and uniqueness of the restaurant. An expensive restaurant doesn't necessarily ensure an enjoyable evening; however, a small, relatively unknown spot could have good food, professional service, and a lovely atmosphere. Therefore, on a purely subjective basis, stars are used to judge the overall dining value (see the star ratings at right). Keep in mind that chefs and owners often change, which sometimes drastically affects the quality of a restaurant. The ratings in this guidebook are based on information available at press time.

The price ratings, as categorized at right, apply to restaurants and hotels. These figures describe general price-range relationships between other restaurants and hotels in the area. The restaurant price ratings are based on the average cost of an entrée for one person, excluding tax and tip. Hotel price ratings reflect the base price of a standard room for two people for one sight during the peak season.

Restaurants

★	Good	
★★	Very Good	
★★★	Excellent	
★★★★	An Extraordinary Experience	
$	The Price Is Right	(less than $10)
$$	Reasonable	($10-$15)
$$$	Expensive	($15-$25)
$$$$	Big Bucks	($25 and up)

Hotels

$	The Price Is Right	(less than $80)
$$	Reasonable	($80-$120)
$$$	Expensive	($120-$180)
$$$$	Big Bucks	($180 and up)

Map Key

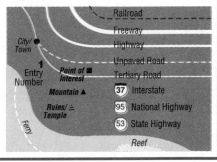

Railroad	
Freeway	
City/Town	Highway
Unpaved Road	
Entry Number Point of Interest	Tertiary Road
Mountain ▲	37 Interstate
Ruins/ Temple	95 National Highway
Ferry	53 State Highway
Reef	

To call Mexico from the US, dial 011-52-area code-number.

Getting to Mexico
By Air

Mexico City's **Aeropuerto Internacional de Benito Juárez** (Benito Juárez International Airport) is Mexico's hub, with connections made by numerous international and regional carriers. Connections can also be made in the capital cities of most states. For more information and local phone numbers, see the orientation of your desired destination in the following pages.

Airlines

Aeroméxico	800/237.6639
AeroCalifornia	800/237.6225
Alaska Airlines	800/426.0333
Continental	800/525.0280
Delta	800/221.1212
Mexicana	800/531.7921
Northwest	800/225.2525

By Car

Drivers bringing cars from the US into Mexico must present the following documents: The car's ownership papers, original vehicle registration, or car rental agreement; a notarized letter from the bank or finance company (if the car is leased or financed) stating that you have permission to take the car into Mexico; an insurance policy from a Mexican insurance company to cover the length of your stay (US insurance is not valid in Mexico); a credit card in the same name as the car owner, to be used to cover the processing fee (without a credit card, you may have to pay a bond equal to the value of the car); a valid driver's license; proof of nationality such as a passport or birth certificate (Latin Americans in particular should carry documentation proving their US residency to avoid trouble leaving Mexico—a driver's license or tax forms will suffice); and a valid Mexican Tourist Card (see "Customs and Immigration" on page 6). US, Canadian, and international driver's licenses are valid in Mexico.

Mexican auto insurance must be purchased at the border or before crossing it. For more information, contact **Sanborn's Mexico Insurance,** PO Box 310, Department FR, 2009 S 10th St, McAllen, TX 78502. 210/686.0711; fax 210/686.0732.

Car Rental Agencies are available at all tourist centers, but you may get a better rate by reserving in advance through one of the following companies:

Avis	800/331.1212
Budget	800/527.0700
Hertz	800/654.3131
National	800/227.7368

Getting around Mexico

Buses Traveling by bus is one of the best ways to fully experience Mexico, and it's becoming a far more pleasant mode of transportation. Granted, if you're determined to ride with the chickens and pigs, you can do so on the agonizingly slow second-class lines that travel to every hamlet and pueblo between two major points. But first-class service is a bargain as well. For a few pesos more you can travel in air-conditioned comfort in an assigned seat with a window. (No matter what class you travel, be sure to carry toilet paper, bottled water, and snacks.) Most major routes are also serviced by luxury motor-coaches with reclining seats, air-conditioning, refreshments, and even music videos on television screens. In major cities the various bus lines are housed in a central terminal, in separate terminals divided into first and second class, or in terminals for specific destinations. Schedules are normally posted on the wall, and you can buy your tickets in advance for the more popular routes.

Driving For information on the myriad requirements one must satisfy before driving in Mexico, see "Getting to Mexico by Car" above.

Taxis The first and most important rule for using Mexican taxis is to confirm the price of your ride *before* the cab starts moving. If language is a problem, have the driver write the amount on a piece of paper in new pesos or dollars. Rates are regulated in many tourist areas, and hotels post the prices for the most common destinations. Mexico City cabs finally have meters, which simplifies matters unless the driver insists the meter is broken. In addition to being an inexpensive and convenient way to travel within a given city, taxis are ideal for getting to and from sights such as ruins and isolated beaches, especially if you can converse with the driver. Some will charge an hourly rate to guide you from one attraction to the next, and are sure to offer unusual observations and tidbits of gossip that you wouldn't get on a more organized tour.

Trains Although trains travel throughout much of Mexico, they vary considerably in comfort and safety. Major routes from Mexico City usually offer a first-class section, where attendants keep the car relatively clean and serve refreshments. First class may be fairly comfortable or totally horrid, depending on the condition of the train and the number of passengers. On long trips the train may be clean at the beginning of your journey, but conditions may rapidly deteriorate into a mess of discarded trash as the trip progresses. The rest rooms are particularly dreadful after a few hours—carry your own toilet paper and practice holding your breath. And unless you are an absolute masochist, forget about second class. The ultimate in comfort are the private sleeping compartments, which are definitely worth the extra cost on long trips.

For more information on schedules and fares, contact **Mexico By Rail,** PO Box 3508, Laredo, TX 78044, 800/228.3225; or **National Railways of Mexico,** Terminal Buenavista, Mexico City, DF 06358, 5/5478972.

FYI

Climate The Pacific and Caribbean coasts are both ideal winter getaways, with little or no rain, air temperatures hovering in the 80s or 90s, and water temperatures in the 70s or above. Both the air and water are warmer the farther south you travel along the Pacific coast; it can be downright chilly in Mazatlán in January, yet hot enough for a sunburn in Acapulco. Los Cabos, at the tip of the Baja California Peninsula, is best in the fall and spring, as it gets windy and cold in January and February and unbearably hot from July through September. The Caribbean is at its best from November through May; the rains and subsequent humidity build through the summer months toward hurricane season in September and October. The high altitude makes Mexico City cool from December through February and rainy from June through September. The best time to visit is in the autumn or spring, when it's warm and dry.

Customs and Immigration Visitors to Mexico are issued a Mexican Tourist Card upon entering the country. You must have a passport or a birth certificate as well as a photo ID to prove your nationality—a driver's license alone will not suffice. The customs official gives you one copy of the Tourist Card (actually a flimsy piece of paper); guard it carefully, since replacing it can be an absolute nightmare. Your copy will be confiscated when you leave Mexico, and you'll need a passport or birth certificate to pass through **US Customs** on the way home. You are allowed to bring $400 in purchases, one liter of alcohol, and one carton of cigarettes from Mexico into the US every 30 days.

Travelers under the age of 18 traveling without parents or guardians must have a notarized affidavit signed by both parents or the legal guardian granting permission to travel in Mexico. This law is occasionally enforced by the customs guards in border towns frequented by teenagers in search of a good time.

Dress Shorts, T-shirts, and bathing suits are acceptable in all the coastal resorts, but this kind of attire is generally frowned upon in Mexico City and in small, conservative towns. Respect local customs and don't wear shorts, tank tops, or halter tops in churches. Men rarely need a full suit and tie unless attending a very formal event.

Drinking Tequila and beer are to Mexico what wine is to France—national beverages that accompany nearly every meal or social occasion. Tequila can be as rough as firewater or as smooth as sherry; drink cheap tequila and you'll regret it for days to come. Be wary of free margaritas served at Happy Hours or on boat tours. They're normally made with the cheapest tequila around—if you feel a stabbing pain in your temples after a few sips, switch to mineral water or beer. Several great beers are brewed in different regions of the country; in the Yucatán try Negro Modelo, León Negra, or Montejo. Wineries in Baja California produce respectable table wines that are much cheaper than the imported wines. Imported liquors such as scotch, whiskey, and gin are extremely expensive.

The legal drinking age in Mexico is 18.

Health Nothing destroys a vacation more effectively than a bout of turista that leaves you glued to the bathroom floor. The diarrhea, nausea, vomiting, and chills can pass in a few hours or linger for days, causing serious health problems. To prevent the onslaught of this dreaded malady, be careful of what you eat and drink. Water is the number one culprit. To be completely safe, drink only bottled water sold in sealed containers. In most of the tourist resorts, the hotels have installed water purification systems and posted signs in bathrooms stating that the water is safe to drink. Some provide complimentary bottled drinking water. In restaurants, order *agua purificada* (purified water) or *agua mineral* (mineral water), and outside of tourist hotels and restaurants, stay away from salads, uncooked vegetables, and uncooked meats and fish (such as ceviche or sushi).

If turista attacks, drink lots of purified water, eat bland foods, and rest until the symptoms pass. Use medications cautiously; some can stop your diarrhea so effectively that they seal harmful germs in your system, which can cause far more serious complications.

Language Though Spanish is Mexico's native tongue, in resorts most Mexicans speak "Spanglish"—a mix of Spanish and English that facilitates communication on both sides. In smaller towns and around the archaeological sites residents may speak one of 50 or more Indian dialects, but if they deal with tourists frequently they'll have a smattering of Spanish as well. See also "Habla Español" on page 68.

Legal Emergencies Your best bet in the event of a legal complication is to get in touch with your country's embassy in Mexico City:

Australian Embassy Jaime Balmes II, Plaza Polanco 5/3959988

Canadian Embassy Schiller 529   5/2543288

New Zealand Embassy Homero 229, Eighth Floor 5/2505999

United Kingdom Embassy Lerma 71 5/2072089

United States Embassy Paseo de la Reforma 305 5/2110042

Or contact one of the following organizations that caters to tourists:

American Express Paseo de la Reforma 234, Mexico City. 5/5330380. Branch offices are also located in most major resort areas.

Citizens Emergency Center Hotline Washington, DC. 202/647.5225. The **US State Department** staffs this organization for US residents who need emergency assistance abroad.

Tourist Help Line (24 hours) Mexico City. 5/2500150. For legal assistance, call 5/5259380 or 5/5259384.

Medical Emergencies Most of the hotels in tourist regions have English-speaking doctors on call for emergencies, and the embassies usually have a list of doctors in various locations who are accustomed to

assisting travelers. Pharmacists in Mexico are also a valuable resource for minor medical problems and can dispense most drugs without a prescription. Be cautious when taking any drugs, and use only the prescribed dosage; stop taking the medication if you notice any side effects. In the event of a serious accident or illness, you can get emergency air transport from Mexico to the US through **Air-Evac** in San Diego, California, 619/278.3822; or in Miami, Florida, 305/772.0003.

Money Mexico's currency is the new peso, or NP. In 1992, the government introduced a new currency, dropping the zeros that had made the peso so unwieldy. The new peso has the same value as the old, for example, 3,000 old pesos is now called 3 new pesos, or 3NP.

The old currency is gradually being removed from circulation, and prices are listed as new pesos. Coins come in denominations of 5, 10, 20, and 50 centavos, and 1, 2, 5, and 10 new pesos. The coins are a bit confusing at first, and it's easy to forget their value. Save those in the lower denominations for tips to children who bag your groceries or sell chewing gum in the street. Bills come in denominations of 10, 20, 50, and 100 new pesos, and look almost like the old pesos of the same value. Always keep a stash of small bills and new peso coins, as change is often hard to come by. Dollars are used as commonly as new pesos in many resort areas.

Traveler's checks usually can be exchanged for new pesos at bank branches in major airports and at large banks in the cities. However, most banks have limited hours for exchanging money, usually between 10AM and noon on weekdays. Some banks will ask to see your passport or Tourist Card. Hotels will usually exchange traveler's checks, though the rate of exchange may be worse than at the banks. A *casa de cambio* (exchange house) is common in tourist zones, and its rates may be slightly better or worse than a bank's. Always change traveler's checks on weekdays, and don't expect to be able to do so in small towns or at archaeological sites. Carry traveler's checks in denominations no larger than $50, and keep a few $20 checks on hand when change is scarce.

MasterCard and Visa are accepted at many first-class hotels and restaurants; American Express is less common. You may be charged an additional fee for using your credit card in some Mexican shops.

Newspapers and Periodicals English-language newspapers (including the *Miami Herald, The New York Times*, and *USA Today*) are available in hotel gift shops in large resort areas, as are magazines such as *Newsweek, Time,* and *People. The News,* an English-language daily paper published in Mexico City, is also commonly available at resorts and carries international news stories, editorials, comics, and columns from US sources.

The bilingual monthly magazine *Mexico Desconocidos* (Unknown Mexico) is published in Mexico City and is a valuable resource for off-the-beaten-path travelers. *Artes de Mexico* is a handsome quarterly coffee-table magazine with articles in Spanish and English and gorgeous photography. The Mexican edition of *Vogue* is always worth a look, even if you can't read a word of Spanish.

Parking In Mexico City parking is a challenge best avoided by using guarded lots. On-street parking is scarce, and if you do find a place, you're likely to be penned in by cars double-parked beside you. In resort areas there are normally plenty of spaces at attractions, restaurants, and shopping centers. Always lock valuables in the trunk of your car whether in a city or at an isolated beach.

Rest Rooms Public bathrooms are difficult to find in cities and towns. When touring, you're best off using the facilities in hotels and restaurants. Rest rooms in airports, bus stations, and gas stations run the gamut from marble stalls with doors, toilet-paper dispensers, and flush toilets with seats, to simple outhouses. Plumbing is primitive in some places, and a wastebasket is often set next to the toilet for toilet paper. Signs are usually posted in the stalls asking you to use either the bucket or the bowl. Toilet paper is sometimes nonexistent or coarse; get in the habit of carrying a packet of tissues (or a roll of toilet paper) wherever you go.

Shopping Closing shop for the afternoon siesta is still an honored tradition throughout much of rural Mexico, but it's a waning practice in the cities and resorts. Many large stores and businesses now stay open from 9AM to 7PM. Smaller shops and galleries and stores in small towns are usually open from 8 or 9AM to 2PM, and 4PM to 7 or 8PM, give or take an hour or two in either direction.

Smoking Cigarette smoke permeates the air in most restaurants and bars, but it has been banned from a majority of buses and trains. Tourist restaurants at the resorts sometimes have no-smoking sections, though these are the exception rather than the rule.

Street Smarts Mexico is no more dangerous for the average traveler than the US, especially if you stick to the tourist areas. In Mexico City use the same precautions you would in Manhattan. Don't walk around alone at night except in heavily trafficked areas such as the **Zona Rosa**. Stay alert in the metro and on buses. Lock your valuables and passport in the hotel safe, or keep them with you in a protected place, such as in a money belt. Most coastal resorts are extremely safe; you're in more danger of being hustled than being robbed outright. Be cautious with street vendors and impromptu tour guides. The easiest way to get in trouble is to overindulge in alcohol and stumble around bars, discos, and streets in a stupor. And stay far, far away from illegal drugs—this is a country that takes drug abuse and transportation of drugs extremely seriously, and you don't want to spend the night or the rest of your life in a Mexican jail.

Try to avoid driving at night in the city or countryside. In some remote areas robbers take great delight in spotting a rental car filled with naive gringos. Talk to the locals before heading off into the hinterlands, and take their advice as to the safety of your route. If there has been a recent rash of robberies, consider heading in another direction.

Taxes A 10-percent value-added tax called *Impuesto de valor agregado (IVA)* is added to all goods and services, including hotel rooms and rental cars. Be sure to ask if the tax is included in the quoted price or added to the final bill. For example, in restaurants, the tax is usually included in the menu prices rather than added to the total.

Telephones Phone calls to, within, and from Mexico are inordinately expensive, and long-distance operators are hard to contact. The least expensive way to make international calls from Mexico is to call collect. Credit card calls cost a bit more, and direct calls are the most expensive. Many hotels tack an additional service charge onto both your local and long-distance calls; ask about the fee before you begin dialing. Some hotels now have direct access to international operators from their guest rooms, yet still add a service charge.

Public pay phones take a 10-centavo coin, as do the new Ladatel phones that have made long-distance calling less expensive. To dial direct from a Ladatel phone, insert a 10-centavo coin and punch the country code and area code for the city (for example, 95/619 for the US and San Diego). The charge per minute will flash on the LCD window. You'll need a walletful of coins to make your call, and you may still have to wait a while for a long-distance operator, but at least you'll bypass the hotel's service fee. AT&T Direct service allows you to contact a US long-distance operator for collect and credit card calls; to reach the operator from a push-button phone push **01; no coins are necessary.

To call Mexico from the US, dial 011-52-area code-number.

To call the US from Mexico, dial 95-area code-number.

To call long distance within Mexico, dial 91-area code-number.

Tipping Traditionally, Mexican taxi drivers have not expected tips, though in the busy tourist areas they are beginning to look scornful if they don't get one. If the driver has been particularly helpful, or has lugged your bags around, add 10 percent to the tab. Bell captains get the equivalent of 50¢ per bag—more if the service warrants it. Housekeepers (who are normally paid abysmally) get 50¢ per day; waiters expect 10 percent of the check but certainly welcome 15 percent.

Closely related to the tip is the *mordida* (bribe), which can greatly facilitate negotiations with Mexican officials in various capacities. Federal, state, and local governments try to limit the use of *mordidas* in tourist areas and caution police officers, in particular, to refrain from soliciting bribes from tourists. If you think you're in a situation that warrants a furtive exchange of cash, ask how much the fine is for what you've done, or what the fee is for what you want done, then negotiate a sum that seems to satisfy the official's need for compensation.

Visitor Information The Mexican Tourist Office has a toll-free number in the US which will connect you to their Mexico City office. The helpful bilingual staff there can provide you with information on Mexico City, as well as other areas of the country. Call 800/482.9832 with you last-minute questions before you go.

Mexico's Famous Feasts and Fiestas

Holidays are celebrated with extreme fervor and passion in Mexico, where any occasion is an excuse for parties, parades, and fireworks. In addition to the national religious and political holidays, all towns celebrate the feast of their patron saint. Most celebrations occur at night, starting with a parade past the main plaza and followed by parties and dances that last until dawn. Foods traditional to the area are sold from carts and stands around the plaza. Banks, post offices, businesses, and stores are closed on national holidays, though in resort areas some shops and tourist-oriented businesses stay open or have abbreviated hours.

January
1 Año Nuevo (New Year's Day) is a national holiday.
6 Día de los Santos Reyes (The Feast of the Epiphany). Mexican children receive gifts from the Three Kings.
17 Fiesta de San Antonio (Feast of St. Anthony). Livestock and pets are blessed and feted.

February
5 The commemoration of the signing of the Constitution of 1917 is a national holiday.
24 Día de la Bandera is Mexico's Flag Day.
Carnival is celebrated throughout Mexico during February or March, most notably in **Mérida, Cozumel,** and **Mazatlán.**

March
21 Fiesta de Benito Juárez. The birthday of President Benito Juárez, Mexico's first Indian head of state, is a national holiday.

March/April
Semana Santa (Holy Week) is observed throughout the country with special passion plays leading up to **Easter Sunday. Good Friday** and **Holy Saturday** are national holidays.

May
1 Día de Trabajo (Labor Day) is a national holiday. Workers, many of whom are union members, take the day off and participate in parades and fiestas.
5 Cinco de Mayo is commonly thought of by foreigners as Mexico's **Independence Day.** Actually, it marks the anniversary of Mexico's defeat of the French in **Puebla** in 1862, and is a national holiday.
10 Día de las Madres (Mother's Day) is celebrated with long, leisurely family lunches and dinners and is essentially a national holiday.

June
1 Día de Naval (Navy Day) is celebrated in most port cities, including **Acapulco** and **Manzanillo.**
18 Fiesta de Corpus Christi (the Feast of Corpus Christi) takes place throughout Mexico with parades and fiestas. In **Mexico City** children are blessed at the **Catedral Nacional** (National Cathedral).
24 Fiesta de San Juan el Bautista (the Feast of St. John the Baptist) is a national holiday.

July
16 Fiesta del Virgen del Carmen (the Feast of the Virgin of Carmen) is marked by fireworks, fairs, bullfights, and fishing competitions.

Late July Fiesta de Santiago (the Feast of Santiago) is a national holiday celebrated with *charreadas* (Mexican-style rodeos).

August
15 Fiesta de Asunción del Virgen Maria (the Feast of the Assumption of the Virgin Mary) includes various religious processions.

September
1 Informe Presidencial. The president gives his annual address to Congress on this national holiday.
15-16 Día de la Independencia (Independence Day) is riotously celebrated in Mexico with fireworks and parades. In **Mexico City,** buildings around the *zócalo* (town square) are strung with red, green, and white lights, and huge portraits of national heroes are made from hundreds of light bulbs in a wire frame. Thousands of people jam the *zócalo* on the night of the 15th for the president's annual *grito* (cry) from the **Palacio Nacional** (National Palace). On the 16th, a national holiday, a military parade attracts thousands of onlookers to **Monumento de la Independencia** (Independence Monument).

October
12 Día de la Raza (Day of the Race) is a national holiday commemorating Columbus's arrival in the Americas and the blending of races within Mexico.

November
1-2 Días de los Muertos (Days of the Dead). All Saints' and All Souls' days are national holidays. Deceased children are honored on the first, adults on the second. Altars to the dead are set up in homes and cemeteries; candles, favorite foods and beverages, and photographs of the departed are surrounded with flowers, especially marigolds. The smell of copal incense fills the air, and candies and breads shaped like skulls and skeletons abound.
20 Aniversario de la Revolución. The Mexican revolution of 1910 is commemorated with a national holiday.

December
12 Fiesta de Nuestra Señora de Guadalupe (the Feast of Our Lady of Guadalupe). This national holiday is celebrated days and even weeks in advance at the **Basílica de Guadalupe** outside **Mexico City.** Pilgrims from throughout the country arrive by the carload and on foot, and approach the Virgin's shrine on their knees. Vendors hawk her likeness on statues, plates, and even gear-shift knobs, and the scene is one of nearly garish revelry. Smaller celebrations are held throughout the country, particularly in towns where Guadalupe is the patron saint.
24 Noche Buena (Christmas Eve).
25 Navidad (Christmas). The 12 days before Christmas are marked by *posadas* (processions) that recall Mary and Joseph's search for an inn. Families come together on the 25th to attend church, exchange gifts, break open piñatas, and share a lavish feast. *Feliz Navidad* is Spanish for "Merry Christmas."

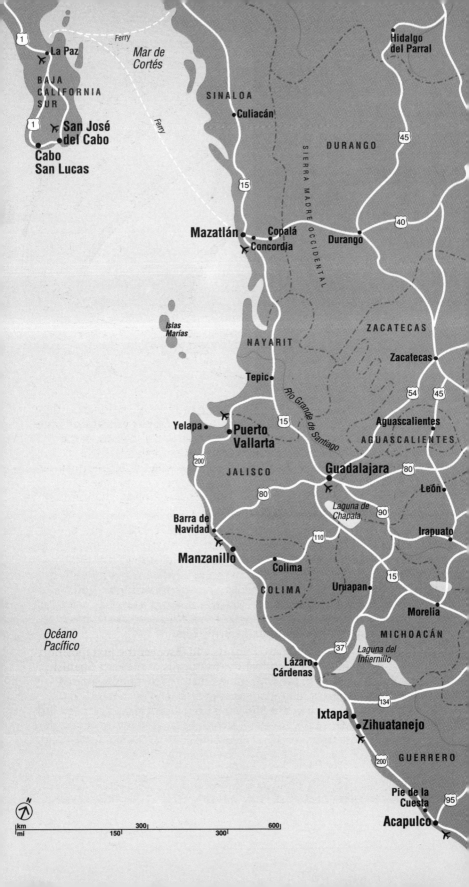

Coastal Resorts

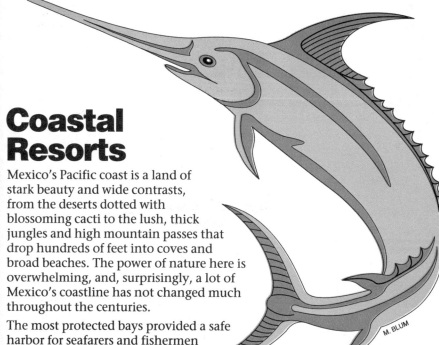

M. BLUM

Mexico's Pacific coast is a land of stark beauty and wide contrasts, from the deserts dotted with blossoming cacti to the lush, thick jungles and high mountain passes that drop hundreds of feet into coves and broad beaches. The power of nature here is overwhelming, and, surprisingly, a lot of Mexico's coastline has not changed much throughout the centuries.

The most protected bays provided a safe harbor for seafarers and fishermen hundreds of years ago, which led to their development as resorts. These are the areas that continue to grow and have become bustling holiday retreats that draw thousands of visitors every year. **Mazatlán** is one of the best sportfishing destinations in Mexico, as well as the site of the yearly Carnival festivities. It's also one of the few coastal cities with remnants of its early colonial era. **Puerto Vallarta** is less than a century old, yet it offers the flavor of Old Mexico with its tile rooftops and steep hillsides. **Manzanillo** is still in the development stage, and many tourists have yet to discover its natural treasures.

Acapulco remains the entertainment hub of Mexico's Pacific coast. It delights all with sophisticated entertainment, gourmet restaurants, and one of the most beautiful bays in the world. Quaint **Zihuatanejo** is a slow-moving Mexican town with low-key, charming hotels just five miles from the more modern **Ixtapa,** which provides glitzy high-rise hotels, golf courses, and tennis courts. And across the **Mar de Cortés** (Sea of Cortez), at the end of the **Baja California Peninsula, Los Cabos** provides an ideal destination for fishing enthusiasts and sun-seekers.

First-time visitors to Mexico's coastal resorts will discover the juxtaposition of modern and colonial-style architecture (footprints of the early Spanish explorers). Bits and pieces of pre-Columbian history are found scattered about in small museums, a reminder of the people who lived here long before tourists began arriving. But Mexico is only just beginning to develop its coastline, and as developers work to accommodate the influx of visitors, concerned leaders are trying to preserve the balance of nature, which they now realize must be handled prudently to ensure its survival.

Los Cabos

For the typical tourist, **Baja California** is both familiar and unique, part Mexican, part psuedo–Southern Californian. Nowhere is this juxtaposition more apparent than in Los Cabos, the southernmost tip of the 1,059-mile-long **Baja California Peninsula**. Los Cabos is a hybrid, spawned by Mexican bankers and politicians in the early 1970s, and nourished by international investors in the 1980s and 1990s. It was formed from two separate towns—**San José del Cabo**, the municipal headquarters, and **Cabo San Lucas**, the center of the commercial and sportfishing industries—with an 18-mile road between them called the **Corridor**. All this is unconnected to mainland Mexico, with only a highway linking it to the United States border at San Diego, California.

The visionaries who turned Mexico into a tourist haven 20 years ago dubbed the area *Los Cabos* (The Capes) and declared that it would someday become a megaresort with golf courses, marinas, lavish hotels, and an endless stream of money-spending tourists. Speculators even debated which location to develop first: Los Cabos or Cancún. Fortunately, Los Cabos lost. Success as a resort destination has come slowly and gradually to Baja's tip, allowing it to grow with a sense of character and surprise.

Long before the developers came, wealthy adventurers were flying or yachting to Los Cabos, then known as "Marlin Alley," for sportfishing. World War II pilots sighted schools of billfish leaping from the waters around Baja's tip; later, astronauts studied the convergence of the **Pacific Ocean** and the **Mar de Cortés** (Sea of Cortez) and knew it would make for a fine fish trap. Legendary outdoorsmen of the John Wayne era roughed it at mountain lodges set in the desert on sandstone cliffs above the sea. Today, those early outposts have become treasured landmarks and four-star hotels serving less rugged adventurers, although some resorts still resist the pressure to put telephones and TVs in every room.

San José del Cabo is the northernmost town in Los Cabos, and also the most Mexican. The offices of **FONATUR** (the National Foundation for Tourism Development) are located here, as is the area's first golf course, several condo and housing projects, and a hotel zone along the shores of the Mar de Cortés. It would be the ideal destination if only the beaches were safe for swimmers. If you're not into swimming in the sea, however, the sound of the crashing waves is the best tranquilizer of all, and San José's sleepy serenity may make this your perfect retreat.

El Arco

MIKE KOHNKE

The **Parroquia de San José** (Parish Church of San José) is the social center of this community that has grown almost overnight to a population of nearly 25,000 full-time residents. Like most of the town's 18th- and 19th-century buildings, the church is simple in style, with none of the grandeur of those in mainland Mexico. Earth-toned brick and stucco boutiques, cafes, and shops line **Boulevard Mijares,** the main avenue, while small-town life goes on a few blocks away in the central market, the *tortillerías* (small stands where tortillas are made), and the rutted dirt streets of the neighborhoods. Along Mijares, locals and travelers conduct official business at the **Palacio Municipal** (City Hall), dine in candlelight under boughs of fuchsia bougainvillea at **Damiana,** and catch up on televised sports at **Tropicana,** all at a leisurely, amicable pace.

The unimaginatively named Corridor is actually the most gorgeous and valuable stretch of real estate in Los Cabos. The windy, two-lane road between the two towns has been replaced with a smooth four-lane highway that cuts through sandstone cliffs over a series of dramatic bays. One-of-a-kind hotels and resorts claim the most scenic clifftops, sequestering guests in luxurious sanctuaries where privacy, peace, and pleasure reign supreme. One of the most enjoyable ways to pass a day in Los Cabos is to embark on a leisurely tour of a half dozen or so hotels in the Corridor. A late breakfast on the **Palmilla's** sun-dappled balcony is a good way to start, followed by drinks, snacks, and hikes to lone beaches and summit trails at the **Meliá Cabo Real,** the **Hotel Cabo San Lucas,** and the **Twin Dolphin.** Plan for a snorkeling break at **Bahía Palmilla, Bahía Santa Maria,** or **Bahía Cabo San Lucas,** and end the afternoon with a sunset cocktail at **Da Giorgio.**

Cabo San Lucas is where the action is. Its origins as the fishing and canning capital of Baja California Sur are still evident despite a more-than-20-year drive to transform the small, dusty settlement into a tourist mecca. Trendy boutiques and bars are jammed together in an unrelated jumble of styles. Too many tourists behave as though Cabo San Lucas were a narcissist's playground, where those who imbibe too much tequila and beer can get away with whatever rowdy behavior might be frowned upon at home. They refer to the town simply as "Cabo," and call the Baja California Peninsula " the Baja."

To appreciate Cabo San Lucas's attributes, visit early in the morning, while the revelers are still nursing their hangovers, and stay out of town when there's a cruise ship in the bay. Start at the main plaza, where the shops carry a tasteful selection of folk art, clothing, and souvenirs, and the restaurants have a character apart from the tourist melee. A miniature maze of short blocks without street signs leads to the waterfront, and it is on these side streets that you'll find a hodgepodge of cafes, bars, arcades, and storefronts ready to be discovered.

Boulevard Marina, along the curve of Bahía San Lucas, is the no-holds-barred tourist strip. The watering holes have cutesy names and blaring music, the restaurants have sidewalk grills offering sizzling treats, and the congested street is filled with mopeds, taxis, and jeeps. Attractive young women and men loiter on just about every street corner in so-called tourist information stands, trying desperately to entice you to visit a time-share presentation (they're paid by commission). Unless you're a glutton for free breakfasts, Happy Hours, and gifts, you'll quickly learn to bolt past these slick sidewalk hustlers and their banter of friendly repartee. At press time, several large buildings were under construction around the marina, and future plans include a yacht club.

Area code 114 unless otherwise noted.

Getting to Los Cabos

Airport

The **Los Cabos International Airport** is 11 kilometers (seven miles) north of San José del Cabo and 35 kilometers (22 miles) north of Cabo San Lucas.

Airport vans called *colectivos* shuttle passengers from the airport to hotels, and are the least expensive route to take, unless you have at least four people to share a taxi. On the way back to the airport, however, you must rely on the cabs, which are extraordinarily expensive. Many hotels have a sign-up sheet at the front desk where you can solicit fellow passengers to share the fare.

Airlines
Aero California.........................30848, 800/258.3311

Alaska Airlines......................20959, 800/426.0333

Mexicana 20960, 800/531.7921

Getting around Los Cabos

Bus Stations
San José del Cabo Doblado 605......................20200

Cabo San Lucas Zaragoza and 16 de Septiembre ......
....30400

Car Rental
Avis 20680, 21080

Budget..30241

Dollar..20671

Hertz...30211

National 20160, 31414

Servitour...30897

FYI

Emergencies
Hospitals
Hospital Raul A. Carillo Calle Manuel Doblado and Colonia 5 de Febrero, San José del Cabo 30102

Police
San José del Cabo 30057

Cabo San Lucas 20361

Money
Banks are open for changing money Mondays through Fridays from 9AM to 1PM. International credit cards and US dollars are accepted in most restaurants, hotels, and shops. There are also *casas de cambio* (exchange houses) in both towns. Try not to be short of cash on Sundays, because it can be difficult to change money on that day, except in some hotels. Always keep bills of small denominations on hand, since it can be difficult to change larger bills (except at banks).

Tours
Baja California Tours has bus tours down the Baja Peninsula from San Diego, California, to Los Cabos, with overnight stops at the major sights along the way. 6986 La Jolla Blvd, Number 204, La Jolla, CA 92037. 619/454.7166; fax 619/454.2703

Baja Expeditions has specialized in adventure travel in Baja for more than 15 years, with hiking, biking, kayaking, and diving trips to all of Baja's natural wonders, including the Pacific and the Mar de Cortés. 2625 Garnet Ave, San Diego, CA 92109. 619/581.3311, 800/843.6967; fax 619/581.6542

Tour Cabos is the main tour operator in Los Cabos, offering scuba and snorkeling trips, sunset cruises, city tours, and other excursions. Plaza Los Cabos, Local B-2, San José del Cabo. 20982

The best way to truly capture the magnitude of the Baja California Peninsula is to drive its length from San Diego to Cabo San Lucas. **M&M Jeeps** rents four-wheel-drive vehicles, and can arrange itineraries with hotels and maps. 2200 El Cajon Blvd, San Diego, CA 92104. 619/297.1615, 800/461.5724; fax 619/297.1617

Visitors Information
Los Cabos does not have a tourism office. The **Oficina de Turismo** (the State Tourism Office) in La Paz distributes some generic information about Los Cabos. PO Box 419, La Paz, Baja California Sur 23010. 112/27722, 27975

A Sight to Miss

Playa de Amor (Beach of Love) This place sounds far more idyllic than it actually is, particularly if you've been lured here by a fast-talking time-share hustler. The standard spiel is that if you agree to tour several time-share properties in Los Cabos, you'll be rewarded with a "free" drive trip. Too good to be true? You bet! Typically, these jaunts consist of a bumpy ride in a *panga* that lets you off at a point that seems too far from shore as you head overboard with your mask and fins, praying the captain will return to pick you up. Once you've reached the small beach, gnats will keep you company as you search for a spot free of seagull droppings and bake in the sand without any drinking water. Savvy locals call this spot "Divorce Beach," referring to the illicit trysts that supposedly take place here. Breakups are more likely to occur during the rough swim back to the boat, however—especially if the water's ripples have turned into waves. Better to admire the beach and fantasize about its potential from aboard a comfortable yacht.

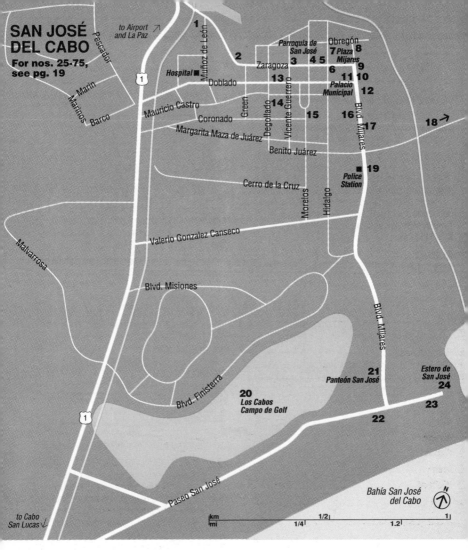

For nos. 25-75,
see pg. 19

**SAN JOSÉ
DEL CABO**

to Airport
and La Paz

1

Pescador

Muñoz de León

2

Parroquia de
San José

Obregón

Marin

Marinos

Barco

Hospital ■

Mauricio Castro

Coronado

Margarita Maza de Juárez

Doblado

Green

Zaragoza

3

7

8

Plaza
Mijares

4 5

9

6

11

10

13

Degollado

Vicente Guerrero

Palacio
Municipal

12

14

15

16

17

18 →

Benito Juárez

Cerro de la Cruz

Morelos

Hidalgo

Police
Station

19

Malvarrosa

Valerio Gonzalez Canseco

Blvd. Misiones

Blvd. Mijares

Blvd. Finisterra

20
Los Cabos
Campo de Golf

21
Panteón San José

Estero de
San José

24

23

22

Paseo San José

Bahía San José
del Cabo

N

to Cabo
San Lucas ↙

km
mi

1/4

1/2

1.2

1

Area code 114 unless otherwise noted.

San José del Cabo

1 Pescaderia El Mercado del Mar
★★★$$ This tiny seafood restaurant is
destined to succeed. Distinguished by an
archway painted with a picture of a crab, its
half dozen tables sit under a *palapa* (a palm-
roof hut) with a bar at one end. Start with
toritos, small yellow Caribe chilies roasted and
stuffed with smoked marlin, or a giant shrimp
cocktail; entrée choices include oysters, clams,
scallops, octopus, calamari, or a fish fillet
rolled around seafood stuffing, all expertly
prepared. You can also buy smoked fish, cured
on the premises in a big brick smoker, or
cooked seafood to go. ♦ Seafood ♦ Daily lunch
and dinner. Hwy 1 (at Zaragoza). No phone

2 Pastelería y Panadería La Princesa
Once inside this pastry shop grab a pair of
tongs and a silver tray, then peruse the
shelves before making your final selection.
Preservatives are nonexistent here, so don't
pile on too much—perhaps a flaky yet dense
palmier (cookie) or a puffy *doña* (doughnut),
a couple of warm *bolillos* (rolls) for lunch, and
some semisweet cookies for afternoon tea.
♦ Bakery ♦ Daily. Zaragoza (between Muñoz
de León and Green). No phone

3 La Fogata ★★$$ The best choice for
reasonably priced homestyle Mexican cooking
is this friendly restaurant. Joel Davida and his
family welcome diners with courtesy and an
intense desire to please. Homesick gringos
love the thick New York steaks served with
baked potatoes and sour cream. ♦ Mexican
♦ Daily breakfast, lunch, and dinner.
Zaragoza (between Vicente Guerrero and
Morelos). 20480

Restaurants/Clubs: Red   Hotels: Blue

Shops/ ☂ Outdoors: Green   **Sights/Culture:** Black

15

Parroquia de San José

ANTHONY QUARTUCCIO

4 Parroquia de San José (Parish Church of San José) Two simple, cream-colored wooden steeples poke humbly above the skyline, marking the town's religious, social, and historical hub. Be sure to examine the tiled mural above the front door, depicting the martyred priest Nicolás Tamaral being dragged to the fire by Pericúe Indians. The missionary invasion of the 1700s was not a beneficial experience for the indigenous residents of this sacred land. Along with their doctrine, the padres brought smallpox and syphilis. By the turn of the century, the local population was virtually eradicated from the area. Though not the first of the California missions, the church, built in 1734, was an early addition to the chain that eventually spread north to what is now Sonoma, California. ♦ Zaragoza (between Morelos and Hidalgo)

5 Plaza and Kiosko The church sits above the town plaza, where taxi drivers congregate with their cabs and children jump off the stairs to the white wrought-iron *kiosko* (gazebo). The small-town, community feeling is strongest on late Sunday afternoon and evening, and the plaza is always a good spot for a rest in the shade. ♦ Zaragoza (between Hidalgo and Blvd Mijares)

6 Copal Heavy carved-wood tables, chairs, and bureaus are set with blue-and-white pottery dishes and glass goblets edged in cobalt blue—inspiration for transforming your home into a traditional Mexican hacienda. At press time the adjacent **Antigua Los Cabos** shop was being remodeled into an art gallery. ♦ Daily. Zaragoza 20 (between Hidalgo and Blvd Mijares). 23070

7 Plaza Mijares Wrought-iron benches and narrow pathways are nearly hidden by trees covered with orange blossoms. The tiny plaza is a pretty place to rest and regroup, and tour buses often pick up their passengers here. This is where many local artists, sculptors, and photographers display their works on Sunday morning during high season. ♦ Off Blvd Mijares (between Zaragoza and Obregón)

8 Damiana ★★★$$ You needn't partake of the aphrodisiacal liqueur (see "Herbal Magic" on page 31) to become enchanted by its namesake restaurant. If you do wish to imbibe, you'll be offered a drink on the house. Husband-and-wife team Luis and Leticia Klein have transformed a crumbling 18th-century hacienda into a serene patio where you feel as if you're dining among friends in a secret hideaway. The restaurant is hidden off Plaza Mijares, beside similar houses where families cluster in front of TV sets. Dining tables sit in the courtyard under a canopy of fuchsia bougainvillea, accompanied by the soothing sound of a gurgling fountain. The pièce de résistance is the imperial shrimp steak, made of chopped fresh shrimp pressed into a patty and grilled. Purists may prefer their gigantic prawns au naturel, sprinkled with bits of toasted garlic. The chateaubriand is sufficient for two hungry carnivores, and the Mexican dishes, especially the *chiles rellenos,* are very good. ♦ Seafood/Mexican ♦ Daily lunch and dinner. Off Blvd Mijares (between Zaragoza and Obregón). 20499

9 Ivan's ★★$$$ Eric and Elsa Gibson, who started in the local restaurant business with the now-defunct **Café Europa,** have moved their operation to a second-story porch and dining room overlooking **Palacio Municipal.** Continuing the European theme, the French chef Didier prepares wonderful pâtés and pastries, Greek and Niçoise salads, and baguettes filled with Polish kielbasa. The all-American half-pound burger rivals any in the area. A great place to escape the heat during a daytime shopping spree, the restaurant is especially romantic at night as colored lights illuminate the fountains below. ♦ Continental ♦ Daily breakfast, lunch, and dinner. Blvd Mijares 16 (across from the Palacio Municipal). No phone

10 Almacenes Goncanseco This one-stop, multipurpose market sells batteries, postcards, cold drinks, snacks, and groceries. ♦ M-Sa; closed at midday. Blvd Mijares (between Zaragoza and Doblado). No phone

11 Palacio Municipal (City Hall) The name is far more grand than the building itself—a pale, sand-colored plaster edifice with a peaked clock tower and a simple inner courtyard. It houses the municipal offices for Los Cabos, where official business for both towns is conducted quite languidly. A plaque at the entrance commemorates the founding of San José (and the building's construction) in 1730. Another plaque observes San José's designation as the municipal headquarters of Los Cabos in 1981, when the original building was renovated and two stories of offices were added around the courtyard. A silent guard stands under the front archway providing directions with a nod of his head. Fountains lit with colored lights at night face the building from the median strip on Boulevard Mijares. ♦ Blvd Mijares (between Zaragoza and Doblado)

12 Galería El Dorado The smallest of three galleries in a chain, the San José branch has a front room filled with wood carvings from Oaxaca, pottery from Puebla, and lacquered boxes from Guerrero. The back room contains sculptures that mimic the work of Sergio Bustamante, one of Mexico's most popular artists. ♦ Daily. Blvd Mijares 20 (between Doblado and Coronado). 30817

13 Tortillería Perla Stop here after shopping at the market to complete the feast with a stack of hot tortillas sold by the kilo. The line is longest early in the morning and midafternoon. ♦ Mexican ♦ M-Sa. Doblado 382 (between Vincente Guerrero and Degollado). 20034

14 Mercado Municipal Though not as spectacular as those on mainland Mexico, San José's enclosed public market has a good enough selection to satisfy your needs for chilies, oranges, mangoes, avocados, and the heady aroma of spices and humanity. ♦ Daily. Mauricio Castro (between Vincente Guerrero and Degollado). No phone

15 Le Bistrot ★★$$ Transplanted Belgians Veronique and Thierry Paquet are bold and daring entrepreneurs, having chosen a tiny cottage far from the main part of town for their French country cafe. During the high season they serve a unique breakfast buffet with fruit crepes and eggs, a nice break from *huevos rancheros.* Dinners usually include imported pâtés and cheeses, and Provençale preparations for the ubiquitous fresh fish. Only seven tables fill the small room, which on the coldest winter nights glow in the firelight from a corner hearth. This restaurant is tough to find, but it's definitely worth the search. ♦ French ♦ Daily lunch and dinner. Morelos 4 (near Coronado) behind the Telemex office. 21174

16 La Casa Vieja A narrow hallway leads to two large rooms filled with a vast array of folk art, clothing, and accessories from throughout Mexico and Guatemala. The selections are refined, and the imaginative displays are always worth another look. When Leticia Klein of **Damiana Restaurant** (above) opened the store on San José's main street in 1982, her neighbors were families living as they had for decades in 19th-century brick and stucco homes. Many of the families have remained through the influx of restaurants, bars, and boutiques. Rows of *flamboyán* trees give a certain measure of privacy, as well as relief from the sun's heat. ♦ M-Sa. Blvd Mijares 27 (between Doblado and Coronado). 20599. Also at: Meliá Cabo Real Hotel, Hwy 1. 30754

Presidential elections in Mexico are held every six years in August, and the victor takes office in December. The time between the election and the inauguration is called El Año de Hidalgo (the year of the nobleman). It is a time of extreme uncertainty, when the president typically pushes through unpopular programs and paybacks with little regard for how they will affect the country. For example, during this period in 1982, then-president López Portillo nationalized the banks, creating economic panic.

17 Tropicana Inn $$ The nicest place to stay in downtown San José is this peaceful and pretty inn with 40 air-conditioned rooms. A tile reproduction of a calla lily painting by Diego Rivera decorates the reception area, and the tile theme is continued throughout the complex, including in the spacious showers. All rooms have two double beds, a satellite TV, and a telephone, and are decorated with pastel-colored cotton spreads and curtains and oil paintings of colonial village scenes. A giant *palapa* covers the pool bar, which is a great place to have a piña colada. The beach is eight blocks away, but all of San José's attractions are within walking distance. ♦ Blvd Mijares 30 (between Doblado and Benito Juárez). 21580; fax 21590

Within the Tropicana Inn:

Tropicana Bar and Grill ★★★$$ An enduring favorite in an area where restaurants struggle to survive, this eatery is alternately romantic and rowdy, depending on the crowd. The bar is popular for televised sporting events and music videos, while the back garden remains serene and picturesque. A blue awning shades sidewalk tables where you can watch the town come alive. The menu offers seafood, an excellent rack of lamb, filet mignon, and other meats imported from the US. Low-priced breakfast and lunch specials are available too. ♦ Seafood/Continental ♦ Daily breakfast, lunch, and dinner. 20907

18 Pueblo La Playa For a true out-of-the-way experience, drive two kilometers (one mile) down the rutted dirt road east of downtown San José to this tiny settlement with the town's original crumbling lighthouse, a newer concrete light tower, and a popular surfing beach. The *pangas* (small skiffs) on the beach are available for sportfishing trips; for information, contact Tomas Cantor at 21195; he also has two beach apartments available for rent. ♦ Take Benito Juárez north from Blvd Mijares and keep going straight.

Within Pueblo la Playa:

La Playita ★★$ Order fresh grilled fish, french fries, and a Corona at this small restaurant surounded by bushes and trees. Then settle in under the *palapa* for a satisfying, soulful meal. ♦ Seafood ♦ Daily lunch and dinner. 21163

19 Mercado de Artesanías Vendors display typical curios at open-air stands shaded with bright blue plastic tarps along Mijares on the southern edge of town. Bartering for cotton serapes, ironwood fish carvings, and silver baubles is expected, and prices are somewhat lower than at the shops in town. ♦ Daily. Blvd Mijares (near Benito Juárez). No phone

20 Los Cabos Campo de Golf Los Cabos's original golf course is about to get some mighty competition from six new courses along the Corridor and in Cabo San Lucas. (Local and federal officials believe that marinas and golf courses will attract the desired class of clientele.) This course, designed by Mario Schjetnan and built by **FONATUR,** has nine well-established and challenging holes. Private homes and condos surround the country club, which sits on a hillside with coastal views. The club also has lighted tennis courts and a clubhouse, and is open to nonmembers. ♦ Blvd Finisterra (off Blvd Mijares). 20900, 20901

21 Panteón San José (San José Cemetery) The entrance to this 19th-century cemetery is hard to find, but is worth the effort for those interested in local culture. Tombs marked by headstones shaped like small churches are half hidden behind tall, dry grass, and colorful plastic flowers are tucked all around plaster angels and crosses. One tomb has 17 brick sides. ♦ Daily. Blvd Mijares (near Paseo San José)

22 Plaza Comercial Part of **FONATUR**'s master plan, this isolated commercial center has been less than successful for shops and restaurants, and now houses business offices, travel agencies, a video rental shop, and a few small restaurants. ♦ Daily. Paseo San José and Blvd Mijares

23 Presidente Inter-Continental $$$ An overwhelming impression of cactus and sand prevails at the oldest of the San José hotel zone's occupants, resting on a solitary piece of land between the sea and the junglelike estuary. Low-rise tan buildings surround what has to be the largest pool in town. The best of the 240 rooms are on the first floor toward the beach, with shaded patios near the sand. Rooms are furnished in earth tones with heavy drapes to block the sun. Mornings, when the estuary's birds are in full chorus, are especially lovely here. There are three restaurants, two bars, and a disco. ♦ Paseo San José (at the Estero de San José). 20211, 800/327.0200; fax 20232

24 Estero de San José The Río San José snakes toward the sea through acres of nearly impenetrable twisting vines and trees along the dry and dusty shoreline. Thus far, the estuary's damp and dense terrain has protected it (and its 200 bird species) from civilization's slow crawl up the coast, but changes are under way. Happily, the government has promised not to destroy the estuary, and has declared it an ecological reserve. ♦ Paseo San José (north of the Presidente Hotel)

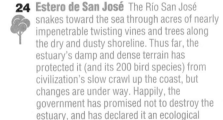

Don't be surprised if a person who walks into a hotel off the street pays more or less than somebody who made a reservation with a travel agent. Prices in Mexico often depend on the supply and demand of the day.

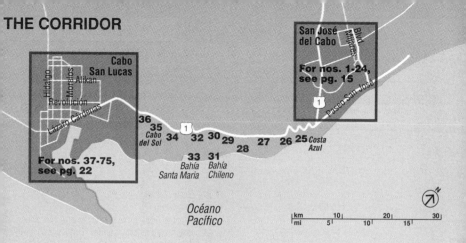

THE CORRIDOR

The Corridor

25 Costa Azul One of the most popular surfing beaches in the area sits in an arroyo (dip) in the highway just south of San José. Die-hard surfers stay in a few worn-down cabanas or camp by the beach, and spend their time in the waves. The annual October Cabo Classic Reggae Surf-Splash contest fills nearby hotels with revelers and attracts thousands to the park. Just south of the beach is a hilltop lookout on the east side of the highway, where you can watch the surfers in action. ◆ Hwy 1 (between San José del Cabo and the Palmilla Hotel)

26 Palmilla $$$$ Gorgeous, luxurious, and classically Mexican, this romantic place never fails to evoke purrs of pleasure from its guests and murmurs of envy from outsiders. Set on one of the most beautiful bays along the coast atop Punta Palmilla, the hotel's property spreads across 900 acres in a gentle rise between the highway and the sea. The 62 rooms are each furnished with Mexican simplicity and an eye for style and detail. Framed embroideries and carved wooden masks hang on the walls, while hand-painted tiles and hand-carved furnishings add color. There are also eight suites, with red-tiled patios, low walls shaped in lacy, layered arches, white wrought-iron tables and chairs, and padded lounges. Two five-bedroom villas are available for those looking for lots of space. There are no TVs or phones in the rooms; those who insist on communicating with the outside world must use the lobby phone.

Wake-up calls are personally delivered by a waiter bearing fresh coffee, orange juice, and croissants. The hotel's fishing fleet is one of the best in Los Cabos, and there is a full-scale dive shop. Guests amuse themselves playing croquet, lounging by the pool, and drinking giant icy margaritas while watching the sunset from the second-story bar. ◆ Hwy 1 (south of San José del Cabo). 20582, 800/637.2226; fax 20583

Within the Palmilla:

La Paloma ★★★★$$$ Even if you're not staying at the hotel, be sure to have a meal here on the second-story patio overlooking the pool and the sea. This has always been one of Los Cabos's best restaurants and has become even better as the menu moves toward lighter, more unusual entrées. You can still get the mixed grill—a bountiful and tasty assortment of sausages and meats—but now there's also oysters Palmilla with spinach and pine nuts, or ravioli stuffed with lobster, cheese, and sun-dried tomatoes. For a total gourmet experience, spend an indulgent Sunday afternoon in the dining room, making your way through a brunch that will remain in your memory for years to come. ◆ Mexican/Nouvelle ◆ Daily breakfast, lunch, and dinner. 21709

 Palmilla Golf Club Located across the highway from the hotel, the **Palmilla's** 27-hole golf course was designed by Jack Nicklaus to take full advantage of the dramatic terrain and coastal views. Ancient cacti loom over emerald greens, and deep arroyos provide natural challenges for golfers of all levels. It's a shame the course can't double as a park for non-golfers; if you get the chance to tour the grounds, don't pass it up. ◆ Hwy 1 (across from the hotel entrance). 20582

Restaurants/Clubs: Red   **Hotels:** Blue
Shops/ ◆ Outdoors: Green   **Sights/Culture:** Black

27 Da Giorgio ★★★$$$ Set on Monte Colorado high above the sea, this restaurant from the outside looks more like a private home than a place to get a meal. (A billboard beside the highway announces the entrance.) The dining area is on the second story of the stone building, and on the upper patio you feel as though you're eating with the stars. Owners Cristina Rodríguez and Giorgio Battaglia managed the **Palmilla** for many years and have brought that hotel's sense of style and Mexican charm to this venture. The Italian chef prepares a mean *penne telefono*, a pasta dish so named because thin strands of mozzarella stretch like phone lines from the pasta as you raise your fork. Other pluses are the textured, crusty breads, pizzas that are baked in wood-burning ovens, and the salad bar that includes fresh greens and herbs grown on the premises. Italian wines, cappuccino, and espresso add to the Mediterranean atmosphere. ♦ Italian ♦ Daily lunch and dinner. Hwy 1, Km 25 (between San José del Cabo and Cabo San Lucas). 21988

Todos Santos

Visitors who never stray beyond Los Cabos miss the best of Baja's natural beauty and potential, which are most evident in the coastal community of Todos Santos, some hundred miles north. Rent a car for a day and drive up the Pacific coastline on Highway 19, along the base of the Sierra Gigante. Take time to stop along the way at solitary beaches to gather driftwood and shells usually found near giant cacti. The scenery grows greener as you enter the town of Todos Santos, home of the nurseries and organic gardens that provide plants and produce for the tourist enclaves farther south.

Though the town may not look luxurious to an outsider, Todos Santos is becoming an artists' colony and an exclusive enclave for Mexicans and expatriates who can afford its rapidly spiraling real estate costs. The crumbling 19th-century brick homes along the main plaza may look unimpressive now, but artists and entrepreneurs are investing hundreds of thousands of dollars in renovations, with promises of galleries, restaurants, and charming inns in the future.

While there, be sure to stop for lunch at **Cafe Santa Fe** (★★★★$$$), owned by Paula and Ezio Colombo. Diners travel south from La Paz and north from Los Cabos just to visit this tiny cafe nestled in a refurbished stucco house. Taking advantage of the locally grown organic produce, the menu includes superb salads and herb garnishes for the freshest fish imaginable. Ezio, who used to supervise the kitchen at **Da Giorgio** in Los Cabos, prepares homemade pastas, pizzas, and calzones that draw rave reviews even from fellow restaurateurs. Be sure not to dawdle too long. You absolutely *do not* want to drive back to Los Cabos after dark.

28 Westin Regina $$$$ Formerly the Conrad Hilton, this new, deluxe hotel is currently the local standard bearer for architecture and services. Set atop a cliff overlooking the Mar de Cortés, it has sleek, terra-cotta-colored buidings with arches that frame views of the sea. The 243 rooms have both air-conditioning and ceiling fans, private balconies with ocean views, sitting areas, and enormous bathrooms with separate bathtubs and showers. It is one of the few hotels in the area with a full fitness center that provides exercise equipment, sauna, steam room, and whirlpool. There are also three outdoor swimming pools. ♦ Hwy 1, Km 22.5 (between San José del Cabo and Cabo San Lucas). 29000, 800/228.3000; fax 29010

29 Meliá Cabo Real $$$ Some say this terra-cotta sprawl of cubes and angles looks like a hospital, but it's much more impressive inside. The grounds are astounding, however, with rock pathways winding past cactus gardens toward white tents billowing in the breeze. Waterfalls, fountains, ponds, and swimming pools appear to blend into a crystal-blue mirage extending into the horizon. A stairway leads down to an immaculate artificial beach and a rock jetty that creates a peaceful miniature bay for swimming and snorkeling. Large and expansive by Los Cabos standards, there are 299 rooms in long five-story buildings that surround the inner grounds. The thoroughly modern rooms have TVs, bathtubs, minibars, and dependable air-conditioning. On-site attractions include a putting green and an 18-hole golf course, horseback riding, and sportfishing. All the amenities, including bars, restaurants, shops, and a health club, keep guests from straying. Construction continues on the adjacent **Cabo Real** development, which has private housing and a golf course. ♦ Hwy 1, Km 19.5 (between San José del Cabo and Cabo San Lucas). 30754, 800/336.3542; fax 305/854.0660

30 Hotel Maria Gaviota $$$ This cozy Mediterranean-style hotel enjoys an ideal setting on a cliff overlooking a small beach. Few of the 40 suites have an ocean view, but all have the sound of the surf and a feeling of seclusion. The one- and two-bedroom suites have kitchenettes, dining areas, and both air-conditioning and ceiling fans. A seaside restaurant sits at the bottom of the cliff—the walk down will help you work up an appetite. For the atmosphere and amenities, it's a better value than other hotels along the Corridor. ♦ Hwy 1, Km 17 (between San José del Cabo and Cabo San Lucas). 33377; fax in La Paz 112/58655

31 Bahía Chileno A dirt road off the highway leads to this secluded clear cove, one of the best along this coastline for snorkeling, scuba diving, and swimming. During high season, a small stand rents snorkeling and dive equipment. ◆ Hwy 1, Km 15 (between San José del Cabo and Cabo San Lucas)

32 Hotel Cabo San Lucas $$$ Looking more like a northwestern hunting and fishing lodge than a tropical oasis, this is one of the Corridor's original hotels, as well as one of its most legendary. This is where weathered, die-hard fisherfolk return for their yearly hunt. But the hotel has lost much of its glory. The 99 rooms are desperately in need of refurbishing, and the air-conditioning system must be overhauled or replaced. The grounds, however, have grown even more spectacular with age, as mature palms, scheffleras, and hibiscus seem to envelop the complex in shade. The dining room and bar are very impressive, made of rock and wood with large windows facing the water. It also features a huge fireplace for chilly nights, and one of the best mariachi groups around. ◆ Hwy 1, Km 14 (between Cabo San Lucas and San José del Cabo). 30664

33 Bahía Santa Maria Another lovely bay where locals and travelers escape from the crowds and snorkel among angel and parrot fish. A stall with equipment rentals is open in high season. ◆ Hwy 1, Km 12.5 (between Cabo San Lucas and San José del Cabo)

34 Twin Dolphin $$$$ Stark, austere, exclusive, and dramatic, it has a dedicated upscale clientele who continually come back. In fact, 80 percent of the guests are satisfied returnees. Rather than try to mimic a tropical paradise, owner David Halliburton Sr. took full advantage of Baja's minimalistic beauty and set the low, long white buildings amid landscaping of rolling hills and stately cacti. Square, white patio umbrellas poke up beside boulders, and the light blue pool shimmers in the sun. Paco, the resident parrot, squawks in his cage in the hotel's entryway. The 44 rooms

reflect the minimalist theme, with low platform beds, small refrigerators, enormous showers , and a state-of-the-art air-conditioning system. An intriguing feature of the place is its reproductions of the peninsula's famed cave paintings, found in remote caves deep in some of Baja's most deserted regions. Artist Cristine Crosby Decker projected slides of the drawings onto the hotel's walls, then sketched over the forms and painted them exactly as the originals appear. Often overlooked, one of the best is on a platform below the hotel's main property to the north, toward Bahía Santa Maria. This is the closest Los Cabos gets to a museum of its history, and you should see the paintings if you can. But remember, rowdy tourists bearing cameras and beer are definitely frowned upon here. ◆ Hwy 1, Km 12 (between Cabo San Lucas and San José del Cabo). 30496, 800/421.8925

35 Cabo del Sol Like a city unto itself, this 1,800-acre resort is beginning to emerge along two miles of the Mar de Cortés coastline, forever changing the landscape of the Corridor. At press time, the Jack Nicklaus-designed golf course was about to open to the public. By the turn of the century, the compound is scheduled to include 2,000 guest rooms in four deluxe hotels, 3,000 custom homes and residential units, and three golf courses. ◆ Hwy 1 (between the Twin Dolphin Hotel and Cabo San Lucas). 21701, 800/637.2226

36 Da Giorgio ★★★★$$$ The owners of this restaurant and its sister eatery at Km 25 excel in choosing settings that make what you eat far less important than where you eat it. At this branch in the **Misiones del Cabo** resort, the restaurant sits right above the sea with an unrivaled view of the rock arches at land's end. There isn't a better seat in Los Cabos for a sunset drink than at these private tables, dotted along small terraces on the oceanside cliffs. The views and atmosphere are so enchanting that it will be hard to move onto more solid fare. However, the spell continues by starlight, under which you can dine on dishes as simple as a shared pizza or as elaborate as butterflied shrimp in white wine. The ample salad bar is a definite plus, and the pasta dishes are satisfying, if unexciting. The sunset, however, is not to be missed. ◆ Italian ◆ Daily breakfast and dinner. Misiones del Cabo, Hwy 1 (between Cabo San Lucas and Cabo del Sol). No phone

The most economical meal in Mexico is the comida corrida, a fixed-price meal including soup, salad, entrée, rice, dessert, and a drink. The lunch is normally available throughout the afternoon at small cafes and restaurants favored by locals.

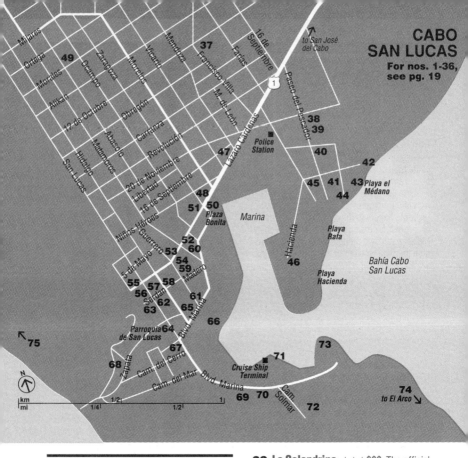

(Map labels, reading top to bottom / left to right:)

Milares • Ortega • 49 • Morales • Ocampo • Atikan • 12 de Octubre • Hidalgo • Matamoros • Abasolo • San Lucas • Zaragoza • Vicario • Mendoza • Morelos • Carranza • Revolución • 20 de Noviembre • Libertad • 16 de Septiembre • Niños Héroes • Obregón • Francisco Villa • Farias • 16 de Septiembre • M. de León • Lazaro Cardenas • Paseo del Pescador

37 • 47 • 48 • 51 • 50 • Plaza Bonita • 52 • 53 • 60 • 54 • 59 • 55 • 57 • 58 • 56 • Serdán • 62 • 61 • 63 • 65 • 5 de Mayo • Madero

Police Station • Marina • 38 • 39 • 40 • 42 • 45 • 41 • 43 Playa el Médano • 44 • Playa Rafa • Hacienda • 46 • Playa Hacienda • Bahía Cabo San Lucas

75 • Parroquia de San Lucas • 64 • 66 • Blvd. Marina • 67 • 68 • Zapata • Cam. del Cerro • Cam. del Mar • Blvd. Marina • Cruise Ship Terminal • 71 • 73 • 69 • 70 • Cam. Solmar • 72 • 74 to El Arco

N • km / mi • 1/4 • 1/2 • 1/2 • 1

1 to San José del Cabo

Cabo San Lucas

37 The Glass Factory Don't even think of trying to find this place on your own. It's hidden in a maze of dusty no-name streets, boatyards, and homes near the highway to Todos Santos, and even locals who've been here frequently get lost. The factory is run by a master glassblower from Guadalajara who oversees a dozen or so workers in a very hot room where huge gas furnaces roar with fire. The craftsmen stick long tubes into the fire and scoop up globs of molten glass, then blow forcefully and gently as they twirl them into goblets. Others concentrate on shaping plates and bowls, then coloring them with streaks of green and blue. Guests are invited to blow their own glass, which is much harder than it looks. Shelves at the front of the work-room display distinctively different mugs, beer steins, shot glasses, and dishes, many unlike what you'll find in town. The prices are said to be wholesale, though they seem a bit high. It's considered polite to purchase some-thing after the show; those little blue shot glasses adorned with emerald green cacti are a lightweight and inexpensive choice. Beware of buying too much, as nothing is more cumbersome than a carry-on bag filled with heavy glass. ◆ M-Sa. Off the Todos Santos Hwy (the northeast side of town). No phone

38 La Golondrina ★★★$$$ The official, unwieldy name is **The Trailer Park Restaurant at La Golondrina,** reflecting the ties between this pretty dining room and the enduringly popular restaurant at the **Faro Viejo** trailer park a few blocks inland. Operated by Douglas Gottfried (son of the trailer park owners) and Tito Roberts (who also owns the local **Domino's Pizza** franchise and **Lukas** disco), this eatery is housed in the oldest building in Cabo San Lucas. During the warm months dinner is served in the courtyard in front; in the winter tables are set up in a cozy dining room with an arched brick ceiling. The menu emphasizes bountiful feasts of barbecued chicken, platters of stir-fried chicken, beef, scallops, or shrimp (prepared as spicy as you wish), huge lobsters prepared five different ways, and at least four different types of fresh fish. Breakfasts are equally enormous. Like its parent restaurant, this place is popular with US expats and tourists who can count on dependable meals and friendly conversation. ◆ Mexican/American ◆ Tu-Sa breakfast, lunch, and dinner. Paseo del Pescador (between Hwy 1 and Playa el Médano). 30542

Approximately 60 native languages are spoken by about 50 indigenous groups in Mexico.

39 Peacocks ★★★★$$$ Chef Bernard Voll and restaurateur Gunter Richter have transformed the San Lucas dining scene with their stylish version of the ubiquitous *palapa* restaurant and their sublime culinary creations. Thick tree trunks support finely woven A-frame *palapas* covering two large rooms, where diners are seated on comfortable bent-willow chairs around bright white tables. Candles glowing in hurricane lamps and flames from the grills in the open kitchen illuminate the space. Chef Voll calls his culinary creations food without frontiers, blending flavors in unusual combinations. The escargots, for example, are served in a spicy Mexican relish; a piquant chicken breast sits atop linguine with pesto made from cilantro.

The menu changes every few days, but always includes the ever-popular fettuccine Alfredo with shrimp and scallops, and the shellfish extravaganza of lobster, crab stuffed with scallops, and skewered shrimp. If they're available, try the chicken liver mousse or baked feta cheese for an appetizer, accompanied by homemade bread and herbal olive oil. The wine list boasts several California labels (including champagne); also ask about the pricier wines not mentioned on the list. Chef Voll's talents soar with his desserts, especially the swan-shaped puff-pastry profiteroles filled with vanilla ice cream and chocolate sauce. Brewed decaffeinated coffee is another rare treat. If you don't make it here for dinner, at least end your day with dessert on the patio. ♦ Nouvelle ♦ Daily dinner. Paseo del Pescador (between Hwy 1 and Playa el Médano). 31858

40 El Rey Sol ★★★$$ Seeing several generations of a Mexican family gathered here for their weekly feast is a good sign that the chefs know their way around a tortilla. This place has been around for years, serving homestyle Mexican meals that haven't been diluted to suit tourist palates. Bring your fresh-caught *dorado*—one of Cabos's most popular catches—and have it fried, breaded, or sautéed, and be prepared for a savory repast. The enclosed brick-and-palm dining room is always cool and shady and is decorated with snapshots and business cards from dedicated clientele. Breakfast is especially good, and is capable of *levantando los muertos*—raising the dead, or at least those sad souls suffering from murderous hangovers. ♦ Mexican ♦ Daily breakfast, lunch, and dinner. Paseo del Pescador (between Hwy 1 and Playa el Médano). No phone

41 Meliá San Lucas $$$ The current headquarters for the local fun set is the swim-up pool bar, *palapa* restaurant, and beach at the more casual of the two Meliá hotels in Los Cabos. The view of **El Arco** (the granite arch where the Pacific meets the Mar de Cortés; see page 31) is outstanding, and the buildings form a staggered horseshoe of tiled roofs, arches, and patios that changes color from sand pale to sunset glow throughout the day. The 168 cool pastel rooms are perfect for escaping the blazing sun, especially if there's a good movie on the satellite TV. As neither the cuisine nor the camaraderie is spectacular in the restaurants and bars, the beachside *palapa* is probably your best choice. Downtown Cabo San Lucas is within walking distance, and the hotel offers a shuttle service to the **Meliá Cabo Real** for a change of scenery. ♦ Paseo del Pescador (between Hwy 1 and Playa el Médano). 31000, 800/336.3542; fax 30420

42 Pueblo Bonito $$$$ A stark white exterior with arches and domes gives this resort on the Playa el Médano a Mediterranean look. The 148 suites, which are also available as time-shares, have kitchenettes, dining areas, oceanfront balconies, and a pleasing blue-and-white decor. Beveled glass doors, chandeliers, and mosaic marble floors give the public spaces a sense of elegance typical of the Pueblo Bonito resorts, which take the time-share concept to new heights. The popular beach area is filled with parasailers, windsurfers, and jet skiers, and a fully equipped health club is available for those who want more exercise. There are two restaurants on site and several more within walking distance. ♦ Playa el Médano (off Paseo del Pescador). 32900, 800/442.5300; fax 31995

43 Playa el Médano Easily the most popular in San Lucas, this beach (its name means sand dune) is filled from sunup to sundown with *panga* (a small fiberglass boat) captains picking up fishing clients, windsurfers, jet skiers, vendors hawking straw hats, and beachcombers. Several small *palapa* restaurants dot the sand: **The Office** restaurant is immensely popular among vacationers, who take souvenir snapshots of each other lounging before the sign. The next beach south is often referred to as Rafa's, the name of a once-popular disco, now gone. ♦ Between the Pueblo Bonito and Hotel Hacienda

---

Restaurants/Clubs: Red   **Hotels:** Blue

Shops/ 🌳 Outdoors: Green   **Sights/Culture:** Black

44 Las Palmas ★$$ This ever-popular *palapa* restaurant owes its fame more to the congeniality of its clientele than to the quality of the meals. If you're craving fresh quail this is your place; otherwise stick to the lower-priced offerings such as simple grilled fish. The seating area spreads to the beach during peak times, and though it looks romantic, you may have a problem with sand flies and gnats. Volleyball games and tournaments are held along this stretch of beach. ♦ Seafood ♦ Daily lunch and dinner. Playa el Médano (near the Meliá San Lucas). 30447

45 Villa Alfonso's $$$$ This petite hotel in a gorgeous white house above Playa el Médano has only eight rooms, each more lovely than the last. All boast custom, handcrafted Mexican furnishings, folk art, and rugs, and some include whirlpool baths. The garden behind the house is a private, secluded area with a lap pool. For those who wish to be completely removed from the masses, this is the perfect spot. ♦ On the road to the Hotel Hacienda (at Playa el Médano). 30739, 800/347.1522

Within Villa Alfonso's:

Restaurant Alfonso's ★★★$$$$ The prix-fixe, six-course dinners served in the small dining room are easily the most elegant in Los Cabos—they even serve sorbet between courses. Each night's dinner includes several choices of appetizers, and entrées difficult to find in Los Cabos, such as lamb chops, veal *picata,* and duckling in orange sauce. Dress is casual, but stylishly so, and the conversation subdued. The main dining room is elegant and comfortable—but for a truly memorable night be sure to call in advance for a poolside table under the stars, with the sound of the surf to serenade you. ♦ Mexican/Continental/Nouvelle ♦ M-Sa dinner. Reservations recommended. 30739

46 Hotel Hacienda $$$ It's easy to see why this hostelry has remained popular for nearly two decades. Set on a spit of land jutting into Bahía San Lucas, from across the water the hotel looks like a whitewashed mission with a bell in its arched tower. Stone carvings of Aztec and Maya gods oversee walkways, town houses, and cabanas, and each turn brings another surprise, such as pastel paper flowers tucked into a bougainvillea arch. The hotel has 112 rooms, with the more expensive accommodations offering seaside balconies, separate living rooms, and marble baths. The beach is just a few steps away and has a great view of **El Arco** and the marina.

The Hacienda is owned by Budd Parr, a Los Cabos pioneer who also runs the **Hotel Cabo San Lucas** in the Corridor. His son Mitch oversees the hotel and visits with guests and their families, some of whom he's known since he was a child. Another long-timer here is the wood-carver Benito Herrera Ortíz, who was born in the state of Oaxaca in 1912 and for years made statues and furnishings in Mexico City. His artistry is evident in the woodwork throughout both hotels. Ortíz now has a small work area near the pool, next to the cage that holds Pancho, a vociferous green macaw. The restaurant offers decent Mexican food and seafood. ♦ Hacienda (off Paseo del Pescador). 30122, 213/655.7777

47 Latitude 22+ ★★$ Jimmy Buffet music and a tropical island style set the theme at this very casual *palapa* bar and restaurant, where the burgers are just like back home and even the Philly cheesesteak sandwich tastes authentic. If you're looking for a good place to hang out with other gringos and watch sports on TV, this is it. ♦ Mexican/American ♦ Daily lunch and dinner. Hwy 1 (between Mendoza and Morelos). 31516

48 Squid Roe ★★$ Part of Carlos Andersen's chain of fun, unbeatably popular tourist hangouts found in most Mexican resort towns. The menus are standardized and dependable, with barbecued ribs (under the "Oink-Oink" column), chicken ("Peep-Peep"), and steaks (yes, "Moo-Moo"). Portions are bountiful, beer comes in silver buckets with six frosty bottles, and waiters do everything they can to convince patrons to try at least one tequila shooter. The decor is junkyard carnival, with objects of amusement dangling from the ceiling and walls. Don't expect a quiet meal, as the noise level is always deafening, even when the place is empty. ♦ American/Mexican ♦ Daily lunch and dinner. Lázaro Cárdenas (between Zaragoza and Morelos) 30655. Also at: Carlos 'n' Charlie's on Blvd Marina. 30973; El Shrimp Bucket at Plaza Marina Fiesta. 32498

Chilies are the most popular seasoning in the world—and Mexicans make great use of the chili in their native dishes. Some chilies pack a surprisingly powerful punch, however, and if you happen to eat one that ignites your sensitive tastebuds, the best antidote is not to guzzle down that ice-cold cerveza, but to eat dairy products, such as milk, yogurt, and ice cream, or starchy foods like tortillas, bread, and rice.

49 El Faro Viejo ★★$$$ Most first-time visitors refer to this enduringly popular gringo hangout as "The Trailer Park Restaurant" for its location in a trailer park several miles northwest of the waterfront. If you arrive after 7PM, you'll probably have to wait for a table in the crowded open-air dining room. The menu includes barbecued chicken and ribs, and shrimp and lobster. Though prices are higher than at the restaurants by the marina (and cab fare adds to the expense), the food is very good, the portions substantial, and the conversations informative (you can pick up some great travel tips by eavesdropping). You'll also get to see how the working people of San Lucas live. ♦ American/Mexican ♦ M-Sa lunch and dinner. Abasolo (between Ortega and Morales). 31927

50 Plaza Bonita There's little chance you'll overlook this bulky, burnt-orange shopping and dining complex as the main road curves to Boulevard Marina and the waterfront at Cabo San Lucas's only traffic light. Part of a complex of offices, condos, and a private marina, the plaza has an Old Mexico feeling with fountains, arches, inner courtyards, and tiled domes. It's within easy walking distance from the **Meliá** and **Hacienda** hotels, along a dirt pathway leading to the marina and town. ♦ Daily. Blvd Marina (between Zaragoza and Morelos)

Within Plaza Bonita:

Salsitas ★$$$ There are few easier ways to while away the afternoon than sipping mango margaritas on a waterfront deck and watching the yachts go by. This eatery is much like a yuppified, California-chain Mexican restaurant—colorful and comfortable. The menu offers a sampling of Mexico's many regional cuisines, including tamales (corn dough wrapped around a meat filling), *huevos motuleños* (fried eggs in a sauce with ham and peas), empanadas filled with meat, and *chiles rellenos* stuffed with shrimp. The quality of the food seems to have diminished of late; order less expensive items until you check it out. ♦ Mexican ♦ Daily breakfast, lunch, and dinner. 31740

Dos Lunas Of the many sportswear boutiques in Cabo San Lucas, this one stands out for its high-quality selection of shorts, T-shirts, and pants, all done in vibrant tropical patterns by Australian designer Ken Done. The prices are as high as in the US, but being in the vacation mode may make you feel like splurging. ♦ Daily. 31969

Cartes Originally a branch of Mexico City's elegant (and expensive) furnishings boutique **Casa Dupois,** this shop still displays gorgeous china, pewter platters, antique furnishings, and woven fabrics. Now under the Cartes name, there also are more affordable inlaid wood picture frames, hand-painted plates, and blown glass vases. ♦ M-Sa. 31770

Libros If you want to get to the literary heart of Mexico, this small bookstore has a good selection of English and Spanish novels and magazines, and some excellent hardback books on Baja. ♦ Daily. 33171

51 Supermercado Plaza No matter where you're staying, it's a good idea to stock up on some groceries at the beginning of your visit. The selection at this supermarket is downright astounding, especially for those who remember the dark ages (several years past) when pickings were slim here. The frozen food cases are stocked with luxuries you thought you'd left behind—gourmet ice creams, frozen pastries, microwave dinners—and there's a wide selection of produce, fresh meats, and sundries. ♦ Daily. In the Plaza Aramburo, Lázaro Cárdenas (between Zaragoza and Ocampo). 31450

52 Temptations The flowing, loose-fitting styles and light-as-air fabrics displayed at this resortwear boutique are perfect for warm climates, and the designs are quite stylish and chic. The shop has a great line of 14K gold jewelry and hundreds of accessories cutely labeled "the great pretenders." You can also find the María of Guadalajara line of cotton gauze clothing in vivid purples, aquas, and pinks. ♦ Daily. Lázaro Cárdenas (between Abasolo and Matamoros). 31015

53 Mar de Cortés $ A longtime favorite with those who spend more time on the sea than in their rooms, this hotel is in the midst of the action, yet surprisingly quiet and cool. The 72 rooms are located in two sections, the oldest of which was built in the 1960s, with brick ceilings, colonial-style hardwood furnishings, and tiled floors. The newer rooms are less traditional, reminding one of the accommodations at standard chain motels. All rooms have air-conditioning, and some have small patios facing the swimming pool. Fishing and diving packages are available. ♦ Lázaro Cárdenas (between Guerrero and Matamoros). 30032; fax 30232. For reservations: PO Box 1827, Monterey, CA 93942. 408/375.4755, 800/347.8821; fax 408/646.0270

54 Cabo Wabo Cantina ★★$ Members of the rock group **Van Halen** opened this cavernous club a few years ago with major fanfare and appearances by several LA groups. Rumors abound every weekend as to what stars are in town and may appear on stage. Most of the time, however, the music is canned. An open-air cantina outside the dance hall serves decent tacos, nachos, and fish-and-chips, and there's even **Waboutique,** where you can buy your very own **Cabo Wabo** T-shirt. ♦ Rock Club/Cantina Tu-Su. Guerrero (between Lázaro Cárdenas and Madero). 31188

55 Pizza Oceano ★★$ Of the many pizza houses proliferating in Cabo San Lucas these days, this one has the best reputation, with locals raving about its high quality. Try the pepperoni or, for regional authenticity, have your pizza topped with chorizo, the Mexican sausage. ♦ Pizza ♦ Daily dinner. Lázaro Cárdenas (at San Lucas). 30932

56 Mi Casa ★★★★$$ The search for good Mexican food in Los Cabos was made easier a few years ago when this small cafe opened in an ancient cobalt blue house facing the plaza. The restaurant quickly outgrew its original dining room (which was turned into a folk art shop) and became an enchanting outdoor dining spot, with tables set on several levels in a courtyard behind the building. The walls surrounding the property are painted in an elaborate mural of village scenes created by artist Rafa Nafa. Spanish is the language of choice, and the menu includes nary a burrito, tostada, or fajita. Instead, those longing for tastes from the mainland enjoy *sopes* (thick tortillas covered with beans, cheese, and tomatoes), *poblano* chilies stuffed with seafood, and *chiles en nogada* (meat-stuffed chilies in a creamy walnut sauce). Even if the names of some of the dishes baffle you, give one a try; you won't find more authentic Mexican cuisine anywhere else in town. ♦ Mexican ♦ Daily lunch and dinner. San Lucas (on the west side of the plaza). 31933

56 Casas Mexicanas This tiny shop is filled with gorgeous pottery, paintings, lacquered boxes, and picture frames, all reasonably priced and difficult to resist. The quality is far better than at most of the souvenir shops; consider purchasing one lasting treasure here. ♦ Daily; closed at midday. San Lucas (on the west side of the plaza). 31933

57 Cabo San Lucas Kiosko and Plaza Cabo San Lucas's true downtown is several blocks northwest of here, but the main plaza is in the tourist zone near the waterfront. Unlike most Mexican plazas, you won't find many families gathered for an evening stroll here, but it is a pretty spot to rest and regroup, and there are several shops and restaurants around the square. ♦ Hidalgo (off Lázaro Cárdenas)

58 The Cheesecake Lady Locals can't start the day without the Lady's fragrant cinnamon rolls and wouldn't dream of celebrating a birthday without one of her elaborately decorated cakes. Her cheesecakes, in dozens of flavors from mango swirl to chocolate caramel pecan, are served in local restaurants and dining rooms; the seven-inch cakes are perfect for a small group of friends to devour while watching movies in a hotel room. At press time there were plans to remodel the space into a coffeehouse and art gallery. ♦ Bakery ♦ M-Sa. Hidalgo (across from the plaza). 30831

59 Antiguedades del Oraciones The owner must be out enjoying the sun, because this cluttered antique shop has very odd hours. It's unfortunate, since the collection of carved wooden *santos* (saints) is quite admirable. If you're interested in seeing more of the treasures inside than you can from the windows, make a point of stopping by whenever you're in the area, or leave the owner a note on the door to arrange a visit. ♦ Madero (between Guerrero and Blvd Marina). No phone

59 Minerva's Baja Tackle and Sportfishing Local anglers say **Minerva's** has the widest selection of tackle and gear in Los Cabos. Try a Mexican flag—a vivid red, white, and green feather—to lure a *dorado*. **Minerva's** also has one of the best fishing fleets around, with Capitan Tony as your guide. ♦ M-Sa; closed at midday. Madero (between Guerrero and Blvd Marina). 31282; fax 30440

60 Giggling Marlin ★$$ Some hardy souls think this spot is the ultimate place for frivolity and food. The wildly whimsical decor certainly makes it seem that way. From the signs at the front door claiming "Broken English Spoken Here" to the ceiling-high fish scale where inebriated patrons dangle by their heels, this place screams fun. Tacos, burgers, and the like are mediocre at best, and the noise is downright deafening, but the patrons seem quite content. ♦ American/Mexican ♦ Daily breakfast, lunch, and dinner. Blvd Marina (at Ocampo). 30606

Anglers Alley

No matter how chic Los Cabos becomes, it will remain first and foremost a fisher's paradise. Your chances of hooking a trophy-sized marlin or sailfish are quite good here, plus there's no shortage of smaller game fish. By dawn, the sea around Cabo San Lucas, which is commonly called Marlin Alley, is filled with everything from state-of-the-art yachts sporting electronic fish-finders to classic Baja pangas captained by fishermen raised on these seas. Fishing is such a big draw here that the annual **Bisbee Black and Blue Marlin Jackpot Tournament,** held at the end of October, carries a prize of more than a half-million dollars. Several smaller tournaments have recently been organized, too.

Naturally, all of this fishing activity has taken its toll on the supply of the really big ones. To help preserve these fish, those invested in the sportfishing industry have established a successful and popular catch-and-release program that encourages people who hook the giant game fish to commemorate their catch with a photograph and certificate (rather than a mounted specimen) and then return the fish to the sea.

With a combined fleet of more than 125 cabin cruisers and countless *pangas,* the sportfishing operators usually can accommodate all potential customers. However, the really great boats are often booked far in advance during the high season (October to Easter) and even in the late summer months when certain species are most plentiful. Most hotels can arrange fishing charters in advance, and several specialized companies advertise in US sportfishing magazines. Some of the top-notch companies with offices in the US and Mexico include:

Finisterra	....	30000, 213/583.3393
Juanita	....	30522, 213/386.3394
Palmilla	....	20582, 800/637.2226
Pices	....	30588, 408/375.3554
Solmar	....	30022, 800/344.3349

Restaurants/Clubs: Red   **Hotels:** Blue
Shops/ 🌳 Outdoors: Green   **Sights/Culture:** Black

Señor Sushi

61 Señor Sushi ★★$$ One of the calmer restaurants on the main drag, this eatery advertises that it serves everything *but* sushi, from barbecued ribs to shrimp scampi. Tables are set on a raised terrace beside the sidewalk so you can view the action without being overwhelmed by it. The early evening dinner specials are a good bargain, and the generous portions of fajitas are a treat for the taste buds as well as the wallet. Half-priced drinks are served during the early evening Happy Hour; live music and dancing start at 8PM. ♦ Seafood/American ♦ M-Su brunch, lunch, and dinner. Blvd Marina (at Guerrero). 31323

61 Galería El Dorado This gallery, the largest branch in a chain of three, displays paintings and sculptures by Mexican and international artists in rotating shows. It also displays an array of fanciful papier-mâché animals and one-of-a-kind silver and gold jewelry. The back-room shop has rows of knickknacks, onyx bookends, chess sets, and inexpensive trinkets from throughout Mexico. ♦ Daily. Blvd Marina 81 (at Guerrero). 30817

62 Restaurant/Taquería San Lucas ★★$ Also known as the Broken Surfboard, this streetside *taquería* is a longtime favorite among San Lucas regulars. The tacos, enchiladas, burgers, and *huevos Mexicana* (scrambled eggs with onions, tomatoes, and chilies) are cheap, filling, and reasonably tasty. ♦ Mexican ♦ Daily breakfast, lunch, and dinner. Hidalgo (between Madero and Zapata). No phone

63 Mamma Eli's A mind-boggling, wallet-draining array of Mexican folk art, clothing, jewelry, and glassware is temptingly arranged over three stories of display rooms, giving the browser a great overview of mainland Mexico's artistic wealth. This boutique is a refreshing discovery after you've gone through the silver baubles, cotton blankets, pottery, and tawdry trinkets at most of the other gift shops. Shop here first for a taste of the best, then compare with the rest. ♦ Daily; closed at midday. San Lucas (between Serdan and Zapata). 31616

"All the vegetation visible to the eye seems to conspire against the intrusion of man. Every shrub is armed with thorns. The cactus tortures the travelers with piercing needles and remorseless fangs. Burrs with barbed thorns cover the ground. The very grass, wherever it grows, resents the touch with wasplike stings that fester in the flesh....A land accursed of God!"J. Ross Browne on Baja California, Harper's Magazine, 1863

Parroquia de San Lucas

ANTHONY QUARTUCCIO

64 Parroquia de San Lucas (Parish Church of San Lucas) You might easily overlook this simple Catholic church, situated as it is on a small side street, but it's worth the search. Atop a wall near its driveway is a large stone book describing the church's origins. It explains, in Spanish, that the area was inhabited by the Pericúe Indians, who called their settlement Anikan. Spanish explorers renamed it Cabo San Lucas in the early 1700s, and the church was established in 1730 by Spanish missionary and priest Nicolás Tamaral (later killed by the Pericúe). A stone archway, which holds a bell sent to San Lucas by the Spaniards in 1750, is inscribed "St. Ignacium, 1746." Fuchsia bougainvillea splashes color along the outer stone walls, but the only fancy touch within is the splattering of glitter in the ceiling plaster. Simple signs near the altar quote the bible: "*Yo soy el pan de la vida*" (I am the bread of life). The faithful, who love their parish church, are ministered to by padres from Italy. ◆ San Lucas (between Zapata and Camino del Cerro)

65 Hotel Marina $ Surprisingly quiet and calm in the midst of the waterfront frenzy, the 30-room hotel sits above a peaceful courtyard with a small pool and hot tub. All rooms, except those facing the street, have tiled baths and pretty flowers painted along the white walls. If you're hungry, you'll have to venture out—there's no restaurant. ◆ Blvd Marina (at Hidalgo). 30030

66 Plaza Las Glorias $$$ Few locals have any kind words for this six-story, four-block-long mass of earth-toned buildings, which houses a 237-room hotel, and several restaurants and bars. The complex effectively blocks the water view and cooling sea breezes from the neighborhood's long-established businesses and residences. After five years, the hotel still seems cavernously bare, with dark hallways leading to nowhere. But it often offers discounted room rates and is certainly the most convenient place to stay if you lack a car and want to be in the midst of the action. The gift shop has a good selection of English-language periodicals. ◆ Blvd Marina (between Madero and Hidalgo). 31220, 800/342.AMIGO; fax 31018

67 Romeo y Julieta ★★★$$ The area's Italian restaurant craze was launched here, and even in low season patrons find themselves crowded elbow-to-elbow in the bar. Owner Luis Bulnes, the Spanish patriarch of much of the cape's tip, who first came to Los Cabos in 1954, has created a sure winner with both his menu and style. Offerings include pizzas and crusty bread from brick, wood-burning ovens, and homemade pastas with authentic flavor and spice. Diners help themselves to marinated vegetables and puffs of fried dough from an antipasto bar at the center of the dining room. The Caesar salad is suitably piquant and the chocolate mousse pie worth saving room for. Newcomers often leap to their feet to snap photos of liquid flames as the waiter prepares a sinfully sweet *café Mexicana flambeau* with Kahlua and ice cream. The refreshingly cool dining room is both romantic and informal, with candlelight and flowers decorating the tables where fishermen gather in T-shirts and shorts. ◆ Italian ◆ Daily dinner. Camino del Cerro (at Blvd Marina). 30225

68 El Pedregal If your rental car has a cooperative transmission and reliable brakes, take a drive up the narrow twisting roads past dump trucks and construction crews to the gorgeous homes where wealthy Cabo devotees take up residence on their extended vacations. Roofs are covered with terra-cotta or hand-painted sunflower-yellow tiles, white archways frame cobbled stairways, and most windows face west to a stunning view above the Pacific. ♦ Camino del Cerro (near Blvd Marina)

69 Hotel Finisterra $$$ The hotel has such a captivating setting that Rolling Stones guitarist Keith Richards and model Patti Hansen chose it as the site for their wedding, and countless other newlyweds have spent their honeymoons here. The 110 rooms in the original sections of the hotel have been refurbished in a pastel color scheme and offer modern amenities. Those on the east overlook the harbor, bay, and downtown Cabo San Lucas, while the west side has both an unfortunate perspective on the hotel's new tower and a breathtaking view of the ocean. A new eight-story building houses 87 large, modern rooms with oceanfront balconies, satellite TV, phones, coffeemakers, and hair dryers.

Other recent renovations include an elevator from the beach up to a bridge leading to the original buildings (in the past, only the hardiest of souls braved the steep climb up and down the cliffs from the hotel to the beach). At press time, a second building was under construction on the beach; the addition will bring the total number of rooms to 300. ♦ Blvd Marina (between Camino del Cerro and Camino Solmar). 30000; fax 30590. For reservations: 18552 MacArthur Blvd, Irvine, CA 92715. 800/347.2252

Within the Finisterra:

The Whale Watcher Bar There isn't a better place in Los Cabos for viewing great gray whales than from this spot. It's easy to while away an entire afternoon in this open-air bar, sipping margaritas, scanning the horizon, and waiting for the sun to set in a blaze of hues. ♦ Daily. 30000

70 El Galeón ★★★★$$ The view of the marina at sunset from the second-story balcony is reason enough to dine here. This restaurant is more sedate and refined than most Cabo San Lucas eateries, with courtly waiters, subdued lighting, and satisfying Italian cuisine. Definitely splurge on the giant lobsters if they're offered. Caesar salad and flaming coffees are prepared tableside, and several veal dishes appear on the menu. You can keep the tab low by ordering pizza or pasta and antipasto. Argentinian pianist Ronald Valentino is a big draw with couples who shun the blaring rock and roll of many in-town restaurants and prefer to listen to a repertoire from Gershwin to Chopin. ♦ Italian ♦ Daily dinner. Blvd Marina (near the cruise ship terminal). 30443

Cruising Los Cabos

Cabo San Lucas is a port of call for several ships sailing the Pacific coast of Baja and the west coast of mainland Mexico. The vessels anchor east of **El Arco** in the Mar de Cortés; passengers are then ferried to the **Bahía San Lucas** marina and sportfishing dock, less than a 10-minute walk from downtown. And that's when the fun begins. Sportfishing enthusiasts can hire a *panga* at the dock for a quick troll out to sea, but don't count on hauling in a big catch because the best action seems to occur at dawn, before the cruise ships have docked. Many people take a glass-bottom boat ride, but if you're short on time, skip it and move swiftly through the open-air artisans' market, unless you're a die-hard treasure hunter (there are some good finds in silver jewelry, if you can tell real from fake). If your aim is to shop, eat, and drink, you'll be satisfied by the establishments along Boulevard Marina and the side streets of Cabo San Lucas.

Energetic hikers will appreciate Baja's natural beauty by walking east across Boulevard Marina and past the **Solmar Suite**'s pool bar to the craggy peak of Baja's southernmost tip, where the Mar de Cortés and the Pacific meet. Walk north along the wide, windswept beach, but don't attempt a solitary swim; the waves are brutal here and even surfers stay clear of these shores.

For equally spectacular scenery with less physical exertion, hire a taxi for a leisurely cruise along the highway between Cabo San Lucas and San José del Cabo. Make as many stops as time allows at the stark, natural bays and dramatic resort hideaways, especially the **Twin Dolphin** and the **Palmilla** hotels, which may change your mind about cruising and prompt you to remain settled on shore.

Cruise lines docking in Los Cabos include:

Carnival	800/327.9501
Commodore	800/832.1122
Princess	800/446.6690
Royal	800/227.4534
Seaborn	800/397.9595
Starlite	800/448.7827

"The very air here is miraculous, and outlines of reality change with the moments. A dream hangs over the entire region."

John Steinbeck, *Log from the Sea of Cortez*

71 Bahía Cabo San Lucas and Marina The busiest waters in the Mar de Cortés have to be along the Cabo San Lucas waterfront, from the sportfishing docks to **El Arco** nearly a mile from shore. Cruise ships anchor nearby and passengers are shuttled to shore by the score. Sportfishing and sightseeing *pangas* clog the wooden docks, while luxury yachts and sailing ships line up in marinas removed from the mobs. Nearly every tourism service has a booth here, with barkers on commission enticing you to go fishing, scuba diving, sailing, and more. Prospective anglers cluster around the southern edge of the marina where fishing boats bring in their haul. If you don't mind flies and the strong smell of fish, visit the sportfishing docks between 1 and 3PM, when the boats come in, and see proud anglers posing beside their catches at the weighing station. Cruise passengers have a waiting lounge with bathrooms and snack shops to the north. Between the docks and the cruise area is an open-air artisans' market, designed to capture the tourist dollar before it gets to town.

The entire marina is a good place to shop and compare. Check out any boat before you board—are there seats, lifejackets, and canopies to shade you from the sun? Does the engine at least look like it will run smoothly? Does the operator provide *cold* drinks and purified water? A trip out to sea is imperative in Los Cabos, and all the more enjoyable if you sail in comfort.

Within Bahía Cabo San Lucas and Marina:

Amigos Del Mar One of the oldest and most reputable scuba companies in Los Cabos has dive trips to the underwater sandfalls (similar to waterfalls, but made of sand) near **El Arco,** or to the coral reef north of Los Cabos at Cabo Pulmo. ♦ Daily. Sportfishing dock. 30505, 800/447.8999; fax 30887

Artisans' Market You'll find a good selection of handicraft-style souvenirs by browsing among the tables and stands at this market on the water's edge. The most unusual and indigenous items are the ironwood carvings of marlin, sailfish, turtles, and whales. The best bargains can be found in silver jewelry, if you can tell the difference between real silver and alloys. Real silver should be stamped "925," while alpaca (known in the US as German silver or nickel silver), the most common silver imitation, is a mix of silver and nickel, and is lighter in color and weight than sterling. ♦ Daily

Operador Pez Gato If you're going out on the water to sightsee rather than dive or fish, consider a sunset catamaran cruise with this operator. The Pacific glows gold as the ship sails along the shore, and if you're lucky, you might see a baby whale off the bow. They also offer snorkeling and sailing tours. ♦ Daily. 33797, 714/673.4705

72 Solmar Suites $$$ These low, white-stucco buildings look like space colony pods against the sandstone foothills of the Sierra Gigante. The rocky ridge extends into the sea at the peninsula's tip, cupping the hotel in stark seclusion. The Pacific pounds onto a dramatic stretch of pristine beach, crowded only in the winter months, when people gather to watch the whales swim a few yards offshore. This resort has by far the most striking setting of any of the local hotels, and does a great job of enhancing, rather than intruding upon, the scenery. Town is just a 10-minute walk away, yet you feel completely removed from the action.

The hotel underwent extensive remodeling in 1993, including the construction of an enormous brick-domed ceiling in the lobby. All the existing 70 rooms and 22 new rooms were turned into suites with sitting areas, balconies, telephones, minibars, air-conditioning, and satellite TV (a blessing on hot afternoons when a cool room and a good movie are requisites). The pool was also completely redone and has a pleasant swim-up bar. A second pool and hot tub were added in the adjacent **Solmar Beach Club** time-share. The renovations have not detracted from the property's stark beauty and sense of isolation—it is the ideal destination for those seeking soothing solitude. ♦ Camino Solmar (off Blvd Marina). 33535; fax 30410. For reservations: Box 383, Pacific Palisades, CA 90272. 310/459.9861, 800/344.3349; fax 310/454.1686

Within the Solmar:

La Roca ★★★$$ The outdoor patio seats at this restaurant command an unequaled view of a pretty palm garden and the sea. And the food is good enough to keep guests from going into town for a meal. Dinner is particularly pleasant as mariachis serenade the diners, backed by the pounding of the surf. Though romantic Mexican ballads are their specialty, don't be surprised if the lead singer bursts into a rousing, Spanish rendition of Elvis Presley's "All Shook Up." The chef goes all out for the Saturday night Mexican fiesta, with a buffet of regional dishes, including great tamales, *chiles rellenos,* chicken mole, and various marinated salads. Staff members present an impressive folk dance show, and all guests get a kick out of swinging a bat at a giant piñata. ♦ Mexican/American ♦ Daily breakfast, lunch, and dinner. 33535

73 Solmar Fishing Fleet This is the largest sportfishing fleet in Los Cabos, with at least 21 cruisers and *pangas.* There are full- and half-day fishing trips from the marina and ships for group charters. Take a gander at the marlin, *dorado,* and sailfish mounted on walls and hanging from ceilings all over the hotel for an idea of what the fishing enthusiasts are so wild about. The newest addition to the fleet is the custom-built 112-foot *Solmar V,* a stunning ship with interiors of gleaming mahogany, brass, and etched glass. There are 12 cabins with private baths and VCRs, and a luxurious dining room and salon. The live-aboard ship travels to nearby dive sites, but its specialty is long-range sportfishing and diving trips to the Socorro Islands some 400 miles offshore. The week-long trips give divers a chance to swim with manta rays, hammerhead sharks, whale sharks, and other giant pelagics; anglers have the opportunity to capture (and release) many types of fish. When not at sea the ship is docked in the marina; look for its distinctive green-and-yellow trim. ◆ Off Blvd Marina. 33535; fax 30410. For reservations: Box 383, Pacific Palisades, CA 90272. 310/459.9861, 800/344.3349; fax 310/454.1686

74 El Arco The granite arch at land's end where the Pacific meets the Mar de Cortés is Baja's trademark. Equally dramatic are the gray-brown granite boulders rising from under the sea south of the arch. Note the skinny tall one that looks like the Baja Peninsula turned upside-down. A cruise past the arch is imperative for any first-timer; chances are good you'll see sea lions sunbathing and cavorting on the rocks, and you'll use up at least one full roll of film trying to capture the arch's natural majesty

75 El Faro de Cabo Falso (The Lighthouse) A small crook of land pokes into the Pacific about five miles northwest of San Lucas, forming a miniature tip that looks like land's end from the sea. The lighthouse was built here in 1890 and served as the peninsula's beacon until it was destroyed by a *chubasco* (hurricane) in 1957; today it still stands, but is in a state of ruin. Since no paved road leads to it, you'll need a four-wheel-drive or off-road vehicle to take you there. When motorcycle groups aren't racing by, it's a secluded and stunning spot, giving a sense of Baja's wild majesty. The lighthouse is also visible from boats on the Pacific. ◆ Eight kilometers (five miles) northwest of Cabo San Lucas

---

A popular saying appropriate to the Baja terrain is "Es tan Mexicano come el nopal" (He is as Mexican as a cactus).

Herbal Magic

Amid the cacti and chaparral covering the dry desert floor grows the *damiana* plant, a nondescript, gray-green jumble of twigs with mystical powers. Herbalists and *curanderos* (healers) believe *damiana* can cure *la gripa* (flu), *letargo* (lethargy), and *escalofríos* (chills). Its most legendary claim, however, is the ability to enhance one's sexuality, turning a timid lover into a proverbial Don Juan.

The dried twigs and leaves of the plant are sold in herb stores throughout Mexico and the US, but in Los Cabos, *damiana* is usually found in markets and liquor stores as a yellow-green liqueur. The legend of this love potion has been enhanced by packaging the brew in a glass bottle shaped like a voluptuous, seated, nude woman. Beware the aphrodisiacal effects of the Los Cabos margarita when concocted with a dash of this potent herbal liqueur.

Bests

Leticia J. Klein
Owner, La Casa Vieja, San José del Cabo

In Los Cabos:

A sunset stroll along **Boulevard Mijares** in San José del Cabo to the *zócalo* (town square). Take a break in front of the mission and watch its twin towers catch fire as the immense, orange sun sets in the background.

December through April is whale-watching season, and you can often spot these large animals with their newborn calves swimming in the sea. The summer months bring huge schools of manta rays, who put on a great show for people on the beach as they leap from the water and virtually fly along the coastline making a clapping sound.

For a real treat, take a boat ride to **El Arco** and **Lovers' Beach.** Regardless of how many times I've done this, the beauty of the area never fails to take my breath away.

Another great spectacle in Los Cabos is the large variety of cacti in full bloom in the autumn.

When I really want to get away from it all, I pack a lunch and head for one of the beaches along the corridor.

Thierry and Veronique Paquet
Chef/Owners, Le Bistrot, San José del Cabo

In San José del Cabo:

St. Maria Beach on Highway 1; it's truly beautiful.

Tropicana Bar and Grill, for the good food.

Los Barriles, a resort on the Sea of Cortés, 60 kilometers (40 miles) south of San José del Cabo.

The **Mercado Municipal** in the town center. It's a great place to pick up fresh fruit.

Restaurants/Clubs: Red	Hotels: Blue
Shops/ ♣ Outdoors: Green	**Sights/Culture:** Black

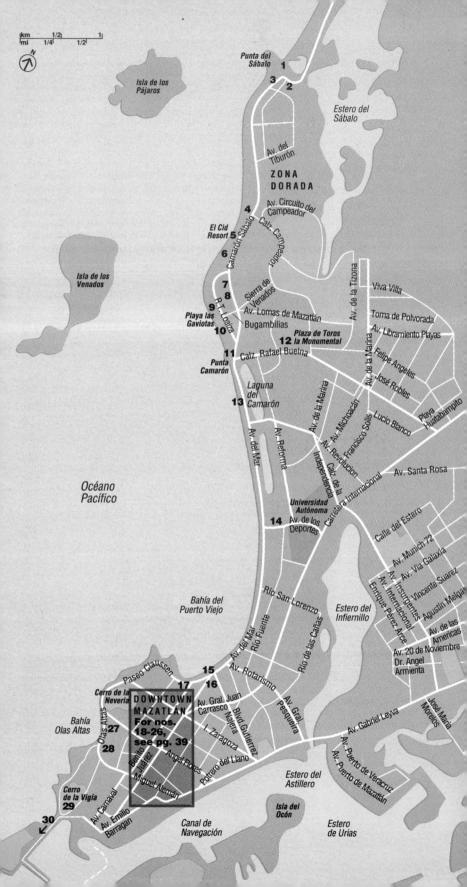

km   1/2   1|
mi   1/4   1/2|
N

Isla de los
Pájaros

Punta del
Sábalo   **1**

3
2

Estero del
Sábalo

Av. del
Tiburón

**ZONA
DORADA**

Av. Circuito del
Campeador

4

El Cid
Resort   **5**

6

Calz. Campeador

Camarón Sábalo

Av. de la Tizona

Viva Villa

7

8   Sierra de
Venados

Av. Lomas de Mazatlán

Bugambilias

Av. de la Marina

Toma de Polvorada

Av. Libramiento Playas

Av. de la Tizona

Felipe Angeles

José Robles

Playa
Huatabampito

Playa las
Gaviotas

R.T. Loaiza

9

10

Plaza de Toros
la Monumental   **12**

11   Calz. Rafael Buelna

Punta
Camarón

Francisco Solís

Lucio Blanco

Laguna
del
Camarón

13

Av. de la Marina

Av. Michoacán

Av. Revolución

Av. del Mar

Av. Reforma

Calz. de la Independencia

Carretera Internacional

Av. Santa Rosa

Universidad
Autónoma

14   Av. de los
Deportes

Calle del Estero

Av. Munich 72

Av. Via Galaxia

Vincente Suarez

Agustín Melgar

Av. de las
Américas

Océano
Pacífico

Av. Insurgentes

Av. Internacional

Enrique Pérez Arce

Av. 20 de Noviembre

Dr. Angel
Armienta

Bahía del
Puerto Viejo

Río San Lorenzo

Río Fuente

Av. del Mar

Av. Gral.
Pesquera

Río de las Cañas

Estero del
Infiernillo

15

17   **16**

Paseo Claussen

Cerro de la
Nevería

Bahía
Olas Altas

Olas Altas

27

28

**DOWNTOWN
MAZATLÁN
For nos.
18-26,
see pg. 39**

Av. Gral. Juan
Carrasco

Blvd Gutiérrez

I. Zaragoza

Najera

Angel Flores

Potrero del Llano

Av. Rotarismo

José María
Morelos

Av. Gabriel Leyva

Av. Puerto de Veracruz

Av. Puerto de Mazatlán

Benito Juárez

Miguel Aleman

Cerro
de la Vigía   **29**

Av. Carnaval

Av. Emilio
Barragan

30

Canal de
Navegación

Isla del
Ocón

Estero del
Astillero

Estero
de Urías

Mazatlán

Mazatlán, a traditional Mexican port city with a stunning coastline, marks the beginning of the **Mexican Riviera** along the **Pacific coast**. Inhabited by almost 450,000 people, Mazatlán was one of Mexico's earliest coastal tourist centers and has some of the best sportfishing around. Thousands visit here each year to enjoy the area's comfortable climate, reasonable prices, and renowned hospitality.

Hotels, restaurants, and shops can be found along the **Zona Dorado** (Golden Zone), an area that includes a 14-mile-long stretch of beach and bustling streets where most people congregate. The zone stretches farther north each year as developers clear the way for new resorts and marinas along acres of prime shoreline. Still, there are isolated, beautiful beaches that can be easily explored. Various travel agencies and hotels offer day trips that include snorkeling, swimming, and picnicking to such uninhabited offshore islands as **Isla de la Piedra, Isla de los Chivas, Isla de los Pájaros**, and **Isla de los Venados**.

Downtown Mazatlán, with its central market, plaza, and cathedral, is the heart of the city's activities and is well worth visiting for those who want a true taste of Mexico. On the edges of downtown lie the crumbling historical buildings of **Mazatlán Viejo**, where historians, architects, and entrepreneurs are working to restore the city's treasures, many dating from the late 1800s and early 1900s. The **Teatro Angela Peralta** (Angela Peralta Theater), centerpiece of Mazatlán Viejo, was reopened in 1992 after decades of neglect, and many buildings in neighboring streets have undergone renewal.

A primary port since the arrival of the Spaniards, Mazatlán is one of Mexico's biggest harbors and home to a thriving commercial fishing fleet and a large fish-packing and export business. The surrounding sea offers anglers the opportunity to land giant marlin and sailfish, and excellent charter boats are available in a range of sizes and prices. (A growing number of sportfishers here are practicing the catch-and-release method; they enjoy the thrill of the fight and capture, then return the graceful fish to the sea to ensure survival of the species.)

For more than a hundred years, Mazatlán has been known as a party town—mainly due to its magnificent Carnival celebration (held for a week in late February or early March), with festivities similar to those in New Orleans and Brazil. It's de rigueur for residents to wear beautiful costumes, attend formal balls, and dance in the streets and cafes until the wee hours of the morning during this week. (Those who return for the celebration annually make their hotel reservations at least six months in advance.) During Easter week, the Zona Dorado is taken over by students on spring break.

Area code 69 unless otherwise noted.

Getting to Mazatlán

Airport

Mazatlán's airport is a 30-minute drive from downtown. Look for the *colectivo* (van) ticket counter at the airport for information on service to your hotel. Returning, you must take a taxi; there are generally plenty waiting at the hotels. Be sure to reconfirm flight reservations at least 24 hours before your departure.

Airlines

Aero California	162190, 862193
Aeroméxico	141111, 823444
Alaska Airlines	852730/1
Delta	142644
Mexicana	812722

Mexico has almost two million square kilometers (761,600 square miles) of land.

Getting around Mazatlán

Buses
For schedules, go to the bus terminal on Río Tamazula (Hwy 15). Call 817625 for more information.

Car Rental
The following agencies have offices downtown or at the airport:

Avis Camarón Sábalo 314............... 140040, 140050

Budget Camarón Sábalo 402 132000

Hertz Ave del Mar 1111 136060

National Camarón Sábalo at Plaza el Camarón ....
....136000

Taxis
Cabs are easily flagged down on the street. *Pulmonías* are open-air jitneys that cost almost the same as taxis. To hire a taxi call 816129, 823189

FYI

Emergencies
Canadian Consulate R.T. Loaiza at Bugambilias........
....837320

Police...148444

Red Cross...816355

24-hour Medical Clinic Carretera Internacional al Norte, Colonia Foviste.................................831090

US Consulate, Circunvalación 120 ....
....852208, 852205

Money
You can change money at the airport, hotels, and banks, with the latter giving you the best rate. Banks are open for changing money Mondays through Fridays from 8AM to 11AM. There are also *casas de cambio* (exchange houses) in town, which are open throughout the day and evening. International credit cards and US dollars are accepted in most restaurants, hotels, and shops. Try not to be short of cash on Sundays, because it can be difficult to change money on that day, except in some hotels. Always keep bills of small denominations on hand, since it can be difficult to change larger bills (except at banks).

Banamex Benito Juárez and Angel Flores 821324

Banca Serfin Camarón Sábalo at Nelson 161595

Banco Mexicano de Occidente Angel Flores and 5 de Mayo 820866

Tours
The following tours are available through several agencies.

City Tour A bus cruise along Mazatlán's oceanside drive provides you with a view of divers leaping from cliffs and a visit to the **Mercado Romero Rubio** (Romero Rubio Market), the **Catedral de Inmaculada Concepción** (Cathedral of the Immaculate Conception), Mazatlán Viejo, and Cerro de la Vigía (Lookout Hill).

Fiesta Cruise A three-hour boat tour of Mazatlán's bay and sheltered harbor.

Mountain Tour A full day of exploring the nearby colonial towns of Copala and Concordia, home of popular hardwood furniture factories (see "Off the Tourist Track" on page 39).

For information and reservations contact:

Marlin Tours 855301

Playa Sol/Alitour...837777

Tour Guide Association................................827534

Visitors Information
Dirección de Turismo (Tourism Office) Banco de Mexico Bldg, Olas Altas 1300 .....851221; fax 851222

Area code 69 unless otherwise noted.

Mazatlán

1 Hotel Camino Real $$$ This aristocrat among hotels commands an exclusive setting on a hillside overlooking the sea. Half of the 169 rooms have a private balcony. Those on the west look out on the Pacific and miles of beaches, while those on the east take in a lagoon and the distant Sierra Madre. Accommodations are spacious, air-conditioned, and decorated in pinks and purples. Guests enjoy gathering at the heated pool, and the two lighted tennis courts are especially popular in the evening. There are also several restaurants.

For even more pampering, request accommodations in the Royal Beach Club. Guests in this section of the hotel have the best views of the ocean, special concierge service, and complimentary continental breakfast, as well as cocktails and hors d'oeuvres every afternoon in the Club lounge. Nancy and Ronald Reagan are among those who have enjoyed the casual elegance of this property. To the north, construction has begun on a separate new marina and megaresort. ◆ Camarón Sábalo (at Punta del Sábalo). 131111, 800/722.6466; fax 140311

2 Sr. Pepper ★★★★$$$ Ask anyone in Mazatlán to recommend a high-quality steak house, and you'll probably end up here, savoring tender Sonora beef barbecued over mesquite coals. Choose between the rib eye, porterhouse, or filet mignon. (These are enormous steaks; if you tell them you want to share, they will cut it in half and bring two plates with all the trimmings.) Start with a huge margarita and move on to the fried zucchini appetizer, which is a treat, as is the complimentary buffet served at the bar Wednesdays through Saturdays. There's also succulent lobster, jumbo shrimp, and cajun blackened fish. After your meal, order *brewed* decaffeinated coffee—this is one of the few places on the Mexican coast that offers it. An intimate candlelit atmosphere, a piano bar, crystal and silver settings, and attentive waiters make each visit a special occasion. Service is excellent, right down to the crumb sweeper after your meal. ♦ International ♦ Daily dinner. Camarón Sábalo (across from the Hotel Camino Real). 140120

3 Pueblo Bonito $$$ This all-suite hotel and time-share resort is one of the most elegant places to stay in town. An opulent chandelier crowns the beautiful lobby, and antique art tastefully fills the public rooms. Its 247 dome-ceilinged rooms all have king-size beds, tiled baths, kitchenettes, and ocean views; most are decorated in pink. All the amenities, including three swimming pools, restaurants, bars, and satellite TV, are offered. ♦ Camarón Sábalo 2121 (between El Cid Resort and the Hotel Camino Real). 143700, 800/442.5300; fax 141723.

4 Tres Islas ★★★$$ Families gather on Sunday afternoons at this *palapa* (palm-thatched hut) on the beach for afternoon-long feasts, which normally include sizzling seafood cooked on clay hibachis. The restaurant is named for the three islands it faces—Isla de los Chivas, Isla de los Pájaros, and Isla de los Venados. Here, you'll feel far removed from the bustle of the tourist zone, actually just a few blocks away. ♦ Seafood ♦ Daily lunch and dinner. Camarón Sábalo (north of El Cid Resort). 143923

5 El Cid Resort $$$$ This city-within-a-city hotel and residential resort sprawls over 900 acres, and consists of three beachfront, five-star hotels; private villas; and an 18-hole golf course. Its thousand rooms are spread out among the Castilla, a 17-story tower that is the hotel's main building; the 25-story El Moro Tower, an all-suite facility with top-floor penthouses; and the less expensive Granada, featuring rooms in low-rise buildings by the swimming pools. The resort is set within lush grounds connected by walkways, bridges, and shuttles. Guests have use of the country club and golf course, the 17 lighted tennis courts (clay and all-weather), 15 restaurants, five swimming pools, a health and fitness club, shops, and a disco. As might be expected, the resort actively pursues potential time-share buyers a bit more aggressively than you'd like. Continuing the megadevelopment theme, the El Cid Marina project is under construction, with plans for more homes and yet another hotel. ♦ Camarón Sábalo (between Calzado Campeador and Rodolfo T. Loaiza). 133333, 800/525.1925; fax 141311

Within the El Cid Resort:

La Concha ★★★$$$ On the beach, this flamboyant restaurant boasts an elaborate *palapa,* illuminated with hanging spotlights. Guests at the resort have been known to eat all three meals here, starting with the bountiful brunch buffet, then a midafternoon snack, and finally a late dinner accompanied by live music. For a total seafood extravaganza, order the *parrillada de mariscos,* one of the more spectacular versions of this ubiquitous Mazatlán dish. Here it includes lobster, shrimp, oysters, and octopus on a bed of lettuce and rice. Dine inside or out, with a view of the ocean either way. ♦ International ♦ Daily breakfast, lunch, and dinner. 133333

Rancho Las Moras

A neglected tequila ranch in the countryside outside Mazatlán has become the area's most innovative and deluxe resort ($$$$). Guests stay in private cabanas filled with folk art and antiques, dine in a restored hacienda, and sunbathe by the pool in ultimate tranquillity. Horseback riding through the mountains to isolated pueblos is the main recreational activity, along with tennis, hiking, and hayrides. Owner Michael Ruíz has also turned the 3,000-acre ranch into a refuge for animals by importing miniature horses and all sorts of birds. Peacocks stroll the grounds beside guinea hens, while wild falcons and hawks soar in the sky. Chickens of every imaginable strain have full run of the property, laying their eggs in window boxes and pottery planters. A white wedding chapel overlooks the property; the original stable is now a glassed-in lounge.

To protect its patrons' privacy, drop-in visits to the ranch are not allowed. You can, however, make reservations in advance to dine at its restaurant (★★★★$$$), an experience not to be missed. Tables covered with embroidered mantillas, and set with painted pottery and blown glass (all made by hand) overlook the grounds and pool. The chef bakes all the bread in an outdoor wood-burning oven, and specializes in outstanding regional Mexican cuisine. Settle in for a leisurely lunch and you may never want to leave. For reservations: Camarón Sábalo 204, Suite 6, Mazatlán. 165044; fax 165045. In the US, write: 9297 Siempre Viva Rd, Suite 15-474, San Diego, CA 92173

Restaurants/Clubs: Red   Hotels: Blue
Shops/ 🌳 Outdoors: Green   **Sights/Culture:** Black

6 Hotel Costa de Oro $$ This 250-room resort is made up of four complexes and sits on both sides of the street. The beach complex is the most popular, with two pools and a restaurant. Rooms in the newer tower are all suites with kitchenettes, and the building offers the privacy of its own pool. Another section is adjacent to three tennis courts. Guests have the option of an all-inclusive program that includes meals, domestic wine, beer, soft drinks, and tax. There are two restaurants and three bars to choose from. Time-shares are available. ♦ Camarón Sábalo (between El Cid Resort and Rodolfo T. Loaiza). 135444, 132005, 800/351.1612; fax 144209

Within the Costa de Oro:

La Carreta Owner Julieta Fuentevilla Alvarez travels throughout Mexico selecting the best folk art and furnishings for her shops. Among the treasures are pillowcases made from *molas*, appliquéd fabric scenes of village life. Her two other shops in the **El Cid** and **Playa Mazatlán** hotels have similar displays, and if you're a true collector you'll want to visit all three. ♦ Daily; closed at midday. 14134

7 Baby Tacos ★$ Taco stands abound throughout Mazatlán and are by far the least expensive places to eat. This one is a step above the street-vendor taco stand, with a clean food preparation area and outdoor seating. Here, you'll pay less than at the fast-food franchises, and get the taste of real Mexico. ♦ Mexican ♦ Daily lunch and dinner. Garzas (between Rodolfo T. Loaiza and Camarón Sábalo). No phone

8 Centro de Artesanías (Mazatlán Arts & Crafts Center) This sprawling center is the hotel zone's version of a public market. Shoppers should allow plenty of time to explore Mexican crafts in the labyrinth of shops in the two-story, thatch-roofed structure. Potters create original ceramics, and carvers work wood into traditional or modern creations. Rug weavers, tinsmiths, and jewelers will fill your personalized request, and orders are taken for custom-made clothing. ♦ Daily. Between Camarón Sábalo and Rodolfo T. Loaiza (north of the traffic circle). 135243

Within the Centro de Artesanías:

No Name Cafe ★★$ A totally north-of-the-border cafe right down to the prices in US currency, this spot is favored by a young crowd drawn to watching sports events on TV. Cold Pacífico beer is the favorite drink; burgers and fries the top menu seller. The patio is a good spot to wait while your friends finish their shoppping. ♦ American ♦ Daily breakfast, lunch, and dinner. 132031

9 Hotel Playa Mazatlán $$ The first hotel built along the Zona Dorada remains one of the most popular. Though not as glitzy as some of the newer additions, this 423-room establishment has a carefree atmosphere reminiscent of Old Mexico. If you want an ocean view and a balcony, make reservations in advance and request one of the 54 deluxe units. The two-bedroom suites have garden views. John Wayne often stayed here. ♦ Rodolfo T. Loaiza 202 (at Playa Las Gaviotas). 134444, 800/762.5816; fax 140366

Within the Hotel Playa Mazatlán:

Fiesta Mexicana This place has had the city's best Mexican fiesta for over 25 years; it's so good even locals attend. The fiesta is held on Sunday nights in low season, and as often as three times a week when tourists abound. The price of admission includes an enormous Mexican buffet and all the tequila and beer you can consume. An excellent folkloric dance show, relatively tame cockfights, ranchero and mariachi performances, and a spectacular fireworks display make up the entertainment. Tickets are available at travel agencies and hotel tour desks. ♦ Admission. Su; more often in tourist season (mid-November through mid-April). 134444, 134455

Terraza Playa ★★★$$ A *palapa* shades the tables on this patio and provides the ideal perch for enjoying a meal and watching beach scenes. This is really a place for a soup-to-nuts dinner—shrimp cocktail, creole soup (with bits of tortillas, green peppers, and cheese), and *churrasco Argentine* (a tender, marinated beef fillet). The chef salad served in a pastry shell is a nice change from heavy meals.

Vendors strolling along the beach will whistle to catch your attention and get you to examine their blankets, straw hats, purses, silver jewelry, and more. If you're not interested, just avoid eye contact. Sometimes you can get good buys, especially if you're skilled at bargaining. Night turns the restaurant into a sparkling setting with a backdrop of stars and music for dancing. On Sunday night the patio tables are good for watching the 8PM fireworks show. No shorts after 6PM. ♦ International ♦ Daily breakfast, lunch, and dinner. 134444, 134455

More than 37 million pounds of shrimp are processed in Mazatlán each year.

Mexico Mexico Women who discover this tiny clothing shop early in their stay will be tempted to invest in a whole new wardrobe. The brightly colored gauze clothing is perfect for tropical climates, especially when personalized with the one-of-a-kind accessories. ♦ Daily; closed at midday. No phone

10 Hotel Los Sabalos $$ One of Mazatlán's newer high-rise hotels where athletic types can enjoy the two lighted tennis courts, pool, sauna, and whirlpool. Many of the 95 rooms have windows that don't open; the suites cost more, but have balconies where you can get fresh air. ♦ Rodolfo T. Loaiza 100 (between Bugambilias and Camarón Sábalo). 835333, 800/351.1612; fax 838156

Within the Hotel Los Sabalos:

Joe's Oyster Bar and Grill ★$ There's no better place to view the beach scene than from this immensely popular seaside cafe, where scantily clad diners quaff cold beers and lemonade after a long sunbathing session. The ambience is far more exciting than the food; stick with simple tacos and seafood cocktails. Patrons get rowdy when the band blares rock and roll favorites nightly after dark. ♦ Seafood/Mexican ♦ Daily lunch and dinner. 135333

11 Valentino's Complex You can't miss the white turrets and domed Arabesque rooftops perched atop Punta Camarón on the south end of the Zona Dorada. Overlooking the sea, this complex enjoys one of the most breathtaking views in Mazatlán. At one time the only tenant was **Valentino's** lively disco, but the distinctive structure continues to grow and now houses a cluster of businesses geared for nighttime dining and entertainment. ♦ Punta Camarón (off Camarón Sábalo)

Within Valentino's Complex:

Valentino's Discotheque No expense was spared in creating this extraordinary dance club. The sound system and laser lights are straight out of Hollywood, and revelers dance up a storm. For those who prefer less noise, **Valentino's** offers another dance floor next door with a quiet, intimate atmosphere, soft music, and the chance to enjoy slow dancing. A game room is available with tables set up for checkers, backgammon, and chess. It's not "in" to arrive before midnight, and customers are expected to dress up. ♦ Cover. Daily. 841666

El Sheik ★$$$ The bubbling waterfall and intimate banquettes scattered about the room provide a cozy setting, and dress is more formal than at most local restaurants (no shorts, please). Seafood is your best bet here, especially the giant Sheik-style shrimp; for the purist, the shrimp brochette is sweet and fresh. Don't order the steak—it's simply not their forte. The waiters put on a great show of flaming coffees and desserts. Even if you're not hungry, consider visiting the restaurant for the spectacular views. Call early and request a table on the balcony where the breeze is balmy and you can see the stars. ♦ Seafood ♦ Daily dinner. Reservations recommended in winter. 141616

12 Plaza de Toros la Monumental (Bullring) Bullfights are presented here every Sunday from Christmas through Easter, and are taken very seriously by aficionados, especially when superstar matadors are in town. Seats in the *sombra* (shady) side of the arena are the most expensive, but you'll appreciate them as the temperature rises. If you haven't been to a bullfight before, be prepared for a gory finale. Tickets are available at travel agents and hotel tour desks. Rodeos (called *charreadas*) are also held at the ring sporadically throughout the year. ♦ Calzado Rafael Buelna (east of Camarón Sábalo). 833598, 841777

13 Señor Frog's ★★★$$ This restaurant is known throughout Mexico as a rowdy hangout where drinking, dancing, and flirting are the norm. If you can handle the unbelievably high level of music and revelry, it's well worth at least one dinner, since the food is very good. Try the *molcajete* (strips of chicken or pork served on a heated clay tray with grilled green onions and melted cheese). Steaks and barbecued chicken and ribs are among the most popular meals, and all the Mexican specialties are exceptionally well prepared. ♦ Mexican/American ♦ Daily lunch and dinner. Av del Mar 225 (between the Zona Dorada and downtown). 821925

Sportfishing

Both commercial and recreational deep-sea fishing are big business in Mazatlán, where world records are often broken. Local captains encourage sportfishers to release their big catches, particularly the large marlin and sailfish for which the area is known. An estimated 12,000 billfish are caught in these waters annually. Several sportfishing fleets operate out of the pier on Boulevard Joel Montes Camarena on the Pacific side of Cerro del Creston. Stop by the pier in midafternoon to see how the anglers are faring and to talk to the captains before choosing a charter. The **Star Fleet**, the largest sportfishing operation in Mazatlan, has an office here. 822665, 823878, 800/633.3085; fax 825155.

14 Acuario de Mazatlán (Mazatlán Aquarium) There are dozens of tanks at this aquarium that are filled with colorful sea horses, eels, lobster, and Day-Glo tropical fish—at least

300 species of fresh- and saltwater fish are on display. Other highlights include the show put on several times a day by California sea lions and singing birds and educational films on the marine world shown in the auditorium. Schoolchildren on field trips visit the adjacent playground and botanical garden; amid the trees in the garden is a small zoo—be sure not to miss the sinister-looking crocodiles. ♦ Admission. Daily. Av de los Deportes 111 (off Av del Mar). 817817, 817815

15 Monumento al Pescador This bronze sculpture was built in 1958 as a tribute to the hardworking fishermen who have built a viable industry that still beats tourism as the leader of Mazatlán's economy. The rather bizarre design of a reclining nude woman extending her hand to a burly, naked fisherman is sure to catch your eye. ♦ Av del Mar (at Blvd Gutierrez Najera)

16 Cenaduría La Negra ★★★$ Maria Luisa Cardenas has been serving excellent traditional Mexican meals for many years, a fact attested to by her loyal fans. The friendly waiters serve large platters of *carne asada* (grilled marinated steak or pork), fried chicken, and pork ribs. It's one of the best places in town for *pozole* (a savory hominy stew). ♦ Mexican ♦ Tu-Sa dinner. Blvd Gutierrez Najera 218 (at Av del Mar). No phone

17 El Marinero ★★$$ A popular local haunt for decades, this classic Mexican seafood house is filled with brightly colored serapes, brick archways, and music from strolling mariachis. The specialty of the house, which easily serves at least two, is the seafood *parrillada* (a clay hibachi loaded with shrimp, frog's legs, oysters, and delicate fish fillets stuffed with seafood, all garnished with onions, peppers, tomatoes, and limes). If you get up early in the morning, you might see owner Miguel Cruz picking and choosing the freshest fish as the boats pull up across the street. ♦ Seafood ♦ Daily lunch and dinner. Paseo Claussen (at 5 de Mayo). 817682

18 Mercado Romero Rubio In the heart of downtown, the enclosed, cast-iron market bustles with residents on their daily errands. Originally built in the 1890s, it was recently renovated for its hundredth birthday. Chickens hang in the open air in the meat section (which can be particularly odiferous); piles of shrimp and fresh fish lie atop ice. Papayas, mangoes, pineapples, and other fruits are stacked beside each other in colorful arrays—bring your camera for some memorable shots. One small section specializes in herbs, incense, and magical potions, another in religious statues and prayer cards. Leather goods, straw baskets and hats, and assorted souvenirs are priced far lower than at shops in the Zona Dorada, especially if you're good at bartering. Visit early in the morning, before the crowds, heat, and aromas become overwhelming. ♦ Daily. Bounded by Benito Juárez and Aquiles Serdan, and Melchor Ocampo and Leandro Valle

19 Cerro de la Nevería (Ice Box Hill) In the 1800s tall-masted ships from San Francisco sailed into Mazatlán's port carrying all types of cargo. One of the most important was ice. A ship would barely be docked before the precious load was rushed up to this hill and placed in tunnels and caves packed carefully with gunnysacks and sawdust. The ice preserved fresh-caught shrimp for the fledgling industry and pampered those who could afford this extravagance.

Before it became an ice locker, the hill served as a lookout station for the Spanish. Soldiers on patrol searched the horizon for the masts of pirate ships commanded by such evildoers as captains Cavendish and Drake, who brought trouble and tragedy to Mexico's coastal cities in their search for Spanish galleons laden with gold and silver. Mazatlán's port was the main shipping point for the neighboring mining communities Rosario, Copalá, and Panuco. Years later during the Mexican Revolution, the hill was used as a repository for munitions. ♦ Vista Hermosa (at Paseo Claussen)

20 Catedral de Inmaculada Concepción (Cathedral of the Immaculate Conception) The two yellow-tiled spires poking into the sky over downtown Mazatlán are relatively new additions to this cathedral of many architectural styles. Construction of the church was begun in 1855 under the orders of Bishop Pedro Lozay Pardave and was completed 20 years later. The facade and central altar are Gothic, while the two side altars are Neo-Classical. The many chandeliers, ethereal frescoes, gilded arches, marble pillars, and formal balconies give the interior a decidedly Baroque effect. The two peaked belfries were added in the early 1900s, and the cathedral was designated a basilica in 1935. ♦ 21 de Marzo (at Benito Juárez)

21 Plaza Revolución Sometimes referred to as Plaza Republica, the town's main square bustles with shoeshine boys looking for business, people chatting on park benches, and children playing. In the center of the park is a two-story wrought-iron gazebo with an interior cafe that looks like a 1950s diner. On Friday evenings families socialize, and vendors sell *elota* (hot ears of corn), balloons, cotton candy, and cold drinks.

In 1913 the plaza's gazebo was the site of the first radio telegraph station in Mazatlán. Cables serving as antennae were stretched to the dome of the cathedral across the street. During the 1920s and 1930s, it was the stage for Carnival dance bands and recently it held a display of moon rocks brought back aboard the *Apollo IX*. The city band plays in the gazebo on Thursday mornings, and a ceremonial color guard lowers the flag every evening at dusk. ♦ Bounded by Benito Juárez and Nelson, and Angel Flores and 21 de Marzo

Off the Tourist Track

Just over an hour's drive from Mazatlán, through low hills covered with rugged bushes and green mango groves, lies the pueblo Concordia, which was founded in the 1500s and inhabited by Spanish settlers and Jesuit missionaries who profited from the success of nearby gold and silver mines. Today the town is a craft center known for its hand-carved hardwood furniture and pottery. There are more than 60 resident cabinetmakers here, most with workshops attached to their homes. Also worth seeing is the town's large plaza, which dates back to the colonial era, and the **Catedral de San Sebastián** (Cathedral of St. Sebastian); the oldest Baroque church in the state, it was built between 1706 and 1785.

A few miles away is the village of Copala, a tranquil retreat to the gold-mining epoch of the late 1800s and early 1900s. This former boomtown is now a well-preserved Mexican pueblo of some 600 full-time residents and a growing population of US expatriates and retirees. **Daniel's Restaurant** (★★$$) at the entrance to town, is a requisite stop for lunch and a piece of banana-cream coconut pie. Owner Daniel Garrison, whose grandmother is buried in the town cemetery, hails from California. A local hangout, the eatery is a serene hideaway, with a calming view of the countryside. If you want to spend the night (well worth it), try the large, comfortable rooms in **Daniel's** small hotel ($). After the tour groups leave, the town settles into bucolic serenity, with the silence broken only by crowing roosters and barking dogs. The cobblestone and dirt streets are lined with century-old white stucco homes, their tile roofs smothered in fuchsia bougainvillea. Neighbors gather at the small central plaza in early evening and stop by the **Catedral de San José** (Cathedral of San José) built in 1641. If it weren't for the electric lights (installed in 1979) and the occasional car, you'd think you had wandered into the past. You can get there by rental car or through arrangements with tour companies, who will drop you off one day and take you back to the city the next.

In the 1800s Mazatlán was rich in precious mahogany and ebony wood, but had no sawmill to make boards. Instead, the local hardwoods were exported, and buildings were constructed of redwood boards imported from San Francisco.

22 Royal Dutch ★★$$ Owners Roelof and Alicia have brought a bit of Holland to this semirestored historical house with their wonderful pastries. Tables are set around the edges of an overgrown courtyard; customers filter in throughout the day for cappuccino and apple strudel, or salads and sandwiches. There's also a mouth-watering selection of carrot cake, homemade breads, and cookies to take out. ♦ Cafe/Bakery ♦ M-Sa. Mariano Escobedo and Benito Juárez. No phone

23 Doney ★★★★$$ A more-than-125-year-old mansion has been cleverly converted into this charming restaurant where locals come to enjoy a fiery *asada al carbon* (Mexican-style barbecued meat), or spicy sausage and fried *platanos* (plantains). On Sunday afternoons the restaurant is filled with families enjoying the *comida corrida,* an entire meal that includes soup, entrée, and dessert. If it's offered, try the sensational *pibil* (pork cooked in banana leaves). On most tables you'll see a pitcher of fresh *naranjada* (orangeade), a sweet and cold treat. Run by the same family for years, the restaurant provides consistently outstanding home-style Mexican cooking. Check out the photos of Mazatlán Viejo and don't leave without having a piece of apple or lemon meringue pie. ♦ Mexican ♦ Daily breakfast, lunch, and dinner. Mariano Escobedo 610 (at 5 de Mayo). 812651

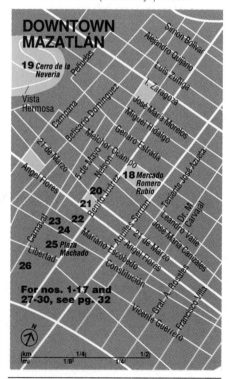

DOWNTOWN MAZATLÁN

19 Cerro de la Neveria

Vista Hermosa

Simón Bolívar
Alejandro Quijano
Luis Zuñiga
I. Zaragoza
José María Morelos
Miguel Hidalgo
Genaro Estrada

Peñuelas
Belisario Domínguez
Melchor Ocampo
21 de Marzo
5 de Mayo
Nelson
Angel Flores
Benito Juárez
Campana

18 Mercado Romero Rubio

20

21

23 22
24
25 Plaza Machado
Libertad
26

Teniente José Azueta
Serdán
Aquiles Serdán
21 de Marzo
Angel Flores
Mariano Escobedo
Constitución
Leandro Valle
José María Canizales
Gral. A. Rosales
Dr. M Carvajal
Vicente Guerrero
Francisco Villa

Carnaval

For nos. 1-17 and 27-30, see pg. 32

N

km
mi   1/8   1/4   1/4   1/2

Restaurants/Clubs: Red   Hotels: Blue

Shops/ ♥ Outdoors: Green   Sights/Culture: Black

39

Mazatlán Viejo

In the late 1800s, when it was the major port for the Pacific coast of Mexico, Mazatlán was quite a wealthy city. Immigrants from Germany, Spain, and the Philippines made their fortunes in silver and gold from mines in the nearby mountains, and from the country's most profitable foundry. Wealthy mine owners and shipping magnates built palatial mansions befitting their social standing just a short carriage ride from the central plaza. As the mines were depleted and other ports thrived along the coast, Mazatlán's boom dwindled, and the old homes fell into decline.

In the late 1980s, the people of Mazatlán began to look to the old neighborhoods in search of their history and tradition. A group of architects and preservationists persuaded the government to delineate a historical center and protect the older buildings from neglect and destruction. The neighborhood now called Mazatlán Viejo radiates inland from a promenade along a particularly gorgeous stretch of sand and sea known as Olas Altas (High Waves), at the foot of Cerro de la Vigía (Lookout Hill). Buildings are gradually being restored as cafes, theaters, and schools, and the area is thriving as a result of its revival. Wander these back streets for a view of the true Mazatlán, filled with architectural surprises and a sense of cultural renewal.

24 Cafe Pacífico ★★$$ The structure that houses this unpretentious cafe was built in 1875; the bar has the original old-style bricks and scorched timbers. The full-length, open-air windows with iron bars (wooden shutters close it up at night) make the place feel like a small Spanish tapas bar. Don't expect fancy fare, just a few seafood dishes, sandwiches, drinks. It's a great vantage point for watching activities across the street at Plaza Machado, especially from the umbrella-shaded sidewalk tables. ♦ Mexican ♦ Daily breakfast, lunch, and dinner. Constitución (across from Plaza Machado). No phone

24 La Casa de Ana ★★$ In a restored building, this may well be the only vegetarian restaurant in downtown—it specializes in Mexican dishes made with meat substitutes. The best bargain is the daily *comida corrida*, a multicourse meal that usually includes soup, salad, rice, beans, an entrée, and dessert. Lighter meals include cream of vegetable soup, soy "beef" burritos, or a bowl of granola with yogurt and fresh fruit. Tables are set under an old ficus tree across the street from the plaza, making it a good place to stop for a cool drink of purified water blended with crushed fruit. ♦ Vegetarian ♦ Daily lunch and dinner. Constitución 115 (across from Plaza Machado). 852839

24 La Hosteria ★★★$$ The sidewalk tables here have become the unofficial hangout for the theater crowd (it's close to the **Teatro Angela Peralta**); the building itself was a glamorous nightclub in the 1920s. Unlike most restaurants in the neighborhood, this one focuses on English and gringo cuisine, with fish-and-chips, steak sandwiches, and seafood chowders among the favorite dishes. Try the banana pancakes topped with ice cream and Kahlua syrup for breakfast if you're in need of a sugar rush. ♦ American ♦ M-Sa breakfast, lunch, and dinner. Constitución 519 (across from Plaza Machado). 855474

25 Plaza Machado The centerpiece of Mazatlán Viejo, this square has a new Moorish-style gazebo surrounded by flowering trees and iron benches. The buildings facing the plaza have been rescued from obscurity and now house trendy cafes where locals and tourists mingle over coffee or beer. ♦ Bounded by Carnaval and Benito Juárez, and Constitución and Libertad

26 Teatro Angela Peralta Mazatlán Viejo's future was guaranteed with the opening of this restored theater a few years ago. In 1869 the theater's original benefactor, Filipino merchant Manuel Rubio, felt Mazatlán needed a cultural center and studied pictures of the grand opera houses of Europe for inspiration. Construction progressed slowly on the **Teatro Rubio,** lapsing for a time after Rubio was lost at sea while on a fund-raising journey. In 1883, the theater was finally ready for its inaugural concert by Mexican diva Angela Peralta. But tragedy struck once again: The star arrived by ship from San Francisco but succumbed to bubonic plague before her performance. Appropriately, the theater was renamed in her honor.

For much of the next century the building served as a cultural, political, and entertainment center for the city, its grandeur often ignored. It was the venue for spirited rallies during the revolution of 1910, and for boxing matches and vaudeville shows. The roof blew away during Hurricane Olivia in 1975, but occasional concerts were still held under the starlit sky. Finally, in 1986, the Friends of the Teatro Angela Peralta was formed to spearhead the theater's reconstruction.

Architect **Juan José León Loya,** who bears a strong resemblance to the theater's original master carpenter, his great grandfather Santiago León Astengo, oversaw the reconstruction. The original tropical

Neo-Classical facade was restored and painted a soft dusty rose; the ornate Baroque interior was rebuilt to be as close to the original as possible. Performances are held sporadically in the concert hall, which is open for public viewing during the day. ♦ Daily. Carnaval (at Libertad). 812236

27 La Siesta $ Favored by travelers who prefer downtown, this place sits across the street from the crashing waves of Olas Altas. It has the advantage of being close to Mazatlán Viejo's historical sites; guests feel like they're staying in a Mexican town rather than a homogenized tourist district. Rooms are on four levels of an old wooden structure painted a cheery white and green. The guest rooms with balconies at the front of the hotel have a view of the sea. All 56 rooms and bathrooms are large and clean, perfectly serviceable, if unexciting. There's a restaurant. ♦ Olas Altas 11 (between Angel Flores and Miguel Alemán). 816350

28 El Museo de Arqueología (Archaeology Museum) The city's small archaeological museum contains artifacts from the state of Sinaloa, as well as changing exhibits of paintings, sculpture, and other works by local artists. ♦ Donations. Tu-Su; closed at midday. Sexto Osuna (off Olas Altas). 853502

29 Cerro de la Vigía (Lookout Hill) Some of Mazatlán Viejo's finest buildings are at the bottom of this hill. While winding toward the top you'll pass the **Universidad de Mazatlán,** housed in an ostentatious 19th-century mansion, and the dull gray **Casa de Eduana** (Customs House) constructed in 1828. Near the top is a lookout point and the **Observatorio** (Observatory), a bunker with gun slits built in 1872. The view encompasses the sportfishing, commercial, and naval piers on the east side of downtown Mazatlán, and the lighthouse atop Cerro del Crestón (Creston Hill). ♦ Carranza (off Olas Altas to the top of the hill)

30 El Faro (The Lighthouse) Perched on the top of Cerro del Creston, this is the world's second-highest lighthouse after the one in Gibraltar. About 505 feet above sea level, its light is seen offshore for 36 nautical miles. It was built during the 1930s, part of a project commanded by **President Porfirio Díaz,** linking what was then an offshore island to the mainland by the construction of a complex breakwater. The hike to the top takes about 30 minutes. Carry along some water and snacks; cold sodas are available from the lighthouse keeper. ♦ Cerro del Creston (off Camerena)

Bests

Professor Gilberto Limon de la Rocha
Director of Tourism Promotion and Marketing, Coordinación General de Turismo del Estado de Sinaloa

In and around Mazatlán:

The sweeping view of the 20 plus kilometers of Mazatlán's sandy beaches at sunset and the orange-hued rays cast on an intense blue sea.

Copalá's captivating charm observed from the main square, the **Church of Saint Joseph** and the 400-year-old buildings make us wonder away to what this enchanting place might have been in 1565 when it was founded.

The beauty of **Stone Island** with its inland canals, walled in by tall thickets of mangrove, the profusion of multicolored birds and the many fish species making the canals their natural habitat.

The **Doney** restaurant close to the Mazatlán city hall; unexcelled food, the famed and savory "enchiladas suizas" are unique. One wonders whether the Swiss gourmets are familiar with enchiladas.

The enticing architecture of the historical and colonial center of Mazatlán. The **Angela Peralta Theatre,** an architectural jewel is the centerpiece of this enchanting area.

The view of Mazatlán's enormous blue bay at sunset ...

The enchantment of the town of **Cosala,** 161 kilometers (100 miles) northwest of Mazatlán, founded in 1562 with its 1780 **Church of St. Ursula** and the incredible 200-year-old clock on top of the

still older city hall. This clock functions by means of a huge rock pulled up to the ceiling by a rope. It takes 24 hours for the rock to reach the floor, then the whole operation is started anew.

Michael Ruiz Loe
Owner, Operator, Rancho Las Moras Guest Ranch, La Carreta Gift Shops

Hotel Playa Mazatlán, sitting at sunset on the terrace with that special someone.

Carnival in **Mazatlán** at the **Plaza la Machado** and be sure to stop and eat at the cafes around the plaza.

Plaza Garibaldi in Mexico City is the best for romantic Mariachi music.

Rancho las Moras, Mazatlán—If you want to see the luxury of old Mexico and get away from the modern tourist destinations, come to the ranch. Here you can see the Mexico of yesterday with all the adventure of the countryside—horses, tennis, swimming—it is a private hacienda where you will feel right at home. Come join me for a "Vampiro," the ranch drink.

Mazatlán was the second city in the world to be bombed by an airplane. In 1914, during the Mexican Revolution, a homemade bomb was hand-dropped from an early-model biplane as it swooped low over the city. It missed the target, soldiers at Cerro de la Neveria, and landed on the street, causing injury to several people.

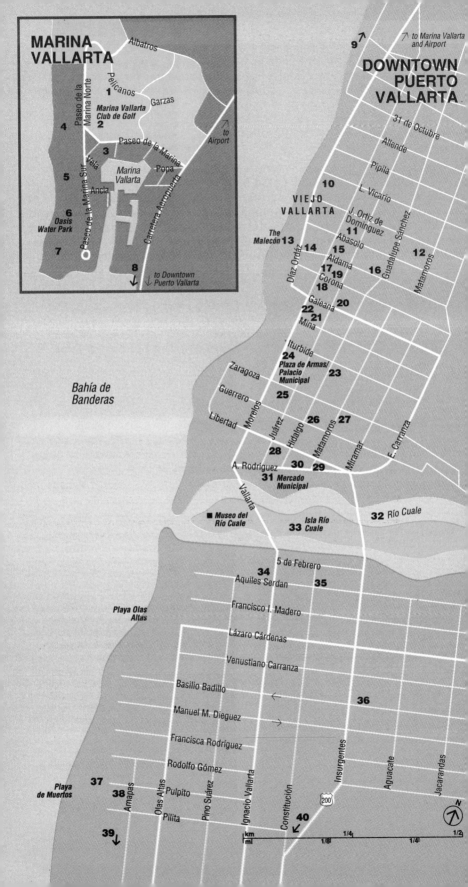

MARINA VALLARTA

Albatros

Pelicanos

1

Paseo de la Marina Norte

Garzas

Marina Vallarta
Club de Golf

2

Paseo de la Marina

to
Airport

3

Vela

Popa

Paseo de la Marina Sur

Marina
Vallarta

Ancla

Carretera Aeropuerto

4

5

6
Oasis
Water Park

7

8

↓ to Downtown
↓ Puerto Vallarta

DOWNTOWN PUERTO VALLARTA

9 ↗

↗ to Marina Vallarta
and Airport

31 de Octubre

Allende

Pipila

L. Vicario

10

Guadalupe Sánchez

J. Ortiz de
Dominguez

11

VIEJO
VALLARTA

The
Malecón **13**

14

Abasolo

15

12

Díaz Ordaz

Aldama

16

Matamoros

17
19

Corona

18

Galeana

20

22

21

Mina

Iturbide

24

Zaragoza

Plaza de Armas/
Palacio
Municipal

23

Guerrero

25

Libertad

Morelos

Juárez

26

Matamoros

27

Hidalgo

Miramar

E. Carranza

28

A. Rodriguez

30

29

31 Mercado
Municipal

Vallarta

■ Museo del
Río Cuale

Isla Río
Cuale

33

32 Río Cuale

5 de Febrero

Bahía de
Banderas

34

Aquiles Serdan

35

Francisco I. Madero

Lázaro Cárdenas

Venustiano Carranza

Playa Olas
Altas

Basilio Badillo

←

Manuel M. Dieguez

→

36

Francisca Rodríguez

Rodolfo Gómez

Ignacio Vallarta

Insurgentes

Aguacate

Jacarandas

Playa
de Muertos

37

38

Amapas

Olas Altas

Pulpito

Pino Suárez

Constitución

200

40

Pilita

39 ↓

km
ml

1/8

1/4

1/4

1/2

N

Puerto Vallarta

Although Puerto Vallarta—nestled alongside the broad **Bahía de Banderas** (Bay of Flags)—is documented in ships' logs from the early 1500s, it didn't develop into a city until centuries later. The first village on the site, **Las Peñas**, began with just a lean-to to shelter workers unloading salt for use in the neighboring mining towns of **Cuale** and **San Sebastián.** By 1880 the village had grown to a population of 1,500, and six years later it was given official political standing. In 1918 the name Las Peñas was changed to Puerto Vallarta, after **Jalisco**'s governor Ignacio L. Vallarta.

It wasn't until the early 1930s that tourists started trickling into town. But by 1963, when Richard Burton and Ava Gardner starred in the film *The Night of the Iguana,* shot in Puerto Vallarta, international publicity attracted droves of curious people. That prompted a building frenzy that almost got out of hand. Hotels, restaurants, shops, and roads sprouted up without much forethought, both downtown and along the northern coastline. Fortunately, civic leaders realized that the city was being destroyed by progress, and undertook a development project that has restored at least some of Puerto Vallarta's original beauty.

On the northern outskirts of town, the **Marina Vallarta** project is nearing completion as a full-scale resort. The road from the marina and airport to downtown has been widened, and downtown traffic congestion has been slightly eased with the construction of a new road leading to the coastal highway that bypasses the city. Downtown streets have been paved with cement and cobblestones, and the web of telephone and electrical wires that once marred the landscape have been buried underground.

The southern coast of Puerto Vallarta still reflects the area's natural beauty. Lush green jungle grows to the edge of the sea and the road seems to be literally cut out of the mountainside, curving, twisting, and climbing along spectacular scenery. The lavish homes gracing this coast are owned by North Americans and out-of-town Mexicans, who make up a large part-time community. Puerto Vallarta has its faithful followers who wouldn't dream of missing their annual journeys to this charming colonial city by the sea.

Area code 322 unless otherwise noted.

Getting to Puerto Vallarta

Airport

Downtown Puerto Vallarta is a 20-minute drive south of the airport; Marina Vallarta is five minutes south, but the trip can be considerably longer depending on how many stops the airport *combis* (vans) make. When making reservations, ask about courtesy pickups provided by some hotels. Otherwise, the *combis* have set fares to the hotels; buy your ticket at the taxi booth before going to the vans.

Airlines

Aeroméxico	10055, 42777
Alaska Airlines	11350, 11352
American	11799, 11927
Continental	11025, 11096
Delta	11032, 11919
Mexicana	11266, 46165
Taesa	11531, 47990

Getting around Puerto Vallarta

Buses

Transports marked "Ixtapa" run north from town to Marina Vallarta; those with a Mismaloya sign run south to Camino Real and Mismaloya. Buses designated *Hoteles* travel between town and the north hotel zone.

The buses can be hot and crowded, but the nominal price (under $1) makes them a great way to get around. Stops are indicated by a blue-and-white sign with a drawing of a bus. Buses begin and end their routes at Plaza Lázaro Cárdenas near Playa de los Muertos.

Car Rental

All the car rental agencies listed below have desks at the airport, as well as at hotels and offices downtown. A car can be an unnecessary burden in town, where traffic gets terribly congested, but comes in handy for side trips to the jungle and isolated beaches.

Avis Carretera Aeropuerto, Km 2.5...................11112

Budget Carretera Aeropuerto, Km 5 22980

Hertz Díaz Ordáz 538 20024

National Carretera Aeropuerto, Km 1.5............20515

Taxis

Cabs are abundant and easy to flag down. Most hotels have signs posting the fares to points around town. Confirm the fare with the driver before taking off.

FYI

Emergencies

Canadian Consulate Hidalgo 217 25398

Hospital Carretera Libramiento, Km 1.5...........44000

Police Palacio Municipal (at Juárez) 20123

US Consulate Insurgentes (at Libertad) 20069

Money

You can change money at the airport, hotels, and banks, with the latter giving you the best rate. Bank hours for changing money are typically Mondays through Fridays from 9AM to 1:30PM. *Casas de cambio* (exchange houses) are scattered around downtown and open throughout the day and evening. International credit cards and US dollars are accepted in most restaurants, hotels, and shops. Try not to be short of cash on Sundays, because it can be difficult to change money on that day, except in some hotels. Always keep bills of small denominations on hand, since it can be difficult to change larger bills (except at banks).

Banamex Juárez (at Zaragoza).........................21998

Banca Confia Morelos (at Libertad) 24464

Banca Cremi Villa Vallarta Shopping Center 25454

Bancomer Juárez (at Mina)..............................25050

Tours

Most hotels have a travel agency or information desk with information on boat tours and driving tours to the jungle (see Jungle Oasis, opposite). Most boat tours leave from the main commercial dock near Marina Vallarta, or a dock at Playa de los Muertos south of town. Contact your hotel tour desk.

Visitors Information

Oficina de Turismo (Tourism Office) is located in the **Palacio Municipal,** next to the plaza on Juárez. The staff here is very helpful and can solve most problems. They are open Mondays through Saturdays. For more information, call 20242/3

Area code 322 unless otherwise noted.

Marina Vallarta

This expanding megadevelopment lies at the north end of town, conveniently close to the airport, but a 25-minute taxi ride to Old Town Puerto Vallarta. The property sprawls along the west side of the airport road with an 18-hole golf course at the northern end. Time-shares, condos, private homes, and hotels surround the 350-slip marina in the center of the development, while five elegant hotels line the beachfront. The area is confusing to newcomers, and distances between various attractions are significant. The best way to get around is by renting a bicycle at your hotel; an abundance of taxis are available as well. A water taxi service also transports guests to various locales around the marina.

1 Bel-Air Hotel $$$$ This hostelry has the same standards as its luxurious, legendary namesake in Los Angeles. Mexican architects **Roberto** and **Ricardo Elias** coincidentally created their hotel in that style, with striking archways, dramatic domes, and the trademark California pink facade. The whimsical masks and pastel fish of the famous Mexican artist Sergio Bustamante hang above the beds in the hotel's 75 suites and villas, many of which have small blue-tile pools and hot tubs on private terraces. Guests lounge in billowing, Moroccan-style tents by the pool amid a landscape of fountains and fish ponds. Privacy is guaranteed since the hotel is surrounded by the marina's golf course—the 18th hole and clubhouse are just a short walk away. ◆ Pelicanos 311 (at the far north side of Marina Vallarta). 10800, 800/362.9170

Within the Bel-Air Hotel:

El Candile ★★★★$$$ One of the best places in town for sampling gourmet regional Mexican cuisine. The restaurant has a circular, trilevel dining room and striking views of the surrounding pools and gardens. Look to the ceiling for a Bustamante chandelier in the shape of a tree covered with birds and wild animals. The menu also includes international dishes. ◆ Continental/Mexican ◆ Daily breakfast, lunch, and dinner. 10800

2 Marina Vallarta Club de Golf Joe Finger designed this 18-hole course that sprawls over the north end of the marina development. It has a pro shop and several clubhouses; membership available to marina residents. Hotel guests can arrange tee times through their concierges. ◆ Paseo de la Marina Norte. 10171, 10173

KITTI HOMME

3 Marina Business Center The promenade around the north shore of the marina is gradually filling up with small cafes, delicatessens, shops, and offices, though many of the 120 commercial spaces are still vacant. **El Faro,** the white lighthouse, stands as a beacon for boats at the harbor entrance. Slips accommodate vessels of up to a hundred feet long, and water taxis transport boaters to their hotels.

Within the Marina Business Center:

El Faro Lighthouse Bar Locals unanimously recommend the glass-enclosed cocktail lounge atop the lighthouse as the most romantic setting for watching the sunset. With its 360-degree view of the marina and sea, it is open only in the evenings, when drinks are served to the accompaniment of romantic ballads. ♦ Cocktails ♦ M-Sa. Royal Pacific Yacht Club. 10233

Captain Morgan's Restaurant ★$$
Shiny brass railings, wood paneling, and heavy wooden captain's chairs welcome all seafarers to this eatery. Dine alfresco on the tile walkway facing the harbor, where stretched panels of canvas protect guests from the sun and rain. The fish chowder is rich and creamy with a dash of Mexican spice, a good beginning for the cajun fish. ♦ Seafood ♦ Daily lunch and dinner. 10262

Las Palomas Doradas ★$$ While this may not be the fanciest-looking restaurant from the outside, it offers excellent local dishes. The small *tampiqueño*-style beef steak (marinated and grilled) is butter-tender, and the tasty trimmings include chicken enchilada, beef *taquito,* spicy *chiles rellenos* (stuffed chili peppers), beans, rice, and great guacamole and chips. For a delightful meal, try dining outside at the wrought-iron tables. ♦ Mexican/Seafood ♦ Daily breakfast, lunch, and dinner. 10470

Jungle Oasis ✓

Those who dream of adventure in the jungle and a tropical-island lifestyle should hop on the shuttle boat from **Puerto Vallarta** to **Yelapa,** a slow-moving fishing village. This is where you can get away from it all—there's no electricity, paved roads, telephones, or even swimming pools. Instead, you'll find US and Canadian expatriates enjoying a laid-back way of life.

As soon as you arrive on shore, representatives from Yelapa's five or six restaurants will approach you and offer a free five-minute boat ride to the other side of the bay if you eat at their establishment. The small cafes serve simple meals (often seafood) and cold drinks.

Probably the biggest draw in Yelapa is the beautiful waterfall with its inviting swimming hole, well worth the 15-minute hike, some of it in jungle terrain. (If you're not feeling hardy enough that day, for a few dollars you can rent a horse to make the trek.) It's everything a remote jungle pool should be, although you *can* buy sodas and beer and relax at the few simple tables and chairs close by. *Raicilla* (local moonshine) is available if you ask for it. Yelapa offers fishing, swimming, and, for bird-watchers, a multitude of winged creatures that stop at the waters of nearby **Río Tuito.** Boats leave Puerto Vallarta's commercial boat docks daily. Similar tours go to the quieter, less traveled fishing village of **Las Animas.**

Restaurants/Clubs: Red   **Hotels:** Blue
Shops/ 🌳 Outdoors: Green   **Sights/Culture:** Black

4 Marriott Casa Magna $$$ Management's desire to immerse guests in supreme luxury is evident throughout this Mexican Taj Mahal. Most of the 433 rooms have private safes, lovely toiletries, a mini-bar, and an iron and ironing board in the closet. You need a map to navigate around multileveled interior stone waterfalls, fountains, and long hallways of polished marble and glittering chandeliers. Outside, immense artificial lakes leave off where the swimming pool begins. A bar under a waterfall is an unusual and cooling place to sip a margarita, and there's also a restaurant. After a good workout in the sophisticated health center, spoil yourself with an expert massage. ♦ Paseo de la Marina 5. 10004; fax 10760

5 Meliá $$$ Part of the Spanish chain, this hotel is run in grand European style. Everything here is spacious, from the 403 large bedrooms to the two-story lobby and bar to the grand-scale swimming pool and the artificial lake that flows through the grounds. This is another huge property where you'll be a bit lost for the first day or two. Several upscale restaurants offer a variety of cuisines and superb wine lists, including some good bottles from Spain. ♦ Paseo de la Marina Sur. 10200, 800/336.3542; fax 10118

6 Oasis Water Park You can't miss the tall, twisting water slides rising atop this children's amusement park. The five-story slides thrill the older kids, who don't seem to mind climbing several steep stairways to the top. Smaller children ride floats along a lazy river, past waterfalls and giant mushroom-shaped fountains surrounding a play area. Lifeguards patrol the activities, while parents lounge poolside or escape to a smaller pool hidden by bushes and trees. Tired tots can rest in a nursery/First Aid Station; older youngsters can fortify their energy with hot dogs and milk shakes at the snack bar. ♦ Admission. Daily. Vidafel Hotel (at the southwest side of the development). 11500

7 Regina Vallarta $$$$ Easily the most architecturally striking hotel in this area, the property was designed by **José Iturbe** in the modern Mexican style originated by **Luis Barragan.** Recessed squares and windows are painted vivid orange and pink against the hotel's cool white facade, and lemon-yellow domes and ceilings brighten the long corridors and spacious rooms. The designers deserve kudos for the extra details that make the 280 guest rooms delightful: Ceiling fans and huge windows allow those who enjoy sea breezes to remain cool and comfortable. The floors are covered with soft woven straw mats, and solid tropical colors (no fussy florals here) have a soothing effect. Islands of blossoms and palm trees break the meandering pool into private areas so it doesn't seem like you're surrounded by other guests. The public spaces are more like galleries than lounges and walkways; don't miss the display of oversized fanciful animals by some of Oaxaca's most noted wood-carvers. There are several restaurants to satisfy hungry guests. ♦ Paseo de la Marina Sur (at the far south end of the development). 11100, 800/228.3000; fax 10121

8 Commercial Boat Docks Cruise ships dock here and deposit their passengers for a fun-filled day in Puerto Vallarta. This is also the place to catch excursion boats to the small island of Yelapa.

8 Krystal Vallarta Hotel $$$ This resort is like a small village where streets are open only to pedestrians and the silent electric golf carts that transport arriving guests to their rooms. *Palapas* (palm-thatched huts) line the beach, and Colonial-style stone water fountains bubble everywhere. The 450 rooms come in a variety of sizes and styles—from standards and suites to villas with private pools. Boutiques, travel agents, bars, coffee shops, specialty restaurants, dozens of swimming pools, a bullring (for bloodless faux bulifights), fiesta grounds, and convention facilities are all easily found on the 42 acres. ♦ Carretera Aeropuerto. 201459, 800/231.9860

Within the Krystal Vallarta Hotel:

Bogart's Restaurant

★★★$$$ As much a stage set as a restaurant, this place is beloved for extravagant, romantic, dress-up dinners. Waiters in red fezzes disappear behind white Arabesque arches and walls and return to deliver a superb meal—maybe the *reina del mar Marraquech* (juicy lobster medallions with a delicious cognac sauce) or the *scherezada* (crispy lettuce, fresh mushrooms, provolone, and Italian dressing). Whatever delightful entrée you choose, be sure to save room for the crepes suzettes—a delicate combination of fresh oranges, limes, brandy, and Cointreau. ♦ International ♦ Daily dinner. Reservations recommended. 21459

8 Sheraton Buganvilias $$$ Location, service, and the friendly clientele make this a longtime favorite of Puerto Vallarta regulars. Downtown is just a 15-minute walk south, and the beach is one of the best for swimming and water sports. Guest rooms in the main tower overlook the pool and beach, and have powerful shower massages in the baths, firm king-size beds, huge closets, and windows

that open to the sea breezes. The all-suite time-share vacation club has its own pool, though everyone seems to congregate at the enormous main pool where there's plenty of shallow space for the kids and a swim-up bar for the grownups. Thick groves of coconut and tan palms wrapped in hardy vines give the grounds a tropical feel, and provide welcome shade during the midday heat. Daily brunch in the coffee shop is quite popular; there are also several restaurants.♦ Carretera Aeropuerto 999. 23000, 30404; fax 20500

Within the Sheraton Buganvilias:

Mexican Fiesta The longest-running and most spectacular fiesta in Puerto Vallarta, drawing a crowd of over 700 revelers in the high season. Emceed by the gregarious Hermi Valdovino, the fiesta includes an endless flow of tequila, a bountiful Mexican buffet, and performances by an outstanding 12-piece mariachi band and folkloric dancers. In the high season the fiesta is held on the beach and culminates with a grand fireworks finale. ♦ Admission. Thursday evenings. 23000

Viejo Vallarta

Red-tile roofs, brick trims, tile floors, and white stucco buildings are the hallmark of Viejo Vallarta (Old Vallarta), which lies within the boundaries of the original village. In Mexican design circles, this architecture is referred to as Puerto Vallarta–style. Civic leaders recognized its value and passed a regulation requiring buildings to be constructed in this manner. Businesses are also encouraged to use old-fashioned signs, and to avoid neon and ultramodern designs.

Still, Viejo Vallarta has been modernized in ways that greatly enhance its charm. Downtown's bumpy, dusty cobblestone streets have been ripped up and improved. Telephone wires are buried underground, no longer marring the view from the hills above town. The streets running inland from the seaside *malecón* are filled with one-of-a-kind galleries, shops, and restaurants well worth visiting.

9 Buenaventura $$ On the edge of Viejo Vallarta and facing the sea is this enduring favorite of families and budget travelers. The five-story atrium lobby is a popular gathering place. Rooms on the fifth floor have balconies overlooking the pool; all 210 guest rooms have pale wood furnishings and a cool yellow-and-white decor. Despite an enforced rule against noise after 11PM, some might find the place a bit loud. The hotel's restaurants are good if you don't want to venture out. ♦ Av México 1301 (between Nicaragua and San Salvador). 23737; fax 23546

10 Cenaduria Doña Raquel ★★★$ Ask anyone where to go for Mexican home-style cooking and they'll mention this restaurant. The *pozole* (a hominy and pork stew) is legendary, and it's hard to find a seat at the few tile-topped tables on Thursday nights, the only night when *pozole*—the mandatory dinner for all true residents—is served. The tostadas are made with beef tongue, *lomo* (pork loin), and *cuerito* (pickled pork skin), though the weak of stomach may prefer shredded chicken or beef or the more predictable enchiladas and *taquitos*. A must for those seeking true Mexican fare that hasn't be adulterated for tourist palates. ♦ Mexican ♦ Tu-Sa dinner. L. Vicario 131 (between Díaz Ordáz and Morelos). 20618

11 Papaya 3 ★★$ This restaurant is so filled with plants, you feel as if you're eating in a beautiful garden. It's a great find for those seeking a break from spicy sauces and fried foods. Fresh vegetables are the restaurant's forte, and the salads are exceptional. Try the mixed salad of shredded carrots and cabbage, lettuce, tomatoes, and onion, topped with fresh tuna. Soft jazz plays in the background, and everything is immaculate. ♦ Health food ♦ Daily breakfast, lunch, and dinner. Abasolo 169 (between Morelos and Juárez). 22718

12 Los Cuatro Vientos $ Make reservations far in advance for one of the 13 rooms in this enchanting hostelry overlooking downtown Puerto Vallarta and the bay. Much of the hotel's business comes from guests who return annually—and for good reason. Pink bougainvillea and the brilliant yellow blossoms of the *copa de oro* (cup of gold) vine are draped over the building and balconies, which frame a small courtyard and pool. Pretty flowers and birds are painted over doorways and arches; rooms are decorated with folk art and antiques. Downtown is within walking distance, and the climb back up the hill to your room will earn you a well-deserved siesta. The restaurant was being renovated at press time. ♦ Matamoros 520 (at Josefa Ortiz de Dominguez). 20161. For reservations: Hotel Los Cuatro Vientos, Apdo 83, Puerto Vallarta, Jalisco 48350, Mexico

13 The Malecón A broad walkway along Puerto Vallarta's oceanfront, this plays an important part in city life. By day, tourists stroll along the promenade enjoying the smell of the sea and the panoramic views. Charming bronze sculptures are scattered about, including the city's symbol: a boy riding a sea horse. On Sunday evenings, families walk together, buying balloons and cotton candy from vendors, and local musicians perform at the small stage and amphitheater at the walkway's south end. Though many downtown shops and restaurants traditionally close on Sundays, some along here open Sunday evening, when locals and tourists gather. ♦ Díaz Ordáz (between A. Rodriguez and 31 de Octubre)

14 Las Palomas ★$$ As soon as guests are seated for breakfast, the waiter pours a steaming mug of Mexican coffee, a good strong brew with a slight cinnamon flavor. The majority of the customers here are high-powered local businesspeople. It's not unusual to see the mayor, a local publisher, or a Puerto Vallarta Rotarian committee discussing a regional issue. For an authentic breakfast, the *chilaquiles* (corn tortilla pieces in a tomato sauce served with fried eggs or shredded chicken) are the best in town; the *pan dulce* (sweet bread) tastes great with coffee. Check out a local specialty, *divorciados*, two eggs separated by a bed of beans. For lunch, pick a favorite Mexican dish, such as the *chiles rellenos*, which are fresh, rich, and spicy. ♦ Mexican/Seafood ♦ Daily breakfast, lunch, and dinner. Díaz Ordáz (at Aldama). 23675

15 Galería Uno One of the city's premier galleries remains a success because of the artists it represents and the hospitality of owners Janice Lavender and Martina Goldberg, who treat their clients like friends. Works by such Mexican legends as Rufino Tamayo and Mañuel Lepe, as well as pieces by contemporary artists, hang in rooms that give the feeling of an inside courtyard. This is a required stop for anyone interested in the local art scene. ♦ M-Sa. Morelos 561 (at Aldama). 20908

Horseback Riding

Puerto Vallarta is perfect horseback riding country, with long stretches of isolated beach, jungle, and mountain foothills; equestrians get a view of the area that most tourists never see. A late-afternoon sunset ride can be particularly nice. Several ranches offer guided horseback riding tours, including transportation to and from your hotel, for all levels of ability:

Cuatro Milpas	47211
El Charro	40114
El Ojo de Agua	48240
Indio	25137
La Primavera	46513

16 Cafe des Artistes

★★★★$$$ In a town with many excellent restaurants, this one stands out for its superb cuisine and sophisticated decor. Chef Thierry Blouet, formerly at **La Perla** in

the **Camino Real** hotel, has reached star status among locals and frequent visitors, and travelers have been known to dine here several times during their stays. His lobster pumpkin soup, served in a gourd bowl, is legendary, and any fresh fish preparation is memorable—try the tuna with *achiote* spices, or red snapper in red and yellow bell pepper saffron sauce. The desserts are exceptional as well, especially the apple and almond cheesecake with kiwi sauce. The soft-gray ceiling, mauve tablecloths, and sparkling votive candles add an air of subdued elegance, enhanced by the pianist's eclectic repertoire. ♦ Nouvelle Mexican ♦ M-Sa dinner. Reservations recommended. Guadalupe Sánchez 740 (at Aldama). 23228

17 El Baul Interiors

Don't enter if you plan on sneaking out of the country without something from one of Mexico's fabulous artists. You'll find striking hand-painted Talavera pottery (characterized by blue-and-white designs) as well as works from local artist Mono Momma (Monkey Mama), who, along with her many children, creates appealing ceramic figures. You almost have to walk sideways to get through the maze of furniture and goods, so allow plenty of time to browse. Most pieces cost a pretty peso, but are worth the splurge. ♦ M-Sa; closed at midday. Morelos 558 (between Aldama and Corona). 30169

18 Arte Magico Huichol

Huichol Indians from northern Jalisco bring their finest work to owners Magua and Mahomedalid, who have dedicated their entire gallery to Huichol yarn and bead art. Huichol art is closely tied to the ancient beliefs of these people, which includes the traditional ritualistic use of peyote (a cactus known for its hallucinogenic properties). The unique, complex wall hangings portray nature, gods, and events in vibrant, multicolored tableaus; ritual masks are beaded in intricate designs. These are one-of-a-kind pieces that take hours of labor, and are priced accordingly. José Benitez, who has successfully exhibited his work in New York, San Francisco, and Chicago, is just one of the fine artists represented. ♦ M-Sa; closed at midday. Corona 164 (between Morelos and Juárez). 24210

19 Galería Pacífico

Specializing in contemporary Mexican works, this gallery presents sculptures, paintings, and unique bronze and wood pieces. Private showings of art that's not on display are offered frequently. The gift shop at the entrance sells posters, graphics, photographs, and other art ranging in price from $5 to $15,000. ♦ M-Sa. Juárez 519 (at Corona). 26768

20 Querubines

Angel collectors are in heaven as they stroll through the many rooms in this folk art shop filled with figures of cherubs. The angels are made from a variety of materials, including terra-cotta, and the store also offers swaths of Guatemalan cloth, Oaxacan rugs and shawls, hand-painted tiles and lightswitch plates, and a host of other gift ideas. ♦ M-Sa. Juárez 501 (at Galeana). 23475

21 Panadería Munguia

★$ Early-morning aromas of fresh bread lead visitors right to the door of one of the best bakeries in town. It was opened in the late 19th century by the grandfather of the present town historian, Carlos Munguia. Check out the cookies, flaky pastries, and typical Mexican *pan dulce*. ♦ Bakery ♦ Daily. Juárez 467 (at Galeana). 22090

22 Brazz Restaurant

★$$ If you like mariachi music, duck in early and have a juicy steak or *queso fundido* (mellow melted cheese served hot over crisp, fried chips) with spicy chilies on the side. The specialty of the house is prime rib, and, though it's good, it's not the familiar cut found in the US or Canada. Get all your talking in before 9PM, when the mariachis arrive and the large room comes to life. Or stay in the small, glassed-in dining room, where you can enjoy the rousing songs and still carry on a conversation. ♦ Mexican ♦ Daily breakfast, lunch, and dinner. Morelos 518 (between Galeana and Mina). 20324

23 La Iglesia de Nuestra Señora de Guadalupe

(The Church of Our Lady of Guadalupe) History says the first Catholic service in Puerto Vallarta was held by Father Ayala under a tree very close to the present church. Ayala began building this masonry structure in 1892 and finished 10 years later. Engineered by Guerrero de Alba, the actual construction was done by the grandparents and great-grandparents of today's Puerto Vallarta residents. On Sunday mornings, it was commonplace to see parishioners on their way to mass picking up as many stones as they could carry.

Two different stories circulate about the origin of the ornate crown replica on top of the building. One says it was copied from the one worn by Carlota, Empress of Mexico, in the late 1860s. Others hold that the crown is the same one seen throughout Mexico in many paintings of the Virgin of Guadalupe. Don't wear shorts or T-shirts when visiting the church. ♦ Hidalgo 370 (at Iturbide)

24 Plaza de Armas Puerta Vallarta's *zócalo* (main square) is next to the **Palacio Municipal** (City Hall) in the middle of town. It's always a busy place, filled with locals and strolling tourists. ♦ Bounded by Morelos and Juárez, and Zaragoza and Iturbide

Minding Miss Manners

Good manners go a long way in Mexico, and are expected in all situations, whether you're negotiating a million-dollar deal or paying a traffic fine. Always start with a general greeting such as *buenos días* (good day or good morning) or *perdón* (pardon me) before launching into the matter at hand. *Por favor* (please) is as valuable as *gracias* (thank you); both should be used liberally in most circumstances. It doesn't hurt to remember *lo siento* (I'm sorry) as well.

Here are some common situations you'll encounter and how you'll be expected to handle them:

- *Mucho gusto* is the polite way of saying "pleased to meet you" or "it's my pleasure" when introduced; to really sweep someone off his or her feet, follow your handshake with *encantada* ("enchanted, I'm sure"). Almost everyone says *hasta luego* (see you later) after an encounter, even the taxi driver who will probably never see you again.

- In restaurants, waiters don't bring the bill until you politely ask for it (*la cuenta, por favor*) or make a motion in the air as if you're signing the check.

- If you smoke cigarettes, always offer one to your Mexican companions before lighting up.

- Be generous with compliments and simple terms of appreciation, such as *muy amable* (you are so kind). Such niceties can seem a bit overdone to the novice, but remember that people in Mexico also say *mi casa es su casa*, without meaning that they're offering you their home for the night. It's just their way of being polite.

- Never wear shorts inside a church, and always put on a shirt when you leave the beach regardless of how hot it is.

- As a courtesy, ask for permission before snapping photos of people.

- Be infinitely more patient than you would ever consider being back home. The *mañana* (tomorrow) attitude is all-pervasive, particularly along the coast.

24 Palacio Municipal (City Hall) Immediately next to the central plaza, this building houses the state tourism office, a good source of information and maps on the area. Be sure to look at the mural on the second-floor stairwell; it was painted by the late Mañuel Lepe, noted artist from Puerto Vallarta. ♦ North side of the plaza

25 Galería Sergio Bustamante Prepare to see some wild flights of imagination by this well-known artist. Wonderful pottery, wood, and papier-mâché creations take the forms of many different creatures, including life-size reproductions of humans in unexpected poses and shapes. Bustamante caused a stir in the Mexican art world with his original designs, which have since been imitated by many artists. ♦ M-Sa. Juárez 275 (at Zaragoza). 21129

26 La Lechuga ★★$$ Climb the green tile stairs to this tiny cafe, where owner Luz Graciela prepares wonderfully healthful meals. Her *comida corrida* (a fixed-price, multi-course lunch) is unlike any other you'll find, and might start with a chilled carrot soup, followed by an entrée of eggplant with chicken, or fettuccine Alfredo. The dinner menu is Italian. Graciela mixes wonderful *licuados* (shakes) with purified water and fresh fruit, and bakes her own delicious baguettes. The best seats are at the three tables on the tiny balcony. ♦ Mexican/Italian/Health Food ♦ M-Sa lunch and dinner. Hidalgo 224 (at Guerrero). 31374

27 Casa Kimberly $$$ The houses of Liz Taylor and Richard Burton have been turned into an intimate hotel with eight rooms and a penthouse. The penthouse (formerly the couple's bedroom) takes up an entire floor, is very private, and has its own patio and views of the city. Though it's an exemplary hotel, most guests come to say they slept where Liz and Richard did. You'll have to go out to eat, since there's no restaurant. ♦ Zaragoza 445 (at Matamoros). 21336, 800/344.8654

28 La Tienda de Maria This closet-size shop specializing in miniatures is a delight for those enamored of Mexico's skull and skeleton art. The shelves are filled with tiny three-dimensional household and village scenes, armies of soldiers, and animals smaller than a fingernail. ♦ Daily; closed at midday. Juárez 182 (between Libertad and A. Rodriguez). No phone

---

Restaurants/Clubs: Red   **Hotels:** Blue
Shops/ 🌳 Outdoors: Green   **Sights/Culture:** Black

South-of-the-Border Books

To better appreciate the people and culture of Mexico, here's a list of good reads that will give you some insight into our multifaceted neighbor.

Art and Time in Mexico: From the Conquest to the Revolution, by Elizabeth Wilder Weismann (1985; Harper & Row)

The Art of Mexican Cooking, by Diana Kennedy (1989; Bantam)

Aztec, by Gary Jennings (1981; Avon)

Casa Mexicana, by Tim Street-Porter (1986; Tabori & Chang)

Children of Sanchez, by Oscar Lewis (1979; Random House)

The Conquest of New Spain, by Bernal Díaz (1988; Shoe String)

Conversations With Moctezuma, by Dick J. Reavis (1990; Quill)

Distant Neighbors: A Portrait of the Mexicans, by Alan Riding (1984; Random House)

Five Families, by Oscar Lewis (1979; Basic Books)

Folk Treasures of Mexico, by Marion Oettinger (1990; Harry N. Abrams)

Gardens of Mexico, by Antonio Haas (1993; Rizzoli)

God and Mr. Gomez, by Jack Smith (1982; Watts, Franklin, Inc.)

Into a Desert Place, by Graham Macintosh (1988; Graham Macintosh)

The Labyrinth of Solitude, by Octavio Paz (1985; Grove Press)

Log from the Sea of Cortez, by John Steinbeck and E.F. Ricketts (1977; Penguin)

Mexico, Places and Pleasures, by Kate Simon (1988; HarperCollins)

Mexican Regional Cooking, by Diana Kennedy (1990; HarperCollins)

Mexico: Some Travels and Some Travelers There, by Alice Adams (1990; Prentice Hall)

Mexico: Splendors of Thirty Centuries (1990; Metropolitan Museum of Art)

Mexico's Feasts of Life, by Patricia Quintana (1989; Country Oak Books)

Reef Fishes of the Sea of Cortez, by Alex Kerstich (1989; Sea Challengers)

A Short History of Mexico, by J. Patrick McHenry (1962; Doubleday)

Sons of the Shaking Earth, by Eric Wolf (1962; University of Chicago Press)

The Mexicans: A Personal Portrait of the Mexican People, by Patrick Oster (1989; Harper & Row)

Tastes of Mexico, by Patricia Quintana (1986; Tabori & Chang)

A Treasury of Mexican Folkways, by Frances Toor (1967; Crown)

29 Gringo Gulch This hilly neighborhood's steep cobblestone streets, often better suited to donkeys than autos, are lined with some lovely homes. Two belonged to Liz Taylor and Richard Burton when their romance sizzled during the filming of *The Night of the Iguana.* Long before that, it was an enclave of thousands of expatriates from the US, hence the name. It's still a popular hangout for North American celebrities. ♦ Overlooking the Río Cuale

30 Chef Roger ★★★★$$$
A native of Switzerland with much of his accent still intact, chef Roger Dreier receives rave reviews from locals and travelers alike, who consider dinner in his small restaurant's candlelit courtyard a sublime event. The eclectic menu includes some of Roger's Swiss favorites—cheese fondue seasoned with kirsch, *fondue bourguignonne* (beef cooked in Burgundy wine), and hearty bratwurst with German mustards—as well as an outstanding Mexican delicacy combining fresh shrimp, *huitlacoche* (a mushroomlike fungus cultivated in corn husks), and squash blossom sauce. Save room for the chocolate marquis, a dense, fudgelike cake with a mint sauce. The ambience is tropical casual and unpretentious. ♦ Nouvelle Continental ♦ M-Sa dinner; also lunch Dec-Mar; closed August and September. Reservations recommended. A. Rodriguez 267 (between Hidalgo and Matamoros). 25900

31 Mercado Municipal Artisan stands line the outskirts of Puerto Vallarta's public market, displaying a wide range of T-shirts, leather items, straw hats, and souvenirs. Housewares and produce fill the market's interior. You won't find many treasures here (the merchandise hardly compares with what can be found in the city's fine folk art galleries), but if you're looking for inexpensive gifts for the folks back home, this may be the place. Bargaining is encouraged. ♦ Daily. A. Rodriguez (between Morelos and Hidalgo). No phone

32 Río Cuale The river begins in the mountains above Puerto Vallarta; during the rainy season it sends down voluminous amounts of water through a river canyon in the middle of town. It rises and rushes in the wet summer months, and dries almost to a trickle in the winter. Old-timers remember when cars were driven right through the low water across the rocky, potholed riverbed before Puente Viejo (Old Bridge) was built. If they had to cross when the water was high, they pulled themselves over the river on a chain. On the other side, they would trade car keys with a friend and go on about their business.

33 Isla Río Cuale (Río Cuale Island) Just below Puerto Vallarta's busy downtown streets lies a small island in the middle of the Río Cuale. Also known as **Isla de los Niños**, it's a lovely park with wide cement and stone walkways, antique wrought-iron benches, flora, and white stucco buildings housing an assortment of shops and restaurants. There are two ways to reach this island: By steps at the beginning of Puente Viejo on Calle Vallarta, or from Calle Insurgentes on the east end of downtown. Two antiquated, suspended wooden swing bridges (for foot traffic only) lead from the island to the south side of town. Plan on some thrills and chills on the swing bridge—a few slats are missing, and kids enjoy jumping on and shaking the bridge when tourists are crossing. It's definitely a rail-clutcher, but apparently no one's been knocked into the rushing river below yet.

On Isla Río Cuale:

John Huston Sculpture In many parks across Mexico, visitors see statues of Benito Juárez, the father of the revolution that freed the poor and broke up the holdings of the rich. Not so on Isla Río Cuale, where a fine, larger-than-life sculpture of John Huston stands at the west entrance. The late film director earned the respect of Puerto Vallartans when he chose their sleepy village, of which he was very fond, as the location for *The Night of the Iguana*. Many feel he was ultimately responsible for drawing attention to the tropical paradise and turning it into one of Mexico's top tourist destinations. ♦ Isla Río Cuale (west entrance)

Le Bistro Jazz Cafe ★★★★$$$ All you need to bring to this popular cafe is an appreciation of good food and jazz. Since 1979, it's been a hangout for well-known (and not-so-well-known) musicians. There's a feel-good atmosphere here, with tall trees creeping over glass roofs on the patio, lush plants, linen tablecloths, a risqué statue of a mermaid, and a great sound system. The decor is a study in black and white, trendy and traditional art, and touches of brass.

The day begins with classical music for breakfast, smooth jazz for lunch, and moves into lively jazz for evening. Dining on the deck overlooking the river, you'll hear the sounds of splashing water along with the syncopated rhythms of Dave Brubeck. And the food here is great, including the creamy spinach enchiladas and the *tampiquena* (a piece of tender marinated beef with a taco, enchilada, quesadilla, guacamole, and *chile relleno*). Dessert lovers should save room for a famous Le Bistro crepe; the only problem will be choosing which one to have. During the high season, expect to wait for a table. ♦ Mexican ♦ Daily breakfast, lunch, and dinner. Isla Río Cuale (west end near the bridge). 20283

Tabu Fabric artist Patti Gallardo creates one-of-a-kind hand-painted jackets, shirts, and dresses splashed with paints and glitter. She's been commissioned to create everything from wall murals to upholstery, and is swamped with orders from faithful customers returning for more on their annual vacations. ♦ M-Su; closed September. Isla Río Cuale (across the walkway from Le Bistro). 23528

Centro Cultural (Cultural Center) Creative artists restored this place and turned it into a meeting ground for artists and art lovers alike. Almost every day, easels are scattered about the white stucco building with painters doing what they love most. Well-known local names such as Rodrigo Lepe and Marta Gilbert are the backbone of the association, and all artists are invited to join. On any day the work of such local artists as Raymundo Gonzalez, Javier Fernandez, Ruben Leyva, or Ramiz Barquet could be on exhibit. Many US artists also enjoy the pleasures of living and creating art in Puerto Vallarta; some, such as Russel Davis, have been part of the scene here for years. ♦ Isla Río Cuale. No phone

Galería Lepe y Nena It's fun to wander through this eclectic gallery owned by Rodrigo Lepe, an artist who paints in the naïf (primitive) style. This soft-spoken man makes colorful hand-painted jewelry as well as avant-garde paintings. The shop is filled with his work and focuses on tiny figures and giant faces of animals and humans. Each shelf and table is cluttered with marvelous bits of art, unique trinkets, colorful jewelry, and Indian reproductions ready to take home as souvenirs. Rodrigo is the brother of the late Mañuel Lepe, a renowned local artist. ♦ M-Sa. Isla Río Cuale. 21277

34 Hotel Molina de Agua $$ A favorite among those who enjoy staying right in town, this tranquil, 65-room hotel is beautifully landscaped with cobblestone paths, fruit trees, and tropical plants. The bungalow rooms are typically Mexican and a bit worn, with red tile floors and colorful flowers painted over the bed; some rooms have etched-glass windows. Newer rooms in the two-story building have air-conditioning, sitting areas, and spectacular views. The restaurant, with its two-for-one margaritas, is a cool, comfy spot by the pool and hot tub. ♦ Vallarta 130 (at Aquiles Serdan). 21957, 21907, 800/826.9408, or 800/423.5512 in CA; fax 26056, 619/755.4596

35 Sr. Quino's ★★$$$ Behind the small, unimpressive facade, a very friendly staff serves unusual seafood dishes. The restaurant specializes in mixed seafood casseroles, including octopus, shrimp, fish fillet, and lobster, served in a variety of sauces. Those with conservative palates will find the white fish fillet sautéed in garlic butter both fresh and sweet. For a great dessert, try the orange cheesecake with a cup of coffee. There are a few tables downstairs, but request one on the open second-floor patio. If you're lucky, the charming Pedro Mancilla may be playing his guitar that evening. ◆ Mexican/Seafood ◆ Daily lunch and dinner. Reservations recommended. Aquiles Serdan 438 (across from the swing bridge). 21215

36 Balam ★★★★$$$ The owner was one of Vallarta's leading commercial fishermen before opening his restaurant, which is quite possibly the best in town for fresh seafood. The ubiquitous red snapper gets a new preparation in the *huachinango globo* (a foil-encased, fragrant blend of snapper, shrimp, tomatoes, onions, green peppers, and cilantro in a savory broth). Ceviche tostadas served as an appetizer are loaded with fresh shredded fish marinated in lime juice; one or two as a side dish with a bowl of *sopa albondigas camarones* (seafood broth with ground shrimp balls) makes a satisfying meal. The eatery is housed in a renovated typical Vallarta home with wood-beam ceilings, brick arches, and a small altar in a recessed bookshelf. ◆ Seafood ◆ Daily lunch and dinner. Basilio Badillo 425 (at Insurgentes). 23451

37 El Dorado ★$$ A substantial increase in prices in the summer of 1993 caused a minor exodus among the expat regulars who consider this *palapa* on Playa de los Muertos a neighborhood hangout. They are bound to return, however, since it's the ideal laid-back spot for an icy beer, fresh red snapper with garlic, and scoping the beach. Stop by for *huevos rancheros* in the morning or a sunset margarita. ◆ Seafood/Mexican ◆ Daily breakfast, lunch, and dinner. Pulpito 110 (off Amapas). 21511

38 La Palapa ★★$ Casual at lunch, this restaurant becomes romantic at dinner. Owner Alberto Perez serenades his guests with guitar ballads accompanied by the sounds of the crashing waves. Dine on calamari almandine, shrimp brochette, or mustard steak on the terrace or under the *palapa*. ◆ Seafood ◆ Daily lunch and dinner. Pulpito (in the La Palapa Condominiums). 25225

39 Meza del Mar Hotel $$ This older, relaxing hotel was among Puerto Vallarta's first all-inclusive resorts. The buildings are rather jammed together, with prolific hanging vines adding to the aged look. Some of the 129 rooms have a musty aroma from the humidity, and the most inexpensive rooms have no view at all. There are two pools, and when you finally get to the bottom floor in the antiquated elevator, you're at the beach level. The oceanside **Papagayo Cafe** offers breakfast, lunch, and snacks all day, and dinner is served in a dining room on the third floor. All-inclusive guests are free to eat and drink whatever they wish.

Prices are surprisingly reasonable, and the location on Playa de los Muertos is popular with locals and visitors alike—the same guests return year after year. ◆ Amapas 380 (near Pilita). 24888, 20716; fax 22308

40 Hotel Playa Conchas Chinas $$ You'll find the lobby at the top of the hill just off the coastal highway, with floors dropping down the face of the cliff to the beach below. All the 39 rooms have views, air-conditioning, and simple decor. Some suites come with Jacuzzis. No restaurant, but at the **El Set** next door guests celebrate a daily sunset along with guitar music. ◆ Carretera a Barra de Navidad, Km 2.5. 20156

40 El Set ★$$$ The name is simply a tribute to the films shot in Puerto Vallarta and to the artists who enjoy the Mexican ambience of this cheery restaurant up on a hill. Celebrities such as Rod Stewart and Kevin Costner have spent pleasant hours here watching the ever-changing sunset, and long evenings sampling Mexican fare. One great dish is the steaming bowl of tortilla soup with chunks of avocado and crispy tortillas served with a cold Pacífico beer. The casual restaurant is splashed with vivid Mexican colors in the red, green, and purple plaid tablecloths and festive decor. The waiters are a fun crew. This is an ideal place to enjoy good food and drink or to wait out a passing rainstorm and watch flashes of lightning on the horizon. ◆ Mexican ◆ Daily lunch and dinner. Carretera a Barra de Navidad, Km 2.5. 20302

Restaurants/Clubs: Red   **Hotels:** Blue
Shops/ 🌴 Outdoors: Green   **Sights/Culture:** Black

40 Hotel Camino Real $$$$ For many frequent visitors, this is the only hotel in town. It often gets awards for its fine facilities and impeccable service. Located a 10-minute drive south of town, the hotel sits on an exquisite bay with a crescent-shaped sandy beach, settled below the highway. Walkways and paths are lined with lush tropical plants and trees. In the lobbies and hallways, cobalt blue walls echo the shades of the sky and sea and are open to the cooling breezes. It was here that Arnold Schwarzenegger watched magenta sunsets after long sweaty days filming in the nearby jungle. Other stars are frequently sighted, though those with unlimited funds hide out in luxurious suites with private pools and hot tubs.

The **Royal Beach Club** is the newest section of the hotel, with 81 minisuites and several larger suites, some with private hot tubs. The 245 rooms in the original building have views of the sea from private balconies. The grounds sprawl along the beach, with several pools and restaurants tucked under towering palm trees. Those seeking peace and quiet stake out one of the 80 shady *palapas* along the beach, raising the flag atop the *palapa* when they want a waiter's attention; more gregarious types hang out at the main pool's swim-up bar. ♦ Carretera a Barra de Navidad. 20022, 800/722.6466; fax 30070

Within the Camino Real:

La Perla ★★$$$ The ocean view from this gourmet restaurant is spectacular, and the food is superb. Mexican cuisine reaches new heights with the *huitlacoche* crepes, made with a mushroomlike fungus that's considered a delicacy by connoisseurs. In keeping with the regional theme, end your meal with *crepas con cajeta* (light crepes drenched in a sauce of caramelized goat milk). ♦ Mexican/Continental ♦ Daily dinner. Reservations recommended. 20022

40 Presidente Inter-Continental $$$ Considered small by some standards, with 120 suites (some with Jacuzzis), this hotel has retained the intimacy of a small inn, while still providing the luxuries that so many demand. The hotel has one of the best beaches in town in a pretty, private cove. A luxurious pool overlooks the sea, and down a small path a coffeehouse serves luscious pastries; there are also several restaurants. Many guest rooms open onto balconies overlooking blue Bahía de Banderas. ♦ Carretera a Barra de Navidad, Km 8.5. 21791, 25191, 800/327.0200

40 La Jolla de Mismaloya Resort & Spa $$$$ This hotel has its own beach surrounded by jungle, and vines and trees dotting the hillsides grow down the cliff almost to the water's edge. Some of the 300 rooms have cooking facilities, and most have great views of immense pools bars, and all the guests never nee restaurant with its for lunch. ♦ Mismal 800/322.2343; fax 81

40 Chico's Paradise ★ ꜱet in the mountains, just 19 kilon. ꜱ (12 miles) south of town, this is the perfect daylong getaway. The restaurant is located back from the road beside a river. The food is surprisingly good for what might be considered a tourist trap; stick with the Mexican dishes. Plan to spend a full afternoon playing in the river and eating. ♦ Mexican ♦ Daily lunch. Hwy 200, Km 20. 20747

Bests

Rodrigo Lepe
Painter, Puerto Vallarta

In Puerto Vallarta:

The art exhibitions at **Central Cultural Center.**

Breakfast at **El Set.**

Go to the beaches at **Nayarit, Punta de Mita,** and **Punta del Burro.**

A walk through the beautiful **Isla Río Cuale.**

End the day with dinner at the **Hotel Posada Río Cuale** restaurant on Isla Río Cuale.

Jim Budd
Freelance Travel Writer

Christmas week, when the denizens of the capital have fled for the beaches, **Mexico City** is empty, the skies are blue and I can see the snow-tipped volcanoes on the horizon.

Coyoacán, the Mexico City neighborhood where Hernan Cortes, Leon Trotsky and Frida Kahlo all chose to live (not at the same time), a Mexico City version of Paris's Latin Quarter or New York's Greenwich Village in the 1930s. Wonderful place to sip coffee and browse for books.

Breakfast at the **Cafe Tacuba,** Tacuba 12, downtown in what's now called the **Historic Center.** Order Oaxaca-style tamales and hot chocolate to be enjoyed in a classic Mexican setting. Remember Oscar Lewis's "Children of Sanchez," a best selling anthropological study back in the 1960s? Sanchez worked as a dishwasher at the Cafe Tacuba.

Lunch at **Villa Vera** in **Acapulco,** munching *huachinango* (red snapper) or lying back and ogling the bodies basking in the sun around the pool at Mexico's tropical version of LA's Bel Air.

Vacationing at **Villa del Sol** in **Zihuatanejo,** lounging in a hammock by the bay outside a luxurious thatched adobe hut only five miles but a world away from the high-rise plastic glitter in **Ixtapa.**

oastal Highway
Manzanillo

South of **Puerto Vallarta**, Highway 200 leads to Manzanillo, running along the ocean and

...ering panoramic vistas of rugged rock formations. **Los Arcos**, a natural underwater preserve, is as striking above the water as it is below, displaying arches carved out by the pounding sea. The two-lane road soon turns away from the seaside, winding through mountains of tall jungle. This area has seen very little development, and miles of beautiful beaches lay pristine and often deserted. Manzanillo, 160 miles south of Puerto Vallarta, is a port city with one of Mexico's most glamorous hotels, the opulent **Las Hadas.** Even more spectacular resorts, including the luxurious **Costa Careyes,** lie along this coastline in private, self-contained compounds where the rich and famous hide out. Most of these places are difficult to reach, requiring flights into either Puerto Vallarta or Manzanillo and then long trips in rental cars or hired taxis. But once you arrive, there is absolutely no reason to leave until you must, ever so reluctantly, head home.

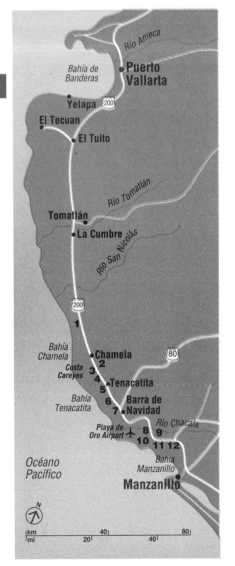

Area code 333 unless otherwise noted.

1 Las Alamandas $$$$ Set within a 1,500-acre private reserve, this exclusive hostelry has room for only 24 guests. Four gorgeous villas (some divided into suites) rest above a white sand beach surrounded by fruit trees, jungle, and bird-filled lagoons. The resort is owned by Isabel Goldsmith, daughter of the Bolivian tin magnate Don Antenor Patiño, who developed nearby **Las Hadas.** Advance reservations are absolutely necessary, since the hotel is sometimes closed for high-powered gatherings. Activities include horseback riding, boat rides, hiking, exercise in the fitness center, and, of course, lounging by the pool. The restaurant specializes in healthful cuisine, with fruits and vegetables grown on the premises and seafood caught just offshore. The villas have fully equipped kitchens, the suites have mini-bars, and all accommodations are decorated with one-of-a-kind folk art, handwoven fabrics, and hand-crafted furnishings. ♦ Hwy 200 (32 kilometers/20 miles north of Costa Careyes). 70259; fax 70161. For reservations: Paseo de las Palmas 755, Lomas de Chapultepec, 11000 Mexico D.F., Mexico. 5/5407657, 800/223.6510; fax 5/5407658

Bel-Air

2 Hotel Bel-Air Costa Careyes $$$$ One of the most exclusive resort communities in Mexico is nestled in the Sierra Madre foothills over a crescent-shaped beach far from any signs of civilization. In fact, the mountain-edged beach area of Costa Careyes lies approximately 154 kilometers (96 miles) south of Puerto Vallarta and 96 kilometers (60 miles) north of Manzanillo. Transportation is available from the Manzanillo airport. The resort was originally designed by Italian architect Gian Franco Brignone in an Italian-Mexican village style, with sweeping palm-frond roofs over pastel-washed terraces that offer stunning views of the sea. Private homes within the resort have been featured in architectural magazines and books as examples of the finest tropical design, complementing the area's natural beauty. The hotel has always attracted a fascinating clientele; in fact, writer Alice Walker credits it in her book *Possessing the Secret of Joy.*

The 60 guest rooms in the main U-shaped hotel complex have been completely renovated with private terraces and soft Mediterranean pastel color schemes. Satellite television and direct-dial telephones, long banned from the rooms, have been added to meet the changing needs of patrons unwilling or unable to endure total isolation. Guests lounge by swimming pools set in lush courtyards and submit to delicious pampering in **The Spa**, a state-of-the-art health and beauty facility. The broad beach is ideal for sunbathing and swimming, and snorkeling is good around the rocky islands offshore. A restaurant, horses, and yachts are also available. ◆ Off Hwy 200 (at Costa Careyes). 70010, 800/6484097; fax 70107

3 Club Med Playa Blanca $$$$ Located near the **Bel-Air Costa Careyes**, this hotel has 590 basic, bright rooms in adobe brick buildings spread around landscaped grounds. Most activities take place around the large pool and along the palm-lined beach. Children over 12 are welcome, but there are no special facilities or activities for them.

An intensive English horseback riding program, scuba diving lessons, circus workshops, and rock-climbing lessons on an artificial wall are all available. Equipment for nearly every water sport is provided, and for those with energy left over, there's a high-tech disco. This is an all-inclusive hotel, with meals and many activities part of the deal. Package prices include airfare, but not airport transfers, which can be very expensive. ◆ Off Hwy 200 (at Costa Careyes). 70734, 800/CLUBMED; fax 70733

4 El Tecuan Hotel and Resort $$ Twenty kilometers (12 miles) south of the **Bel-Air Costa Careyes** turnoff, the sign to this resort is marked by a small *faro* (lighthouse). The road meanders through mango plantations and jungle growth and is quite narrow in places—watch the curves and be prepared to stop in a hurry; you're apt to come across a herd of cows or goats taking an afternoon siesta on the pavement. Built on top of a hill, the hotel's greatest asset is its view of a lake and the ocean. This is a favorite of Mexican families from Guadalajara and those seeking isolation. The strong surf makes it dangerous for swimming, but there's a pool shared by most of the 36 rooms. A few villas have private pools, and waterskiing is available on a nearby lagoon. A private airstrip accommodates small planes up to a light twin-engine size. The restaurant and bar offer simple meals and mixed drinks. ◆ Hwy 200, Km 33.5 (between Chamela and Tenacatita). No phone. For reservations: El Tecuan, Garibaldi 1676, Guadalajara, Jalisco 44100, Mexico. 36/160055

5 Los Angeles Loco $$$ Part of the Fiesta Americana chain, this all-inclusive hotel is designed to keep guests active and happy with a pool, tennis courts, and horseback riding. All 217 rooms have ocean views and balconies. Three meals, snacks, and unlimited Mexican beverages are included along with a variety of water sports and games on the Bahía Tenacatita. Guests can shop on the property or take a special trip to Puerto Vallarta or Manzanillo. The Manzanillo airport is about 45 minutes away, and transport to the hotel costs extra. ◆ Hwy 200 (at Bahía Tenacatita). 70220, 800/343.7821

6 El Tamarindo $$$$ Scheduled to open at press time, this hotel is located in a 2,000-acre natural reserve. It is part of a resort village on a spectacular jungle-edged cove, and is managed by the **Bel-Air Costa Careyes.** The village includes 60 private villas, a championship golf course, an equestrian center, a yacht marina, a restaurant, and nine miles of private coastline. ◆ Hwy 200 (20 minutes north of the Playa de Oro Airport). 332/10800, 800/648.4097

7 Melaque Also known as San Patricio, this small beach town sits in the middle of Bahía Navidad near the town of Barra de Navidad. It is only a few blocks square, with simple accommodations. Along the beach, small, low-key hotels lure those on a budget. Open-air cafes serve strong coffee and simple but good meals. On St. Patrick's Day the sea is the scene of a festive *flotilla* (parade) during which the boats are blessed and everyone parties. ◆ Off Hwy 200 (five kilometers/three miles northwest of Barra de Navidad)

7 Barra de Navidad On another beautiful out-of-the-way beach, this low-key resort town has a variety of casual cafes and shops. Rumor has it the area will soon explode with heavy tourism. But for now enjoy long walks on the sand, small hotels, and fresh-caught seafood fixed in a variety of ways. ◆ Off Hwy 200 (between Bahía Tenacatita and Manzanillo)

Mexican writer Octavio Paz won the Nobel Prize for literature in 1991.

Within Barra de Navidad:

Hotel Cabo Blanco $$ One of Barra de Navidad's nicest and largest hotels was named after the Charles Bronson movie of the same name. The grounds are well kept with 74 rooms, two pools, outdoor dining, and a lovely indoor restaurant specializing in Mexican food. It is located slightly inland on canals that were supposedly used in the colonial era to repair Spanish ships traveling along the Pacific coast. ♦ Pueblo Nuevo. 362/70168; fax 362/21936

Manzanillo

The small coastal city of **Manzanillo** in the state of **Colima** is south of **Puerto Vallarta** in the middle of lush jungle. It began as a railhead, where cargo was transferred between ships and trains, and the shipping business is still located in the center of downtown. Most visitors to Mexico who weren't fishing enthusiasts hadn't heard of Manzanillo until 1974, when Bolivian Don Antenor Patiño completed his fairyland getaway, the flamboyant **Las Hadas** hotel. Soon after that, the hotel's **Mantarraya Golf Course** began to attract world attention.

While not a major tourist mecca, Manzanillo is a gathering place for visitors from all over the world (20 percent are from Japan) who enjoy outdoor activities. For excellent insight into colonial times, you can travel north and east to Colima, the state's capital, where the **Museo de la Cultura Occidental** (Museum of Western Culture) and the **Museo de Historia** (Museum of History), along with a charming, old city center and 19th-century cathedral, make a great day trip (travel agents in Manzanillo can make arrangements for you).

Mexican holidays are definitely not the best time to visit the small resort towns, especially along the coast, because Manzanillo is very popular with Mexican families and every room is booked well in advance. The traffic around the bay is jammed, and the beaches are crowded during the holidays, too.

If you're not traveling by car, try visiting Manzanillo with a group. Let someone else navigate the way through the maze of small streets that climb around hills overlooking **Bahía de Santiago** and **Bahía de Manzanillo.** And ask your travel agent about all-inclusive resorts. This area is noted for sportfishing, and anglers will no doubt find many good package trips.

Don't miss downtown Manzanillo, which has a lovely old plaza, though it's close to the railroad. The small shops here can surprise and delight with unusual finds, and several restaurants offer good, simple fare.

Bahía de Santiago is an up-and-coming area. Stores and restaurants are springing up and a new marina and several new hotels were under construction at press time. Right now, the hotel gift shops are the best source for local arts and crafts, as well as the arts boutique **Grivel,** which is located in Plaza Santiago.

Getting to Manzanillo
Airport

Playa de Oro Airport is located about 32 kilometers (20 miles) northwest of Manzanillo. Transportation is provided from the airport by *combi* (van) direct to your hotel.

Airlines
Aeroméxico 21267, 800/237.6639
Mexicana 21972, 800/531.7921

Getting around Manzanillo

Few numerical street addresses are used in Manzanillo. People designate their location by neighborhood or street, so don't waste your time looking for numbers.

Car Rental
In Manzanillo rental cars are expensive but necessary if you wish to visit out-of-the-way beaches and resorts.

Budget 31445
National 30611

Taxis
Plenty of cabs are available and are usually parked in front of the larger hotels.

FYI

Emergencies
Hospital B, Colonia de San Pedrito 20029
Police 21004

Money
You can change money at the airport, hotels, and banks, with the latter giving you the best rate. Bank hours for changing money are typically Mondays through Fridays from 9AM to 1:30PM. *Casas de cambio* (exchange houses) are scattered around downtown and open throughout the day and evening. International credit cards and US dollars are accepted in most restaurants, hotels, and shops. Try not to be short of cash on Sundays, because it can be difficult to change money on that day, except in some hotels. Always keep bills of small denominations on hand, since it can be difficult to change larger bills (except at banks).

Visitors Information
The **Oficina de Turismo** (Tourism Office) is located at Juárez 244 (yes, they have a street number; the problem is, they are seldom around). M-Sa. 20181, 21117

Travel agencies also can provide information:

Recorridos Turísticos Manzanillo ....
Plaza Las Glorias Hotel 30435

Viajes Anfitriones Mexicanos Club Maeva 31940

Area code 333 unless otherwise noted.

8 Club Santiago This is a bustling neighborhood of condos with villas, apartments, and private homes. The location is quite nice and near an active, two-mile stretch of beach. There are plenty of restaurants, bars, tennis courts, and a nine-hole golf course close by to keep you busy. ♦ Playa Santiago (between Barra de Navidad and Bahía Manzanillo). 30413

9 Club Maeva $$ Families with children love this place. There are playgrounds and pools just for kids and a dance club and tennis courts to keep the adults happy. The little ones especially like the pool with its long, curving water slide. There are 514 rooms; some bungalows come equipped with kitchenettes. You can take a bridge across the busy highway to the beach on the other side. All inclusive. ♦ Playa Miramar (between Barra de Navidad and Bahía Manzanillo). 30595, 800/GO.MAEVA; fax 30395

10 Plaza Las Glorias Hotel $$ Painted a deep ocher color, this hotel looks like a tiny pueblo clustered on the side of the hill. A small cable car carries guests and luggage to the hotel entrance at the top. All 86 rooms and 15 suites are comfortable and pleasantly furnished, although those by the pool can be noisy. Some are more desirable than others, with Jacuzzis in the bedrooms; always ask to see your room before you sign on the dotted line. If you wish, furnished kitchenettes are available. The hotel is a little rundown, although swimmers don't seem to mind the chipped paint on the child-filled pool, and everyone seems to be having a good time. In the dining room you'll enjoy a great view of the **Mantarraya Golf Course** along with good Mexican food. The prices are good and the staff is friendly and helpful. ♦ Tesoro (between Playa Miramar and Bahía Manzanillo). 30440, 800/342.AMIGO; fax 31395

LAS HADAS

10 Las Hadas Hotel $$$$ This became the best-known hotel in Manzanillo after Dudley Moore and Bo Derek romped here in the movie *10*. One of a kind, it was built by Bolivian millionaire Antenor Patiño as a playground for his family and friends. Spanish architect **José Luis Ezquerra** spent a decade (1964-1974), supervising construction of Patiño's fantasy village that seems straight out of the Arabian Nights. The 224 rooms and four suites are all white, spacious, and aging, but spotlessly clean with elegant decor, including marble floors. Most have balconies with breathtaking views. Brilliant trees line walkways, and fuchsias tumble over stark white turrets, domes, and walls. On the beach and around the pool, Arab-style tents protect delicate skin from the tropical sun. Cushy lounges under more tents surround the swimming pools.

Three restaurants offer a choice of seafood and international and Mexican fare, and there are outstanding shops and boutiques, along with a pizza parlor and minimarket. You can keep busy during the day with water sports, tennis, and golf, and at night you can listen to live music filtering through the palms or dance until dawn. Guests at other hotels can use the facilities here, but are required to rent beach towels at a hefty price. ♦ Rincón de las Hadas (between Playa Miramar and Bahía Manzanillo). 30000, 800/228.3000; fax 30430

Within the Las Hadas Hotel:

Legazpi ★★$$$ For a gastronomical treat, have dinner here, where candlelight sparkles on crystal and silver and the atmosphere is full of romance. Gourmet food is presented beautifully with special touches: tender filet mignon, cooked vegetables served in delicate pastry boxes, raw vegetables carved into shapes of flowers, and fresh-baked pastries. ♦ International ♦ Daily dinner. Reservations recommended. 30000

10 Mantarraya Golf Course Though expensive, this 18-hole, par-71 course is a challenge for golfers who loft balls over sea-filled gorges. Designed by Pete and Roy Dye, it is considered one of the top five courses in Mexico, as well as one of the hundred best in the world. A full 18-hole game will take you right down to the beach. During tournaments, golfers make use of a traveling golf cart filled with cold soda, beer, and any other desired liquid refreshment. ♦ Daily. Off Hwy 200 (east of Playa Miramar) 30246

> The average Mexican consumes more than half a kilo (about one pound) of tortillas per day.

Restaurants/Clubs: Red   **Hotels:** Blue
Shops/ 🌳 Outdoors: Green   **Sights/Culture:** Black

Beyond Your Basic Bean Burrito

The cuisine of Mexico is far more varied than most travelers realize—it has been influenced by the ancient Aztec and Maya, the Spanish conquistadores, the French occupation, and the modern-day invasion of expatriates and travelers from the United States, Europe, and the Far East. The Indians provided corn and beans, the basics from which all Mexican cuisine emerges. Beef and cheese came from the Spanish; spices and coffee arrived on trading ships from Africa and the East. To get the real flavor of Mexico, bypass such internationally generic fare as hamburgers and pizza and seek out the authentic regional food, which varies throughout the land.

Beans, rice, corn, tortillas, and fiery chilies are eaten throughout Mexico, but even these staples vary in preparation and flavor. In the north, cooked pinto beans are often mashed and fried; in the south, they are served as a runny soup. Other differences come from products indigenous to the area. Sonora, for example, is the source of prime beef raised on the state's wide-ranging cattle ranches. Coastal areas are known for their seafood cocktails (such as ceviche) and fish preparations, which again vary according to the types of chilies and vegetables that are grown locally. Yucatán cooks season their meats and fish with sour orange juice, wrap them in banana leaves, and bake them; in Veracruz red snapper is smothered with a zesty sauce of onions, tomatoes, and green peppers.

Most major cities and resorts have one or two restaurants specializing in the regional cuisines of Mexico, where travelers can sample *pozole* from Jalisco, mole from Puebla, and delicate cheeses from Oaxaca. For the best representation of local dishes, try the *comida corrida* (the set menu). These multicourse midday feasts typically include soup, beans, rice, and an entrée of fish, poultry, or meat prepared in the local fashion. Lunch is the main meal of the day, usually consumed at one or two in the afternoon, followed by a siesta; dinner is a light meal served after 8PM.

For those diners who are not interested in trying the unknown, here's a glossary of common Mexican foods:

Achiote Annatto seeds or oil; used for flavor and color.

Antojitos Appetizers; also called *botanes*.

Carne Asada *Carne* (meat) usually refers to beef. *Carne asada* is a grilled and marinated thin strip of beef served with beans, rice, tortillas, and guacamole.

Cerveza There are many popular regional brands of *cerveza* (beer) in Mexico, including Tecate, Dos Equis, Corona, Carta Blanca, and Superior.

Ceviche A seafood cocktail of raw fish, lobster, conch, or shrimp pickled in lime juice with chopped onions, tomato, and cilantro. As a rule, raw fish is not the safest food to eat unless you know it is fresh and was caught in unpolluted waters.

Chayote A member of the squash family and one of the most common vegetables in Mexico, usually served steamed or boiled with carrots.

Cilantro The leaves of the coriander plant (also known as Chinese or Mexican parsley). A common seasoning in salsas and guacamole.

Chilaquiles Pieces of corn tortillas cooked in a savory broth; sometimes served with eggs and cheese.

Chile Relleno A green chili (of the Anaheim variety) stuffed with cheese and/or meat, and covered with a corn batter and baked.

Flan Caramel custard.

Guacamole Mashed avocado with cilantro and lemon juice; some varieties include onion, garlic, tomato, and/or sour cream.

Huachinango a la Veracruzano Traditionally made with red snapper in a sauce of tomatoes, green peppers, and onion; other fish fillets are also used.

Huevos Mexicana Eggs scrambled with diced onion, green pepper, and tomato.

Huevos Rancheros Fried eggs on steamed corn tortillas covered with a tomato-based sauce.

Huevos Revueltos Scrambled eggs.

Licuados Drinks made from water, ice, and pureed fruits; usually the cup is dipped directly into the mixture, which is stored in large glass bottles. The flavors are determined by the region and may include watermelon, papaya, strawberry, or pineapple. *Licuados* are wonderfully refreshing, but it's hard to tell if they are made from purified water unless you're in a tourist-oriented restaurant.

Limonada Lemonade made with fresh lemon juice, sugar, and water; purified water is used at most restaurants and bars.

Mole A sauce used on meats and vegetables, it originated in Puebla and Oaxaca and is made from a blend of spices and, usually, bitter chocolate.

Pozole A hearty stew made from pork and hominy.

Salsa A blend of tomatoes, onions, hot peppers (usually jalapeños, though the type of pepper may vary with the region), lemon or lime juice, and other seasonings. Salsas come in a wide range of flavors and degrees of spiciness; always try a drop first before spooning it over your food.

Sopa de Tortilla Seasoned chicken-broth-based soup with thin strips of deep-fried corn tortillas, chunks of cheese, avocado, and sprigs of cilantro.

Tamales Cornmeal paste formed around a filling of seasoned meat, vegetables, or fruit, then wrapped in corn husks and steamed.

11 Days Inn Hotel Fiesta Mexicana $ Though not overly luxurious, this hotel has a wonderful location on the beach. It's always crowded with Mexican tourists, and the 200 rooms and public places are attractively decorated with local handicrafts. The reasonable **Restaurant-Bar El Palmero** serves good Mexican and international food. This is a festive place, filled with families and the music of mariachi bands. ♦ Hwy 200, Km 8.5, Carretera Manzanillo Santiago. 32023; fax 32180

12 Willy's ★$$ Owner/chef Michel and his wife, Jeanne Françoise, serve French specialties and seafood to please the gourmet palate. The barbecue sizzles with lobster and shrimp kabobs grilling over a mesquite fire. Guests can dine and watch the sunset at a reserved table that is theirs for the entire evening. ♦ Seafood ♦ Daily dinner. Reservations recommended. On the beach (near Crucero Las Brisas). 31794

12 Carlos 'n' Charlie's Bar, Grill & Clothesline ★★$$ Can anything go wrong in one of Carlos Andersen's chain of well-known restaurants? It's fun times, cluttered decor, and good food for all. Mexican specialties are a sure thing here, as are the ribs. ♦ Mexican ♦ Daily lunch and dinner. Santiago-Manzanillo Rd (near Crucero Las Brisas). 31150

12 Osteria Bugatti ★★★$$$ Both locals and out-of-towners who know well-prepared Italian-style seafood return year after year. Be sure to try the oysters or the lobster diabolo. The chef also prepares rich pasta and shrimp dishes. ♦ Italian ♦ Daily lunch and dinner; closed the last two weeks of September. Santiago-Manzanillo Rd (near Crucero Las Brisas). 32999

12 ¡Que Barbaro! When it's time for a romantic evening, stop here for a drink and listen to mesmerizing music from the past 50 years. The air-conditioning is refreshing when the place fills up. Drinks and light food are served. ♦ Daily. Near Crucero Las Brisas. 31650

Mexico has a lot to offer if you like beach resorts, mountains, and the desert. You can learn about Mexican history through the pyramids, the colonial cities, and the most modern and industrialized cities.

What I especially love about Mexico is:

Mexico City, where you can stand inside the ruins of the **Templo Mayor** in the city center and see architecture from the colonial era in front of the modern buildings that show you how big and developed Mexico is.

Cancún, with its white sand beaches and crystal waters, is one of the best and most modern resorts in the world. You can find fun nightlife, too. Once you're there, be sure to visit the impressive amd always mysterious pyramids in **Uxmal, Chichén Itzá, Tulúm,** and several other nearby archaeological sites.

Puerto Vallarta is wonderful and very romantic. You'll find a great combination of nice beaches and an old downtown that reminds you of a typical Mexican *pueblito*. Locals tell you that Liz Taylor loves this place; it is where she fell in love with Richard Burton when he filmed *The Night of the Iguana.*

Do you want to have fun? Come to **Acapulco,** the most traditional resort in Mexico. It has great hotels and the most fabulous nightlife, discotheques, and restaurants. Or you can just watch the sunset while lying on the sand or sitting on the balcony of your luxurious suite. Do you like silver? Well, you're in the right place to get the greatest jewelry and crafts.

Take a trip to **Baja California,** the "strong arm of Mexico," if you like water sports, with a stop in **San Felipe** on the **Sea of Cortés.** You'll find triathlons, sailing, fishing and off-road car and motorcycle races. **Los Cabos, Loreto,** and **La Paz** are also great places for sports. Even the most skeptical divers are overwhelmed by the abundance of life in the Sea of Cortés. We are visited by migrating whales, dolphins, and seals.

In any coastal Mexican city, you can enjoy the best seafood—the biggest lobsters and shrimp, of course—with the various flavors of Mexico, a country with one of the most popular cuisines in the world.

Although the site may not be open to tourism until early in the next century, a major discovery of a "lost" pre-Columbian city on the gulf coast northwest of Veracruz was made in 1994. Named **El Pital,** after the nearest village, the sprawling area covers over 40 square miles and originally had more than a hundred structures—including some pyramids over 130 feet high—that had been completely hidden by dense jungle vegetation. It will take archaeologists many years to completely uncover the city.

Ixtapa/Zihuatanejo

Combine a modern hotel zone with a traditional fishing community and you have the two-in-one destination of Ixtapa (pronounced Ees-*ta*-pa) and Zihuatanejo (pronounced See-wah-ta-*neh*-ho), in the state of **Guerrero**. Only six kilometers (four miles) apart, each town has its own gorgeous bay and beaches, and both are favorite hideaways for experienced travelers. Those seeking luxurious creature comforts head to Ixtapa, which opened as a resort area in 1975.

Zihuatanejo, a fishing town with ancient roots, attracts those in search of the true Mexico, without glamour and glitz. Wherever they unpack their bags, most travelers shuttle back and forth between the two, sampling the best each place has to offer. Ixta/Zihua (a nickname that saves a lot of syllables) is well worth a vacation of a week or more, with a day or two for visiting isolated beaches, another for scuba diving or fishing, a day for shopping in both towns, and, of course, as much time as possible for simply relaxing on the beach or by the pool.

Ixtapa is small, fashionable, and blissfully free of the overdevelopment so common in planned resorts—the town's movers and shakers seem intent on keeping the resort under control. The two-mile-long hotel zone along **Playa del Palmar** and **Boulevard Ixtapa** contains fewer than a dozen hotels. The **Marina Ixtapa** complex is low-key and spacious, and the two 18-hole golf courses at opposite ends of the tourist zone offer stretches of green undisturbed by buildings.

Zihuatanejo was something of a cult destination long before the jungle and palm groves were cleared from Ixtapa's shores. Over the years artifacts found during various building projects support the belief that Zihuatanejo dates back to the pre-Columbian matriarchal Cuitlateca society. The **Museo Arqueológico de la Costa Grande** (Archaeology Museum) on the shores of the town's main beach contains displays of figurines with a decidedly feminine theme.

Changes to Zihuatenjo have enhanced its charm without destroying its character—roads and businesses now exist where small planes once landed, and there is an international airport 15 minutes from town. Revitalization projects continue—dirt streets are paved with decorative brick, and the **Paseo del Pescador** (Fisherman's Walkway) runs along the bay. Locals congregate around the beachside basketball court, which doubles as an amphitheater for weekend entertainment. The public market is still the main place to buy food, as well as the shorefront where fisherfolk sell their day's catch.

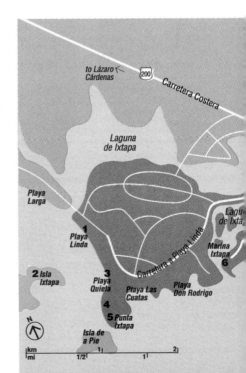

Getting to Ixtapa/Zihuatanejo

Airport

The **Ixtapa/Zihuatanejo Airport** is 16 kilometers (10. miles) east of Zihuatanejo. *Colectivos* (vans) run to hotels in both towns and cost far less than private taxis.

Airlines

Aeroméxico	42208
Delta	43386
Mexicana	42227, 32208

Driving

Ixtapa/Zihuatanejo is 150 miles northwest of Acapulco, a three- to four-hour trip on a well-paved highway with gorgeous mountain and coastal scenery. The highway travels through several small towns where you may want to stop for a cold drink and a bit of local color. From Mexico City, the drive is seven hours. Ixtapa and Zihuatanejo both have Pemex gas stations.

Getting around Ixtapa/Zihuatanejo

Buses

Buses run regularly between the two towns, and less frequently into Marina Ixtapa and out to Playa Quieta. Daily buses leave from the terminal on Airport Highway to most cities in Mexico. About eight trips a day are made to Acapulco. For more information, call 42175, 43477.

Car Rental

Although a car isn't necessary, it comes in handy for traveling between the two towns, to Playa la Ropa, and to out-of-the-way hotels. As rates are astronomically high, plan on doing your driving around in a day or two. There are several agencies at the airport and hotels.

Ixtapa

Avis	42248

Zihuatanejo

Budget	43060
Dollar	42314
Hertz	42952

Taxis

Cabs are easily found on the streets and in front of all major hotels, shopping centers, and restaurants.

FYI

Emergencies

Hospital General de Zona 8, Carretera Nacional Acapulco-Zihuatenejo No. 1, Zihuatenejo 42285

Police	42040
Red Cross	42019

Money

You can easily change money at your hotel, but the best rates are at the banks, which are open Mondays through Fridays from 9AM to 1PM. *Casas de cambio* (exchange houses) in both towns are open in the evenings and on weekends. International credit cards and US dollars are accepted in most restaurants,

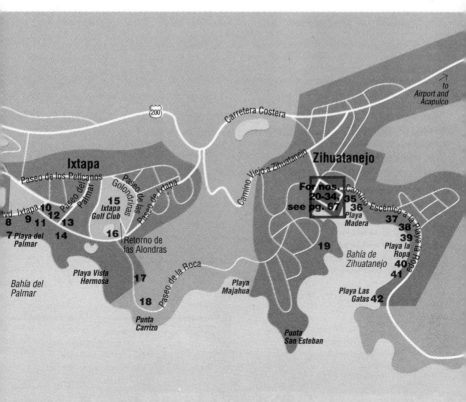

hotels, and shops. Try not to be short of cash on Sundays, because it can be difficult to change money on that day, except in some hotels. Always keep bills of small denominations on hand, since it can be difficult to change larger bills (except at banks).

Banamex Cuauhtémoc 4, Zihuatanejo ....
....42181, 42196

Travel Agents
Paseos Ixtapa Krystal Ixtapa Hotel lobby 30343

Visitors Information
The government tourism office is in Ixtapa at **La Puerta Mall**. It is open Mondays through Fridays. For information, call 31967.

Area code 753 unless otherwise noted.

Ixtapa

1 Playa Linda Total escape is possible at this undeveloped beach, which is backed by groves of coconut palms, glistening sand, and the jungle. Horses are available to rent by the hour or the day, and a few palm-roofed stands on the beach serve drinks and snacks. ♦ Off Carretara a Playa Linda, north of Club Med

2 Isla Ixtapa Called Isla Grande, this jungle island just off the coast is a wildlife preserve of sorts, though only the gulls and pelicans can withstand the steady stream of sun worshipers, skin divers, and bird-watchers making the trip here from Playa Quieta. Day-trippers have three beaches to choose from: Cuachalalate, the main beach with *palapa* (palm-roofed) restaurants and a dive shop; Varadero, on the windward side of the island, where you can rent snorkels and masks; and Playa Coral, a haven where fish and turtles congregate in the clear waters. It's a 10-minute boat ride to the island from Playa Quieta (buy a round-trip ticket and don't miss the last boat back, which leaves before dusk).

3 Playa Quieta "Quiet Beach" lies on a calm stretch of water protected by **Isla Ixtapa**. The sheltered bay makes this long beach ideal for all kinds of water sports, and it's common to see Windsurfers, sailboats, and skiffs on the water, many from **Club Med**. ♦ Carretara a Playa Linda (past the Punta Ixtapa development, about 20 minutes from the hotel zone)

4 Club Med Ixtapa $$$$ Although the beach may be quiet, its famous resort is not. A 20-minute drive from Ixtapa's hotel zone, this club is one of the "family villages" with a Kids Club (for ages 10 months to 11 years) and a circus workshop. Children and adults learn to fly on a high trapeze, and at the end of a week, guests and talented GO's (the staff) put on a great show, complete with makeup, funky wigs, and costumes. The days are packed with snorkeling, tennis, volleyball, and other activities. Meals are served buffet style, and while every dish is not a gourmet delight,

many are above and beyond the norm, with outstanding breads and pastries baked fresh daily. ♦ All inclusive. Reservations required. Playa Quieta. 43340, 43380, 800/CLUBMED

5 Punta Ixtapa Bulldozers and the sound of hammers have replaced the iguanas and armadillos on this natural point at the northwest end of Playa del Palmar. This is destined to become a luxurious residential development, with lots costing up to one million doallars each, and houses expected to be worth three times as much. The construction will take most of the decade to complete. The complex includes the beaches Don Rodrigo and Las Cuatas, where rocks jut from the sea just offshore, and Playa Linda, just two kilometers (one mile) away.

6 Marina Ixtapa A channel at the end of Playa del Palmar leads yachts into this gorgeous new marina complex. Condominiums with Mediterranean and hacienda-style architecture edge the 622 yacht slips, which accommodate vessels of up to a hundred feet long. Restaurants and shops are clustered around a handsome terra-cotta–colored lighthouse, and its 18-hole golf course provides a scenic landscape. ♦ Playa del Palmar (west end)

Within Marina Ixtapa:

Marina Ixtapa Golf Course Recently opened, this is Ixtapa's second 18-hole course. Designed by Texan Robert von Hagge, the championship-caliber par-72 course is quite challenging, measuring approximately 6,900 yards from the back tees. The greens are designed to incorporate a variety of pin areas that can be used to determine the difficulty of the course; walking the course is not allowed here, but there are 125 carts to help you navigate the layouts. For those interested in other sports, there is also a clubhouse, tennis courts, swimming pool, gym, spa, and restaurant. More than a mile of canals run through the course, allowing condo owners to take water taxis to the greens. ♦ Moderate greens fees. Daily. 31410; fax 30825

Local lore has it that Zihuatanejo received its name from one of Spanish conqueror Hernán Cortés's captains. When the captain reached Bahía de Zihuatanejo, his guide told him the area was called Cihuatlán in the Nahuatl language, meaning "the place of women." The captain added the Castilian suffix *nejo,* meaning small and insignificant, to the name—which may be why the conquerors left the area alone.

Restaurants/Clubs: Red   **Hotels:** Blue
Shops/ 🌳 Outdoors: Green   **Sights/Culture:** Black

Beccofino

Beccofino ★★★$$$ The name in Italian means fine beak, or, colloquially, the ability to discern good taste. Owner Angelo Rolly Pavia has used excellent taste in this restaurant reminiscent of the Italian Riviera. The view of handsome yachts in the marina evokes a mood of extravagance, and this is definitely the place to go all out. The menu, in Italian and Spanish, is an adventure for those unfamiliar with the cuisine, but even the uninitiated can appreciate swordfish ravioli or shrimp in pink pepper sauce. Meatless meals include a sublime cannelloni with spinach and cheese and pasta Beccofino with pesto and peas. There's a daily special for every course, and a tempting array of desserts, including tropical fruit tarts. Imported wines include the popular Batasiolo Pinot Grigio, Chiantis, and Champagnes, and a bracing grappa that is sure to clear your head (momentarily, that is). ♦ Italian ♦ Daily breakfast, lunch, and dinner. Reservations recommended. Marina Ixtapa (near the lighthouse). 31770

7 Playa del Palmar The center of Ixtapa's tourism zone, this two-mile-long stretch of sand is backed by more than 10 luxury hotels. In pretourist times there was only wild grass growing to the edge of the sand; thick groves of coconut palms now provide a junglelike setting. Several *morros* (rocky islands) lie offshore, creating exquisite settings against the sunset. The surf here can get rough, so swimmers should take note of the daily conditions announced by the flags: red, dangerous; yellow, use caution; green, go ahead and swim. ♦ Off Blvd Ixtapa

8 Carlos 'n' Charlie's ★$$ Dancing beneath the stars goes on throughout the night in this branch of Carlos Andersen's chain of zany cafes where fun is king. The Mexican decor offers a few surrealistic touches, and the fare is the usual ribs, seafood, and regional dishes. ♦ Mexican ♦ Daily lunch and dinner. Blvd Ixtapa (next to the Hotel Posada Real). 30085

8 Hotel Posada Real $$ A simple, chain-style hotel with 110 small, nondescript rooms, sitting on the same beach as the upscale giants. A large pool, beach *palapas,* and grassy gardens provide ample relaxation areas, while the two adjacent restaurants are among the rowdiest around (choose your room accordingly). One note: It's the farthest hotel from Ixtapa's shopping centers; unless you're an energetic walker, you may spend as much on taxis as you save on your room. ♦ Blvd Ixtapa (at Playa del Palmar). 31925, 800/334.7234; fax 31805

8 Euforia Disco The action at this all-night disco doesn't even get started until nearly midnight. A high-tech laser display and sound system plus floor fog make this a popular hangout for the young crowd. ♦ Cover. Daily. Blvd Ixtapa (at Playa del Palmar). 31190

9 Omni Hotel $$$ You can't miss this hotel, one of the monoliths on the beach. It features a giant pool with a swim-up bar and 281 comfortable rooms that have bougainvillea streaming from the balconies. Bright flowers are painted above every archway, while wood carvings and floral arrangements add touches of elegance. The lobby bar is a relaxing place for a cocktail before dinner, and the umbrella-topped tables are perfect for sitting under the massive skylights. ♦ Blvd Ixtapa (at Playa del Palmar). 30003, 619/233.1008, 800/223.7755; fax 31805

Within the Omni Hotel:

La Gran Tapa ★★★$$$ Occasionally, a truly unusual restaurant appears among the resort chains. For Ixtapa, this is one of them. Though larger and more formal than your average tapas bar, the restaurant has all the requisite ingredients for a taste of Madrid. Bullfighting photos and posters fill the walls, small cafe tables in the lounge and raised dining area provide a good view of the crowd, and sangria and hearty red wines are the drink of choice at the bar. As with most tapas places, you can run up a hefty tab sampling the menu's delights; your best bet is to share an assortment with friends. Favorites include olives stuffed with anchovies, empanadas stuffed with black beans and machengo cheese, and chicken livers in sherry. You may find yourself returning again and again, for the food and for the convivial crowd, which reaches its peak about 11PM. ♦ Spanish ♦ M, W-Su dinner. Reservations recommended. 30003

9 Krystal Ixtapa $$$ The beachfront hotel has raised the level of vacationing to a fine art form. One of three highly respected properties designed and operated by Mexico City's de la Parra family, this well-cared-for hotel has 260 comfortable rooms and suites with exceptional views of the ocean and beach. The oversized lobby has classic and modern Mexican touches, striking wall hangings, and embroidered cushions, while sitting areas are bathed in sunshine from the broad skylights. Clusters of trees and flowers fill the rambling grounds, and a huge pool meanders around a grand sun deck. With a variety of daytime activities available, along with several intimate bars and cafes, there's always something to keep you busy. ♦ Blvd Ixtapa (at Playa del Palmar). 30333, 800/231.9860; fax 30216

Within the Krystal Ixtapa:

Bogart's ★★$$$$ This expensive, elaborate restaurant is a shrine to the late Humphrey Bogart and his much-loved movie *Casablanca.* Life-size posters of Bogey, romantic piano music, subdued lighting, ceiling fans, and white-on-white Moroccan-style architecture help set the scene. The somewhat pretentious decor and attitude are carried through in the elaborate menu, which includes a vast array of flambéed entrées and desserts. Highlights include the Casablanca Supreme (chicken breast stuffed with lobster), and Muslim salad (a combination of bacon, nuts, lettuce, and tomatoes in a warm vinaigrette dressing). Pianist Esther Walter plays soothing music at a white grand piano set on a pedestal at the rear of the restaurant. ♦ International ♦ Daily dinner. Reservations recommended. 30333

Christine's An elegant yet fun disco is housed in a lovely building. The round dance floor is surrounded by ficus trees, and tiny flashing lights crisscross the floor. During the floor show, waiters dance along with the most flamboyant laser light show around. Stars shine through the glass-domed ceiling, while US stars perform on-screen in the most current video clips. ♦ Cover. Daily. 30333

9 Hotel Dorado Pacífico $$ A soaring 15-story atrium lobby with glass elevators and splashing fountains leads to a long swimming pool with a swim-up bar. The 285 rooms on the ocean side have sliding glass doors leading to small balconies. The suites have mini-bars, spacious sitting areas, and a fold-out couch, and all rooms have been refurbished with blond wood furnishings (though they still have rotary phones). Families are welcome, and there's a separate wading pool and two water slides for kids. The cafeteria offers large buffets, and it's a great spot for a late-night snack of french fries and gazpacho before heading to the discos. ♦ Blvd Ixtapa (at Playa del Palmar). 32025, 800/448.8355; fax 30126

Within the Hotel Dorado Pacífico:

La Brasserie ★★$$ A tinkling mellow piano mingles with the murmurings of happy diners at this gourmet restaurant in an elegant garden atrium. The French dishes on the menu are outstanding, including escargots and flambéed dishes prepared tableside. Ask about their French wine-and-cheese tasting parties. ♦ International ♦ M, W-Su dinner; closed May through November. 32025

La Cebolla Roja ★★$$ Grilled meats and fish are the specialty at this alfresco dining area right on the sand. Candles flicker in hurricane lamps, and the crashing waves provide the music. A trip to the salad bar accompanies most meals; try the mixed grill, with a sampling of Mexican-style meats. ♦ Mexican/Seafood ♦ Daily dinner. 32025

10 Raffaello ★$ A pale pink Mediterranean terrace surrounded by twinkling lights creates the perfect setting for dinner. Italian specialties include beef *picata,* baked octopus, and the delicious pasta Raffaello (a blend of pasta, bacon, and ham in a green chili sauce). ♦ Italian ♦ Daily lunch and dinner. Blvd Ixtapa 6 (across from the Hotel Dorado Pacífico). 32386

10 Los Mandiles ★★$$ An old-timer by Ixtapa standards, this restaurant has a steady following of locals who congregate over fishbowl-size margaritas or jars of fruit juices and dependable Mexican food. The fajitas, enchiladas, and similar standbys are good, though overpriced. The ambience is the main attraction, with hanging lamps made of giant sombreros, a somewhat subdued rowdiness (without the mandatory tequila slammers standard at similar restaurants), and a general sense of merriment. ♦ Mexican ♦ Daily lunch and dinner. Punta Carrizo (at Isla de Apie, behind Galería Ixtapa). 30379

10 La Puerta Mall At one time this property was part of a large hacienda, surrounded by thousands of coconut palms. The hacienda has been replaced by some fine shops and restaurants in a series of Spanish-style one-story stucco buildings arranged around a courtyard (none of Ixtapa's shopping malls is of the glitzy glass-and-chrome variety so popular in Cancún). As the first mall on the strip, it is now battling competition from at least three other plazas. The tourism office is located here, as well as a miniature golf course called **Golfito.** ♦ Daily. Blvd Ixtapa (across from the Presidente Hotel). No phone

Within La Puerta Mall:

Mamma Norma Pizzeria ★★$$ This tiny cafe is consistently recommended as the best pizza place in Ixtapa (and they deliver!). The

Mexican pizza is topped with beans and chorizo (sausage), the marinara comes with tuna, sardines, and chopped egg. Photos of Italy line the walls, and meals are accompanied by recorded Italian tunes. ♦ Italian ♦ Daily lunch and dinner. 30274

Ixcama ★★★$ This tiny green-and-white cafe can't be beat for a quick, inexpensive lunch or snack. Fruit shakes and juices are made to order, as are the excellent *tortas* (hot sandwiches made with French bread, ham, cheese, avocado, and a sprinkling of chopped jalapeños). The homemade vegetable juice is a tangy eye-opener, and the excellent ice creams (especially pineapple) are wonderful on a warm afternoon. ♦ Sandwiches/Ice cream/Fruit ♦ Daily breakfast, lunch, and dinner. No phone

Mic-Mac A vast selection of embroidered T-shirts and dresses, Guatemalan belts, and gorgeous postcards fill this small shop, owned by the same people who have the larger La Fuente in Los Patios. ♦ Daily; closed at midday. 31733

11 **Presidente Ixtapa Forum Resort** $$$ Now an all-inclusive hotel, this was one of the first hostelries built in Ixtapa, and it wears its age well. From the street all you see is the newer high-rise, dubbed "the computer card" by some because of its tiny square windows. But once past the tower you see the true hotel, with a front plaza and iron gazebo, carved stone entryways, and Colonial-style fountains. There are a total of 400 rooms, most with tile floors, marble countertops, rattan furniture, large balconies, and king-sized beds on request. The newer building has a glass elevator and great views of the sea. ♦ Blvd Ixtapa. 30018, 800/327.0200; fax 32312

Within the Presidente Ixtapa Forum Resort:

La Isla ★★$$$ Who can resist the romance of watching a smoky purple sky tinged with pink and violet while sipping a glass of chilled white wine? Savor the moment until the skies turn black and starry, then order meat or fish prepared to perfection in a simple or sizzling *picante* style. The atmosphere is elegant and relaxed, and there are several dishes that must be tried, including the clam soup and the wonderful Neptune's seafood platter. ♦ International ♦ Daily breakfast, lunch, and dinner. 30018

12 **Los Patios** In the row of shopping centers across from the hotels, this one stands out for its excellent folk art shops and galleries. The building is a two-story, U-shaped, rust-colored affair, the first of the malls on Boulevard Ixtapa. ♦ Daily. Blvd Ixtapa (across from the Fontan and Aristos hotels)

Within Los Patios:

Golden Cookie Shop ★★★★$ At breakfast time in high season you're almost destined to stand in line for a seat at this German bakery and cafe, but it's worth the wait. Owners Esther (from Singapore) and Helmut (from Germany) Walters serve great breakfasts of eggs, hash browns, and melt-in-your-mouth sweet rolls. But Chef Helmut really shines with his bratwurst, knockwurst, chicken curry, *nasi goreng* (an Indonesian rice dish with vegetables), and fried bananas. The pastries, strudel, and cookies are beyond compare, and you're not likely to find homemade rye bread anywhere else in town. ♦ International/Bakery ♦ Daily breakfast and lunch; dinner November through May. Second floor. 30310

La Fuente This is surely the only place you'll find lacquered wicker desks and tables sporting smiling wicker jaguar faces, or three-foot-high blown glass vases. Hand-painted plates rest upon distressed antique buffets and dining tables; mirrors with embossed tin frames hang on the wall. The shop carries only the best Mexican folk art and furnishings, which make you long to ship them all home. ♦ Daily; closed at midday. First floor. 30812

Galería San Angel Owner Rosa Elena Quesnel de Vitard has filled her small gallery with a sampling of some of Mexico's finest artists, including religious paintings by Jorge Ritter, designer of the Mexican pavilion murals at the 1964 New York World's Fair. Hand-tooled crosses made of silver and cedar designed by Brother Gabriel Chávez de la Mora of Cuernavaca, surrealistic brass boxes and mirrors by Enrique Zavala, and filigreed replicas of the gold jewelry found at the Zapotec temples at Monte Albán in Oaxaca are also available here. ♦ Daily; closed at midday. First floor. 43611

12 **Plaza Ixpamar** Yet another small shopping center, this one is distinguished by the black iron gate and archway at its entrance. Many of the spaces here have yet to be rented out, but it's a cool, shady place to wander through the existing shops. ♦ Daily. Off Blvd Ixtapa (behind Los Patios)

Within Plaza Ixpamar:

EL AMANECER

El Amanecer This two-story shop is chockablock with reasonably priced folk art and crafts from all over Mexico. An extensive collection of expressive terra-cotta angels from Metepec covers one wall; rustic clay candelabra have a woodlike shine due to a technique developed by Don Heron Martinez of Puebla. Rows of embroidered dresses hang by the windows, and tables are covered with wood and clay skeletons, magic powders, and *milagros* (religious charms). ♦ Daily; closed at midday. 31902

13 Mercado Turisticos Ixtapa (Ixtapa Tourist Market) The vendors who once plied their wares on the sidewalks and beaches now congregate in this tile-roofed artisans' market across from the **Sheraton** hotel. It's well worth a visit here for the requisite T-shirts and souvenirs, and the sampling of folk art from Guerrero artisans. Bargaining is expected. ♦ Daily. Blvd Ixtapa (across from the Sheraton). No phone

14 Sheraton Ixtapa Resort $$$ The sound of the rushing waterfall in the open-air atrium lobby immediately calms stressed-out visitors. A tropical landscape of pools, beaches, and gardens provides plenty of room for privacy, though you may prefer to relax on your balcony and survey the scene from above. Though many think of this hotel as a business traveler's haven, that's not so: The entire 332-room hotel was designed for pleasure and relaxation, with spacious rooms in cool, soothing colors. ♦ Blvd Ixtapa (near Paseo del Palmar). 31858, 800/325.3535; fax 32438

Within the Sheraton Ixtapa Resort:

La Fonda ★★★$$ If you came to Mexico for the food, then this is the place for you. Here it's called gourmet Mexican, with such specialties as ceviche, *chicharron de queso* (grilled cheese rinds), quesadillas with cheese, *huitlacoche* (a mushroomlike fungus cultivated on corn husks), and squash blossoms. The dining room is reminiscent of a colonial plaza, with walls washed in soft blue, yellow, and pink, huge star-shaped piñatas hanging from the ceiling, and a fountain at the entryway. And the strains of Mexican ballads, sung and strummed by a guitarist in the adjacent lobby bar, complete the dining experience. ♦ Mexican ♦ Daily dinner. 31858

Veranda ★★$ Dining in the open atrium lobby under bright white suspended tents has a cool, cosmopolitan feeling. The Mexican breakfast buffet is set up for early birds who choose from fruit, fresh juices, pastries, and cereals before digging into such Mexican specialties as *chilaquiles* (corn tortillas in broth), quesadillas, *huevos rancheros,* and much more. For those who don't want that much spice in their life, there are pancakes, eggs and bacon, and club sandwiches with fresh-roasted turkey. This is the perfect place to escape the midday sun. ♦ Mexican/International ♦ Daily breakfast, lunch, and dinner. 31858

15 Ixtapa Golf Club

Designed by Robert Trent Jones Jr., this green oasis with palm trees scattered alongside cool reflecting lakes and ponds (it's a natural refuge for flamingos, cranes, parrots, rabbits, iguanas, and the occasional alligator) makes for an exciting game of golf. The 18-hole course is 6,898 yards, par 72, with a capacity for 250 players. Clubhouse facilities include showers and lockers, a pro shop run by golf pro Eduardo Medina, a boutique, and a restaurant-bar. Adjacent to the clubhouse are five lighted, professional-size tennis courts and a large swimming pool with a bar and lounge area. Other amenities include caddies, electric carts, and a roving bar cart to quench your thirst on the course. Golf tournaments are held here in November and June. ♦ Moderate greens fees. Daily. Blvd Ixtapa (at Retorno de las Alondras). 31062

G. L. G.

16 Villa del Lago $$ It's a golfer's dream to stay in this elegant six-suite bed and breakfast right next to the sixth tee; there's also a small pool overlooking the rolling greens and the lake. Daily rates include greens fees, breakfast (served on your terrace or near the pool), and afternoon wine and cheese. Dinner is available on request for an extra charge. Nightlife consists of stargazing from the terrace while sipping a drink, but transportation is available to whisk you off to the shows, bars, and discos just five minutes away on Playa del Palmar. ♦ Reservations recommended. Retorno de las Alondras 244 (next to the golf course). 31482; fax 31422

17 Westin Brisas Resort Ixtapa $$$ Sitting on its own little bay on Playa Vista Hermosa, this 428-room pyramid-shaped hotel provides the ultimate in privacy. The air is filled with the sounds of exotic birds who live in the nearby jungle; pleasant walkways meander past swimming pools with waterfalls. Guests in the lanai rooms have ocean views from their hammocks; those in the **Royal Beach Club** have use of a private lounge where complimentary continental breakfast and afternoon cocktails with hors d'oeuvres are served. Not to be overlooked are the standard rooms, which are still luxurious compared to other hotels. Nonsmoking rooms are available. Fresh flowers and fruit are brought in daily, and a shady beach *palapa* is reserved at your request.

Every restaurant within the complex is excellent, and shoppers get their fix at high-end galleries and boutiques. In fact, some guests never leave the grounds. ♦ Playa Vista Hermosa (off Paseo de Ixtapa). 32121, 800/228.3000; fax 30751

Within the Westin Resort Ixtapa:

El Mexicano ★★$$ Gourmet Mexican food tastes even better on a tree-lined patio decorated in bold colors. Jumbo prawns in tamarind sauce are outstanding, and the baby abalone in *chile chipotle* sauce is a memorable appetizer. For a different approach to fish, try the cream of coriander seafood dishes. ♦ Mexican ♦ Daily dinner. Reservations recommended. 32121

Portofino Restaurant ★★★$$$ When you're in the mood to splurge on a special evening, this restaurant offers intimate dining with crystal and candlelight. This is the best Italian food in town, including scrumptious beef scallopini and the biggest and freshest shrimp you've ever eaten. The antipasto buffet not only looks good, but it has all the familiar tastes of your favorite trattoria in Rome. Save room for dessert—the choices seem endless, but try the sabayon dressed with fresh strawberries. ♦ Italian ♦ Daily dinner. Reservations recommended. 32121

18 **Villa de la Selva** ★★★$$$ Take all the time you wish and linger over a Spanish coffee or a glass of cognac high on the southern hills overlooking Playa Vista Hermosa and the impressive **Westin Resort.** Once the lovely home of an ex-president, it has been converted into a series of dining rooms, each with open terraces and views of the sea. Classic Mexican dishes and outstanding steaks are on the menu, along with a great wine list. ♦ Mexican/International ♦ Daily dinner. Reservations recommended. Paseo de La Roca (off Paseo de Ixtapa). 30362

Zihuatanejo

19 **Puerto Mío** $$$ Few hotels can claim their own cove and marina; this one has all that and more. Hacienda-style buildings in pale pastel colors perch on the side of a steep bluff that appears to be climbing into the sky. All 30 rooms have unparalleled views of Bahía de Zihuatanejo and are gorgeously furnished with folk art; some have private hot tubs. The rooms in the mansion atop the property's highest hill are enormous, with gauze canopies draping over the beds, shells embedded in the bathroom walls, and vibrant handwoven cotton fabrics contrasting with white stucco walls. Swimming pools seem to flow over the edge of the cliff; barrel cacti tower beside fuchsia bougainvillea, giving the property a surrealistic desert-jungle effect. There also is a scuba center, with boats departing from the hotel's marina; dive packages are available. ♦ Cerro del Almacen (between Punta San Esteban and downtown). 42748; fax 42048

Within Puerto Mío:

Restaurant Puerto Mío ★★★★$$$$ The terrace and formal dining rooms overlooking the small cove help make this the most revered restaurant in Ixta/Zihua these days. Locals say it has the best food, service, and ambience in the area, and since the menu changes every few days, it's well worth more than one visit. Come for the sunset, best viewed from the adjacent lounge; as night falls, torches are lit along the cliff tops over the sea. Begin your meal with a salad of sliced tomatoes and full-bodied Oaxacan cheese, or delicate shrimp crepes. Move on to fresh tuna with pepper sauce, or snapper with peanut sauce, or whatever fresh fish the chef has prepared. Linger over a brandy afterward, then wander up the hill to the *palapa*-covered, open-air nightclub, where the music is right for dancing or romantic conversation. ♦ Nouvelle Mexican/Seafood ♦ Daily dinner. 42748

20 **Muelle Municipal** Cruise ships, fishing boats, and yachts all anchor off this short wooden pier, a favorite spot for evening strolls. A white obelisk monument marking the beginning of Paseo del Pescador is just right of the pier; the navy is headquartered to the left, next to the fishing cooperative. Fisherfolk beach their *pangas* (small skiffs) along this stretch of sand, and stash their gear in blue wooden lockers. They pull out before dawn and return before noon with their catch. If fresh fish isn't your idea of a souvenir, check out the adjacent display of coral and shells at the open-air **Mercado Conchas Marina** (Seashell Market). ♦ Off Paseo del Pescador (at Playa Municipal)

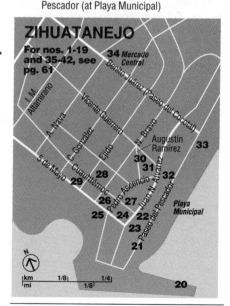

ZIHUATANEJO

For nos. 1-19 and 35-42, see pg. 61

34 *Mercado Central*

I. M. Altamirano
A. Nava
V. Gonzalez
Vicente Guerrero
Ejido
Cuauhtemoc
5 de Mayo
Benito Juarez (Paseo del Cocotal)
N. Bravo
Augustin Ramirez 33
30
31
32
29
28
Pedro Ascencio
Juan N. Alvarez
26 27
25 24 22
23
21
Paseo del Pescador
Playa Municipal
N
km 1/8 1/4
mi 1/8
20

Restaurants/Clubs: Red   **Hotels:** Blue
Shops/ 🌳 Outdoors: Green   **Sights/Culture:** Black

¿Habla Español?

Relax. Mexicans don't assume that gringos speak Spanish. Most are very patient with your possibly flawed attempts, and are generally pleased that you've tried. Here are some basics to get you started.

¡Buen viaje! (Have a good trip!)

Hello, Good-Bye, and Other Basics

Good morning	*Buenos días*
Good afternoon	*Buenas tardes*
Good evening	*Buenas noches*
How are you?	*Cómo está usted?*
Good-bye!	*Adiós!*
Yes	*Sí*
No	*No*
Please	*Por favor*
Thank you	*Gracias*
You're welcome	*De nada*
I beg your pardon/ Excuse me	*Perdón?/Con permiso*
I'm sorry	*Lo siento*
I don't speak Spanish.	*No hablo español.*
Do you speak English?	*Habla usted inglés?*
I don't understand.	*No comprendo/ No entiendo.*
Do you understand?	*Comprende?/Entiende?*
More slowly, please.	*Más lento, por favor.*
I don't know.	*No sé.*
My name is	*Me llamo*
What is your name?	*Cómo se llama?*
miss	*señorita*
madame, ma'am	*señora*
mister	*señor*
good	*bueno/a*
bad	*malo/a*
open	*abierto/a*
closed	*cerrado/a*
entrance	*entrada*
exit	*salida*
push	*empujar*
pull	*jalar*
What time does it open/close?	*A qué hora se abre/ se cierra?*
today	*hoy*
tomorrow	*mañana*
yesterday	*ayer*
week	*semana*
month	*mes*
year	*año*

Hotel Talk

I have a reservation	*Tengo una reservación*
I would like	*Quisiera*
a double room	*una habitación doble*
a quiet room	*una habitación tranquila*
with (private) bath	*con baño (privado)*
with air-conditioning	*con aire acondicionado*

Does that price include	*Está incluído en el precio*
breakfast?	*el desayuno?*
taxes?	*los impuestos?*
Do you accept traveler's checks?	*Acepta usted cheques de viajero?*
Do you accept credit cards?	*Acepta tarjetas de crédito?*

Restaurant Repartee

Waiter!	*Camarero!/Mesero!*
I would like	*Quisiera*
a glass of	*un vaso de*
a bottle of	*una botella de*
a liter of	*un litro de*
The check, please.	*La cuenta, por favor.*
Is a service charge included?	*Está incluído el servicio?*
I think there is a mistake in the bill.	*Creo que hay un error en la cuenta.*
lunch	*la comida*
dinner	*la cena*
tip	*la propina*
bread	*pan*
butter	*mantequilla*
pepper	*pimienta*
salt	*sal*
sugar	*azúcar*
soup	*sopa*
salad	*ensalada*
vegetables	*verduras*
cheese	*queso*
beans	*frijoles*
meat	*carne*
chicken	*pollo*
veal	*ternera*
fish	*pescado*
seafood, shellfish	*mariscos*
pork	*carne de cerdo*
ham	*jamón*
bacon	*tocino*
chops	*chuletas*
dessert	*postre*

As You Like It

cold	*frío/a*
hot	*caliente*
sweet	*dulce*
(very) dry	*(muy) seco/a*
broiled, roasted	*asado/a*
baked	*horneado/a*
boiled	*hervido/a*
fried	*frito/a*
raw	*crudo/a*
rare	*jugoso/a*

medium	medio/a
well done	bien cocido/a
spicy	picante

Thirsty No More

hot chocolate (cocoa)	un chocolate caliente
black coffee	un café negro
"American-style" coffee	un café americano
coffee with hot milk	café con leche
milk	leche
tea	un té
fruit juice	un jugo de fruta
water	agua
purified water	agua purificada
mineral water	agua mineral
ice	hielo
without ice	sin hielo
beer	una cerveza
red wine	vino tinto
white wine	vino blanco

Sizing It Up

How much does this cost?	Cuánto cuesta ésto?
inexpensive	barato/a
expensive	caro/a
large	grande
small	pequeño/a
long	largo/a
short	corto/a
old	viejo/a
new	nuevo/a
used	usado/a
this one	esto
a little	un poquito
a lot	mucho

On the Move

north	norte
south	sur
east	este
west	oeste
right	derecho/a
left	izquierdo/a
highway	carretera, autopista
gas station	la gasolinera
Go straight ahead.	Siga todo derecho.
here	aquí
there	allí
bus stop	la parada de autobuses
bus station	la estación de autobuses
train station	la estación de ferrocarril
subway station	la estación de metro
airport	el aeropuerto
tourist information	información turística
map	el mapa
one-way ticket	un boleto de ida
round-trip ticket	un boleto de ida y vuelta

first class	primera clase
second class	segunda clase
smoking	fumar
no smoking	no fumar
Does this train go to …?	Va este tren a …?
Does this bus go to …?	Va este autobús a …?
Where is/are …?	Dónde está/están…?
How far is it from here to …?	Qué distancia hay desde aquí hasta …?

The Bare Necessities

aspirin	aspirina
Band-Aids	curitas
barbershop, beauty shop	la peluquería
condom	el condón
dry cleaner	la tintorería
laundromat, laundry	la lavandería
letter	carta
post office	el correo
postage stamps	estampillas, timbres
postcard	tarjeta postal
sanitary napkins	toallas femininas
shampoo	el champú
shaving cream	la espuma
soap	el jabón
tampons	unos tampones
tissues	Kleenex
toilet paper	papel higiénico
toothpaste	pasta de dientes
Where is the bathroom?	Dónde está el baño?
Where are the toilets?	Dónde están los sanitarios?
Men's Room	Caballeros/Señores
Women's Room	Damas/Señoras

Days of the Week
(usually lowercased in Spanish)

Monday	Lunes
Tuesday	Martes
Wednesday	Miércoles
Thursday	Jueves
Friday	Viernes
Saturday	Sábado
Sunday	Domingo

Numbers

zero	cero
one	uno
two	dos
three	tres
four	cuatro
five	cinco
six	seis
seven	siete
eight	ocho
nine	nueve
ten	diez

21 Paseo del Pescador A decorative brick promenade runs from the municipal pier the length of downtown Zihua and the Playa Municipal (or Playa Principal), where locals sun on the sand and play in the waves. Open-air seafood restaurants line the walkway from the pier to the basketball court at the foot of Cuauhtémoc, where there always seems to be a game under way. A small stage at the water side of the court is used for musical performances on Sunday evenings, and the wide brick plaza on the street side of the court serves as a gathering spot. More cafes appear as the road leads eastward to the **Museo Arqueológico de la Costa Grande.** The walkway was extended along the rock cliffs to Playa Madera, but severe storms recently wiped it out. At press time, the *paseo* was under repair; possible plans include extending it to Playa la Ropa.

22 Casa Elvira ★★$$ One of the oldest restaurants in Zihua, it is packed on weekend afternoons with locals feasting on large seafood platters of red snapper, lobster, shrimp, and octopus. The chips are freshly fried throughout the day, and taste great with the chunky guacamole. The parade of people on the *paseo* is visible from most tables, as is a saltwater aquarium mimicking the local underwater scenery. If you're tired of fish, there's also good spaghetti, a great grilled meat platter, and cheese-filled *chiles rellenos.* ♦ Seafood/Mexican ♦ Daily breakfast, lunch, and dinner. Paseo del Pescador (near the basketball court). 42061

22 La Zapoteca A collector's dream, hand-woven wool rugs with ancient Zapotec designs fill the shelves and walls in this shop on the *paseo* dedicated to Oaxacan art. The shop also carries embroidered clothing, pottery, hammocks, and other folk art. ♦ Daily. Paseo del Pescador (near the basketball court). 42061

23 La Sirena Gorda ★★★$$ Owner Luis Muñoz knows his way around a fish, especially when it's wrapped in a fresh corn tortilla. Fish tacos are his specialty, and shouldn't be missed. Fillings include smoked sailfish, shrimp topped with crumbled bacon and onion strips, conch with nopales cactus, and *pescado al pastor* (fish roasted on a spit and served with fresh cilantro). Chances are you'll keep coming back until you've sampled them all; there also are hefty burgers and fish dinners. The restaurant's name means "happy mermaid"; the lovely sea creature is depicted in paintings and drawings done by creative customers. Early risers can watch the anglers head out to sea while lingering over a breakfast of eggs or fish tacos. ♦ Seafood ♦ M, Tu, Th-Su breakfast, lunch, and dinner. Paseo del Pescador (near the pier). 42687

24 Ziwok ★★★$$$ The owner of **La Sirena Gorda** moved his second restaurant from the cliffs over Playa la Ropa to the town center in 1994, solidifying his position as the premier restaurateur in downtown Zihuatanejo. Though the adventurous Japanese/Mexican menu has changed a bit, the food is still exceptional. The sushi and sashimi are gone, but you can still try chicken stir-fried with nopales cactus and jicama, fresh fish in a chili sauce, or flaky tempura. ♦ Japanese/Mexican ♦ Tu-Su dinner. Juan N. Alvarez (at 5 de Mayo). 43136

24 El Patio ★★★$$$ Candles shimmer in an intimate garden dining area perfect for quiet conversations. The street-side part of the restaurant serves as a bar in high season and a dining room at other times. Precious hand-painted Talavera vases and plates are displayed in antique china cabinets, and blue-and-white tiles from Oaxaca line the counters of the open kitchen. Dinners begin with complimentary, appetizer-size corn patties with chopped lettuce, meats, onions, and cheese atop a thick corn tortilla. Mexican specialties include a *nopalito* (cactus) salad and shrimp-stuffed *chiles rellenos;* seafood shines in the tuna brochette. There's live music in the high season, including Andean flutes or Spanish flamenco. ♦ Mexican/Seafood ♦ Daily breakfast, lunch, dinner. 5 de Mayo 3 (at Pedro Ascencio). 43019

25 Mercado de Artesanía Turístico Vendors who used to ply their wares on the beach have set up shop in this four-block-long market with 255 permanent stands. Clean, shaded, and filled with fascinating goods, the market is a great place to learn about local folk art. Artists paint colorful scenes of village life on bowls and plates, or glue tiny seashells into statuettes. T-shirts abound, and though they may seem light and flimsy, they're perfect for this humid climate and dry quickly. A careful shopper will find items from most of Mexico's craft centers, and with some skillful bargaining could end up with some worthy treasures. ♦ Daily. 5 de Mayo (between Juan N. Alvarez and C. González). No phone

26 Iglesia de la Virgen de Guadalupe
(Church of the Virgin of Guadalupe) Zihua's
main church is a simple one, with a metal roof
and ceiling fans. A box is set by the front door
with a sign in English requesting donations for
the church's refurbishing. ♦ 5 de Mayo (at
Pedro Ascencio)

27 Zihuatanejo Scuba Center Zihua is
beginning to gain fame as a prime diving
destination. Manta rays, eagle rays, and the
occasional shark or humpback whale provide
that extra jolt of excitement divers crave, and
with at least 28 dive sites to choose from,
deep-sea devotees find enough variety to
satisfy them. It's run by Ed Clarke, an ex–San
Francisco business executive, and Juan
Barnard Avila, a marine biologist. Both are
experienced certified divers, and run a first-
class, safe operation. Divers must have a
certification card, and are taken in small
groups to sites that include coral gardens and
underwater caves. Certification courses are
available. ♦ M-Sa. Cuauhtémoc 3 (between
Juan N. Alvarez and Pedro Ascencio). 42147;
fax 44468. Also at: Puerto Mío Hotel, 42748.
Scuba and hotel packages are available
through **Destination Consultants,** World
Trade Center, Suite 100, San Francisco, CA
94111. 415/781.5588; fax 415/781.0213

27 Ruby's Joyeria y Galería Jewelry and
accessories in silver, gold, and precious gems
are displayed, with prices ranging from
downright cheap to thousands of dollars. Lots
of jewelry shops line this pedestrian-only
stretch, but this store has the highest quality
pieces, many signed by the artist. ♦ Daily;
closed at midday. Cuauhtémoc 7 (between
Juan N. Alvarez and Pedro Ascencio). 43990

28 Nueva Zelanda ★★★$ First-rate
breakfasts plus great sandwiches, *tortas,* and
enchiladas keep the seats full throughout the
day. Diners check their choices on a printed
menu/order form, and waiters deliver the
orders quickly. Sit at the counter and watch
the waiters put papaya and water or milk in
the blender for thick *licuados* (fruit drinks).
♦ Mexican/American ♦ Daily breakfast and
lunch. Cuauhtémoc (at Ejido). No phone

29 Boutique D'Xochitl Known for her
elaborate style of dress, Xochitl was an Aztec
queen in the time of Cuauhtémoc. Modern
women can dress equally extravagantly in
flowing gauze skirts by Maria de Guadalajara
and appliquéd jackets by Girasol, two of

Mexico's top designers of resort wear. This
boutique carries both lines, plus glamorous
hats and accessories to complete the look.
♦ Daily. Cuauhtémoc (at Ejido). 42131

30 Coconuts ★★★$$ This upscale outdoor
restaurant sparkles with trees covered
with tiny white lights. The eatery has a good
(and well-deserved) reputation for its
international menu and friendly bar. It's
closed during the rainy season, so call ahead.
♦ International ♦ Daily dinner; closed August
through November. Reservations recom-
mended. Augustín Ramírez 1 (at Vicente
Guerrero). 42518

31 Coco Cabaña It's fun to browse through
this boutique's large selection of Mexican folk
art, complete with whimsical animals from
Oaxaca, unique Guerrero masks, and
handwoven cloth from Chiapas. Prices are a
bit higher than in the bigger cities, but the
quality and variety are excellent. ♦ Daily.
Vicente Guerrero (at Augustín Ramírez).
No phone

31 El Buen Gusto $ A steady stream of people
enter this bright pink house to peruse shelves
filled with delicious *bolillos* (crusty rolls),
dense sugar cookies, and flaky pastries.
Resist temptation and buy only what you can
eat within the day, then return tomorrow to
see what new treats are fresh from the oven.
♦ Bakery ♦ Daily. Vicente Guerrero 8 (at Juan
N. Alvarez). 43231

32 Hotel Avila $ The rooms on the beach side
of this immaculately kept budget hotel have
the best seats in town for viewing the scene
along the Paseo del Pescador. Two large
terraces with upholstered couches, tables,
and chairs face the sea; from this lofty perch
you have a panoramic view of Bahía
Zihuatanejo. Each of the 27 large, white rooms
has two double beds, giant showers, ceiling
fans, and powerful air-conditioners (which
you only need in the height of summer).
Sliding glass doors open onto balconies and
patios, providing a nice sea breeze. Rooms on
the street side aren't nearly as nice, since you
lose the breeze and gain traffic noise. The
restaurant downstairs is a good spot for a
quick bite or cool drink. Since this is the only
downtown hotel right at the beach, it fills up
quickly in the winter months. ♦ Juan N.
Alvarez 8 (between Cuauhtémoc and Vicente
Guerrero). 42010

**33 Museo Arqueológico de la Costa
Grande** (Archaeology Museum) Inaugurated
in 1992, this small museum is located in a
handsome river-rock building at the end of
Paseo del Pescador, practically on the sand.
Displays include paintings of the pre-
Columbian Cuitlateca people, and artifacts
from archaeological sites in the state of
Guerrero. ♦ Admission. Tu-Su. Paseo del
Pescador (between Vicente Guerrero and
Benito Juárez). 32552

34 Mercado Central Housewives fill their shopping bags with seasonal vegetables, fresh meat, poultry, seafood, and medicinal herbs. There's also a wide variety of tropical fruits such as papaya, coconut, bananas, and tamarind. The candy paste made with tamarind can be sugary sweet, or, for something really different, chili flavored. ♦ Daily. Benito Juárez (at A. Nava). No phone

35 Bungalows Pacíficos $ High on a hill overlooking the bay, this small hotel offers large patios where guests can sit among the wild indigenous plants and catch the breezes and vistas of Zihuatanejo. The six apartmentlike rooms are simple, with twin beds and kitchens. Owner Anita Hahner Chimalpopoca is friendly and full of useful information and suggestions, and the best part of staying here is getting to know her (made easier by the fact that she speaks English, Spanish, and German). She is vitally interested in the archaeology of the area and has been collecting artifacts for more than 20 years. Playa Madera is at the base of a long, downhill climb, and you can reach town along the cliffside path from here. ♦ Cerro de la Madera (near Playa Madera). 42112

Sportfishing

Knowledgeable anglers head for Zihuatanejo from December through March, when marlin, dorado, sailfish, and other big game fish come within a few miles of shore. According to the experts, the San Andreas Fault cuts deep canyons not far from the shoreline, creating ideal conditions for large fish who demand plenty of space. The **Ixtapa/Zihuatanejo Billfish Classic** tournament held in January and the May **International Sailfish Tournament** both attract serious sportfishers and produce record-breaking catches—recently an angler landed a thousand-pound marlin after battling for several long hours. Sportfishing boats from *pangas* to cabin cruisers are available for charter at the fishing cooperative in Zihuatanejo (Paseo del Pescador, 42056).

> The tiny islet of Punta Ixtapa is called Isla de Pie (Island on Foot), since you can walk to it during low tide.

Restaurants/Clubs: Red	**Hotels:** Blue
Shops/ Outdoors: Green	**Sights/Culture:** Black

36 Playa Madera This sunbathing spot, the smallest beach along the bay, is named for its early days as a loading point for logs (*madera* means timber) that were cut from the surrounding jungle and exported. There are small inexpensive hotels and cottages along the shore and on the bluff above. ♦ Off Camino Escénico a la Playa la Ropa, east of downtown

36 Hotel Irma $ Just look for a pinker-than-pink building with a broad awning at the arched entrance. Set on a cliff above Playa Madera, this rustic, Mexican-style hotel has pink granite walls, red tile floors, brick archways, and 75 simple rooms. Complimentary transportation is provided to and from Playa la Ropa, popular because of its restaurants and shops. The hotel is a favorite of Mexican families, and the **Zihuatanejo Scuba Center** uses one of its pools for diving lessons. Excellent Mexican food is served at **El Zorito's,** but the coffee shop is just average. ♦ Near Playa Madera. 42101, 42025; fax 43738

37 La Casa Que Canta $$$$ Considered one of the most beautiful hotels in Mexico, and a member of the Small Luxury Hotels of the World, this place lives up to its name—the house of song. Each of the 18 suites (two with private pools) is named after a popular Mexican ballad, and each has a mood of its own. The cool white-on-white decor is accented with gorgeous furnishings from Michoacán, engraved and painted by hand into fanciful pastel scenes. The arms of a couch are carved into bright red-and-yellow parrots; soft blue monkeys swing on a nightstand. Several rooms have wooden desk chairs decorated with reproductions of Frida Kahlo paintings. All guest rooms have telephones, but TV sets are nonexistent. Children under the age of 18 are not allowed.

The walls surrounding the property are made of rough adobe and give off a faint, earthy aroma of straw and clay. In addition to the beach, there are both fresh- and saltwater swimming pools. Breakfast and lunch are intimate affairs, served on the private balconies or at the guests-only *palapa* cafe. ♦ Camino Escénico a la Playa la Ropa (between Playa Madera and Playa la Ropa). 42722, 42878, 800/525.4800; fax 42006

Within La Casa Que Canta:

La Casa Que Canta ★★★$$$$ Private dining areas are scattered down the many levels of the main building, nestled in niches looking out to the sea. The menu changes every few days, but may include a tomato and Oaxaca cheese salad, chilled curried chicken soup, or crayfish with ginger sauce. ♦ Mexican/International ♦ Daily dinner. Camino Playa la Ropa. 42722, 42878, 800/525.4800; fax 42006

38 Hoteles Catalina and **Sotavento** $$ These two hotels have the same owner and share the same property; there's a total of 84 breeze-cooled rooms perched on a cliff overlooking the sea. The sister hotels have been around awhile and show their age, but the location in the midst of tall trees and a jungle environment is one of the best in Zihuatanejo. Terraces with hammocks and lounge chairs afford total relaxation. Music and amiable guests, some of whom have been returning here since the 1960s, make for a pleasant dining experience. An elevator (when in operation) eases the long trek to and from the beach below. ♦ Camino Escénico a la Playa la Ropa (between Playa Madera and Playa la Ropa). 42032; fax 42975

39 Playa la Ropa (Beach of Clothes) Centuries ago one of the trading ships from the Orient floundered and sunk in Bahía de Zihuatanejo, and, for days afterward, fine silks and rich clothing washed ashore—hence the name. Many say this is the best swimming beach in town, and it's usually filled with locals and guests from adjacent hotels. Several hotels and outdoor cafes are located right on the sand, and a few more are nestled in the hillside overlooking the road that overlooks the beach.

40 Villa del Sol $$$$ Take all the ingredients of a great Mexican hotel—comfortable beds, tropical ambience, luxurious amenities, and purified water—and add a friendly staff, 36 spacious rooms with delicate transparent white draperies around the bed (romantic and mosquito-proof), a sitting area, and a terrace

with hammocks. Put it all on the most beautiful beach in Zihuatanejo and you have this hotel, a member of the Small Luxury Hotels of the World.

The property sits in the middle of Playa la Ropa, with its own sandy lounge area separated from the main beach. Hand-painted tiles, fountains, and Mexican art decorate the rooms and public spaces, with winding, shady paths leading to the two pools and the **Villa del Sol Restaurant,** where the gourmet meals will make a substantial dent in your wallet. When business is slow, outsiders are welcome to use the restaurant and facilities for a fee. Proper attire is required—no bathing suits in the restaurant, no shorts after 6PM.

An MAP plan (rates include breakfast and dinner) is de rigueur in high season (15 November-30 April) and optional in the summer. Children over 14 are welcome during winter, and younger children are accepted during the summer season. ♦ Reservations required. Playa la Ropa. 42239, 800/525.4800; fax 42758

41 Rossy ★★$ There are two floors of lawn chairs, tables, and inviting hammocks, all open to cool breezes at this eatery at the far end of Playa la Ropa. Feeling adventurous? Try limpets (a mollusk that lives on the rocks) in a soup or cocktail. The cold beer and excellent coffee are priced amazingly low. ♦ Mexican/Seafood ♦ Daily. Playa la Ropa. 44004

42 Playa Las Gatas (Nurse Shark Beach) At the southern end of Playa la Ropa is a peninsula; on its seaward side is the **Faro de Potosí** (Potosí Lighthouse); on the bayside is a beach that locals consider to be the most beautiful in the entire bay. According to local lore, a Tarascan king built the breakwater of rocks that protect the lush palm-lined beach to create a private beach for his daughter. Unless you're a mountain goat, you must get here by boat (catch one from the downtown pier). There are several *palapa* restaurants specializing in lobster, charcoal-broiled red snapper, clams, and oysters; the best is **Chez Arnoldo** (★★★$$$). Scuba, snorkeling, and other water sports equipment is available for rent.

Every day around 7PM in Zihuatanejo, hundreds of swallows circle the town and land on the telephone wires near the movie theater. They chatter and twitter together for about 45 minutes, then fly away to their nighttime habitat. No one knows why they come to this particular spot, but for as many years as anyone can remember this has been an evening ritual. Strangers learn the hard way not to park their cars under the telephone wires.

Acapulco

Since the 1950s, when it became Hollywood's beach club where such stars as Rita Hayworth, Eddie Fisher, Errol Flynn, and Cary Grant used to play, Acapulco has been synonymous with glamour, wealth, and fame. It still attracts all types of celebrities, and has hosted such disparate events as Liz Taylor and Mike Todd's wedding, Pat and Richard Nixon's 25th anniversary, and Bill and Hillary Clinton's honeymoon. Given the number of private enclaves and guarded hideaways, there's room for all, even the average tourist with an unremarkable name.

Acapulco is divided into several districts, each with its own distinct characteristic. On the west side of the bay, **Acapulco Viejo** (Old Acapulco) and the **Playa Caleta** area were once the center of glamour, but they have settled into a comfortable obscurity that attracts laid-back wanderers and nostalgia buffs. **Costera Miguel Alemán**, lined with high-rise hotels, shopping malls, restaurants, discos, and beach bars, runs parallel to the bay's center shoreline, with the golf course, **Centro Acapulco** (Convention Center), and lavish hillside houses on the east end. The hills along **Carretera Escénica**, winding from the Costera southeast to the airport, are dotted with spectacular private homes and resorts, most hidden from sight. Gourmet restaurants and exclusive discos command stunning views from along the roadside. The beach side of this scenic road is the site of a miles-long

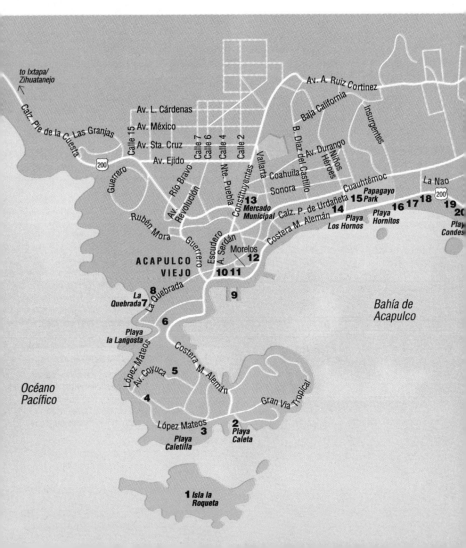

megadevelopment called **Acapulco Diamante.** When finished (at press time, the completion date was projected to be after the turn of the century), the area will include several deluxe resort hotels and private homes priced in the millions.

Such grand-scale planning is Acapulco's style. An aura of monied narcissism seems to pervade the sultry sea air, and definitely influences the local ambience. *Acapulqueños* and their guests follow a time schedule far different than fast-paced US residents are accustomed to. Early morning simply doesn't exist, except for the working class. Breakfast is a late-morning affair, after 10AM or so. Lunch doesn't start until 3PM, and it seems gauche to dine before nine. The night doesn't really begin until midnight, when lines of smashingly dressed revelers of all ages form outside glittering discos and stylish clubs. Sleep is an afterthought, and siestas are imperative if you plan to keep up with the pace.

Naturally, there are other ways to spend your time and money. Shopping for everything from sandals to sculptures is excellent. Sunbathing, preferably with an iced drink in hand, is the daytime activity of choice. Dining can be as adventurous as you wish, be it fish tacos, sushi, beef burgers, or flaming filet mignon. Acapulco is home, at least part-time, to many who have seen and done it all. Still, they keep returning for more.

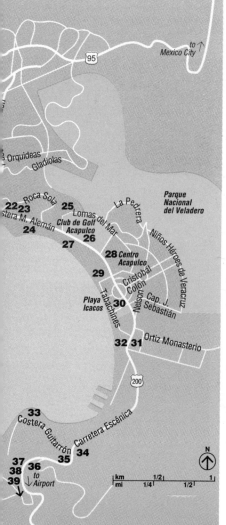

Area code 74 unless otherwise noted.

Getting to Acapulco
Airport

Juan N. Alvarez International Airport is a 25-minute drive southwest of downtown. Call 669476 for information.

Airlines

Aeroméxico	840709, 669109
American	669248, 669260
Continental	669063, 669046
Delta	669331, 669005
Mexicana	846890, 841215
Taesa	811214, 864576

Driving

Highway 95, a new roadway between Mexico City and Acapulco, has cut the driving time nearly in half, but there's one catch: high tolls. In fact, when the highway first opened, bus companies refused to use it. On the positive side, driving is still significantly less expensive than flying between the two cities.

Getting around Acapulco

The city is divided into the old and the new sections, connected by the Costera Miguel Alemán, a broad waterfront boulevard that winds around the harbor from east to west. Buses, cabs, and horse-drawn carts transport people along this busy thoroughfare.

Buses

Take the bus to most tourist destinations. Look for the yellow stands and blue *parada* (bus stop) signs—some even include a pay phone, mail box, and color-coded maps of the bus routes mounted on the wall. Buses marked "Base-Costera-Zócalo-Hornos" run along the length of the main tourist zone to the zócalo in Acapulco Viejo and the beach below the cliffs of La Quebrada (avoid those labeled "Cine Rio," unless you want to take the marginally scenic and impressively congested trip through the streets of downtown Acapulco). Those marked "Base-Caleta" run to Playa Caleta at the southwest tip of the bay.

Car Rental

Avis	841633, 842581
Budget	848200, 810596
Dollar	843066, 843769
Hertz	858947, 856889
National	848234, 844348

Taxis

Besides being inexpensive, this is the easiest way to travel around Acapulco. You can usually flag down a cab on the main boulevard anytime of day or night. Cabs parked in front of hotels (by the sign marked *sitio*) can cost more than the independent taxi cruising the streets, especially during the slow seasons. You can run up quite a tab traveling to the hotels and restaurants in the area around **Las Brisas** hotel and Acapulco Diamante. Always establish the price with the driver before climbing in.

FYI

Emergencies
Canadian Consulate Hotel Club del Sol 856600

Hospitals
Hospital General Ave Ruis Cortines, Colonia Alta Progreso 851730

Hospital Privado Maghallanes Ave Wilfredo Maseu 2, Acapulco 856706

Police..868220

Locatel is a 24-hour hotline (811100) offering assistance with legal and medical emergencies, as well as other information, to tourists.

US Consulate, Hotel Club del Sol 856264

Money
You can change money at the airport, hotels, and banks, with the latter giving you the best rate. Bank hours for changing money are typically Mondays through Fridays from 9AM to 1:30PM. *Casas de cambio* (exchange houses) are scattered around downtown and open throughout the day and evening. International credit cards and US dollars are accepted in most restaurants, hotels, and shops. Try not to be short of cash on Sundays, because it can be difficult to change money on that day, except in some hotels. Always keep bills of small denominations on hand, since it can be difficult to change larger bills (except at banks).

Banamex Costera M. Alemán 2085 859020

Bancomer Costera M. Alemán (at Laurel) 848055

Banpais Costera M. Alemán 2083 857127

Travel Agents
Most hotels have their own travel agents. Many others are available throughout Acapulco, including:

American Express Costera M. Alemán 709-A............
....846887

Fantasy Tours Costera M. Alemán 50.............842528

Viajes Dorado Pacífico Costera M. Alemán 127 ....
....863280

Visitors Information
The **Oficina de Turisma** (Tourism Office) on Costera M. Alemán (in front of the Centro Acapulco) is open daily. Call 847050 or 844973 for information.

Area code 74 unless otherwise noted.

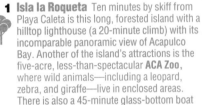

1 Isla la Roqueta Ten minutes by skiff from Playa Caleta is this long, forested island with a hilltop lighthouse (a 20-minute climb) with its incomparable panoramic view of Acapulco Bay. Another of the island's attractions is the five-acre, less-than-spectacular **ACA Zoo**, where wild animals—including a leopard, zebra, and giraffe—live in enclosed areas. There is also a 45-minute glass-bottom boat cruise that includes a peek at the underwater *Virgen de Guadalupe* statue.

On Isla la Roqueta:

Palao's Restaurant ★$ Stop here for a quick bite while visiting the zoo, or come in the evening by boat to this beachside Polynesian-style compound for dinner and salsa music. Ask at your hotel or a local travel agent for schedules. The Mexican and seafood dishes are predictable, but the setting is lovely. ♦ Mexican/Seafood ♦ Daily lunch and dinner. Isla la Roqueta. No phone

2 Playa Caleta Once the hangout for the glamour set, this park and the surrounding residential and shopping neighborhoods are typically overlooked by tourists. But the area has much to offer for those seeking a sampling of traditional Mexico. The beach here is immensely popular with locals, who seem to cover every grain of sand on weekends. City buses travel between the Costera, the Zócalo, and Playa Caleta regularly. ♦ Gran Via Tropical (at Costera M. Alemán)

2 Mundo Mágico A combination amusement park, aquarium, and beach club, this place is packed on the weekends with families. The indoor and outdoor exhibits include displays of tropical fish, turtles, alligators, and seals frolicking and splashing. Windows let you see both above and below the water level. Other diversions include a water slide, swimming pool, sheltered saltwater cove, jet skis, Windsurfers, a scuba school, and a lookout tower with a telescope that lets you survey Isla la Roqueta and the zoo (US quarters accepted for the telescope). ♦ Admission. M, W-Su. Playa Caleta (off Gran Via Topical). 831215, 831193

3 Boca Chica Hotel $ European and US travelers seeking charm and tranquillity instead of glitz keep rediscovering this small pink-and-white inn, built into the hillside over a small bay next to Playa Caleta. A favorite of the Hollywood crowd, the hotel lost much of its following in the 1970s and 1980s as fancier spots opened on the Costera and the east bay. But Miguel Angel Muñoz, son of the original owner, is intent on keeping the hotel as inviting as ever. The 45 rooms are simply furnished and air-conditioned, though guests may prefer to keep their doors open to the sea breezes. Satellite TVs are gradually appearing in the rooms, but most guests prefer to spend their time at the secluded beach, where the water is crystal clear and snorkelers collect shells along a rocky point (non-guests can spend the day here for a small fee, which is credited toward the purchase of refreshments at the restaurant). If that's not enough, Playa Caleta is within easy walking distance, and the rest of Acapulco is readily accessible by public bus. ♦ Playa Caletilla (off López Mateos). 836601, 836741, 800/346.3942; fax 839513

Within the Boca Chica Hotel:

Marina Club and Sushi Bar ★$ Those in the know make the trip regularly to this seaside restaurant to enjoy the unlikely marriage of two cuisines. The Mexican chef spent several years in Japan, and the sushi and sashimi are prepared to order from the freshest fish. For a north-of-the-border variation, try the Philadelphia rolls with salmon, cream cheese, and cucumber. The wasabi, seaweed, and even the rice are all imported (Mexican rice doesn't stick together as well as Japanese). The Mexican food is just as good, judging by the number of locals here, and the mango mousse shouldn't be missed. ♦ Mexican/Japanese ♦ Daily breakfast, lunch, and dinner. 836601, 836741

The Cora Indians from the state of Nayarit have their own version of the origin of the revered Mexican chilies. Legend has it that a man named Narama was attending a banquet when he suddenly jumped on the table. His testes turned into chilies, and he sprinkled the spicy seeds onto the food. The guests had their first taste of the spice of life and it has been an important part of the culture ever since.

4 Hotel Los Flamingos $ This hotel was built in the 1930s, when most of Acapulco's visitors were very rich and sailed in by yacht. It wasn't until the 1950s that it became a Shangri-la for the "Hollywood Gang." The select group, including Cary Grant, John Wayne, Johnny Weissmuller, Roy Rogers, Errol Flynn, Red Skelton, and Richard Widmark, loved it so much they bought it for a short time (fond memories of the gang are kept alive in the photo gallery in the hotel lobby). It's still a charmer, with one of Acapulco's most beautiful gardens. The food is good, the 84 rooms are clean, the ambience is quiet, and a warm nostalgia hangs in the air. Though no longer the luxury hotel it once was, it's perfect if you want tranquillity, a view of the sea, and a five-minute drive to downtown. ♦ López Mateos (near Av Coyuca). 820690; fax 839806

5 Coyuca 22 ★★$$$ This converted villa offers elegant dining in four open terraces that look down the side of the mountain at the lights of Acapulco. Eating in the beautifully lit garden is like visiting a good friend who just happens to fix divine lobster and steak. ♦ Seafood/Steak ♦ Daily dinner; closed May-November. Reservations recommended. Av Coyuca 22 (between López Mateos and Costera M. Alemán). 835030, 823468

6 Mariscos Mi Barquito ★★★$$ The climb up several flights of stairs to the top of this house on a hill above Playa la Langosta is rewarded with a cool breeze, spectacular view, and wonderful meal. A true Mexican seafood cafe, meals here include ceviche the consistency of soup (order fish ceviche with shrimp floating on top), plus a hot seafood soup worthy of high praise. Snapper, octopus, shrimp, baby shark, and the daily catch are prepared a variety of ways, and paella is the big draw on Saturdays. Lunch for hours on end as *Acapulqueños* do, giving yourself plenty of time to sample several dishes. The restaurant's bright white facade and blue lettering make it easy to spot near the foot of the street to La Quebrada. ♦ Seafood ♦ Daily lunch. López Mateos 30 (at Playa la Langosta). 823595

Restaurants/Clubs: Red　　**Hotels:** Blue
Shops/ ♠ **Outdoors:** Green　　**Sights/Culture:** Black

7 La Quebrada Cliff divers plunge from this 130-foot cliff night and day carrying flaming torches into a small pocket of the rushing sea. (See "Perilous Plunges," page 82.) ◆ Daily. La Quebrada (off Guerrero)

8 El Mirador Plaza Las Glorias $$ When this place was first built by Teddy Stauffer, he invited his Hollywood cronies to come discover Acapulco—making the hotel *the* hangout for the stars. Over the years its luster faded, and the only real attraction was a glamorous history and a great location overlooking the rocks and cliffs of La Quebrada. Today, the hundred renovated rooms attract those who appreciate the view and the low rate and don't mind the distance to beaches and restaurants. You can run up a hefty taxi tab from here; those on a budget may wish to stay elsewhere. ◆ La Quebrada 74 (off Guerrero). 831155, 831221, 800/342.2644; fax 820638

Within the Plaza Las Glorias:

La Perla $$ Although this restaurant/nightclub is a popular spot for a drink, it's known for one show only—La Quebrada's cliff divers (see "La Quebrada" above). You're best off dining elsewhere. Try to get here 15 minutes early for a good seat. ◆ Admission. Daily. 831221

9 Pesca Deportiva (Commercial Boat Docks) Fishing enthusiasts come here to watch the big commercial boats unload their catch. This is also a docking point for cruise ships and a favorite promenade for Mexican families who enjoy tourist-watching as much as tourists enjoy observing them. For a day of deep-sea fishing, visit the fishermen's cooperative shack across from the Zócalo. First-timers might feel more comfortable making arrangements through their hotel. ◆ Off Costera M. Alemán

10 Zócalo Acapulco Viejo's central plaza is opposite the city's crowded fishing harbor and is filled with aged trees providing heavy shade and thick, low branches for young climbers. Shoeshiners do a thriving business in the cool shadows. Local women trade gossip while children play tag nearby, and the men meet at outdoor cafes and discuss life over a game of dominoes and cups of black coffee. The atmosphere is relaxed, and a world apart from the luxury hotels in "new" Acapulco. ◆ Off Costera M. Alemán (at Escudero A. Serdán)

11 Sanborn's ★$ This full-service boutique/restaurant/bookstore is *the* best choice for homesick US travelers. The familiar glass cases offer everything from books and magazines to jewelry and trinkets. For a great breakfast, order hotcakes and coffee at the lunch counter, or drop in for a lunch of enchiladas or quesadillas. A more modern branch is at Playa Condesa.
◆ American/Mexican ◆ Daily breakfast, lunch, and dinner. Off Escudero A. Serdán and Costera M. Alemán. 26167. Also at: Costera M. Alemán 1226 (at Playa Condesa). 844465

12 El Fuerte San Diego (Fort San Diego) The only bit of history intact from Acapulco's beginnings is this star-shaped fort. Strategically placed on a hill next to the army barracks in 1616, its vantage point enabled soldiers to spot a distant pirate ship and fire mounted cannons before the marauders got too close. The original fort was destroyed in the 1776 earthquake, then rebuilt before 1800. Mexican troops drove out the Spanish and took over the fort in 1818. Today, the fort's moat separates it from small houses, shops, and neighborhood cafes.

Under the direction of Mexico City's **Museo de Antropología** (Museum of Anthropology), the fort has been restored and houses the **Museo Histórico de Acapulco** (Acapulco's Historical Museum). Well worth a visit, it portrays life in the pre-Columbian era.
◆ Admission. T-Su. Costera M. Alemán (at Morelos). 823828

13 Mercado Municipal For a look at the life of *Acapulqueños*, take an hour or two to wander through the public market where locals shop for necessities. There's no touristy glitz, just everyday goods displayed in a labyrinth of stalls where meats and vegetables, leather goods, hand-carved wooden items, baskets, and baubles are sold. A huge flower market has blossoms and buds, plus roots, herbs, and magic potions for any purpose. Pottery and leather sandals are real bargains, but you're better off going to a reputable uptown jewelry store for silver. The best time to arrive is early in the morning, since many vendors call it a day by 1PM. ◆ Daily. Constituyentes (at Hurtado de Mendoza)

14 Chiles' Verdes ★★$$ At first glance, this dining spot has the appearance of a trendy **Carlos 'n' Charlie's** restaurant. But once you settle in for lunch (which doesn't really get going until 3:30PM), you discover a true Mexican hangout. Businesspeople huddle at tables under ceiling fans, devouring hefty portions of such Mexican dishes as *molcajete* (marinated strips of meat served with melted cheese) and enchiladas that seem guaranteed to put them to sleep. The restaurant sits at the edge of the auto-repair district, not a scenic or picturesque neighborhood, although those who wander the back streets will get a much more authentic picture of Acapulco than they'll ever see on the Costera.
◆ Mexican ◆ Daily lunch and dinner. Malaespina 20 (between Costera M. Alemán and Cuauhtémoc). 855276

15 Papagayo Park A natural treasure ignored by most tourists, this park is named for a hotel that once was a waterfront resort. The main attraction here is a children's amusement park, with bumper boats and life-sized reproductions of the space shuttle *Columbia* and a Spanish galleon. At press time, this section of the 52-acre park was closed for a complete overhaul. But the playgrounds and the aviary, where tropical birds perch for photos along winding paths, still make it worth a stop. ♦ Costera M. Alemán (between Insurgentes and Aviles)

16 Paraíso Radisson $$ Within walking distance of Acapulco Viejo, but still on the main hotel strip, this place is immensely popular with families and tour groups. Even the grandest suites are moderately priced when compared to rates at nearby hotels, and special packages make this the best bargain in town. The 422 rooms are functional and well kept, and there are ice machines on every floor. The top-floor restaurant has a great view of the skyline. Two drawbacks: The elevators are noisy and the pool is small. The largest of Acapulco's artisans' markets is next door. ♦ Costera M. Alemán 163 (at Playa Hornitos). 855050, 800/333.3333; fax 855543

17 Howard Johnson Maralisa Hotel and Beach Club $$ Once a beach club for a luxurious hotel, this place is now a member of the famous US chain. Much of the hotel's grandeur has faded—the intricate tile work and stone lion fountains look worn and neglected, and the guest rooms have an outdated decor, with dark wood furnishings, and garish green bathrooms. But the rates are remarkably low for this stretch of the Costera, and with only 90 rooms and balconies overlooking the two small pools, the setting is a pleasant reprieve from its massive neighbors. No restaurant. ♦ Alemania (at Costera M. Alemán). 856677, 800/446.4656; fax 859228

18 Plaza Bahía Shopping Center Take a break from the midday heat in this air-conditioned mall, with three floors of shops and cafes. Clothing stores include familiar names such as **Benetton, OP, Esprit,** and **Dockers,** and the movie theater usually shows first-run US hits with Spanish subtitles. If you need a pharmacy, eyeglasses, money changer, photo shop, travel agent, or souvenirs, take a look around. ♦ Daily. Costera M. Alemán 123 (near Insurgentes, next to the Acapulco Plaza Hotel)

Acapulco was originally called Acatíl Pulco in the Nahuatil language, meaning "place of reeds."

18 Acapulco Plaza Hotel
$$$ If you're looking for a hotel that has something going on all the time, check out this beachside high-rise complex. Three separate towers house 418 rooms and suites, and all the usual amenities are offered, including a bilingual staff and two large pools. For the really active, two health clubs, the **Oasis** and **Mirage,** offer exercise equipment, saunas, steam baths, Jacuzzis, and massage. Tennis buffs can play into the evening on the hotel's four outdoor, lighted courts. Seven good restaurants and an assortment of bars make dining and drinking a special event here; on Tuesday and Thursday evenings, there's a great Mexican fiesta. ♦ Costera M. Alemán 123 (near Insurgentes). 859050, 800/FIESTA-1; fax 855285

Scenic Pie de la Cuesta

When the rush and crush of Acapulco's crowds get to be a bit too much, rent a car or jeep and set out to explore Pie de la Cuesta, a peaceful fishing village just 10 kilometers (six miles) north, for a good view of what Acapulco was like before the tourism explosion. The small town is situated between the open sea and a tranquil lagoon, which is the center of activity. Young boys in skiffs fish here, alongside white cranes. Women socialize along the shore of the lagoon while doing the family wash. On the ocean side, the roaring surf continuously pounds the sand with giant white breakers, making swimming hazardous (there are reports of sharks, too). Shelling is a favorite pastime along the miles of broad white beach; other than that, the main attraction is visiting one of the many oceanfront restaurants to watch the gorgeous sunset.

If a sudden shower interrupts your activity, the nearby **Ukae Kim Hotel** ($$$) welcomes all to the *palapa* bar next to the pool. One of the few hotels in town, it is low-key, intimate, a little worn, and decorated in a bright Mediterranean style. Charming touches include flowered lavatory sinks and yellow hand-painted tiles. Fresh seafood is served in the small dining room. And even in the summer, your chances of finding a room without reservations are good. 600727 or 5/7895910; fax 5/7607955.

A few minutes away, on the lagoon, **Steve's Hideaway** (★★$; no phone) is a pleasant place to spend a few hours over a cold drink. Owner Steve Garcia has traveled the world, learning the restaurant business in US cities such as San Francisco, Beverly Hills, Miami, and New York. His tiny cafe is perched on a rickety wooden pier over the lagoon and is a favorite haunt for gringos who gather here every year under the thatch roof to relax and socialize. Try Steve's Aztec pizza; it bears little resemblance to US-style pizza and is made with whatever's in the icebox, Mexican style.

19 Galería Rudic Owner Myrtille Rudic de Rullán displays a fine collection of Mexican artwork in her attractive gallery. Sculptor Armando Amaya's full-bodied, expressive women pose at the gallery's entrance; if it hasn't sold yet, you must see the lithe bronze man riding a soaring manta ray by Gustavo Salmones. Painter Alejandro Camarena captures the character of Mexico in scenes from typical plazas, and rotating exhibits provide a glimpse of the country's exciting art scene. ♦ M-Sa; closed at midday. Pinzón 9 (at Costera M. Alemán). 844844

20 Continental Plaza Hotel $$ Though this hotel recently received a much needed face-lift, its 435 rooms will never be elegant. The grounds, however, are spectacular, with landscaping grown thick and junglelike over the years, and pools that wind under bridges and along rock paths in a seaside maze. The hotel is going partially time-share, and you may grow tired of being accosted by enthusiastic salespeople. ♦ Costera M. Alemán (at Playa Condesa). 40909, 800/USA.AMIGO; fax 42081, 42120

Within the Continental Plaza Hotel:

TONY ROMA'S
◆ A PLACE FOR RIBS ◆

Tony Roma's ★★★$$ The proliferation of US chain restaurants in Mexican resorts can be overwhelming; surely you didn't travel to Acapulco for a Big Mac. But sometimes the longing for home-style cooking does overtake even the most stalwart adventurer. When that happens, head here. The meats are imported, so you can get ribs, steaks, and burgers just like back home, and you can be sure the bountiful salads are prepared with purified water. Much calmer than other US-style restaurants, with a subdued, spacious sense of relaxed dining, this is a refuge for homesick travelers who've grown tired of raucous bars. ♦ American ♦ Daily lunch and dinner. 40904

Restaurants/Clubs: Red   **Hotels:** Blue
Shops/ 🌳 Outdoors: Green   **Sights/Culture:** Black

21 Paraíso/Paradise ★★$$ Another of the wild places where vacationers leave their restraints at home, especially if they're in the under-30 crowd. If you don't know how to dance, you'll do it anyway, and if it's your birthday, who knows what will happen. Seafood is the specialty, and portions are large. Remember, the music is loud, the waiters are crazy, and the salsa is hot. ♦ Seafood ♦ Daily lunch and dinner. Costera M. Alemán (at del Prado). 845988

22 Cafe Pacífico ★★★$$$ Pianist Ricardo Arcos is the main attraction at this small restaurant and lounge, which starts filling up with his fans after midnight. Before then, the setting is one of romantic dining, with flames leaping from chafing dishes as solicitous waiters flambé shrimp with Pernod or cognac, or sauté fresh spinach with bacon. With fewer than ten tables, the dining room fills up quickly after 9PM, though you won't mind waiting while Ricardo's playing. ♦ Continental ♦ Daily dinner. Costera M. Alemán (at del Prado). 842538, ext 241

23 Hard Times ★$$ Anyone who needs a burger fix should rush to this casual restaurant, where they'll get the best hamburger and fries, homemade vegetable soup, and even a great chocolate milk shake. You might end up sitting under a street sign from back home or see a wall decoration that used to be part of the car you were driving last week. ♦ American ♦ M-Sa dinner. Costera M. Alemán (at Costera Viejo). 840064

23 La Tablita ★★★$$$ Travelers in Mexico sometimes complain that they just can't find a good steak. This Argentine-style steak house solves that problem with a vast selection of simply grilled steaks, smothered with sauces, or cooked on a tabletop grill with jalapeños and mushrooms. Steaks are served with Argentine *chimichurri* sauce, a vinegar-and-spice concoction guaranteed to pique your taste buds. ♦ Steaks ♦ Daily dinner. Costera M. Alemán 82 (at Fracc. Club Deportivo). 811276

24 Hotel El Presidente $$ The 400 rooms (including suites and penthouses) at this hotel were recently redecorated, making it an even more ideal place to stay than before. The location is terrific, with sun and clean sand luring guests away from the pool to one of the

finest beaches on the strip. Supervised poolside activities and water games keep young and old occupied all day. The rooms are simple, and there are comfortable public spaces, restaurants and bars, and a disco for those who choose to dance the night away. ♦ Costera M. Alemán 89 (at Fracc. Club Deportivo). 841700, 841800; fax 841376

25 Villa Vera Hotel and Raquet Club $$$$
One of the first to entertain Hollywood's "in" crowd, this hotel was built in the 1950s by Carl Renstrom, wealthy Nebraska inventor and businessman, as a villa for his family. He later added five smaller villas for business associates, and the hotel soon became a tropical hideaway for the celebrities of the day: Liz Taylor married Mike Todd here, with Debbie Reynolds and Eddie Fisher as attendants; President Eisenhower visited at the same time Elvis Presley was filming *Fun In Acapulco;* Pat and Richard Nixon celebrated their 25th wedding anniversary here; and Lana Turner even lived in the hotel for three years.

Set on a quiet hillside away from the bustle of downtown, the hotel, now run by Carl's daughter Lisa, has 80 rooms, a restaurant, 20 swimming pools, and three red-clay tennis courts. Thick trees and lavish gardens around the property provide privacy and seclusion. Four luxurious homes on the grounds are available for rent, either by the week or day, and come fully staffed with maids, cooks, and gardeners. The **Beauty and Fitness Center** provides good equipment and trainers. Bodies are pampered and muscles soothed either in your room or by your private pool. Children over 16 are welcome. ♦ Lomas del Mar 35 (near Costera M. Alemán). 840433, 800/525.4800; fax 847479

26 Club de Golf Acapulco This public nine-hole course is the scene of tournaments throughout the year. Located behind and around the **Centro Acapulco,** it's not as aesthetically pleasing as the course at the **Acapulco Princess** (page 39). No carts are allowed. ♦ Fee. Daily. Costera M. Alemán 840781

Baseball caps with logos from the US *Constellation, Kitty Hawk,* and other ships are treasured by locals who get the chance to tour US Navy vessels anchored in Bahía Acapulco for R&R.

The new Acapulco–Mexico City Highway has 62 underpasses for cattle and pedestrians, and the highest bridge in the country, with pillars standing 618 feet tall.

27 Elcano $$$ The most exciting new hotel on the strip is actually one of the oldest, thoroughly remodeled under the direction of architects **Carlos Villela and** Ramiro Alatorre. The glamour of the 1950s has been re-created with a unique design and style, a nautical blue-on-white scheme that echoes the sky and sea. The 340 rooms are filled with creature comforts—sloping navy blue tiled backrests by the firm double and king-size beds, slatted wood lounge chairs on the balconies, high-backed white wicker chairs by the marble-topped dining tables, and both air-conditioning and fans. Blue-and-white patterns in the tile floors carry the nautical theme throughout the hotel, and are even used in the cement around the pool. There is a health club with the latest in fitness machines, and a beauty salon that's always crowded. The hotel has an ideal location, set back against the bay a few blocks from the **Centro Acapulco,** blessedly removed from the frenetic noise of the Costera.

Most enchanting of all is the hotel's artwork. Artist Cristina Rubalcava, a Mexican expatriate living in Paris, has created a series of paintings evoking the myths and memories of Acapulco. She's painted the cliff divers of La Quebrada hurtling toward mermaids in the sea, and Rita Hayworth dancing on the beach, encircled by a fanciful boa trailing the words of a favorite song, *La Boa.* The paintings hang in the guest rooms and are printed as complimentary postcards for guests. If you're not staying at the hotel, you can still see some of Rubalcava's work in **La Victoria** restaurant, and on the wall facing the elevators at pool level. ♦ Costera M. Alemán 75 (near Las Palmas). 841950, 800/222.7692, 305/715.9940; fax 842230

Within the Elcano:

La Victoria ★★★★$$ A romantic, tranquil gourmet restaurant that rivals any in the city. Arrive before 10PM and you'll be serenaded by the soulful guitarist performing in the cocktail lounge; after that a spirited trio entertains diners. Seafood stars on the menu, from the piquant ceviche to shrimp in champagne sauce, crab cakes, and grilled salmon. The desserts are incomparable; stop in for a *cafe Español* and a sweet treat with some friends so you can try them all.
♦ Seafood/International ♦ Daily dinner. Reservations recommended. 841950

Bambuco ★★★$$ A classy seaside cafe with impeccable service, this restaurant draws a local following for power breakfasts of *huevos rancheros* and mushroom omelettes. The mix of vacationers and power brokers gives the cafe a cosmopolitan feel, relaxed yet buzzing with seemingly important conversations. The lunch and dinner menu includes some of the selections from **La Victoria** (including the desserts), plus salads and sandwiches. ♦ Mexican/International ♦ Daily breakfast, lunch, and dinner. 841950

28 Centro Acapulco (Convention Center) One of the largest convention centers in Mexico, it hosts business meetings, concerts, and cultural events throughout the year. The famous acrobatic **Papantla Flyers** have become a permanent fixture on stage here, thrilling audiences as they leap from a tall pole and fly in ever-enlarging circles attached to a rope. Just as the upside-down flyer gets perilously close to the ground, the rope is totally unfurled, and he lands gracefully on his feet.

Ballet Folklorico is presented Tuesday and Sunday nights during the winter season. For the lively crowd, the center's **Disco Laser** offers what its name suggests: flashing lights, live and taped music, and a lot of fun; things get rolling about 11PM. There are several crafts and gift shops on the beautifully landscaped grounds with artwork from around the country. ♦ Costera M. Alemán (near Las Palmas). 847050; fax 846252

Perilous Plunges

One of Acapulco's most popular year-round attractions is the high-divers at the cliffs of La Quebrada. Hundreds of tourists watch the young, muscular divers from terraced viewing platforms. This daring feat is even more spectacular at sunset, when the divers, often in pairs, carry flaming torches as they plunge 130 feet into the sea.

After kneeling and praying at a small shrine, each diver in turn stands poised on the cliff's edge, arms pointing down, muscles tense with concentration as he studies the timing and rush of the crashing surf. At the right moment he leaps forward and hurtles down in a graceful swan dive, slipping into the water as it rushes into a small cove. One wrong move could be fatal.

This dangerous spectacle, performed by a select fraternity of trained men, dates back to 1934. But who's to say when it all began? Maybe pre-Columbian Indians tested their strength against the powerful sea in the same way.

To witness this memorable sight, you can climb up to the observation point, where you will be charged a small fee. Or you can enjoy one of the best vantage points for the show on the terrace of the adjacent La Perla at the **El Mirador Plaza Las Glorias** hotel, which overlooks the cliffs. For more information, call 831155 or 831221.

29 Super Super For your not-so-basic shopping spree, this enormous supermarket has just about everything you might be craving—and some things you never dreamed of. The fruit counter provides an introduction to the more bizarre tropical fruits, including the gorgeous hot pink *pitajaya,* and papayas as big as watermelons. The deli counter offers take-out chicken with mole, flan, various salsas and salads, and a selection of imported goods—from frozen waffles to gourmet ice creams—that is truly astounding. ♦ Daily, 24 hours. Costera M. Alemán (near Cristóbal Colón). No phone

29 Moishe's Kosher Deli ★★$ If you want a pastrami sandwich, search out this tiny lunch counter. Located just off the sidewalk by **Super Super,** the deli features kosher hot dogs, bagels and lox, corned beef, roast beef, spaghetti, and tacos. Despite its name, not all ingredients here are kosher, but it's the closest you can get in Acapulco. ♦ Deli ♦ Daily lunch and dinner. Costera M. Alemán (near Cristóbal Colón). No phone

29 Copacabaña Hotel $$ This 1950s-style hotel is one of the hottest spots on the beach, yet close to the action downtown. Everything here is done on a grand scale: The bar is huge and has many tables, a wooden floor enables couples to dance to a live band on the beach under the stars, and the slightly worn 480 rooms have large terraces with great views. Many families from Mexico City return yearly. There's a restaurant, and a waterskiing show just offshore during the winter season. ♦ Luis Maya 11 (near Costera M. Alemán). 847730, 42155, 800/221.6509

CICI

30 CICI Parque Acuatico (CICI Water Park) Families settle in for the day at this amusement park where water is the greatest attraction. Children (and a few adults) scream as they speed down water slides, watch trained seals and dolphins cavort, and play in a swimming pool with built-in wave action. Toddler-size attractions include small slides, gentle waterfalls and fountains, and a relaxing river ride. Adults set up housekeeping in cool, shaded areas, and for refreshments, the park's many snack bars rise to the occasion. ♦ Admission. Daily. Costera M. Alemán (at Cristóbal Colón)

The first road from Mexico City to Acapulco was opened in 1927; the trip took at least a week.

31 Restaurant Suntory Acapulco ★★$$$
This low-key restaurant specializes in *shabu-shabu* (beef and vegetables dipped in steaming broth), *teppenyaki* (meat, seafood, and vegetables cooked at the table on a sizzling hot-plate), and sukiyaki (meat, bean curd, and vegetables). If you want to try something really fresh, catch your own crayfish in the tank and have it cooked before your eyes. It's part of a worldwide, high-quality chain that originated in Mexico City in 1970. ♦ Japanese ♦ Daily lunch and dinner. Reservations required. Costera M. Alemán 36 (at Ortiz Monasterio). 848088, 848766

32 Hyatt Regency Acapulco $$$$ Set on beautiful Bahía de Acapulco (Acapulco Bay), this hotel opens onto the sea and sand, and most of the 600 rooms have great views. The verdant palm-thick grounds are dotted with pools, above-average cafes, and bars. Though rather staid, the guest rooms are comfortable, and the service is good. If you're looking for something special, try the **Regency Club.** Two upper floors are set aside with a private lounge where complimentary continental breakfast and afternoon wine and cheese are served daily. The huge, spreading ceiba tree in front of the hotel is said to be over 250 years old. ♦ Costera M. Alemán 1 (at Ortiz Monasterio). 842888, 881234, 800/233.1234; fax 843087

33 Acapulco Sheraton Hotel $$$ The dramatic lobby, with floor-to-ceiling windows across the ocean side of the entire room, provides views that won't quit. Furniture and carpets are rich in teal, burgundy, and purple. Even the lobby bar piano is painted a shiny rich burgundy. Striking sculptures are scattered about; note the *Neptune* in the lobby and another in the **Bahía Restaurant.**

The 226 rooms are very comfortable, with tile floors, luxurious bathrooms, soothing colors, and air-conditioning. One peculiarity is the manner in which you must get to your room. If you're staying in one of the 13 villas, you must take as many as three elevators and crossover walkways to get there. A colorfully painted cable tram brings guests from the lower sections of the property to the upper levels. One swimming pool is set in a blooming garden, and the other is near the beach. The hotel is built on the side of the hill overlooking Playa Secreto (where a former

Mexican president is said to have brought his mistress for romantic interludes). ♦ Costera Guitarrón 110 (off Carretera Escénica). 812222, 800/325.3535; fax 843760

34 Extravaganzza Acapulco's discos are legendary for their lavish decor, stylish clientele, and psychedelic special effects. This place lives up to its name, with an unbelievable dose of nonstop music, flashing lights, floor fog, and fireworks. Smile nicely at the doorman; on a busy night he decides who gets in and who doesn't. Under no circumstance should you come dressed in shorts, T-shirts, or sandals. ♦ Cover. Daily. Carretera Escénica (between Costera M. Alemán and Las Brisas). 847154, 847164

35 Señor Frog's ★★★★$$ Set atop a cliff facing Bahía de Acapulco, this place is as popular with local VIPs as it is with partying tourists. The food is bountiful and delicious, with an emphasis on barbecued ribs and chicken, Mexican platters, and seafood. On Thursday afternoons, *pozole*, a hominy stew, is the requisite meal, and lunches last until sunset. Several tables are permanently reserved for prominent local dignitaries, who gather religiously for this meal. It traditionally begins with a plate of *botanes* (appetizers), including tamales, *taquitos,* and hunks of Oaxacan cheese, then continues on to the main course of *pozole.* Finish with dessert and you'll be full well into the next day. The place really kicks into action at night, when the music is raucous, the crowd rowdy, and the tequila flowing in abundance. ♦ International/Mexican ♦ Daily lunch and dinner. Carretera Escénica, Lote 28 (at La Vista Shopping Center). 848020, 848027. Also at: Costera M. Alemán 999 (at del Prado). 841285

36 Las Brisas Hotel $$$$ This elegant 267-room grande dame is more than 30 years old, but still holds the reputation as the loveliest hotel in Acapulco. She holds court on 110 acres built into the contours of a mountain ensconced in fuchsia blossoms, pink hibiscus, feathery vines, and tall trees. The small casitas (villas) continue to lure honeymooners and others with romance on the mind. Guests enjoy private pools at 253 of the bungalows. The resort is sparkling white, dashed with its hallmark pink color scheme, pink-and-white jeeps, and fresh pink flowers floating in the pools. The Royal Beach Club casitas are the most recently renovated accommodations, with silent high-tech air-conditioners and handsome carved wooden furniture.

The hotel pampers its guests, and many come back year after year. On the fifth visit, you receive a discreet, hand-painted sign, notifying all who pass by that your casita has been named in your honor (at least for the duration of your stay). A breakfast of fresh fruit, sweet rolls, and steaming hot coffee is deposited daily in the "magic box" (in a wall with a double opening) to greet you each morning.

The streets of this small village are steep, and hardy guests can get good cardiovascular exercise just walking to the lobby; or you can pick up the phone and dial for a jeep, which arrives at your bungalow within minutes and will take you anywhere on the grounds. The grounds include **La Concha,** the private seaside beach club at the bottom of the mountain, a spa and health club, an art gallery, a variety of boutiques, a deli, and tennis courts. At the very top, the **Capilla de Paz** (Chapel of Peace) sits 1,300 feet above sea level. The three restaurants are closed to non-guests except for special events, including a reservations-required Wednesday steak-and-lobster dinner at **La Concha.** A service charge covering all tips (waiters, porters, etc.) for your entire stay is included in the bill. Jeeps are available for rent from the hotel. ♦ Carretera Escénica 5255. 841650, 800/228.3000; fax 852748

Acapulco Cleans Up Its Act

When travelers to Mexico started bypassing Acapulco in favor of newer resort destinations more than a dozen years ago, state leaders began to heed the complaints of tourists. Topping the list of irksome problems was the swarm of vendors who would continually harass visitors. A law was enacted making street and beach vending illegal. To help the vendors maintain a living, a work-training program with a million-dollar budget was established, and low-interest loans have been made available to help vendors open stalls in the flea markets. There's also a shelter offering education to abandoned children who used to support themselves by begging or selling chewing gum in the street.

The colorful stalls are filled with T-shirts, clothing, papier-mâché figures, silver jewelry, puppets, and countless other crafts. Practice your bargaining skills, or just window-shop and walk away when you've seen enough. Markets in Acapulco include: **El Parazal** (five blocks from the Zócalo), **Mercado Noa Noa** (in front of Playa Los Hornos), and **Mercado de Artesanías El Pueblito** (across from the **Acapulco Plaza** hotel).

37 **Madeiras** ★★★$$$$ Within walking distance of the **Las Brisas** hotel, you can sit in an open pavilion built of rich hardwoods and enjoy one of the most sumptuous meals in the city. Cooling breezes and sparkling views of the Acapulco shoreline are captured through large open windows. The setting is elegant and the food is out of this world. The four-course prix-fixe menu offers your choice from among a gourmet listing that runs the gamut from a starter of Thai pasta to terrific cold soups to main dishes that include veal tips in white wine—all topped off with a superb selection of desserts and coffee. Reservations can be difficult to get, so many people make them months in advance—yes, it's that good. ♦ International ♦ M-Sa dinner. Reservations required. Carretera Escénica (between Las Brisas and the airport). 844378

38 **Kookabura** ★★★$$ Bahía de Acapulco is a sight you never tire of, and this restaurant has one of the best panoramic viewing spots. Fortunately, the north-of-the-border-style food is also quite good. Choices include boneless breast of chicken, potato skins stuffed with cheese, mahimahi in garlic butter, strawberry crepes, and delicious French vanilla ice cream. ♦ American ♦ M-Sa dinner. Carretera Escénica (between Las Brisas and Acapulco Diamante). 844418

CASANOVA

38 **Ristorante Casa Nova** ★★★$$$$ From the moment you step into the elegant entrance graced by an immense flower arrangement, you know you are in for a fabulous evening of fine Italian cuisine. Steps take you down the mountainside to the restaurant where you can dine in indoor air-conditioned comfort or outdoor terraced seating, both with spectacular views of the bay. The extensive menu presents perfectly prepared pastas, plus international delicacies such as fresh Norwegian salmon or thick New Zealand lamb chops. ♦ Italian ♦ T-Su dinner. Reservations required during winter. Carretera Escénica 5256 (between Las Brisas and the airport). 846815/16

Though saltwater shrimp are on most menus, locals swear the best shrimp in Acapulco comes from the freshwater Tres Palos Lagoon.

39 Acapulco Diamante A massive resort development that stretches along the coastline from **Las Brisas** all the way to the **Acapulco Princess** hotel near the airport, this is like a second, self-contained city within the city limits of Acapulco. By early in the next century, the area will include several luxury private home developments and condo complexes, two marinas, three 18-hole golf courses, and several hotels.

The bright orange sculpture at the entrance near the airport is called *Pueblo del Sol,* and was created by sculptor Pal Kepenyes. (To view Kepenyes's work, especially his dramatic sculpted jewelry, check with local galleries or call his studio at 843738.) ♦ Carretera Escénica (between Las Brisas and the airport)

39 Camino Real $$$$ A winding, rocky road twists past palatial private homes in various stages of completion toward a jewel-toned bay, a wonderful backdrop for this hotel. Green tiled roofs and creamy stucco walls echo the colors of the surrounding terrain; natural rock platforms and lounging areas perch above the sea. The buildings afford water views from the 155 superdeluxe rooms, each decorated in moss green, beige, aqua, and lavender. Amenities include sandalwood-scented toiletries, deep bathtubs, hair dryers, shaving mirrors, and satellite TV. Eight elevators transport guests to the pools and restaurants, and complimentary airport shuttle service is available. ♦ Baja Catita (at Carretera Escénica). 812010; 800/722.6466

39 Acapulco Princess Hotel $$$$ One drawback of a 1,019-room hotel is that while it can handle very large groups of people, solo travelers can be intimidated. For long, quiet walks on the beach, the hotel offers lovely white sand dotted with tall trees, and acres of well-manicured grass. The three high-rise, pyramid-style buildings are visible from the main road, and the hotel has a glowing, well-deserved reputation for luxury and excellent service.

Guests stay in tropically decorated rooms with cane furnishings, and entertain themselves with five swimming pools, nine outdoor and two indoor tennis courts, nine restaurants, and a decidedly upscale shopping arcade. Golfers have a choice of two 18-hole courses, and a fully staffed and equipped pro shop. The hotel is a long way from the activity along the Costera, and the all-inclusive (MAP) rates are mandatory during the high season. ♦ Carretera Escénica (at Playa Revolcadero). 843100, 800/223.1818; fax 888020

39 Pierre Marqués Hotel $$$$ Built in 1957 as J. Paul Getty's hideaway, this is now a luxurious 344-room hotel (open only during high season) within the **Princess** compound. The rooms resemble those at the **Princess**

and there are three pools and eight lighted tennis courts. Villas and bungalows with roomy patios are available, and for those who yearn for activity, a complimentary shuttle travels between the two hotels; all of the facilities are available to guests at either hotel. Together they cover an area of 240 acres along Playa Revolcadero. ♦ Nov-May. Carretera Escénica (at Playa Revolcadero). 842000, 800/223.1818; fax 848554

39 Vidafel Mayan Palace $$$ Another grand-scale project that will eventually have more than a thousand rooms, an 18-hole golf course, a water park, a monorail, and various other attractions, this time-share resort and hotel is located on the spectacular Playa Revolcadero. At press time, the first 380 rooms were open, but you get a good sense of the scope of the project from the surrounding acres of ongoing construction and the magnificent entryway. Gigantic replicas of Maya carvings set in green marble niches, a long reflecting pool, and polished black-and-white marble floors give the hotel a museumlike appearance, with the reception area set off to the side. The swimming pool flows past waterfalls and boulders to the beach, where it parallels the sand. With the time-share concept in mind, most suites have kitchens, sofa beds, and dining areas. The resort is meant to be self-contained, and has two restaurants currently open, with more on the way. ♦ Carretera Escénica (at Playa Revolcadero). 690102, 800/VIDAFEL; fax 620008

Bests

Luis Fernando Sánchez Tena
Former Director of Sales, Hotel Las Brisas, Acapulco

The cliff divers are one of the most unique sights in the world.

Barra Vieja Lagoon, a native fishing village southeast of Acapulco.

The sunset at **Pie de la Cuesta Beach.** Just eight miles from Acapulco, it's a very quiet, relaxing, and romantic place.

Fort San Diego Museum, for history on the area.

Isla La Roqueta, with its zoo and aquarium.

Restaurants/Clubs: Red   Hotels: Blue
Shops/ 🌴 Outdoors: Green   **Sights/Culture:** Black

Yucatán Peninsula

The 43,000-square-mile Yucatán Peninsula sits like an independent nation bordered by the **Gulf of Mexico**, the **Caribbean Sea,** and the wilderness of **Guatemala** and **Belize**. The peninsula bears the slashes of *sacbes* (ancient limestone roads) connecting the ruins of the Maya ceremonial centers of **Chichén Itzá, Uxmal,** and **Cobá.** Today, asphalt highways link the peninsula's three states—**Campeche, Yucatán,** and **Quintana Roo**—with **Mexico City** and the national government. The connection seems almost superficial, however. In character, cuisine, and geography, the Yucatán Peninsula is more Caribbean, European, and Maya than Mexican.

Campeche, on the Gulf of Mexico, is the peninsula's unknown territory, a stretch of impenetrable jungle covered with Maya ruins and bordered by a coastline known more for its ports than its beaches. The state of Yucatán is wedged between the peninsula's two other states in the center of the northern coast where the gulf meets the sea. **Mérida**, the capital of Yucatán, was built by the Spanish conquistadores atop the ancient Maya city T'Ho, and best represents the contrasts and similarities of the ancient Maya and their Spanish, French, and Mexican conquerors. The largest city on the Yucatán peninsula, it is a great launching point for a Yucatán adventure, with monuments, markets, and museums serving as an introduction to the peninsula's history and mystique.

The state of Quintana Roo is largely composed of a limestone shelf covered with scrubby jungle and white sand beaches that line a chain of coral reefs in the Caribbean. This region was the province of pirates, smugglers, and Maya villagers until developers set their sights on **Cancún** in the early 1970s. Within two decades, Cancún has become the nation's number one tourist destination, with the nearby island resorts of **Cozumel** and **Isla Mujeres** getting their share of attention as well. Travelers in search of a secluded and much less tourist-oriented retreat head for the sparsely populated beaches and Maya outposts along Quintana Roo's mainland coast, stretching south of Cancún to the capital city of **Chetumal** and the border of Belize.

Mérida

In addition to Mérida's having the distinction of being probably the safest and most European capital city in Mexico (and possibly Central America), it encompasses all that is fascinating about the **Yucatán Peninsula.** Gracious and ebullient, *Meridanos* (as the 600,000 or so inhabitants of the city are called) embrace both neighbors and strangers with genuine goodwill. Narrow brick streets shaded by laurel trees pass by Moorish palaces and archways dating back to the time of the Spanish conquistadores who built their 16th-century capital from the rubble and ruins of the ancient Maya capital, T'Ho. Bits of limestone blocks from temples destroyed in 1542 can still be detected in the walls of 16th-century Franciscan churches where the Maya of today follow the Catholic rituals their ancestors resisted 400 years ago. Approximately 500,000 Maya were killed by the Spanish, led by Francisco Montejo, in a 15-year battle for control of Mérida's land, commerce, and soul. But the Maya spirit is resilient, and their descendants retain a distinct Indian appearance and an ancient language that is still spoken in traditional villages and along the city streets.

The history of this area is alive and very much a part of the culture, architecture, and social life of Yucatán's capital city. Nowhere is this more evident than in the central plaza, which has remained Mérida's heart from the time of **T'Ho,** through the conquest, and into today. Maya men from tiny villages outside the city drape colorful hammocks on their shoulders and entreat tourists to buy their wares. Businessmen with distinctly European appearances read Spanish newspapers while having their shoes shined by Maya boys. Young girls in miniskirts and high heels stroll past Maya women in lavishly embroidered costumes selling woven bracelets and shawls.

A mural depicting the violent and vivid blending of the Maya and Spanish peoples into the Mexican race is painted on a wall of **Palacio Municipal** (City Hall); portraits of the tormentors and benefactors who controlled Yucatán's political and religious evolution hang in the **Palacio Gobierno** (Government Palace). *Meridanos* of all ethnic ancestry gather by the plaza to watch folk dancers perform a wedding dance or to listen to festive marimbas and military bands.

The city's European heritage and proximity to the Caribbean give it a flavor and look of its own. Mérida's cuisine is a mix of Yucatecan, continental, and Middle Eastern fare. Residents dress for the tropics, the men in short-sleeved *guayabera* shirts that hang loose outside their trousers. Everyone, including politicians and bankers, forgoes suits and ties and wears *guayaberas* to civic events. The lightweight, intricately woven Yucatecan hammock is preferred over the bed by many residents, and even the most elegant homes have hammock hooks in the walls.

Europe's impact on Mérida is most evident along **Paseo de Montejo**, a 10-block-long boulevard lined with laurel, tamarind, flamboyant trees, and a procession of palatial mansions. The city was a center of wealth and power during the late 1800s. *Hacendados* (hacienda owners) controlled vast parcels of land, running corn and cattle plantations with the labor of indentured Indians. Henequen, a strong fiber from the agave plant that is used for making rope, became a valuable export in the 1900s; agave fields flourished in the peninsula's heat, and vast fortunes grew from its cultivation. The *hacendados* created city neighborhoods fashioned after the Champs-Elysées, commissioning French and Italian engineers and architects to design pompous, ornate homes, which they filled with imported marble, crystal, and antiques. Many of these mansions still stand along the Paseo de Montejo and surrounding streets, though some have fallen into unfortunate disrepair. The frothy peach-and-white **Palacio Cantón** is one of the best preserved of these homes and now serves as the **Museo Regional de Antropología** (Regional Anthropology Museum).

Perhaps the best way to fully appreciate Mérida's charms is to hire a *calesa* (horse-drawn carriage) for a Sunday afternoon ride, when traffic is least oppressive. Start at the main plaza and head north on Calle 60 past the parks to Paseo de Montejo and its side streets, then southwest to the **Parque Centenario**. Keep your camera handy, for Mérida is filled with picturesque places.

Area code is 99 unless otherwise indicated.

Getting to Mérida

Airport

Mérida International Airport is six kilometers (four miles) southwest of the city. Minibuses run from the airport to downtown and to major hotels.

Airlines

AeroCaribe	461678, 286786
Aeroméxico	279455, 461400
Aviacsa	461926, 269087
Aviateca	461296, 246228
Continental	461826, 461826
Mexicana	461362, 235253
Taesa	461358, 461826

Getting around Mérida

Buses

The **Terminal de Autobús** (main bus station) at Calle 69, No 544 (between Calles 68 and 70) has daily departures for **Chichén Itzá, Uxmal**, the coast, Campeche, Villahermosa, Palenque, and Mexico City.

Car Rental

Avis Paseo de Montejo 500 (at Calle 45) ....282810, 236191; airport 464606

Budget Calle 60 (at Calle 57) 236191; airport 461308

Executive Calle 60 (between Calles 49 and 51).......... ....233732; airport 461387

National Calle 60, No 486 (between Calle 57 and 55) 232493

Taxis

Cabs do not circulate around Mérida looking for fares; instead, they congregate at taxi stands at most of the city's parks and major churches, and by **La Catedral**. To request a cab, call 285322 or 231221.

FYI

Emergencies

Hospital O'Horan, Av Itza (at Av Jacinto Caneti) 238711

Police 282553

US Consulate, Av Paseo de Mentijo (at Av Colón) 255011

Money

Banks are open Mondays though Fridays 9AM to 1:30PM. You can change money at the airport, hotels, and banks, with the latter giving you the best rate. *Casas de cambio* (exchange houses) are scattered around downtown and open throughout the day and evening. International credit cards and US dollars are accepted in most restaurants, hotels, and shops. Try not to be short of cash on Sundays, because it can be difficult to change money on that day, except in some hotels. Always keep bills of small denominations on hand, since it can be difficult to change larger bills (except at banks). A reliable place to cash your traveler's checks is Banamex (in Casa de Montejo at Plaza Mayor), and the branch also has a 24-hour cash machine where you can get pesos by using some credit cards.

Tours

Most hotel desks and tour companies can arrange trips to the ruins of **Uxmal** and **Chichén Itzá** and sightseeing tours of Mérida.

Discover Mérida is a tourist bus with two-hour sightseeing tours of the city; it departs daily from **Parque Santa Lucia.** For information and tickets contact your hotel's front desk or call 272476, 276119.

Ecoturismo Yucatán runs group and customized cultural, adventure, and bird-watching tours on the Yucatán Peninsula and in southern Mexico, Belize, and Guatemala. It is located at Calle 3, No 235 (between Calles 32-A and 34). 252187; fax 259047.

Mayaland Tours operates hotels at **Uxmal** and **Chichén Itzá,** and offers bus tours with overnight stays at the ruins and packages including reduced rental car rates. For information, contact them at Avenida Colón 502 (off Paseo de Montejo). 252246, 800/235.4079; fax 257022.

Viajes Novedosos has group and individualized tours to the Maya ruins of Yucatán and to the Ruta Maya, incorporating Maya sites in Mexico, Guatemala, Belize, Honduras, and El Salvador. It is located at Calle 58, No 488 (at Calle 43). 245996; fax 239061.

Yucatán Trails has English-speaking travel agents to assist with local tours, and information and reservations for destinations throughout Mexico, as well as reservations to get you home. Their office is at Calle 62, No 482 (between Calles 59 and 57). 282582, 285913; fax 244919.

Visitors Information

The **Oficina de Turismo** (Tourism Office) is in the **Teatro José Peón Contreras.** Open daily, it is located at Calle 60 (between Calles 57 and 59). 248386.

Area code is 99 unless otherwise indicated.

1 Plaza Mayor Mérida's main plaza, surrounded by monuments to commerce and Christianity, is at its best on Sundays, when the surrounding streets are closed to vehicular traffic, and *Meridanos* dressed in their best gather to spend most of the day in a whirl of music, color, and festivity. Vendors selling plastic Donald Ducks, embroidered baby clothes, and peace symbols on leather neckbands set up stands along the plaza's periphery. Carts sit at every corner, offering tamales, homemade potato chips, corn on the cob, and sweet meringues. Teenagers ogle their friends from balconies in the **Palacio Gobierno,** while toddlers race about with joyful abandon under the adoring gazes of adults. The plaza is less enchanting on other days, when traffic noise on the narrow streets remains a constant distraction. But it's always a pretty place to relax, study your map, and get a shoeshine. ♦ Bounded by Calles 60 and 62, and Calles 61 and 63

2 La Catedral Looking more like a prison than a church, this cathedral is said to be the oldest in North America. It was built by Maya laborers over a 36-year period in the late 1500s using stones and rubble from the ancient Maya city **T'Ho.** Much of the present floor is made of marble tombstones from the 1800s. Narrow gunnery slats shed the only natural light inside this Gothic monolith lined with altars to the Virgin and saints. Statues of benefactors, noted doctors, and priests stand near the entrance, along with supplicants sitting on the floor, begging for coins.

This cathedral lacks the ornate glitter and gold normally seen in Mexican churches, as it was supposedly looted during the revolution. Religious pictures, rosary beads, and *milagros* (tiny silver, gold, or tin replicas of human body parts to pin on a statue of the saint who helped heal your wounds) are sold at two small stands by the front doors. ♦ Calle 60 (between Calles 61 and 63). No phone

3 Palacio Gobierno Designed by engineer David Casares, this 100-year-old palace houses state offices. The inner courtyard is filled with perfect palms and ferns in tall terra-cotta vases that line the gray tile floor; netting over the courtyard keeps the pigeons out. Be sure to note the mysterious gray, red, and yellow mural, *Evolución Social de Hombre de Yucatán* (The Social Evolution of Man in Yucatán), painted by Yucatecan artist Fernando Castro Pacheco in 1972. A regal ballroom upstairs, replete with crystal chandeliers and a grand piano, serves as a gallery for Pacheco's moving and startling portraits of Yucatán's historical personages and social themes. Several wrought-iron balconies face the plaza from off the ballroom and are a nice spot for a breather.

The mood here is formal and sedate. Visitors are expected to act with decorum, except on Sundays, when the liveliness from the plaza prevails. Small newsstands and cafes line the covered arcade along the front of the palace, where you can pick up a copy of *The News* (a Mexico City–based, English-language paper) and a cup of *tamarindo* sorbet. ♦ Daily. Calle 61 (between Calles 60 and 62). No phone

La Catedral

LAWRENCE MILLS

4 Pan Montejo There are several branches of this bakery around the city, but this is the best of those near the plaza, with shelves of cookies, breakfast pastries, and breads, and a select display of special treats at the counter. Don't miss the nut tarts. ◆ Bakery ◆ Daily. Calle 61 (between Calles 60 and 58). 210462

4 Museo de la Ciudad de Mérida (City Museum) In a former convent and hospital, this museum holds the prints, drawings, photos, and models of early Mérida. The building is one of the first structures built after the Spanish conquest. ◆ Admission; free on Sundays. T-Su; closed at midday. Calle 61 (at Calle 58). 612258

5 Gran Hotel $$$ Built in 1901, Mérida's first hotel is grand indeed, with Greek pillars, tiled floors, wrought-iron banisters along curving stairways, and two levels of balconies looking down on the central courtyard. The hallways are filled with gorgeous antiques and china cabinets displaying porcelain brought to Mérida by European immigrants in the early 1900s. The noise from the hotel's position at the edge of **Parque Hidalgo** has been diminished by heavy sliding glass doors on the rooms facing the park, and air-conditioning has been added to some of the 34 rooms. Enormous carved wooden beams frame the windows in the high-ceilinged rooms, which have one or two double beds, modern tiled showers, small closets, tiny televisions, and standard furnishings (the good antiques are in the public spaces). Purified water is available in large dispensers on each floor. This is a great place to soak in the ambience of old and new Mérida, surrounded by history inside the hotel and the jumble of traffic and parks outdoors. ◆ Calle 60, No 496 (between Calles 59 and 61). 247730; fax 247622

Within the Gran Hotel:

El Patio Español ★★★$$ Tables are set beside the courtyard and in small dining rooms inside the hotel, giving a pleasant respite from the sun. The food is surprisingly good for a hotel cafe; try the excellent *sopa de lima* (a large bowl of savory broth with shredded chicken, strips of fried tortillas, and slices of lime), served with warm *bolillos* (rolls). The paella and Yucatecan dishes are also very good. ◆ Yucatecan/International ◆ Daily. 247730

5 Parque Hidalgo Calle 60 north of the plaza is lined with hotels, restaurants, and parks, none more popular than this courtyard (sometimes called Parque Cepeda Peraza) with benches and a small gazebo. Sidewalk cafes and aged hotels frame the walkways, and marimbas play throughout the day. On Saturday and Sunday nights young people wait up to an hour in long lines wrapping around the plaza to get into Cine Apolo, the most popular movie theater in town, where first-run Spanish-language films are screened. The park is a great spot to linger over a coffee or beer, write postcards, and watch the scenery. Artisans sometimes set up tables here, and hammock sellers are always present. ◆ Calle 60 (between Calles 61 and 59)

5 Giorgio ★★$ Part of the attraction of this popular, though unelaborate, cafe are its reasonably priced pizzas and pastas. Another is the ongoing parade of vendors, travelers, and locals through the park. ◆ Italian ◆ Daily breakfast, lunch, and dinner. Parque Hildago (in front of the Gran Hotel). No phone

5 Hotel Caribe $$ A longtime favorite on **Parque Hidalgo**, this converted three-story colonial home has a gorgeous central courtyard. The 56 remodeled rooms are decorated in soft pastels and floral prints, and have telephones and air-conditioning. Most rooms are set back around the courtyard and don't have a view of the plaza. The rooftop pool area, however, has a nice view of downtown. Two restaurants are also available. ◆ Calle 59, No 500 (at the rear of the park). 249022; fax 248733

LAWRENCE MILLS

6 Iglesia de la Tercera Orden (Church of the Third Order) The Jesuits set up a miniature dynasty here in 1618, building a Baroque, carved-stone church, a boys' school, a theater, and the **Parque de la Maternidad** (Mother's Park). If you look closely at the church's outer walls facing Calle 59, you'll notice Maya latticework designs in the stones, taken from the rubble of the ancient Maya capital, T'Ho. ◆ Calle 60 (between Calles 59 and 57)

Restaurants/Clubs: Red   **Hotels:** Blue
Shops/ 🌳 Outdoors: Green   **Sights/Culture:** Black

6 Parque de la Maternidad (Mother's Park) This small, quiet park has a graceful, white statue of the Madonna and Child surrounded by S-shaped benches known as *confidenciales*. It's one of the prettiest places to escape from the activity on the street ♦ Calle 60 (between Calles 59 and 57)

6 Teatro José Peón Contreras Designed by Enrique Deserti (who also created the Palacio Cantón, home of the **Museo Regional de Antropología,** see page 94) in 1908, when *Meridanos* were thoroughly enamored with European design, this ornate Italianate theater has a sweeping Carrara marble staircase and frescoed dome. Art shows are sometimes held in the lobby, and the **Ballet Folklorico** (Folkloric Ballet) of the **Universidad Autónomo de Yucatán** (University of Yucatán) puts on a weekly show illustrating the history of the state through music and dance. ♦ Shows: Tu. Calle 60 (between Calles 57 and 59). 243954

Within the Teatro José Peón Contreras:

Oficina de Turismo (Tourism Office) English- and Spanish-speaking clerks armed with an immense knowledge of their city staff this excellent tourism office. Brochures and pamphlets are kept behind the desk, so you must ask for what you need and sign the guest book. ♦ Daily. 248925

Cafe Péon Contreras ★$$ This pretty indoor/outdoor cafe would be ideal if the food were better; unless it improves, come here for the ambience. It's best to stick with the coffee, espresso, cappuccino, and desserts, especially the carrot cake. Still, it's a peaceful place to sit—the street it fronts is closed to traffic. Callejon Congresso (at Calle 60). No phone

7 Fernando Huertas Mexican clothing designer Fernando Huertas does amazing things with Guatemalan and Mexican textiles, creating gorgeous fitted jackets, dresses, and vests that command high prices. Distinctive pieces of silver jewelry, and leather and cloth accessories are scattered about the shop, where salespeople treat all customers as valued clients. ♦ M-F. Calle 59, No 511 (between Calles 60 and 62). 216035

8 La Bella Epoca ★★★★$$ Mérida's best tables for a leisurely, sumptuous dinner are set on the small second-story balconies of this elegant, yet casual, restaurant.

While the menu is perhaps a bit too ambitious, offering pages of Mexican, Yucatecan, Middle Eastern, and vegetarian fare, the chef manages to prepare most dishes very well. His roster of regional Mexican specialties is particularly impressive—for a savory tour of the country's cuisine, start with *crepas de huitlacoche* (crepes with a delicate fungus that's grown on corn) or *sikil-pak* (a dip of pumpkin seeds and grilled tomatoes and onions), followed by *pollo pipian* (chicken with a sauce of ground pumpkin seeds) or *carne asada* (tender marinated beef with guacamole, beans, and rice). The vast selection of desserts makes decision-making difficult; the *crepas cajeta* (crepes with caramel sauce) are superb, but you should also try mangoes flambéed with tequila, or pumpkin-seed marzipan. The service is excellent and the clientele fascinating, particularly after 10PM when *Méridanos* accustomed to midnight repasts fill the dining room with laughter and chatter. ♦ Continental/Mexican/Yucatecan ♦ Daily lunch and dinner. Calle 60 (between Calles 59 and 57). 281928

8 Universidad Autónomo de Yucatán (University of Yucatán) A Moorish archway straddles a street corner where students congregate before class. Beyond it sits a bare patio which is center stage for the university's musical concerts on Friday nights. The university was established in 1831 on the site of Mérida's first university, built by the Jesuits in 1618. In and around the library are portraits of the school's founders and patrons (such as Andres Quintana Roo and Cepeda Peraza, both highly revered military generals), and a mural telling the story of the reconstruction and reopening of the university by Governor Felipe Carillo Puerto in 1941. The school has a fine intensive Spanish program and a Maya studies course for foreigners. ♦ Calle 60 (between Calles 59 and 57)

9 Casa del Balam $$$ You don't realize the charm that lies within this seven-story, 54-room hotel until you walk past the drab facade and up a red tile path to the entrance and courtyard filled with ferns, bougainvillea, and palms.

"House of the Tiger" would be by far the best hotel in town, were it not for the traffic noise at this corner. To cut down on the noise, several rooms have been remodeled and have air-conditioning, which definitely helps. The newer rooms have satellite TV and mini-bars; all rooms have wrought-iron headboards, red-and-white tile floors, woven blue spreads, and touches of Old Mexico. You'll be charmed by the cane-backed rocking chairs in the rooms and courtyard, and the inner balconies where you can almost forget the city outside. **Bougambilias** is a simple dining room where the waiters appear to have lived their entire lives, bearing trays of typical hotel fare. If you're not staying here, stop in for a cool drink in the courtyard and soak in the ambience of Old Mérida. ♦ Calle 60, No 488 (between Calles 57 and 55). 228844, 800/624.8451; fax 245011

huge, with king-size beds and windows overlooking the courtyards, while others are as small and simple as a monk's cell. Under a more-than-80-year-old tree, there's a long lap pool. Rivero has a second 62-room hotel of the same name a block away, designed in an equally unconventional style, and guests there have use of this hotel's swimming pool. Beverages and snacks are available at the small cafe. ♦ Calle 60 (between Calles 53 and 51). 232463

10 El Pórtico del Peregrino ★★★$$$
Romance and tranquillity are guaranteed at this small restaurant, which doesn't look like much from the street. Once you walk down a narrow passageway, though, you're in a tropical garden where vines wrap around tree trunks and candlelight casts a peaceful glow. Just off the garden is an air-conditioned dining room furnished with antiques; another cool room by the street provides a nice spot for lunch. *Berenjenas al horno* (baked eggplant layered with tender chicken, melted cheese, and a savory tomato sauce) is the best dish in the house. The chicken-liver shish kebab also has a loyal following. There is a mainstream selection of grilled chicken and fish dinners. ♦ Middle Eastern ♦ Daily lunch and dinner. Calle 57, No 501 (between Calles 60 and 62). 286163

10 Cafetería Pop ★★★$ Plain, simple, and unadorned, this is tops in Mérida for fresh-brewed coffee and breakfast served all day long. Students and professors from the nearby university congregate at its 12 tables; however, the proprietors discourage loitering during the busiest hours of the morning, and do not sell beer or wine unless it's ordered with a meal. Hamburgers here are better than most in town, and the restaurant makes a good pit stop for a cup of coffee and a slice of cake or pie when your energy flags. ♦ American/Mexican ♦ M-Sa breakfast, lunch, and dinner. Calle 57, No 501 (between Calles 60 and 62). 286163

11 Parque Santa Lucia A quiet, plain square with a few *confidenciales* (benches) and shade trees. It fills with locals and guests for the Thursday night concerts and the Sunday flea market and book sale. ♦ Calle 60 (between Calles 55 and 53)

12 Hotel Trinidad Galería $ Those drawn to the bizarre and unusual will enjoy this eccentric hotel, owned by Manolo Rivero, an avid collector of antiques and modern art. The lobby is filled with potted palms (one sporting a stuffed monkey), and 17th-century statues are scattered along the rambling hacienda's stairways and corridors. Eclecticism reigns in the 30 rooms, with a jumble of mismatched antique chests and beds. Some rooms are

Izamal

When Pope John Paul II visited Mexico in August 1993, he held a momentous audience with the indigenous peoples of Mexico and Central America in this town 72 kilometers (45 miles) east of Mérida on Highway 80. Wearing their traditional dress, Maya and mestizo groups from all over the region met in the main plaza in a gathering at least 3,000 strong (the official estimate, considered low by observers). One of the oldest cities in Mexico, Izamal holds particular importance both to the Maya and to those of the Catholic faith because of its Maya temples and impressive convent and monastery.

Izamal was once ruled by the ruthless Bishop Diego de Landa, a Franciscan zealot responsible for nearly obliterating the Maya in the 1700s. Along with torturing and killing thousands of Maya, Diego de Landa burned their sacred codices, the written history of Maya culture. The monastery at Izamal (overlooking the main plaza) was built from the rubble of a Maya temple and cenote wall that were dismantled by Maya slaves under the direction of Fray Juan de Mérida, a Franciscan monk who supervised the construction of several churches in the area. Northeast of the main plaza, the ruins of the Maya temple **Kinich Kakmó** rise atop a hillside with an astounding view of the flat countryside. On a clear day, you're able to see **Chichén Itzá** from its top.

Known as the "Ciudad Amarillo" for the unrelenting yellow color scheme of its buildings, Izamal got a fresh coat of paint and other improvements for the pope's visit. The town is becoming a stop on organized tours of the area, and the government has built a **Parador Turistica** (Tourism Center) near the entrance road to town. The center includes a museum, artisans' shops, and other attractions. The best store in town is **Hecho a Mano,** owned by Hector Garza and Jeanne Hunt, who have spent years collecting folk art throughout Mexico. Some of their collectibles and Hunt's photographs are displayed in their tiny shop on Calle 33 across from the monastery. The restaurant **Kinich Kakmó** (★★★$; Calle 27, No 299) is the perfect spot to sample Yucatecan cuisine. Owner Miriam Azcorra has created a pretty courtyard setting for her restaurant, which sits practically in the shadow of the ruins. Stop here for lunch on the way to **Chichén Itzá.** Izamal is well worth visiting—it combines much of Yucatán's history in a picturesque colonial setting. Make sure you have plenty of film!

13 Posada Toledo $ Europeans and budget travelers are justifiably enamored of this hotel in a converted colonial mansion. The 15 rooms have high wood-beamed ceilings, antique furnishings, hardwood floors, and tiled baths. Fresh air is at a minimum, since few rooms have windows to the street; it's common for guests to keep their doors open to the central courtyard. Two rooms at the front of the hotel have been converted into a master suite with pale blue walls, ornate woodwork along ceilings and doors, a crystal chandelier, air-conditioning, and a separate living room. The rate for this palatial suite is far less than a typical double room in a more modern hotel; it might be the perfect honeymoon suite for the right couple. No restaurant. ♦ Calle 58 (at Calle 57). 231690; fax 232256

14 Hotel Mucuy $ Mérida has an outstanding selection of budget hotels, and this one is right up there. Much of its charm is due to the hospitable hosts, Alfredo and Ofelia Comín. The building's architecture isn't as remarkable as at the colonial-style hotels, but the 22 rooms are comfortable and immaculate; all have ceiling fans and face a pretty garden. There's a communal refrigerator, bookshelf, and clothesline, and tables and chairs by the garden. The hotel arranges some of the most economical trips to the ruins available in town. No restaurant. ♦ Calle 57, No 481 (between Calles 56 and 58). 285193; fax 237801

15 Paseo de Montejo The Champs-Elysées of Mérida, this boulevard has a landscaped central divide and wide, shaded sidewalks perfect for a leisurely stroll. Though not as elegant and picturesque as in its prime, it's still a prestigious address. Many airlines and banks have their headquarters in the faded mansions that were the heart of high-society life at the turn of the century. Some families whose ancestors built these palatial estates have been unable to maintain their former glory, allowing several to fall into disrepair. ♦ Calles 56 and 56-A (between Calle 47 and Paseo Colón)

16 Cerámica Mayakat Hand-painted porcelain tiles and dishes line the walls of this tiny shop, where you can design a plaque for your home or office and have it custom-made in less than a week. They also stock the town's best selection of obscure and scholarly books and pamphlets on Mérida and Yucatán. ♦ M-Su. Paseo de Montejo, No 498-B (between Calles 45 and 43). 236385

17 Museo Regional de Antropología (Regional Anthropology Museum) The museum is located inside the frothy peach-and-white **Palacio Cantón**, a grand and suitable home for the state's impressive collection of Maya art and artifacts. The palace was built for Governor General Francisco Cantón Rosado (who enjoyed it for only six years before dying in 1917) and was used as a school of fine arts in the 1930s. In 1948 it became the official residence of the Governor of Yucatán and in 1977 was transformed into the museum. Allow plenty of time to examine both the building, built in 1911, with its Doric and Ionic columns, sweeping white marble staircases, crystal chandeliers, and Beaux Arts ornamentation, as well as the displays.

The histories of the Maya and Yucatán are covered extensively. Of special interest are the exhibit of the wooden boards used to press Maya children's foreheads into a sloping shape to make them beautiful (a custom that continues today), and significant structures at **Chichén Itzá** and **Uxmal.** The second floor is devoted to pieces from **Oxkintok,** a hidden Maya city near Uxmal that was partially excavated and studied by Spanish archaeologists from 1986 to 1991. The museum has an excellent bookstore, though much of the literature is in Spanish. ♦ Admission. T-Su. Calle 43 (between Paseo de Montejo and Calle 58). 230557

18 Hyatt Regency Mérida $$$$ For years the four-star **Holiday Inn** was the only hotel at the edge of Mérida's wealthy neighborhoods; it attracted business travelers and those seeking the comforts of home. The area is fast becoming a tourist center, and this hostelry is the first (at least three more are on the drawing board) of the deluxe high-rise hotels that are joining the pioneer. The tallest hotel in town at 17 stories, it has 300 luxurious rooms that far outshine the competition. Services new to Mérida include in-room movie channels on satellite TV, 24-hour room service, a swim-up bar at the pool, and a full-scale business center. Several bars and restaurants keep hungry guests fed. ♦ Calle 60, No 344 (at Paseo Colón). 256722, 800/228.9000; fax 257002

Restaurants/Clubs: Red   **Hotels:** Blue
Shops/ 🌳 Outdoors: Green   **Sights/Culture:** Black

20 Los Almendros ★★★$ Locals and travelers pack this eatery at lunchtime for traditional Yucatecan and Maya meals that last for hours. Along with branches in Ticul and Cancún, the restaurant has been serving the same basic menu for nearly three decades—*pok-chuc* (pork chop grilled with spices), *cochinita* or *pollo pibil* (pork or chicken baked in banana leaves), *pavo de relleno* (turkey stuffed with olives, capers, raisins, and cheese), and other regional fare. The cavernous dining room echoes with spirited conversations, and the menu is printed with photos and English descriptions for neophytes. ◆ Yucatecan ◆ Daily breakfast, lunch, and dinner. Calle 50-A, No 493 (between Calles 57 and 59). 285459

21 Iglesia Mejorada (Church of Improvement) Modeled after a Spanish church of the same name, this massive, forbidding structure was built in 1640 by the Franciscans and used as a hospital in the mid-1800s. Though rarely open, it is interesting from the outside, looming over the pretty plaza and brick streets of the church's namesake neighborhood. The side streets are filled with gorgeous mansions from the turn of the century; most are rundown and some are abandoned, but it's not difficult to imagine how grand it all must have been. ◆ Calle 50 (between Calles 59 and 57)

21 Museo Nacional de Artes Populares (National Museum of Popular Arts) An impressive collection of folk art fills the rooms of this colonial hacienda. Of particular interest are the conch-shell carvings, hammock looms, and pottery reproductions of Maya huts. The upstairs galleries display a large collection of costumes and masks from Chiapas, Oaxaca, and Michoacán. ◆ Free. T-Su. Calle 59 (between Calles 48 and 50). No phone

22 El Arco de los Dragones In the 17th century the Spanish fortified the city by building a massive stone wall around it with 13 arched gates. One of the few remaining arches looms over Calle 61 by the overgrown wall and grounds of a deserted Spanish military base. Moorish in design, the arch has three spires on top and gated guard stations at each side (*dragones* means guard in Spanish). ◆ Calle 61 (between Calles 50 and 52)

23 Mercado Municipal You haven't really been to a Mexican municipal market until you've tried to absorb this overwhelming labyrinth of commerce. The square-block-deep enclosed market itself is fairly predictable, with the lower floor devoted to Maya women and children hawking trinkets and other items, while the men sell dead chickens and pigs. However, on the second floor is an artisans' market filled with treasures, most of which can also be found in the rows of tiny shops lining the surrounding streets. This is where you're bound to get lost at least once, trying to find the section devoted to hammocks, *jipis* (straw hats), regional clothing, and woven bags. Do *not* bring your car into this area. ◆ Daily. Calle 67 (between Calles 56 and 58)

24 Mercado de Artesanías Garcia Rejón (Artisans' Market) Embroidered dresses and *huipiles* (blouses), brightly striped woven belts, henequen hammocks and bags, and pottery decorated with Maya designs fill this arts and crafts market. Many of the products are machine-made and flimsy, but you can find one-of-a-kind treasures if you're patient and persistent. ◆ Daily. Calle 65 (between Calles 60 and 58)

LAWRENCE MILLS

25 Casa de Montejo (House of Montejo) Francisco Montejo Jr., the son of Mérida's conqueror, began building the family palace in 1549, using Maya laborers and artisans and rubble from **T'Ho.** An appalling reminder of this heritage can be seen at the entrance of the building in the stonework portraits of Spanish soldiers in full imperial regalia standing on Maya heads. Successive generations of Montejos occupied the house until the 1970s, when Banamex had it remodeled by renowned architect **Augustín Legoretta** and turned it into its Mérida headquarters.

Little remains of the inner house, which had been refurbished during the late 19th century in the ornate French style of the day. Visitors can stroll the inner gardens and cash traveler's checks during banking hours. ♦ M-F. Calle 63 (between Calles 60 and 62)

26 Palacio Municipal (City Hall) A true city hall, always bustling with activity, this building was constructed in 1542 as the town's headquarters and jail. Throughout the next four centuries, the original wooden building was rebuilt and replaced several times by other structures. The current pretty yellow palace with its ribbonlike white trim was finally completed in 1928, replete with an ornate archway from a nearby Dominican convent and a clock tower that chimes on the quarter hour. On Sundays and several evenings during the week, the street is roped off and a wooden stage is erected for performances of a traditional wedding dance or concerts by a local band. The building next door on Calle 61 is a tourist plaza with two stories of shops and restaurants. ♦ Daily. Calle 62 (between Calles 63 and 61). No phone

27 Casa de las Artesanías The selection at the folk art shop in this restored monastery is enough to overwhelm even a die-hard shopper. Baskets, weaving, pottery, glassware, embroidery, wood carving—it's all here, at reasonable, set prices. Be sure to check out the building itself and the courtyard in the back, where art exhibits are often held. The monastery is also used for art and Maya-language classes. ♦ M-Su. Calle 63, No 513 (between Calles 64 and 66). 235392, 286676

28 Cafe Louvre ★★$ More interesting for its ambience than its food, this cafe has two small doors on the street leading into an outer coffee shop buzzing with conversation. At first glance, the back room looks like a beige dungeon filled with men reading newspapers and families in a feeding frenzy. Once your eyes adjust to the dim light and your ears adjust to the cacophony, it seems more like a train terminal where you can sit and drink coffee for hours watching the working class at rest. On Calle 62 north of the cafe are some marvelous Art Deco buildings, including a deserted theater made of glass bricks. ♦ Mexican/American ♦ Daily breakfast, lunch, and dinner. Calle 62, No 499-D (between Calles 59 and 61). 245073

29 Hotel Colón $$ To enjoy your stay you have to overlook the ravages of time and appreciate the architectural novelties incorporated in the 1920s design of one of Mérida's first hotels. Whether you're a guest or a visitor, be sure to check out the tiled *baños de vapor* (steam baths). Separate areas for women and men have elaborate hand-painted tile showers and narrow rooms with shallow pools surrounded by benches, where bathers soak in the steam. (Baths are open to non-guests for a fee and are rumored to be popular for secret liaisons.) The swimming pool in a back garden is one of the nicest in town. The rest of the 66-room hotel is eclectic, starting with the huge painted plaster dogs guarding the front desk. Rooms have tattered red-and-gold brocade bedspreads and drapes, and the yellow-and-blue tiled stairways and arches are faded and chipped. Still, a stay here is an experience you'll never forget. A coffee shop provides light meals and snacks. ♦ Calle 62, No 483 (between Calles 59 and 57). 234355, 234508; fax 244919

29 Alberto's Continental Patio

★★★$$$ For more than 30 years Alberto, Nery, and Pepe Salum have graciously served their guests exquisite Lebanese meals in a carefully restored home built in 1727. Giant rubber trees dripping with Spanish moss shade a central patio, yet allow diners to see the stars at night. Two inner dining rooms are decorated with antique religious statues and paintings, gilded mirrors, copper pots, and candles sparkling in hurricane lamps on the heavy wood tables.

The menu runs the full gamut of fish, beef, and fowl, with a good selection of Maya specialties. For a Yucatecan feast order the complete dinner of ceviche, *sopa de lima* (lime soup), broiled snapper with achiote sauce, fried bananas, and coconut pie. But the chef's true love is Lebanese fare; try a subtly spicy hummus or tabbouleh (a salad of cracked wheat and fresh mint), followed by cabbage rolls stuffed with ground beef. Finish with a cup or two of their thick dark Turkish coffee and you'll be sure to stay up all night. ♦ Lebanese/Mexican ♦ Daily. Calle 64, No 482 (between Calles 57 and 59). 285367

30 Casa Mexilio $$ Owners Roger and Jorge have teamed up to transform a turn-of-the-century stone-and-stucco structure into a distinctive guest house with only eight rooms.

The entrance leads to an immense kitchen painted and tiled in bright yellows and blues, with a communal table set with traditional Mexican pottery where breakfast is served.

Each room has a character of its own, with some combination of white walls, loft beds, tiled sinks, antique wardrobes, black and terra-cotta pots dangling from ropes, and Mexican and Guatemalan textiles and rugs. You may want to take your coffee and sit beside the small pool in the shaded courtyard, where the resident cats lounge. The neighborhood is quiet, and it's usually easy to find parking on the street. ♦ Calle 68, No 495 (between Calles 57 and 59). 214032, 303/674.9615, 800/538.6802; fax 303/674.8735

31 Hotel Residencial $$ A logical and comfortable hotel for those traveling by car is this Pepto-Bismol pink, French-Colonial–style hotel. The formal entrance leads into a courtyard with a small kidney-shaped swimming pool; the noise and traffic of guests coming and going keeps the pool from being relaxing. White pillars and wrought-iron railings support the balconies on the four floors above. The decor within the 66 guest rooms is far less opulent than its exterior, but the air-conditioning and showers are powerful, and the mirrored closet big enough to store clothes for a year. There is a gated parking lot and a pretty little neighborhood park nearby. There is also a restaurant. ♦ Calle 59, No 589 (between Calles 76 and 78). 243899, 243099; fax 212230

Favorite Finds in Mérida

The Yucatán Peninsula is well known for its distinctive regional folk arts—particularly its hammocks and clothing (designed to alleviate the discomfort of the tropical heat) and the woven blankets and hand-crafted pottery incorporating Maya symbols and portraits of revered gods. Savvy visitors begin their journeys through the peninsula with a trip to the local market to buy a hammock for beach siestas, and a *jipi* (straw hat) to shade their brows while climbing the ruins. The market and surrounding shops in **Mérida** are the best sources for regional crafts, but good buys can also be found in Cancún, Cozumel, and in most town squares, where vendors from the area display their wares, including the following three favorite Yucatecan creations.

Hammocks: Woven of flimsy, multicolored strings in a loose yet supple hanging cradle, the Yucatecan hammock is coveted the world over for its comfort, durability, and beauty. Silk hammocks are works of art and cost a fortune. Nylon hammocks are tough yet silky, and they don't fade or shred in the sun. Cotton is the most common and least expensive material used. Henequen and other scratchy fibers are unacceptable for a hammock, unless you have ascetic tendencies. Yucatecan hammocks come in three sizes: *sencillo* (designed for one person, but often not large enough for the average gringo's body), *doble* (to hold two people snugly or one comfortably), and *matrimonial* (big enough for two adults and a child).

If you have the time and transportation, consider visiting a hammock weavers' town, such as Tixkokob, on Highway 80 east of Mérida. Hammock looms sit on nearly every front porch, and families are delighted to show you their techniques and wares. Often the man of the family is in the city, wandering through the plaza with his pile of homemade hammocks, but the women and children genuinely enjoy visitors and will most likely invite you into their homes to practice swinging in their family hammocks strung across the living space. If you can't get away from Mérida but still want to shop knowledgeably, visit **El Aguacate** (Calle 58, No 604;

286265) near the market district and **La Poblana** (Calle 65, No 492; 216503)—both shops will take the time to show you how their hammocks are made and discuss the qualities of each variety.

Jipis: These popular hats (commonly called Panama hats by tourists) are made from the fibers of the jipijapa plant, grown in Campeche. They are crushable, bendable, wonderfully wearable lightweight straw hats that are perfect for the Yucatán climate; a well-made *jipi* will hold up for years. Judge its quality by the coarseness of the fiber and the tightness of the weave. Soft, tightly woven hats of the highest caliber are surprisingly expensive and not really necessary for casual use. Try the middle grade and stay away from cheap, loosely constructed hats, unless you plan to dispose of it after your trip. *Jipis* are woven in dark, damp caves in the small towns of Campeche, including Becal, on Highway 80 between Mérida and the city of Campeche. In Mérida, you'll find good examples of the various *jipis* at **La Casa de los Jipis** (Calle 56, No 526; no phone).

Guayaberas: Foreign men who spend a lot of time in the Yucatán almost always end up adopting the *guayabera* look, which makes great sense given the heat. *Guayaberas* are shirts that button up the front to an open neck and collar, have short sleeves, and hang outside the trousers. They typically are made of lightweight cotton, but also come in polyester (which destroys their breathing ability). The shirt fronts are usually embroidered in the same color thread as the shirt (white is the most traditional color, and blue is very popular) or pleated with tiny tucks. Custom-tailored and off-the-rack *guayaberas* are available in Mérida at **Camisería Canul** (Calle 59, No 496; no phone), **Jack's** (Calle 59, No 505; no phone), and other shops in the same neighborhood.

Mexicans sometimes refer to Yucatán as La Hermana Republica de Mexico (the Sister Republic of Mexico), an acknowledgment of the area's individualistic, independent character and spirit.

32 Parque El Centenario A fantastic display of youthful merriment and family togetherness takes place every Sunday at this botanical-zoological amusement park, which was inaugurated in 1910 at the eastern edge of Mérida. Rides in the amusement area are designed for children and Maya adults (who tend to stand little more than four feet tall). There's a sky ride that dangles 10 feet above a shallow lake. Shaded brick pathways wander past the zoo's interesting collection of indigenous monkeys, lizards, and snakes. The park sits at a corner where traffic from the airport and points east veers into downtown. Behind it is an interesting cemetery and residential area. ♦ Free. Daily. Itzáes (between Calles 59 and 65). 285815

33 Hotel D'Champs $$ This thoroughly modern hotel (by far the nicest within walking distance of the bus station) pays tribute to Mérida's  French period with its architectural details mimicking the ornamentation of the mansions of Paseo de Montejo. A pale gray-and-peach color scheme carries throughout the lobby and into the 30 rooms decorated in floral pastels. The dining room and bar sit off a garden at the end of a long swimming pool. White wrought-iron tables under shade trees provide a good spot for enjoying a cool drink before returning to your room for a quiet siesta. ♦ Calle 70, No 543 (between Calles 65 and 67). 248655, 248829; fax 238024

34 Ermita Santa Isabel (Saint Isabel Hermitage) The botanical gardens alongside this Jesuit hermitage, built in the mid-1700s, are filled with Maya figurines, stone fountains, wishing wells, and indigenous flowers and trees, many labeled with their Spanish names. Located in a quiet neighborhood with brick roads, the hermitage was a popular resting spot for travelers en route to Campeche in the 1800s, and was restored in 1966. Folk dancers perform in a small park across the street from the church on Friday nights. ♦ Calle 66 (between Calles 77 and 79)

Mérida to Chichén Itzá

The easiest, fastest route from Mérida to Chichén Itzá is on the new *autopista,* an eight-lane toll road that slashes through the jungle all the way to Cancún. Future plans include another toll road from Nuevo Xcan to the coast near **Akumal.** The tolls are high, as are the speeds, and thus far the road is fairly free of buses and trucks. You can cover the 120 kilometers (75 miles) from Mérida to Chichén Itzá in less than two hours on the new road, or take a more leisurely drive on Highway 180 east. Bus and truck drivers on this highway share the road somewhat reluctantly with meandering wanderers, and you're best off just letting them pass. Side trips off Highway 180 include a half-hour drive about 32 kilometers (20 miles) east on Highway 80 to **Tixkokob,** a small town where nearly every home has a wooden loom outside the front door. If you're in the market for hammocks (this is the best place to buy hammocks; see "Favorite Finds in Mérida" on page 97), take time to wander from house to house for an on-the-spot lesson in hammock weaving and the Maya life-style. It's also one of the best opportunities to visit a typical *na* (an oval hut with a thatch roof). In many homes the interior is unpartitioned, with hammocks hanging in the middle for sleeping and sitting, and a cooking/eating area near the back door. More modern homes here have tables, chairs, and shelves, but rarely will you see a bed.

Two kilometers (1 mile) east of Tixkokob, an unnamed paved road heads north to **Motul,** birthplace of Felipe Carillo Puerto, one of the most revered Governors of Yucatán, who was assassinated in 1924. This drive takes you through henequen plantations, where the tough agave plant, Yucatán's most valuable crop, is harvested by Maya laborers wielding machetes. One of the most ornate monasteries from the time of the Spanish conquest is located by Motul's plaza. Continue east (less than an hour's drive) on the Motul road or Highway 80 to **Izamal** (see "Izamal" on page 93), then south about 32 kilometers (20 miles) from Izamal to reach Highway 180 east to **Piste** and **Chichén Itzá.**

Ermita Santa Isabel

LAWRENCE MILLS

Bests

Alicia del Villar de Blanco
General Director, VN Travel and Viajes Novedosos

Mérida This city of bleached-white roofs and sparkling clean streets has a charm that's hard to describe. It's one of the safest places in Mexico, probably because there is no drug problem among the young; the family structure is very solid and adolescents feel wanted and cared for here. Mérida has impressive historical sites: the ornate **Cathedral;** the **Palacio Gobierno,** a beautiful 17th-century building housing city offices; the **Teatro José Peón Contreras,** an architectural jewel; the **Universidad Autónomo de Yucatán;** and **Paseo de Montejo,** which is filled with elaborate mansions and happy inhabitants.

Chichén Itzá Along with Palenque and Tikal, this is one of the most extensive Maya archaeological sites. Grandiose temples, pyramids, a ball court, and other structures speak highly of a most amazing and ancient civilization. Among many achievements, the Maya invented the concept of "zero," an exercise in abstract thought that the Europeans started using in the early Middle Ages, when the Maya were already in decline. The **Temple of Kukulcán,** also known as **El Castillo,** is magnificent and is the focus of a biannual equinox in March and September, when the play of light from the setting sun suggests a serpent undulating down the principal staircase. You'll also see ancient steam baths, a ceremonial ball court with amazing acoustics, temples to Venus and the Jaguar, and much more.

Uxmal All the majesty and grandiosity of Chichén Itzá cannot compare with the rare beauty of Uxmal, where the creators outdid each other in their artisanship. Delicate structures are graced with a stone filigree not seen anywhere else in the world. Among the many buildings worth touring are the **Pyramid of the Magician;** the **Quadrangle of the Nuns,** with rooms resembling Spanish cloisters; and the **Governor's Palace,** one of the most stunning pre-Columbian structures. Every night there is a spectacular hour-long light and sound show, in Spanish at 7PM and in English at 9PM.

Izamal This harmoniously built colonial city 72 kilometers (45 miles) east of Mérida is famous for its immense **Convent,** built by **Diego de Landa** in the 16th century atop an ancient Maya pyramid. You reach it by climbing the pyramid's original steps. Three platforms make the complex asymmetric, and it's surrounded by many arches.

Valladolid Yucatán's second-largest city after Mérida gives a good overview of provincial colonial life, with a main plaza where the locals congregate nightly to visit. Valladolid is renowned for its many elaborately built churches, with altars made of fine wood covered with gold and silver leaf.

Patricia Alisau
Bureau Chief, *Travel Age West* Magazine

Dining on exquisite *sopa de lima* (lime soup) in **Alberto's Continental Patio** restaurant which exudes the atmosphere of the old hacienda it's located in.

I love the people. They are so shy and neat and have the best sense of humor in all of Mexico. I love the independence of the people that made them want to create a separate Republic within Mexico many eons ago.

The cool white *huipiles* of the native women and tropical *guayabera* shirts of the men. Just looking at them cools the atmosphere down a few degrees in the steamy city.

I always spend a few hours shopping for hand-woven hammocks and the famous "panama" hats which you can squish and fold into a suitcase. They always bounce back into their original shape when you unpack and they are so cheap, a perfect buy for a globetrotter as myself.

When a local trio plays, "La Peregrina," I think of US journalist Alma Reed and her tragic love affair with the governor of the Yucatán. This romantic song her lover had created for her will continue to keep the memories alive even though they both are gone.

At **Chichén Itzá,** climbing to the top of the temples, especially the one dedicated to the Warriors with the ever-serene **Chac Mool** with its gaze fixed on a far horizon.

Walking the jungle paths at **Cobá** to discover a stately stele or stairway to a pyramid still shrouded in ancient foliage. This less-visited site is free of crowds and so still that you can hear the sounds of the forest clearly.

Red-and-white bas-relief plaques depicting elephants, lions, and snakes hang at the corners of old buildings at intersections throughout Mérida. They are reproductions of the signs that designated the street names before uninspired civic planners chose to adopt the current monotonous and confusing numerical system.

Though conquered and subjugated by the Spaniards and their mestizo descendants, the Maya of Yucatán gathered in 1847 to wage a bloody guerrilla war against their oppressors. More than half the Maya population of the peninsula died in the War of the Castes, which lasted until 1901.

Fragrant white mariposas bloom throughout Mérida in the summer months, making the humid air heavy with their scent. The flower resembles a gardenia and it's believed to grow only in the Yucatán.

Restaurants/Clubs: Red   **Hotels:** Blue
Shops/ Outdoors: Green   **Sights/Culture:** Black

Uxmal

Hidden in the rolling green hills of the **Puuc** territory (*puuc* is Maya for hill), **Uxmal** is the **Yucatán's** most architecturally beautiful Maya site. Its pyramids and palaces are decorated with incredibly ornate and intricate latticework friezes that from afar look like delicate lace held up against the azure sky. The elliptical and enchanting **Pyramid of the Magician** echoes the form of the surrounding terrain, looming above the angular planes and geometric designs of the **Quadrangle of the Nuns**.

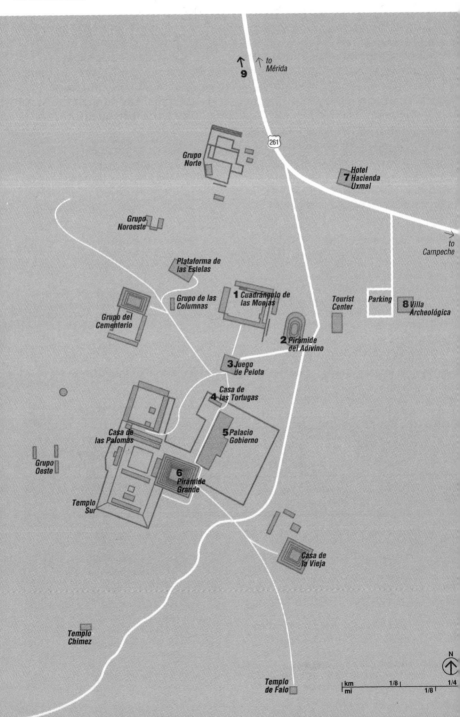

9 ↑ ↑ to Mérida

261

Grupo Norte

7 Hotel Hacienda Uxmal

→ to Campeche

Grupo Noroeste

Plataforma de las Estelas

Grupo de las Columnas

1 Cuadrángulo de las Monjas

Tourist Center

Parking

8 Villa Archeológica

Grupo del Cementerio

2 Pirámide del Adivino

3 Juego de Pelota

Casa de **4** las Tortugas

Casa de las Palomas

5 Palacio Gobierno

Grupo Oeste

6 Pirámide Grande

Templo Sur

Casa de la Vieja

Templo Chimez

Templo de Falo

N

km   1/8   1/4
mi   1/8

Tour guides will tell you that **Uxmal** means "thrice built"; archaeologists, however, have found that it was occupied and rebuilt at least five times. The area first flourished in the seventh century and was abandoned and reoccupied sporadically through the ninth century. A tribe known as the Tutul Xiú (believed to have been influenced by both the Toltecs, who reigned in central Mexico, and the Itzá, a warfaring Maya tribe) invaded **Uxmal** in the early 10th century and held on for about 400 years, a period of war and strife between the Yucatán's Maya tribes. When the Spaniards arrived in the mid-15th century, **Uxmal** was essentially deserted.

Archaeologists have yet to completely understand why **Uxmal** was inhabited and deserted so many times. One clue can be found in the abundance of masks and sculptures of the snout-nosed rain god, Chac. The people of **Uxmal** had good reason to fear and revere Chac, for water is scarce in these parts. There are no cenotes (natural wells or sinkholes in the limestone terrain), which soak up rainwater as quickly as it falls. And though the Maya dug *chultunes* (cisterns) for collecting water during the infrequent storms, drought may well have driven them away.

Most travelers visit **Uxmal** for just a few hours on day trips from Mérida, 50 miles north, and also stop at other major sites in the Puuc region. It is far better to spend the night near the ruins; you'll be able to explore them early in the morning and evening, when the tour groups are gone, and can return at night for the sound-and-light show, the best of its kind in Mexico. The colorful display brings out architectural details easily missed in daylight, and the site takes on an eerie sense of mystery, especially in the glow of the moon. **Uxmal** is open daily; there is an admission fee and an extra charge for using a video camera. The sound-and-light show is presented twice nightly— once in Spanish and another time in English.

Area code 99 unless otherwise noted.

1 Cuadrángulo de las Monjas (Quadrangle of the Nuns) The Spaniards named this group of four buildings surrounding a central plaza. Archaeologists suspect the Maya used it as a school for the military or royalty, housing the students in some 70 small rooms. A fine example of a corbeled arch marks the main entrance at the south side. The facades are strikingly ornate, with stone latticework friezes at the top of each building, interspersed with masonry masks, snakes, and miniature representations of the *na* (a classic Maya hut), still seen in villages throughout the Yucatán Peninsula.

2 Pirámide del Adivinador (Pyramid of the Magician) Said to be the only Maya structure built in an ellipse, this graceful, beautiful pyramid faces west, toward the sun, and stands 92 feet high. Its western stairway slopes at a 60° angle; the eastern stairway is even steeper, but the view is worth the climb. A doorway shaped like the grotesque face of Chac leads into the small temple at the top (you pass through his mouth). Several legends explain the origin of the pyramid— some say it was built in one night by a magical dwarf, others that it housed a magician dwarf king who overthrew an evil leader with

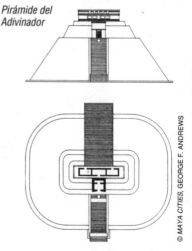

Pirámide del Adivinador

© MAYA CITIES, GEORGE F. ANDREWS

cunning, trickery, and the help of a giant bat speaking for the gods. The original pyramid was rebuilt five times, each new version covering the last and maintaining the basic oval form. The best times to take photos are at sunrise and sunset, when the limestone walls take on a golden glow. At night, in the full moonlight, the pyramid has an ethereal beauty that could never be captured on film.

Campeche

Nestled between the Gulf of Mexico and the jungles of Quintana Roo, Campeche is the most overlooked of the three states on the Yucatán Peninsula. The capital city, also called Campeche, is the most frequently visited part of the state, although only about 50,000 tourists make it here each year. In the early 1500s, the capital was an entry point to the peninsula for the Spanish, who fortified it against pirates in the 1600s with *baluartes* (massive stone walls and gates) that still surround the city.

Much of this state is wild and sparsely inhabited, with a population of only about 700,000. Few roads run to the south and east, where many of the animals that have disappeared from the peninsula—jaguars, ocelots, and deer—roam undisturbed in natural preserves. Maya sites, many of which have barely been explored, are hidden in the rainy jungles to the south and the dry plains to the north. The largest Maya burial ground on the peninsula is on Isla Jaina off Campeche's northwest coast, which is closed to tourists. Some of the most beautiful statues, carvings, and jewelry from the Maya world have been found in burial jars on the banks of Jaina's rivers; most of those treasures are now in museums and collections around the world. **Edzná** is the most frequently visited Maya site in the state, and sits south of the highway between Campeche and **Uxmal**. Built and inhabited between 300 BC and AD 900, **Edzná** is best known for its **Temple of Five Stories,** a stepped pyramid with intricate details. Nearby, the site of **Xtampak** is undergoing sporadic excavation, as are **Becan, Chicana, Xpujil,** and **Calakmul** in the southern part of the state. Tourism services are scarce in this area, though the sites can be reached on a long day trip from either the capital city or Chetumal, on the Quintana Roo coast.

Most of the capital's urban attractions can be seen in a day and are concentrated along the waterfront and the main plaza (bordered by Calles 5, 10, 55, and 57). The **Baluarte San Carlos** (Admission fee; Tu-Su; Circuito Baluartes Sur, at Justo Sierra; no phone) has a small museum of the city's history. **Baluarte Santiago** (Calle 8, at Calle 51) surrounds a lush botanical garden, while **Baluarte de la Soledad** (Tu-Su; Calle 8, at Calle 57; no phone) offers a sweeping view of the town and waterfront from its gun towers, and an enclosed collection of stelae from the state's many Maya archaeological sites. Campeche's **Catedral** (Calle 55, at Calle 8) was constructed from 1650 to 1850 and is far more ornate and Gothic than the one in Mérida. And the **Museo Regional de Campeche** (Admission; Tu-Su; Calle 59, at Calle 44; 981/69111) was originally built for the royal governor in 1804, and houses a respectable collection of artifacts from Maya ruins. For brochures and maps of Campeche, go to the tourist information office in the **Baluarte Santa Rosa** (Circuito Baluartes, at Calle 14; 981/65593). The best hotel in the city is the waterfront **Ramada Inn Campeche** ($$$; Ruíz Cortinez 151, at Calle 59; 981/62233, 800/272.6234), the least expensive hotel in the Ramada chain. Fishing is one of Campeche's leading industries, which means seafood stars on local menus.

Clay ocarina, from Isla Jaina

FROM MAYA DESIGNS

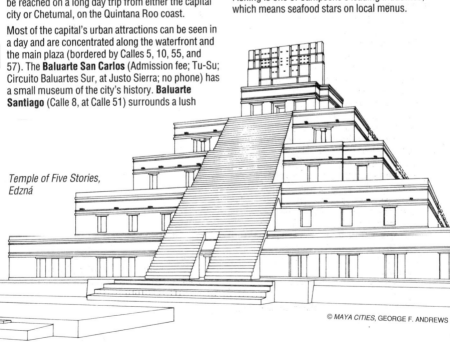

Temple of Five Stories, Edzná

© *MAYA CITIES*, GEORGE F. ANDREWS

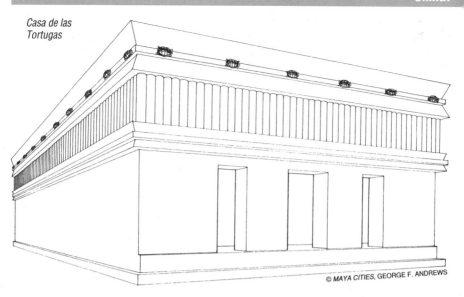

Casa de las Tortugas

© MAYA CITIES, GEORGE F. ANDREWS

3 Juego de Pelota (Ball Court) Set within viewing distance from **Uxmal**'s major buildings, this was the site of ritualistic games involving human sacrifice. This court is far smaller than the one at **Chichén Itzá** and has not been restored.

4 Casa de las Tortugas (House of the Turtles) The upper cornices of this small, simple temple are embedded with a turtle motif. Some of the seven tiny rooms inside have platforms about 16 inches high. Archaeologists have yet to figure out the purpose of these platforms.

5 Palacio Gobierno (Palace of the Governor) Considered by some to be the finest example of pre-Hispanic art in Mesoamerica, the 320-foot-long palace is separated by three corbeled arches, creating narrow passageways or sanctuaries. The intricate friezes along the uppermost section of the palace are made up of geometric carvings overlaid with plumed serpents and Chac masks. What looks like a carved chain at the top cornice is actually a representation of undulating serpents, whose heads once protruded from the corners, but now are gone. The limestone mosaics decorating the building are said to have required more than 20,000 individually cut stones set into a rubble core. The Spaniards gave the palace its current name, but it is believed the Maya used it as a center for astronomy. The building faces east, toward Venus, and every eight years the planet rises on the horizon to a point that is perfectly aligned with the palace's main door.

6 Pirámide Grande (Great Pyramid) Also called the **Pyramid of the Macaws** for the carvings of birds in flight that decorate its walls, this pyramid rises 65 steps in nine levels above **Palacio Gobierno.** Though the view from the **Pyramid of the Magician** is said to be the finest at **Uxmal,** photographers should climb up here for panoramic shots of the city's buildings set against the impenetrable jungle. From here you can see rounded mounds overgrown with grass and trees, probably covering even more buildings waiting to be excavated.

7 Hotel Hacienda Uxmal $$ This was the first hotel at **Uxmal,** and it feels like a private hacienda where the Maya housekeepers, porters, and waiters are considered part of the family. The 80 rooms are furnished with wood-and-wicker rocking chairs, dressers, and headboards. Air-conditioning and cable TV with movie channels have been added to some rooms; hot water is usually abundant. Tropical flowers and trees shade the swimming pool. The restaurant has improved considerably and offers a full breakfast, lunch, and a three-course dinner. The **Cafe Nicte-Ha** has less expensive sandwiches and pizza; snacks are also served at the poolside bar in high season. ♦ Hwy 261 (about 100 yards north of the ruins). 247142. For reservations: Mayaland Tours, Colón 502, Mérida 97000, Mexico. 252122, 800/235.4079; fax 257022

Restaurants/Clubs: Red   **Hotels:** Blue
Shops/ 🌳 Outdoors: Green   **Sights/Culture:** Black

The National University of Mexico (UNAM), created in 1551, is the oldest university in the New World.

On the Road to Ruins

Several small and fascinating Maya sites are scattered along the highways south of Mérida and around **Uxmal.** You can cover most of them on a day trip from Mérida, or spend the night at **Uxmal** and give yourself more time to explore. The most popular route is a circular drive beginning south of **Uxmal** on Highway 261.

*Chac Mask
from Kabah*

Once connected to **Uxmal** 22 kilometers (14 miles) northwest by a now overgrown limestone road called a *sacbe,* **Kabah** is fascinating for its **Palacio de los Mascarones** (Palace of the Masks) and **Codz-Pop** temple, both covered with hundreds of hook-nosed images of the rain god Chac. An unnamed road marked with signs for the ruins turns east off Highway 261 south of Kabah. **Sayil,** five kilometers (three miles) southeast, is undergoing excavation of its three-story palace. Reliefs of Chac adorn the second level of the palace, along with a solitary replica of the Descending God, who is normally associated with **Tulum. Labná,** another eight kilometers (five miles) south, is marked by a large, ornate ceremonial arch with two reproductions of the classic *na* and the ubiquitous Chac. All sites are open daily, and charge admission fees.

About 29 kilometers (18 miles) northeast of **Labná** are the **Caves of Loltún,** an underground system of enormous caverns and passageways with Maya sculptures and surrealistic shapes formed by stalactites. The name Loltún means "flower of the rock," possibly referring to the petal-shaped rooms off one corridor. Visitors must take part in a guided tour of the caves and are not allowed to wander about alone. Tours are offered daily (check at the information desk at **Uxmal** for tour hours), and there is an admission fee.

Mani is a contemporary Maya town at the northeast point of the Maya route loop and is infamous as the site where Fray Diego de Landa, a Spanish Franciscan zealot, burned nearly all the Maya books and documents. A huge 16th-century church and monastery stands in the center of town and was built in an amazingly short seven-month period with the labor of the Maya, who were beaten for honoring their gods. Mani also has the cenote where the wicked mother of the magical dwarf who built the **Uxmal** pyramid is said to live. Legend has it that she would make the well run dry and demand that babies be tossed in as a sacrifice to get the water flowing again.

Ticul, a Maya town near the intersection of Highway 261 and Highway 184, is a good place to stop for lunch, though the bicycle and truck traffic is horrendous. Its main restaurant, **Los Almendros** (★★★$; Calle 23; 207/20021), has a reputation for serving the best Yucatecan cuisine around, and the prices are moderate. The outdoor patio is pleasant when there's a breeze. **Arte Maya,** at the west side of town on Calle 23, is a must-see gallery of Maya sculptures, created by a cooperative of artists who trained with the late original master of Maya carving, Wilbert Gonzalez.

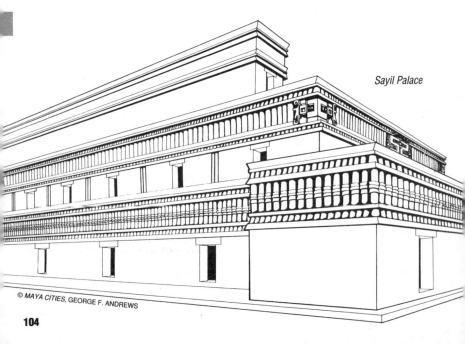

Sayil Palace

© *MAYA CITIES,* GEORGE F. ANDREWS

8 Villa Archeológica $$ Club Med manages the hotel closest to the ruins, a very popular choice with European travelers and tour groups. A two-story white stucco building framing the swimming pool houses 44 small, air-conditioned guest rooms. The dining room serves the best and most expensive food at Uxmal. ♦ On the road leading to the ruins off Hwy 261 (about 20 yards from the entrance to the ruins). 247503, 800/CLUBMED

9 Rancho Uxmal $ Your only option for inexpensive rooms near the ruins is this simple 26-room inn with a very good, moderately priced restaurant and a swimming pool. The rooms have soft mattresses, fans, and private bathrooms with hot showers. It's at least a 45-minute walk to the ruins, but the manager will give you a ride or help you flag down a bus; buses traveling back to Mérida from the ruins will give you a ride to the hotel. ♦ Hwy 261 (about three kilometers/two miles north of the ruins). For reservations: Rancho Uxmal, Calle 26, No 156, Ticul, Yucatán 97860, Mexico. 997/20277, or 99/231576 in Mérida

Bests

Katharine A. Diaz
Group Editor, *Mexico Events & Destinations* Magazine

Mazatlán, Sinaloa
You've heard of Carnival in Rio de Janeiro and New Orleans? Well, right up there with those celebrations are the ones held in Mazatlán. Enjoy parades of elaborate floats, marching bands, beauty queens and much more! But make your reservations early. (Carnival is usually celebrated the few days before Lent.)

Traveling with the kids? Spend an afternoon at the **Mazatlán Aquarium.** There's a fun seal show. In the exhibit area, look for the pejelagarto fish, an unusual lizardy-looking fish that is a living relic from the distant past.

Mazatlán is the shrimp capital of Mexico, so enjoy it for breakfast, lunch, and dinner!

Puerto Vallarta, Jalisco
Sun worship on the area's beautiful beaches, even the ones that can only be reached by boat. But don't leave without exploring the town's cobblestone streets.

Because of the resident and semi-resident artist community in PV, the art galleries are a must-see.

Ixtapa/Zihuatanejo
The **Hotel Villa del Sol** is one of those truly romantic, one-of-a-kind hotels everyone wishes they could stay at at least once in their life. If you can't, you can dine in its outdoor restaurant and let warm ocean breezes create romance under a setting sun.

Yucatán Peninsula
When in **Mérida,** the capital of the state of Yucatán, you'll enjoy the weekly schedule of cultural entertainment. Through the week different squares host programs featuring traditional music or dance. Just ask at the Tourism Office where the action is.

Since you'll probably visit one Maya archaeological site or another (**Chichén Itzá** and **Uxmal** are among the best known), a stop at the **Regional Anthropology Museum of Yucatán** will give you good background information and reveal some of the ancients' secrets. It is housed in an elegant mansion in the posh Montejo district.

Elsewhere on the peninsula, **Campeche,** the capital of the state of **Campeche,** is loaded with history. It is one of the first settlements established by the Spanish, and infamous pirates regularly ravaged it. A walled city, its forts **San Francisco, Soledad, Santiago, Santa Rosa, San Pedro, San Juan,** and **San Carlos** testify to colonial defense strategies. A great divided highway, #180, leads to the city.

Mexico General
Mass Transit Take public mass transit. It's cheaper and real. Try buses, *colectivos,* and, when in Mexico City, the subway. It's clean, user-friendly, and puts New York's to shame.

Public Markets The heart of any town is the public market where buying fresh is still the name of the game. Take the time to notice the variety of herbs, chilis, beans, fruits, vegetables, and cuts of meats. A true cultural experience. You also may find souvenirs cheaper here than in shops.

Food Before visiting a city or region of Mexico, find out what the local specialties are. Is the local dish a special tamal wrapped in cactus leaves? Order one. Is the town known for its sweet bread? Visit a bakery.

Arts and Crafts Like food, traditional arts and crafts vary from region to region and from town to town....

Lifetime Goal Having been bitten by the archaeology bug, I now want to visit every archaeological site in Mexico. That means years of travel.... The Aztec, Maya, Toltec, Totonac, Mixtec, and others left behind a rich legacy.

There are a few small structures along dirt paths leading away from Uxmal's main buildings, including the Casa de la Vieja (House of the Old Woman), reportedly the home of the witch who raised the legendary magician king. Farther on down the trail is a series of buildings—the Colección de Falo (Phallus Collection) including the Templo de Falo (Temple of the Phallus)— known for their unusual representations of phallic symbols (some of which are used as water spouts on the sides of buildings). The Maya are not typically known for their erotic art, and the phallus is not a common ornament except for here. The Grupo del Cementerio (Cemetery Group) was named for the reliefs of skulls and crossbones that were found on the buildings' walls. See the map on page 100 for the precise locations of these structures.

Chichén Itzá

The most famous of the Maya sites, **Chichén Itzá** covers about one square mile of jungle, and the area surrounding the ruins has been cleared and planted with green lawns. Hordes of tourists arrive by the busload from Mérida and Cancún, swarming over the sacred buildings. Tour bus engines drone incessantly as their drivers wait in air-conditioned comfort. But there is a way to appreciate **Chichén Itzá's** grandeur with some sense of isolation— just be at the gates the minute they open (8AM). Shutterbugs who wish to

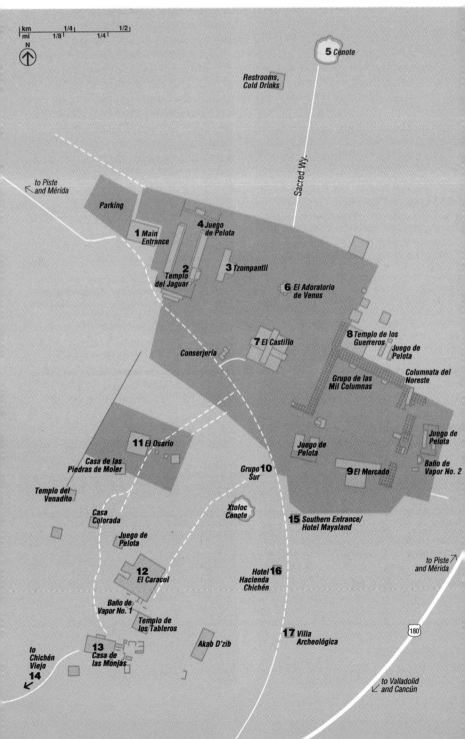

km 1/4 1/2
mi 1/8 1/4

N

5 Cenote

Restrooms,
Cold Drinks

Sacred Wy.

to Piste
and Mérida

Parking

1 Main
Entrance

4 Juego
de Pelota

2 Templo
del Jaguar

3 Tzompantli

6 El Adoratorio
de Venus

7 El Castillo

8 Templo de los
Guerreros

Juego de
Pelota

Conserjería

Columnata del
Noreste

Grupo de las
Mil Columnas

11 El Osario

Casa de las
Piedras de Moler

Juego de
Pelota

Juego de
Pelota

Baño de
Vapor No. 2

Templo del
Venadito

Grupo 10
Sur

9 El Mercado

Casa
Colorada

Xtoloc
Cenote

15 Southern Entrance/
Hotel Mayaland

Juego de
Pelota

to Piste
and Mérida

12 El Caracol

Hotel 16
Hacienda
Chichén

Baño de
Vapor No. 1

180

Templo de
los Tableros

13 Casa de
las Monjas

Akab D'zib

17 Villa
Archeológica

to
Chichén
Viejo

14

to Valladolid
and Cancún

photograph the ruins sans humans should definitely arrive early. Then take a break at midday, when the crowds are at their peak, and return in the midafternoon, about the time the out-of-towners are loading up for their journey back to the cities. Naturally, this schedule works best if you spend the night at one of the captivating hotels nearby .

Giving yourself a couple of days to fully explore **Chichén Itzá** allows you to follow its development chronologically and architecturally. The ceremonial center of **Chichén Itzá** went through several incarnations. At the far southern edge of the site are the oldest buildings, believed to have been constructed around AD 400-600, during the Maya classical period. In AD 900, the site was invaded by the Itzáes, a Maya tribe from the south associated with the Aztecs. The Itzáes were then joined by the Toltecs from around Mexico City in the latter part of the 10th century; the combined groups altered existing buildings and constructed others in a style blending elements from both cultures. The buildings in the **Grupo Sur** (Southern Group), including **El Caracol**, show the beginnings of Toltec influence, with pure Maya elements. Those in the north group have distinct Toltec designs, emphasizing war, struggle, and sacrifice in the carvings. **Chichén Itzá**'s most famous buildings, especially **El Castillo** temple, were completed in this era. At press time, for the first time in many years, some excavations were going on, and certain areas may be roped off when you visit. The major buildings aren't affected, however, and it's interesting to watch the archaeologists and laborers painstakingly working to unearth ancient structures from beneath mounds of trees and dirt.

A dirt road divides the north and south groups; if you have the time, spend one day at each. If you only have a day to see **Chichén Itzá**, plan on spending at least four hours at the site, and more if you wish to climb the several steep buildings and survey the scenery. Guides are available at the entrance, and will entertain you with a mix of fact, folklore, and fantasy for a reasonable sum. Wear comfortable shoes and sunscreen, and carry a bottle of water.

The evening sound-and-light show was completely revamped in 1993, with improved technical systems and a more factual text. The show is worth seeing, plus it gets you into the ruins at night (though you are not allowed to wander about). Wear insect repellent and carry a flashlight. There are two entrances—one from the main parking lot, the other from the south road leading to the hotels. **Chichén Itzá** is located on Highway 180 between Mérida and Cancún, and is open daily. There is an admission fee. The nightly sound-and-light show is presented twice each evening, once in Spanish and once in English.

Area code 985 unless otherwise noted.

1 Main Entrance The Mexican government has prettied up the entryways to many major archaeological sites, putting in parking lots (with parking fees), restricting vendors to permanent stalls, and creating a central gathering place for groups. At **Chichén Itzá**, you enter through a cement corbeled arch to a central shopping/dining area with rest room facilities adequate for busloads of tourists. Backpackers can check their gear at the ticket counter. A large model of the site gives you a good overview of what you will see. Facilities include an excellent bookstore, an ice-cream parlor, a jewelry store, a decent restaurant, and a small museum where several carvings from the buildings are protected from the elements.

Within the Main Entrance:

Cultur Servicios (Shopping Center) This large store is divided into several small shops. There are two excellent sections selling books on the Maya and Mexico, a camera and film department, and a money-exchange counter (however, it offers a dreadful exchange rate for US dollars). You must purchase each item at its corresponding counter. ♦ Daily. No phone

Restaurante Ruinas de Chichén Itzá

★★$ Better than would be expected, this cafeteria-style restaurant serves breakfast all day (including a refreshing fruit plate), plus tourist-oriented treats such as fried chicken, spaghetti, and tuna sandwiches. Some tables are scattered away from the rest under big trees, a perfect spot for writing postcards. ◆ Cafeteria ◆ Daily. No phone

2 Templo del Jaguar (Temple of the Jaguars) A chamber at the base of this temple is decorated with frescoes of warriors in elaborate regalia, with some of the original green and red paint intact. Beehives hang from the ceiling, perhaps in the hope that they will discourage visitors from loitering in the chamber and leaning on the walls, thus rubbing off the paintings. A jaguar sculpture in the middle of the chamber is the last such intact carving at **Chichén,** and has oversized claws and a leering grin much like that of the Cheshire cat. The standing jaguar's back is flat, making a tempting perch for souvenir photos. Consider the cumulative damage of thousands of tourists straddling this ancient cat and refrain from adding to the destruction.

3 Tzompantli Four walls carved with hundreds of skulls surround a four-foot-high platform littered with more freestanding skulls, some with red paint still intact. This is probably where the heads of enemies and ball players (see below) were displayed, impaled on stakes. Carvings of warriors and serpents can be seen on the wall facing the **Templo de los Guerreros** (Temple of the Warriors).

4 Juego de Pelota (Ball Court) This ball court may be the largest in the Maya world, at 272 feet long and 99 feet wide. Sheer cut stone walls run the length of the court on each side, and stone rings protrude near the top of the walls. The game played in this court is believed to have resembled soccer. Players used their heads, shoulders, and feet (but not their hands) to pass a small rubber ball through the rings. It seems the games ended in ritual sacrifice, though it still is not clear whether the winners or losers lost their heads. Sacrifice to the gods was, after all, considered to be an honor, though it may be hard to imagine people playing their hearts out to make such an offering. The acoustics of the court are excellent; a person can hear whispering or clapping at the other end of the court, though the chatter and yelling from your fellow visitors may frustrate your attempts to replicate this experiment.

5 Cenote (Sacred Well) A wide dirt road, which was paved with limestone at one time, leads north from the main cluster of ruins to this oval-shaped sinkhole measuring 198 feet long, 194 feet wide, and 69 feet deep from ground level to the water's surface. The upper sides of the cenote are clogged with tree roots and vines, but the limestone walls become slick and slippery closer to the water.

It was first believed that young female virgins were hurled into these waters to appease the rain gods, but diving archaeologists have since discovered skeletons belonging to individuals of all ages and both sexes. Some believe that the society's castoffs (the sick, old, or degenerate) were sacrificed here to the rain god. Another story is that men, women, and children were all thrown into the well to satisfy the gods in the early morning. The slippery walls were impossible to climb, and most could not swim well enough to survive until noon. Those who remained on the surface were lifted from the water to relate the stories of what they had learned from the spirits in the water. Thousands of artifacts of gold and jade, items highly precious to the Maya, have also been found in the murky depths, which undoubtedly hold more treasures. Several underwater archaeological digs have taken place here, including one headed by Jacques Cousteau. A refreshment stand and rest rooms are located by the cenote.

Piste

The archaeological site of **Chichén Itzá** sits at the edge of Piste, a small village in need of beautification. Acting as the service center for the ruins, Piste has a gas station, a bank (where it may be difficult to change large traveler's checks—bring along the cash you will need), and several restaurants and hotels. For the most part the restaurants are geared toward the tour bus trade and are alternately packed full or totally empty. **Pueblo Maya** (★$; 62777) a tourist attraction on the main road through town, is the best choice for a reasonably priced buffet lunch served in a mock Maya village with artificial streams and artisans' workshops. Piste's hotels have lower rates than those right at the ruins, and most are within easy walking distance of the site. The **Pirámide Inn** ($$; Carretera Mérida-Vallo; 62462) has 44 motel-like rooms, a large pool and courtyard, a good restaurant, and information on tours to other Maya sites. The best budget hotel in the area is the **Hotel Dolores Alba** ($; 99/285650; fax 99/283163), on the highway south of the ruins toward Valladolid. The basic rooms, some with air-conditioning, are more than adequate and hammocks hang beside the small pool. Breakfast and dinner are served in the lobby restaurant. The owners are extremely accommodating—they'll drive you to the ruins in the morning, and flag down buses en route to Valladolid or Mérida for you to continue on your travels.

Restaurants/Clubs: Red Hotels: Blue
Shops/ 🌳 Outdoors: Green **Sights/Culture: Blac**

6 El Adoratorio de Venus (The Temple of Venus) Serpent monsters with human heads coming out of their mouths are carved along the stairways. It is believed these carvings represented the planet Venus. The temple is also known as the **Temple of Chac Mool,** for a statue of this figure that was buried inside (now displayed at the **Museo de Antropología** in Mexico City). A large Chac Mool (a stone carving), patched with cement, stands beside the temple.

El Castillo

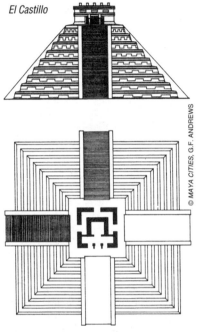

© MAYA CITIES, G.F. ANDREWS

7 El Castillo (The Castle) Also known as the **Temple of Kukulcán,** the grandest of **Chichén Itzá's** ceremonial buildings (loosely called pyramids) looms 98 feet above ground in a regal mass of gray limestone befitting its name. It dominates the site in stark symmetry and tells us much about the Maya concept of time. Four stairways facing the cardinal directions have 91 steps each. Visitors can climb the west stairway, a steep and somewhat frightening ascent and an even more terrifying descent; you can hold onto the rusted chain running down the center. The steps in the four stairways, combined with the single step up to the temple at the top, total 365. Fifty-two panels on the sides represent the years of the Maya calendar, while the 18 terraces each represent a month of the religious year (each month consisting of 20 days, plus a five-day month, equaling 365).

The building is topped by a temple to Kukulcán (known as Quetzacoatl in other parts of Mexico), the deity that led the Toltecs on their migration to Yucatán, and who is represented by a feathered snake. Archaeologists have discovered a more ancient temple inside the pyramid. A slippery damp stairway leads from a small doorway under the north steps up to an altar holding two statues. One is a Chac Mool, a stone carving of a reclining figure with a dish on his chest—where the hearts of sacrificed victims were placed in offerings to the gods; the other is a bejeweled red tiger that originally wore a mosaic disc of jade and turquoise, now in the **Museo de Antropología** in Mexico City. The inner temple is open to the public only a few hours in the morning and again for a few hours in the afternoon. Those prone to claustrophobia should take heed: The stairs are narrow, dark, and winding, and most days there is a line of tourists going both ways, making the trip somewhat frightening.

A great stone serpent head protrudes from the base of the stairway. At the spring and fall equinox, (21 March and 21 September), the afternoon light and shadows strike the stairway and form a picture of Kukulcán undulating out of his temple and wriggling down the pyramid to bless the fertile earth. The engineering skill that went into this amazing project boggles the mind. Thousands of people travel to **Chichén Itzá** to witness the sight, particularly in the spring, since there is always the chance that the fall rains will spoil the spectacle. It's wise to make hotel reservations well in advance—a year ahead is not unreasonable.

8 Templo de los Guerreros (Temple of the Warriors) Also known as **The Temple of a Thousand Columns,** this sits east of **El Castillo.** Stand near the open-mouthed serpent's head at the northwest corner of **El Castillo** for a great photo of the ornate serpent and the towering pyramid juxtaposed against a lineup of white limestone pillars. The temple is much like the **Temple of Venus** in the Toltec center of **Tula** north of Mexico City. Archaeologists speculate the Toltecs carried plans for the building from their homeland to **Chichén Itzá** when they traveled to Yucatán and overtook the Maya in AD 900. The columns, running in straight rows in front of the temple and along its southern side, are carved on all four squared-off facades with re-liefs of warriors, most carrying lances. Rising above the columns,

FROM MAYA DESIGNS

Feathered-serpent column

the temple has several distinctive characteristics. The side of the front stairway is shaped in a corbeled arch, and masks of the snout-nosed rain god, Chac, protrude

Chac Mool

GERARD GARBUTT

from the sides of the stairway. A reclining Chac Mool sits near the top of the steps, and carvings of feathered serpents, jaguars, and warriors are still visible on the walls.

9 El Mercado (The Market) Southeast from the **Templo de los Guerreros,** a narrow pathway leads to this little-visited cluster of ruins. A large columned portico extends to the north side forming two parallel galleries. In one of these is an altar with bas-reliefs. In the rear is a rectangular courtyard surrounded by columns, which some suspect may have been covered with palm thatch and used as a market area. At press time, there was some reconstruction going on in this area.

10 Grupo Sur The old road from Mérida used to cut right through **Chichén Itzá,** dividing the ruins in the north from those in the south. A pathway now leads from the remains of this road to the Southern Group (also called the Central Group). There is a refreshment stand at the beginning of this trail, with tables and chairs shaded by a *palapa* (thatch-roofed hut).

11 El Osario (The Tomb of the Great Priest) This tomb looks today like a 20-foot-high pile of rubble. Most of its importance lay in the six tombs found inside, particularly in one beneath the earth's surface, which contained a skeleton and offerings of jade, pearls, and gold. At press time, archaeologists were reconstructing this building and excavating other structures in this area.

12 El Caracol (The Observatory) To some, this is the most beautiful building in the Maya world. A circular tower sits atop two tiered platforms, with small windows facing the four cardinal points. A spiral staircase inside the platforms winds to the top, but it is not open to the public. The name means "the snail," and supposedly refers to this staircase. The building is believed to have been used by astronomers. It is particularly beautiful late in the day, when its tower glows gold in the light of the setting sun.

In Mexico any beach that is 60 feet from the high-water line is accessible to everyone—at no charge. Hotel owners cannot keep anyone from enjoying the beach or the sea no matter how close it is to their establishments.

13 Casa de las Monjas (House of the Nuns) The Spaniards believed virgins who were destined to be sacrificed lived in this building, and thus they gave it this monastic name. Climbing the pyramid gets more difficult every year, as the limestone steps continue crumbling, but the view is well worth the fright. Crouch behind the small door at the top for a spectacular photo of **El Caracol** and **El Castillo.** There are several small chambers at the base of the building in back.

Voyage to Valladolid

Highway 180 is the most scenic route east from **Chichén Itzá** to Cancún and passes right through Valladolid, the second-largest city in Yucatán. The new *autopista* bypasses the city, but it's worth the time to exit the highway long enough to tour this colonial gem. Valladolid's civic leaders are beginning to realize the value of tourism, and are making a concerted effort to clean up and revitalize the central area. The narrow streets leading to this pleasant, provincial city's main square are lined with auto repair shops, hardware stores, and gas stations. Buses, trucks, cars, and bicycles clog the streets, competing for the right of way; once you reach the plaza, pull into a parking place for a break from the confusion.

Young girls and women selling woven bracelets, embroidered dresses, and hammocks will most likely descend upon you the second you open the car doors. If you're not interested in their wares, just say "*no, gracias*" and keep walking toward the peaceful Plaza Principal. Take note of the central fountain, with its rather garishly painted statue of a woman bearing a water jug surrounded by green plaster frogs. The side streets off the plaza are filled with tiny luncheonettes and shops selling paper products, fabrics, plastic wares, and clothing. Valladolid is the center of commerce for the region between Mérida and the coast, and residents from rural villages make regular trips here for everything from machetes to high heels.

It's also a favorite of travelers who wish to visit the ruins of **Chichén Itzá** without paying high prices for accommodations. The ruins are about an hour away by bus or car, and by staying here you have the advantage of being in a traditional colonial city with few of the trappings of tourism. **El Mesón de Marqués** ($$; Calle 39, on the north side of the plaza; 62073) is the best hotel in town, with 30 rooms in a converted 18th-century home and a newer addition. The rooms facing the plaza have the best view and the most traffic noise; those near the courtyard pool are quiet. Amenities are negligible, but there is a fairly good restaurant, which is a comfortable place to stop for a cool drink on your drive through town. The **Hotel María de la Luz** ($; Calle 2, on the west side of the plaza; 62070) is another good option, with 28 rooms (some air-conditioned) and a small restaurant. Once you've toured the town, consider purchasing a hammock from the local vendors. Nearby villages are known for their high-quality hammocks, and the prices are much less than those in Cancún.

14 Chichén Viejo A pathway just west of the **Casa de las Monjas** leads to the oldest ruins of **Chichén Itzá,** which are only partially excavated. The farther you wander on this isolated jungle path, the more you begin to understand what it must have been like when early explorers first stumbled upon the ruins. Overgrown mounds on both sides of the path are labeled with rickety signs that point out the **Temple of the Phallus** and the **Temple of the Lintels.** The carvings on these buildings are similar to those found in the Puuc region of **Uxmal,** with lacy latticework and distinctive Chac masks. Maya guides are usually waiting at the beginning of the path, and can lead you deep into the jungle, away from the tourist-oriented parts of **Chichén Itzá** into a world that seems untouched by modern influences.

15 Southern Entrance The old road that once carried traffic through **Chichén Itzá** leads to a rear entrance of the ruins and past a few hotels to join the main road again. Area Maya residents still use the road as a shortcut, riding their bikes over dirt ridges and ruts past a steady stream of tourists. In the high season Maya women hang clotheslines by the tour buses and sell T-shirts, blankets, and shawls. Several tour companies park their buses just outside the back gate, where you can pay the entrance fee and come and go from the ruins to the hotels. Guests at the three hotels along this road have easy access to the ruins and can take a break at midday to swim, eat, and sleep.

15 Hotel Mayaland $$$ Enchanting and unrelentingly romantic, this hotel sits in a hundred-acre jungle of red ginger blossoms, fuchsia bougainvillea, and towering trees nearly hiding guest cottages resembling Maya huts. Inside the 62-room hotel, mosquito nets hang over beds that have Maya designs carved in their mahogany frames. Wooden shutters cover screened windows, ceiling fans lazily stir the tropical air, and low-slung cane and mahogany chairs sit on front porches. More modern rooms in the main building have air-conditioning, TVs, antique furnishings, and tiled balconies overlooking the gardens; those at the front of the building have a breathtaking view of **El Caracol.**

The food in the restaurant here is the only flaw—dinners consist of only two or three choices of entrées, all mediocre. It would be far better if the Maya cooks were allowed to prepare their culture's cuisine instead of chicken breasts and fish fillets covered with undistinguished sauces. ♦ Off Hwy 180 (at the southern road to the ruins). 62777. For reservations in Mérida: Mayaland Tours. 99/252122, 800/235.4079; fax 99/257022

16 Hotel Hacienda Chichén $$ So mysterious they seem almost haunted, the 20 rooms here are located in small cottages scattered about the grounds, many with secret paths leading from their porches into the jungle to **Chichén Viejo.** The main building and stone archway in front of it are the remains of a 17th-century hacienda, complete with a small Catholic church said to be the oldest on the peninsula.

The hotel is only open during the high season (roughly from 1 November to 30 April), and advance reservations are strongly advised. At press time, the owners were considering opening in the low season as well, so it's worth checking before you book a room elsewhere. Meals are served in the central dining room and on the main building's porch looking over the grounds. An old railroad track runs by the church into the jungle, serving as a path to the ruins. Another trail runs to **El Caracol** from behind the cottages. The Maya workers at the hotel can guide you along these walks during their off hours (for a tip). ♦ Off Hwy 180 (at the southern road to the ruins). No phone. For reservations in Mérida: Calle 60 No 488, Mérida, Yucatán 97000, Mexico. 99/248844, 800/624.8451; fax 99/245011

17 Villa Archeológica $$ One of several hotels built by the government near archaeological sites and managed by Club Med, this place is typically filled with tour groups from the **Club Med** in Cancún, though individual guests are welcome. The 32 small, air-conditioned rooms are decorated with local folk art, and there's a good library on the Maya. The pool is a cool, shaded spot perfect for relaxing after climbing the ruins. There's also a French restaurant, easily the most expensive dining spot around. ♦ Off Hwy 180 (at the southern road to the ruins). 62830, 800/CLUBMED

Thirteen Mexicans made *Forbes's* list of billionaires in 1993; Mexico now ranks fourth worldwide in the number of billionaire residents.

Mexico Insight, 1 Aug 1993

Restaurants/Clubs: Red   **Hotels:** Blue
Shops/ 🌳 Outdoors: Green   **Sights/Culture:** Black

Cancún

Just like a teenager, Cancún is audacious, flamboyant, and terribly absorbed with its image. When the kid of the Caribbean was only 15 years old, its backers spent millions of dollars to host the 1989 Miss Universe Pageant, and the new resort area became the tropical backdrop for viewers from all over the world. Naturally, the coverage brought Cancún international attention and a willing audience. The next year, more than 1.5 million tourists stopped by to see if the sand was as white and the water as crystalline as it appeared on television.

They found a 14-mile-long island whose windward side was a nearly uninterrupted stretch of talcum sand so white it never burned their feet. Glitzy, glamorous hotels stood proudly in line facing the endless horizon of sky against sea. Languid sunbathers lounged under the shade of *palapas* (thatch-roofed huts) or sipped piña coladas at swim-up bars. What they found was tropical mystique, Mexican style.

Cancún is designed to dazzle and mesmerize, to fill visitors' days with sun, sea and shopping, and nights with a whirl of music, dining, dancing, and gazing at star-filled skies. Palms wave lazily beside shimmering pools, and rock music collides with mariachi tunes, which blend into reggae or salsa in a constant throbbing beat. Parasailers float high above the shore, while neon-bright Windsurfers fly by, skimming the surface of the sea like a gull. Swimmers and snorkelers move leisurely from their towels to the water and back, skin glistening with oil and sweat.

Standing on the beach you'd hardly know you were in Mexico, save for the occasional drift of conversational Spanish. Margaritas and guacamole are popular snacks by the pool, but it's not as though you have to adapt to another culture. Cancún was born to be a resort that would lure and captivate foreigners, and it does just that. The first tourist hotels opened in 1974; by the end of 1994 there were more than 126,000 rooms and suites in some 118 hotels, in varying degrees of luxury. There's no scarcity of lavish accommodations, such as at the recently opened, European-style **Ritz Carlton**, but the good news is Cancún is becoming more affordable for the tourist of moderate means. Package deals and charter flights are now common, lowering prices far below what you are quoted if you just show up at the front desk.

The relaxation in foreign trade arrangements under the presidency of Carlos Salinas de Gortari brought a proliferation of US franchises to Cancún, where the golden arches are commonplace and delivery men carry pizzas strapped to their mopeds. There are 17 shopping centers here and more than 300 restaurants—more than enough to satisfy the most demanding visitor.

Beyond the hotel zone is the backbone of Cancún—a city of 250,000 residents primarily immigrants from throughout Mexico and the world. Most travelers venture into the downtown area along **Avenidas Tulum** and **Yaxchilán**. But to really appreciate Cancún's geographical and cultural heritage, you need to get *out* of town. Ferries and tours frequently head east across the Caribbean to **Isla Mujeres**, a traditional favorite of the getaway traveler. Tour buses ply the roads from Cancún to the Maya ruins of **Chichén Itzá, Cobá, and Tulum**, all within a half day's distance. The hundred-mile-long Cancún-Tulum Corridor is filling up rapidly with one-of-a-kind hideaway hotels and overwhelming master-planned resorts. If you have at least a week's vacation, rent a car for a day or two and explore. Once you are about 10 miles out of town, surrounded by scrubby jungle interspersed with thatch-roofed Maya huts, Cancún slips away like an aberration. You'll understand why a handful of bankers and politicians flew over the eastern wilderness of the **Yucatán Peninsula** and decided to create a tropical paradise.

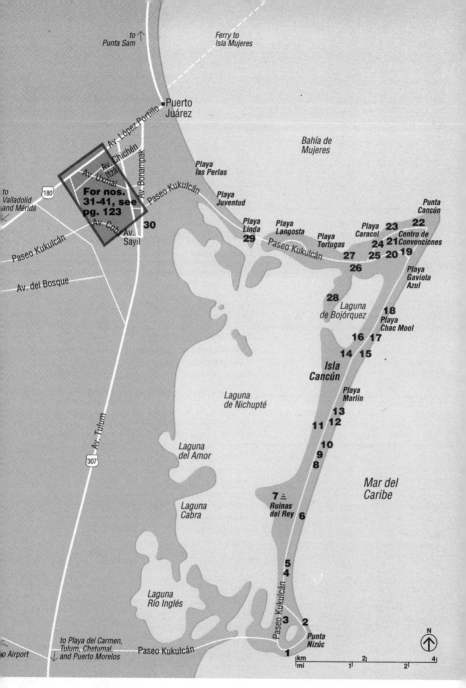

to
Punta Sam

Ferry to
Isla Mujeres

●Puerto
Juárez

Bahía de
Mujeres

Av. López Portillo
Av. Chichén Itzá
Av. Uxmal
Av. Bonampak
Av. Cobá
Av. Sayil
Paseo Kukulcán

to
Valladolid
and Mérida

180

For nos.
31-41, see
pg. 123

30

Playa
las Perlas

Playa
Juventud

Playa
Linda
29

Playa
Langosta

Playa
Tortugas

Playa
Caracol

23
24
27
25
26
20

22
21
19

Punta
Cancún

Centro de
Convenciones

Playa
Gaviota
Azul

Av. del Bosque

Paseo Kukulcán

28

Laguna
de Bojórquez

18
Playa
Chac Mool

16 **17**

14 **15**

Isla
Cancún

Playa
Marlin

Laguna
de Nichupté

13
11 **12**

10
9
8

Av. Tulum

307

Laguna
del Amor

Mar del
Caribe

Laguna
Cabra

7
Ruinas
del Rey **6**

Laguna
Río Inglés

5
4

3 **2**
Punta
Nizúc

1

Paseo Kukulcán

to Playa del Carmen,
Tulum, Chetumal,
and Puerto Morelos

to Airport

Paseo Kukulcán

N

km
mi   1   1   2   2   4

Area code 98 unless otherwise noted.

Getting to Cancún

Airport

Cancún International Airport is 10 kilometers (six miles) south of Punta Nizúc, the southern end of the hotel zone, and 14 kilometers (nine miles) southwest of Cancún.

Minibuses run from the airport into the downtown area and to the hotel zone, and cost far less than individual taxis.

Airlines

AeroCancún	860140
AeroCozumel and **AeroCaribe**	842000, 860083
Aeroméxico	843571, 860079
American	860055, 860151
Aviateca	843938, 871386
Continental	860040, 860169
Lacsa	873101, 875101
Mexicana	874444, 860120

Northwest	860046
Taesa	874314, 860085
United	860025, 860158

Getting around Cancún

Sidewalks and a bicycle path run along the short arm of the hotel zone's "7" shape, but for the most part Paseo Kukulcán is friendlier to cars than pedestrians. The longer north-south leg of the "7" has some scenic stretches on the lagoon side of the road; the hotel side is filled with ramps and driveways and is not a safe place to stroll absentmindedly. Except when traveling short distances, you're best off taking a cab or bus.

Buses

Ruta 1 and *Ruta 2* city buses go to the beaches along Paseo Kukulcán and to Punta Nizúc in the hotel zone. *Ruta 8* goes to Puerto Juárez and the ferry to Isla Mujeres. Catch the bus in front of the tourist office on Avenida Tulum, or at stops along Paseo Kukulcán. **Autocar Cancún** buses travel the length of the hotel zone into downtown until midnight, and are the least expensive way to get around. Bus stops are marked, though these buses will stop nearly anywhere you flag them down.

The bus station is located in downtown Cancún at the intersection of Tulum and Uxmal. Call 841378 or 843948 for schedule information.

Car Rental

The following agencies have offices at the airport and in hotels:

Avis	842328, 830828
Budget	840730, 840204
Econo-Rent	841826, 841435
National	860152, 851000

Taxis

Cabs wait at most hotels and can be easily flagged on the street.

FYI

Emergencies

Canadian Consulate Plaza Mexico 843716

Clínica Quirúrgica del Caribe (24-hour medical clinic), Supermanzana 63, Lote 13..............842516

Hospital Americano (open 24 hours), Calle Viento 15 ....846133, 846430

Police 841913, 841202

Red Cross...841616

Total Assist (24-hour assistance), Calle Claveles 5.... ....848082, 848017

US Consulate Ave Nader 842411

Money

You can change money at the airport, hotels, and banks, with the latter giving you the best rate. Banks are open Mondays through Fridays from 9AM to 1:30PM. Some have special hours for changing money, usually from 10AM to 1 or 2PM. *Casas de cambio* (exchange houses) are scattered around downtown and open throughout the day and evening. International credit cards and US dollars are accepted in most restaurants, hotels, and shops. Try not to be short of cash on Sundays, because it can be difficult to change money on that day, except in some hotels. Always keep bills of small denominations on hand, since it can be difficult to change larger bills (except at banks).

Tours

Archaeological Travel agencies and tour companies abound in Cancún. Most offer the same basic side trips with assorted themes and amenities. Probably the single most popular excursion is a trip down the mainland coast to the Maya ruins of **Tulum**, with a stop at **Xel-Há**, an underwater preserve. The **Chichén Itzá** trip is popular and enjoyable, although it's somewhat grueling, since the drive takes about three hours each way. If you're an archaeology buff, consider spending a night near the ruins rather than trying to see everything in one day.

Check your hotel's tour desk for an overview of your options, and ask fellow travelers about their experiences with the different companies.

Mayaland Tours (Hotel America, Av Tulum (at Av Brisa); 872450; fax in Mérida 99/252397) operates at hotels in **Chichén Itzá** and **Uxmal,** and has several options for short and extended explorations, including an economical car-rental package combined with stays at their hotels. Their **Chichén Itzá** tour includes transportation in the most comfortable tour buses around, and meals at the **Mayaland Hotel.**

Cruises and Water Activities There are more than a dozen marinas in the hotel zone, at least as many boat tour operators, and countless opinions about the quality and price of their services. Talk with as many people as possible about their experiences before you choose a company; much depends on the crew aboard a particular ship, which can change frequently. Among the more popular boat trips are day tours to Isla Mujeres with snorkeling, lunch, and shopping, or evening tours with dinner and a show; submarine tours at the reefs; snorkeling trips; and sunset cruises. Most marina operations conduct other water tours and also rent water runners.

Aqua Tours (Paseo Kukulcán, Km 6.5, across from **Fat Tuesday;** 830400, 831137) has a dive center and cruises to Isla Mujeres.

Marina Aqua Ray (Paseo Kukulcán, Km 10.5; 831763, 831773) is a full-service water sports center with locations around the hotel zone.

Nautibus, a floating submarine, tours the lagoon and the reef from the Playa Linda dock (833552, 833602).

Playa Linda is headquarters for many of the sightseeing boats, specialty cruises, fishing boats, and transport to Isla Mujeres. The complex includes a taco stand, long-distance telephone and fax office, and representatives from most of the cruise companies. On Paseo Kukulcán across from Plaza Nautilus, it's a worthwhile place to stop to check out your options.

Visitors Information

The **Oficina de Tourismo** (Tourism Office) is open daily. It's located at Avenida Tulum 29 (between Avs Cobá and Uxmal). 848073.

Area code 98 unless otherwise noted.

1 Club Med $$$$ This 300-room resort claims one of the most spectacular and isolated fingers of land at the far southern end of the hotel zone, jutting between Laguna de Nichupté and the Caribbean on Punta Nizúc. It's close to the airport and the coastal highway to **Tulum**, yet far enough away from downtown Cancún to make visiting here a special excursion. The all-inclusive system here is probably one of the best values around, since restaurant tabs and hotel rates in Cancún are high by Mexican standards. Scuba divers and water sports enthusiasts really get their money's worth, and can easily spend a week exploring the sea from the compound without getting bored. Side trips to **Chichén Itzá** and **Cobá** with meals and overnight stays at the excellent Club Med–run **Villas Arqueológica** are well worth the extra charge. There are no facilities for children under 12. ♦ Paseo Kukulcán (between Hwy 307 and Punta Nizúc). 842409, 800/CLUB.MED; fax 842090

2 Restaurant Punta Nizúc ★★★$ A small fishing cooperative provides the catch of the day at this rustic restaurant beyond the hotel zone. The anglers have built a wooden walkway along the mangrove-lined shore, leading to the eatery. Order the whole fish (you can choose from snapper, grouper, or dorado—whatever's in season) either grilled, fried, or *tikin-xic* (Maya style, baked in banana leaves). The meals and drinks (including the popular Cuba Libres made of rum, Coca-Cola, and lime) are inexpensive, and the experience more authentically Mexican than most in Cancún. ♦ Seafood ♦ Daily lunch. Paseo Kukulcán (at the foot of the Punta Nizúc bridge). No phone

3 Westin Regina $$$$ This hotel gets major points for its attention to detail. From the outside, the soaring structure seems almost forbidding, but the 385 guest rooms are delightfully comfortable and luxurious, and have windows that open and allow you to fall asleep to the sounds of the surf and the cool breeze. The mini-bar in each room has a sink, and ice machines are located on every floor. The shower is in a separate stall from the bathtub, and toiletries include laundry soap.

Though far from the majority of restaurants and shops in the hotel zone, this property is close to the airport and Highway 307, and has

its own dining spots and boutiques. It sits between the sea and the lagoon, with deep blue swimming pools on both sides. The surf gets rough here, and though the rocky point seems like a perfect snorkeling spot, the waves make it nearly impossible for you to keep your snorkel clear of water. The hotel's lagoon-side pool is a calmer spot for reading and relaxing in the sun, and is by far the best spot for viewing the colors of the Caribbean sunset. ♦ Paseo Kukulcán (between Punta Nizúc and Punta Cancún). 850444, 850086, 800/228.3000; fax 850666

For the Birds

Isla Contoy, 30 kilometers (19 miles) north of Isla Mujeres, is a nearly four-mile-long national wildlife preserve with more than 70 species of birds that inhabit the swamps and lagoons undisturbed. Day tours to the island from Isla Mujeres and Cancún include a bird-watching cruise along the island's edge, and a stop for snorkeling, swimming, and lunch. Pink flamingos migrate to the island in April, and sea turtles lay their eggs on the beaches from June through August. The boat trip is at least 1.5 hours from Mujeres to Contoy, and three hours from Cancún. For optimum comfort, choose a boat with a bathroom, sun covering, life jackets, and cold drinks. The ride can be rough if the winds are up. Check at the Fishermen's Cooperative office (Av Rueda Medina; 987/70274) on Isla Mujeres or with travel agents in Cancún for information on boat trips.

Río Lagartos (Alligator River) is actually an estuary visited by thousands of pink flamingos every spring and summer during mating season, and a national park with few facilities. Birders and naturalists are attracted to the park, 266 kilometers (166 miles) northwest of Cancún, year-round; its residents include egrets, herons, cormorants, and an occasional falcon or hawk. The flamingos are the big draw, however, filling the sky with a rush of pink feathers in flight. The alligators (for which the area was named) were hunted into near-extinction and are now protected. Check with travel agents in Cancún for trips to **Lagartos.**

The **Sian Ka'an Biosphere Reserve** on the Boca Paila Peninsula south of Cancún is a prime bird-watching spot. Day trips to the preserve can be arranged through **Amigos de Sian Ka'an** in Cancún (845629). It's much easier, and preferable, to go with a group; there are no boats for hire at the preserve to tour the lagoons—the highlight of the trip.

4 Solaris $$ With 184 rooms, this is an intimate, secluded hideaway in the midst of the hotel zone. The narrow buildings are stacked in graded heights to provide optimum views of the pool and the endless sea. Curved walls and arches frame and separate alcoves in the public areas and rooms, giving a sense of privacy and space. A Mediterranean theme prevails in the architecture and decor, with stark white walls and blue sea and sky reminiscent of hillside villas on the Greek isles. It's a great place to escape, relax, and indulge in your fantasies; there's also a restaurant. ♦ Paseo Kukulcán, Km 20.5 (between Punta Nizúc and Punta Cancún). 850100, 800/368.9779, 713/266.9797; fax 850354, 713/266.9909

5 Puerto al Sol $$$$ Taking the wallet-free theme to new heights of luxury, this hotel offers amenities more typical of the glitzy pay-as-you-go hotels, including in-room whirlpool tubs, daily wake-up calls with a carafe of coffee and basket of *pan dulce* (sweet bread), ocean views from all the rooms, and a variety of suites and combinations of interconnected rooms to accommodate families and friends. As in most all-inclusive resorts, the emphasis here is on food, drink, and fun, with a choice of restaurants and bars, and scheduled activities such as aerobics, volleyball, and mock bullfights presented by local matadors. The hotel's health club is a major plus, with its state-of-the-art exercise equipment and indoor lap pool. Tours to surrounding ruins are available at extra cost, or free with certain package deals. ♦ Paseo Kukulcán, Km 20 (between Punta Nizúc and Punta Cancún). 851555, 305/371.7208; fax 852040, 305/375.9508

6 Days Inn El Pueblito $$ Dwarfed by the competition in size and style, this is the least expensive hotel on this stretch of beach, yet it is also more attractive than you might expect. Colonial-style buildings in white stucco with bubble gum–pink trim are staggered down a hillside beside five swimming pools with the requisite volleyball net and swim-up bar. On the south side of the complex a water slide flows from the top of the hill to the bottom. The 239 rooms are far from luxurious, but most have balconies facing the pools or the sea, and all have cable TV and phones. A good choice for those on a budget who care more about being near a fabulous beach than staying in a fancy room. The coffee shop/restaurant is a dependable place, but nothing special. ♦ Paseo Kukulcán, Km 17.5 (between Punta Nizúc and Punta Cancún). 850672, 800/90014, 800/325.2525; fax 850731

7 Ruinas del Rey Overlooked and neglected thus far, this modest Maya site has become the centerpiece of an 18-hole golf course that was scheduled to open at press time. The small temples and burial site were first excavated in 1954 and restored in 1975, and are hardly impressive if you've been to the larger Maya sites. You may visit the site even if you don't plan to play. ♦ Daily. Paseo Kukulcán, Km 17 (on the lagoon side)

8 Fiesta Americana Condessa $$$$ Offering spectacular sea views from every vantage point, the terra-cotta buildings at this 500-room property are terraced around gardens, streams, waterfalls, and swimming pools. Cool marble floors, pale wood furnishings, and plant-filled balconies make the rooms comfortable havens during the midday heat, especially if there's a good movie on cable TV. You'll have to take a bus or cab from here to the hotel zone's major malls, which isn't a drawback if you like being away from the crush of traffic and tourists. The cafe and the French and Italian restaurants are far better than you'd expect in a hotel, and you can work off the calories on the tennis courts or in the health club. The long, uncrowded white sand beach is perfect for solitary walks. ♦ Paseo Kukulcán, Km 16.5 (between Punta Nizúc and Plaza Kukulcán). 851000, 800/FIESTA1; fax 851650

9 Up & Down There's no shortage of discos and dance clubs in Cancún, with new places opening all the time and old ones revamping their decor and their light shows. But this one is certainly unique—it's a gourmet restaurant, romantic nightclub, and state-of-the-art disco all in one. Wear your glitziest outfit here—no shorts or sandals are allowed. ♦ Cover. Daily. Paseo Kukulcán, Km 16.5 (near the Mélia hotel). 852910

10 Ritz Carlton $$$$ Decidedly European in decor and service, this brought a new level of elegance to Cancún when it opened in 1993. From the street, the pale pink hotel is understated, but the beveled glass doors opening into the lobby dispel such perceptions. Glistening crystal chandeliers, gleaming marble floors, and French provincial furnishings project an opulent style that is reflected throughout the property. All 369 rooms and suites have televisions and mini-bars hidden inside elegant armoires; glassed-in showers separate from the bathtubs; and balconies looking out on the formal landscaped gardens, pools, and beach. Within the building, the hallways leading to the guest rooms face a nine-story central atrium with a stained-glass dome ceiling. The service throughout the hotel is excellent, and even more so in the private **Club Lounge,** where gourmet treats are offered throughout the day, and secluded seating areas overlook the atrium. The health club, steam rooms, saunas, and massage are all included in the room rate. Locals have discovered the **Club**

Grill restaurant, beloved for its extraordinary desserts and romantic dance music in the lounge. If you are accustomed to impeccable service and European style, this is the place for you. ♦ Paseo Kukulcán (at Retorno del Rey). 850808, 800/241.3333; fax 851015

11 **Mexico Magico** With US dollars accepted as readily as pesos, and fast-food franchises more prevalent than taco stands, Cancún doesn't really feel like Mexico. To make up for this lack of cultural identity, a make-believe, sanitized version of Mexico was recently built on the lagoon at the ever-expanding Isla Dorado housing development. Garish walls painted in vivid blue, pink, and yellow surround a complex of plazas and buildings that supposedly represent the various regions of Mexico. Construction is ongoing, and, ultimately, the park will feature musical shows in nine theaters, eight restaurants, discos, and shops. ♦ Admission. Daily 6PM to midnight. Paseo Kukulcán (at Laguna de Nichupté). No phone

12 **Casa Turquesa** $$$$ More like a private villa than a hotel, this hostelry has 28 elegantly furnished suites set behind a guarded gate. Oceanfront balconies with private hot tubs, in-room CD players and VCRs, huge dressing rooms, and an abundance of Caswell-Massey toiletries add to the comfort level. Striped blue-and-white awnings shade guests by the swimming pool and on the pristine white beach, and there's a charming restaurant for those who want to extend the tranquil mood to mealtimes. A member of the Small Luxury Hotels of the World, it's less fussy than the **Ritz Carlton,** but still exudes an air of grand luxury. ♦ Paseo Kukulcán, Km 13.5 (behind Plaza Kukulcán). 852924, 800/525.4800; fax 852922

13 **Plaza Kukulcán** This is the newest of Cancún's many shopping malls in the more recently developed stretch of the hotel zone. The enclosed, air-conditioned plaza has the usual sprawl of sportswear, jewelry, and folk art shops, trendy bars and restaurants, plus two movie theaters, and Cancún's only bowling alley. ♦ Daily. Paseo Kukulcán, Km 13 (between Punta Nizúc and Punta Cancún). 852200

Within Plaza Kukulcán:

Cenacolo ★★$$ The name loosely means a gathering of artists, poets, and writers, though at this restaurant it's hard to tell the artistic leanings of the patrons, all of whom are wolfing down plates of pasta. Locals seem willing to venture into the hotel zone for fried calamari with aioli, *pasta puttanesca* (anchovy, tomato, and olive sauce), and seafood fettuccine. Outdoor tables overlook the traffic and lagoon; indoors is more clublike, with regular patrons mingling at the bar. ♦ Italian ♦ Daily lunch and dinner. 872888, 853603

14 **Flamingo Plaza** If you're feeling the least bit homesick for US-style shopping, you'll be comforted by the layout and content of this modernistic, Maya-decor mall. A food court contains a dazzling (or appalling) array of familiar chain pizza, sandwich, and burger stands. Many of the shops are name-brand outlets (Gucci, Disney), with a few bargains amid the high-priced trendy togs. ♦ Daily. Paseo Kukulcán, Km 11 (between Punta Nizúc and Punta Cancún). 832855, 832945

Within the Flamingo Plaza:

Artland You'll get an abbreviated education in Maya culture just by studying the works of art on display at this gallery that specializes in batiks and rubbings of Maya carvings. There are also paintings of the ruins, many with printed explanations of the deities and their purposes. ♦ M-Sa. 832855, 832945

Gold's Gym Yes, this is a branch of the bodybuilding emporium that turns out muscled, bronzed gods in LA. There's even a display of its workout wear, in case you want hip souvenirs. Daily and weekly rates are available for tourists. ♦ M-F until 10PM; Sa-Su until 9PM. 832933

Xcaret A maze of Mexican curios, from tacky coconut-shell gorillas bearing tequila bottles to *muñecas* (painted pottery dolls) by Oaxacan artist Josefina Aguilar. Check out the rain sticks—three-foot-high bamboo poles strung on the inside with beads that sound like falling rain when the pole is inverted. ♦ Daily until 10PM. 832855

15 **Continental Villas Plaza** $$ You can't miss this lineup of 26 pink villas and a 635-room hotel curving along the boulevard across from the businesses on Laguna de Bojórquez. The location is ideal, at the beginning of the hotel zone's busiest stretch of hotels, restaurants, and shops; there are water sports facilities on both the Caribbean and the lagoon. Arrayed like a frothy strawberry whipped-cream confection on a thin strip of land between the road and the beach, the resort has seven restaurants and bars, including **Le Buffet,** which serves nightly all-you-can-eat spreads. The pastel color scheme carries through into the light and airy rooms and suites. ♦ Paseo Kukulcán, Km 11 (between Punta Nizúc and Punta Cancún). 831022, 800/88.CONTI, 713/448.2846; fax 851403, 713/448.0417

Isla Mujeres

ISLA MUJERES

Punta Norte
Isla Mujeres
Ferry to Puerto Juárez
Isla Chico
Airport
Mar del Caribe
Parque de las Tortugas
Av. Rueda Medina
Laguna Makax
Salina Grande
Bahía de Mujeres
Hacienda Mundaca
Playa Pescador
Playa Lancheros
Parque Garrafón Nacional
Playa Garrafónes
Punta Sur
Manchones Reef
N
km
mi
1
1
2

The Island of Women, just eight miles east of **Cancún,** is the perfect destination for those seeking peaceful surroundings, moderate prices, and the ambience of a small Mexican town.

Unlike Cancún, the island has no high-rise hotels, discos, or shopping malls, and few distractions from its main attraction: the beach. The relaxed mood is contagious: visitors quickly settle into a languid routine, alternating between the sand and sidewalk cafes. Some who initially plan to spend a night or two end up extending their stays, convinced that they've discovered the ideal Caribbean hideaway.

All travelers to Isla Mujeres must pass through Cancún, since the island has no airport. A passenger ferry runs several times daily from **Puerto Juárez,** three miles north of Cancún, to Isla Mujeres, and takes about 40 minutes each way. There also is a car ferry that leaves from nearby **Punta Sam** (north of Puerto Juárez) seven times a day. Innumerable tour boats ply the waters between the two destinations; most have a cruise theme of some sort—pirate, dinner, sunset, and so on. Some travel at night to a seemingly secluded beach for a Mexican/Caribbean floor show on the sand.

The five-mile-long, two-and-a-half-mile-wide island can be explored easily on a rented moped or by taxi in four hours or less. Ferries and tour boats discharge passengers at the pier in the heart of downtown on **Avenida Rueda Medina.** If you arrive

early enough for breakfast, walk north to **Playa Coco,** also called **Playa Norte,** the most popular beach in town. Several inexpensive restaurants and hotels are clustered along Playa Coco, where laid-back vacationers sun on the sand and stroll to and from town. **Hotel Posada del Mar** ($$; 987/70300; fax 987/70266), on Avenida Rueda Medina near the beach, has an extremely loyal following and an excellent streetside restaurant, **Pinguino** (★★★$), that is great for breakfast and even better for lobster dinner followed by dancing. Next in line is the **Condo Nautibeach** ($$$; 987/70259; fax 987/70487), where condo rentals can be a bargain if you're traveling with a group. Its restaurant, **Chez Magaly** (★★★$$$; 987/70259), is one of the most expensive on the island, with gourmet meals worth paying for. The best tables are on the terrace facing the ocean. **Buho's** on Avenida Carlos Lazo ($; 987/70179) is a good breakfast stop for a plate of *huevos motuleños* (eggs served Yucatán style on a corn tortilla). Nearby is the **Cabañas María del Mar** ($$; 987/70179; fax 987/70213), an enormously popular and friendly collection of hotel rooms and bungalows where you can rent mopeds by the day. **Na Balam** ($$; Calle Zacil-Ha 118; 987/70279; fax 987/70446) is a pretty, small hotel right on the beach, decorated with folk art from Chiapas; one of the best dining spots on the island—**Zacil-Ha** (★★★$; no phone)—is located here. Several *palapa* restaurants on the beach serve fresh fish, cold drinks, and snacks. At the far north end of Playa Coco, a small bridge leads to the remains of the **Del Prado** hotel. Once the keystone resort for the island, the hotel suffered serious damage from Hurricane Gilbert in 1988, and had not yet reopened at press time.

South of Playa Coco, back by the ferry pier, is the island's downtown, a jumble of unnamed streets with homes, restaurants, and shops in various states of repair. You can spend an hour or two wandering, watching a basketball game in the plaza, and browsing the shops for souvenirs, which tend to be less expensive than in Cancún. **Casa del Arte Mexica** (Av Hidalgo 6, at Morelos; 987/70459) is exceptional for its limestone carvings and rubbings of Maya designs and its batik T-shirts and sarongs. **La Loma** (Guerrero 6, at the main square; 987/70223) has a nice collection of masks from throughout Mexico. The nearby **Hotel Perla del Caribe** ($$; 987/70120; fax 987/70011) is perched over the ocean on the east side of downtown, overlooking the seaside *malecón* (boardwalk) that is filled with locals out for an evening stroll. **Pizza Rolandi** (★★★$; Av Hidalgo, at Av Madero; 987/70430) is a great place to stop for thin-crust pizzas, garlic bread, and a cold beer in a convivial courtyard. **Cafecito** (★★★$; Av Juárez, at Matamoros; no phone) serves the best coffee on the island, along with fresh-fruit crepes.

If you have a car, drive south from downtown to Playa Pescador, then turn right and double back along the narrow strip of land that curves around Laguna Makax to a lighthouse looking back across Bahía de Mujeres (Bay of Women) toward downtown.

Several private residences and small time-share/condo complexes have sprouted up along here. Back along the main road is the **Hacienda Mundaca,** a pirate's hideaway that has been partially restored and is open to the public. Near Isla Mujeres's southern tip is **Parque Garrafón Nacional,** an underwater preserve where the snorkeling is far better than off the beaches of Cancún. It's a little more difficult as well, since you enter the water by climbing over limestone rocks rather than strolling in from the sand. The park has dressing rooms, showers, food and souvenir concessions, and equipment rentals, and is open daily during daylight hours. Tour boats from Cancún discharge hordes of passengers at the park around noon, and the water gets quite crowded. Still, this is the best place on the island to stop for a swim. Farther south is the lighthouse and the crumbling remains of a Maya temple set on steep cliffs over the crashing waves. The lighthouse keeper sells cold drinks and handwoven hammocks to explorers who venture down the dirt road to his home. The road is navigable for mopeds and VW Bugs if you take it slowly. Return to town on the windward side until the road cuts west around a navy base. The view of rugged, undeveloped beaches facing the open sea is spectacular.

Las Cuevas de los Tiburones Dormidos (The Caves of the Sleeping Sharks) is Isla Mujeres's most famous underwater attraction. The caves, about three miles northeast of the island in the open sea, were first discovered by Carlos García Castilla, a local fisherman who came upon them while diving for lobster. He noticed that the sharks in the area seemed unusually lethargic, and found some within the caves actually sleeping with their eyes open (since sharks have no gills, normally they must be constantly on the move to oxygenate their bloodstream). Ramon Bravo, Mexico's leading shark expert, Jacques Cousteau, and a diving expedition from *National Geographic* magazine have all studied the phenomenon, and attribute the sharks' somnolent state to the high salinity of the water and lack of carbon dioxide in the caves. The steady currents through the undersea warrens supply them with the necessary oxygen.

The sleeping sharks are a big attraction for scuba divers, but only the most experienced should attempt the dive. Local dive masters say you must go at least 80 feet underwater to see the sharks (which may or may not be there when you are) and divers must also deal with the risk of encountering wide-awake, hungry sharks as well as sleepy ones. Isla Mujeres has several other good dive sites, including the coral reefs at Los Manchones at the southern end of the island. Local dive shops include **Bahía Dive Shop** (Av Rueda Medina 166, across from the ferry pier; 987/70340) and **Buzos de Mexico** (Av Rueda Medina, at Av Madero, one block north of the pier; 987/70131).

16 Gypsy's ★★★$$ Dinner shows are inevitable in a place like Cancún, where nearly anything goes in the drive to outshine the competition. This place showcases outstanding flamenco dancers, who dazzle the diners with their stomps and swirls in a rustic *palapa* above Laguna de Bojórquez. Red-and-yellow tablecloths and elaborate matador capes swinging from the ceiling are meant to evoke visions of Old Spain. But the show is more important than the cuisine, which seems geared simply to satisfying a full house. A decent paella and Spanish chorizo (sausage) fulfill the motherland's obligations to the menu. There's also a daily breakfast buffet, but be forewarned: Like many of the bargain breakfasts offered around town, this one is staffed by persuasively personable time-share salespeople. ♦ Spanish/Seafood ♦ Cover. Daily breakfast and dinner. Paseo Kukulcán, Km 10.5 (between Punta Nizúc and Punta Cancún). 832120, 832015

17 Hyatt Cancún Caribe $$$$ Elegant, sophisticated, and quieter than most Cancún hotels, this is one of the few in the tourist zone to have earned Mexico's Gran Turismo rating, which means that it exceeds the standards for five-star hotels. The classiest of the 140 rooms are in the villas, with private pools, Jacuzzis, and lounges, and gorgeous settings atop a limestone bluff overlooking the sea. The decor is an opulent blend of golden marble pillars and floors, black wrought-iron banisters, and dark, carved wood hutches and étagères. Little touches of tropical safari are thrown in: The bellmen are dressed in adventure attire and resident peacocks spend much of their time outside lying by the glass doors. The beach is narrower than most, but is also more dramatic with the presence of limestone boulders jutting out of the sea. ♦ Paseo Kukulcán (between Punta Nizúc and Punta Cancún). 830044, 800/50777, 800/233.1234; fax 831514

Within the Hyatt Cancún Caribe:

Galería Sergio Bustamante You've seen copies of the master's works in every handicrafts shop on the island; now view the originals in this small gallery. Bustamante first gained attention with his life-size papier-mâché, copper, and brass sculptures of flamingos, lions, and giraffes. This gallery goes beyond what have become common images and now offers displays of his newer

Restaurants/Clubs: Red   **Hotels:** Blue
Shops/ 🌳 Outdoors: Green   **Sights/Culture:** Black

paintings and sculptures, many with a sea life theme. ◆ M-Sa; closed at midday. 830044

Blue Bayou ★★★$$$ The sounds of a flowing waterfall mingle with soft jazz and murmured conversations in this elegant restaurant filled with tropical plants. Spicy creole and cajun dishes are the specialty. There are also plenty of Mexican dishes and grilled fish specialties that are more soothing to the palate. The blackened steaks are thick, tender, and delicious. Be sure to save room for the sublime pecan pie. Stop by the adjacent cocktail lounge for an after-dinner drink and some live jazz. ◆ Daily dinner. Reservations recommended. 830044

18 Chac Mool ★★★$$$ One of the few non-hotel restaurants on the shores of this part of the Caribbean, this dining spot takes full advantage of its sensual setting—the white sand beach is flooded with light and strains of Vivaldi. Romantics can select a pricey bottle of Moët Champagne to enhance their dinner of shrimp in puff pastry, escargots, lobster, and crepes Alaska. The dining room is glassed-in to protect diners from any errant winds, but opens to the sea breezes on balmy nights. An inexpensive all-you-can-eat breakfast is also available. ◆ Seafood/Beef ◆ Daily breakfast and dinner. Paseo Kukulcán (at Playa Chac Mool). 831107

19 Coral Negro Mercado de Artesanías (Artisans' Market) An outdoor handicrafts market with stand after stand selling similar cotton blankets, T-shirts, gauze dresses, and souvenirs, with a few special finds buried among the knickknacks. ◆ Daily. Paseo Kukulcán, Km 9 (near Punta Cancún). No phone

20 Victor This small gallery is a must for shoppers looking for authentic Mexican art. The owner also has branches in Mexico City and Oaxaca, and has specialized in collecting antiques, carvings, weavings, and figurines from the country's art centers since 1940. On display are antique carved wood *santos* (statues of saints), Oaxacan wool rugs, woven wall hangings from Chiapas, and a great selection of *nacimientos* (nativity sets) and Day of the Dead skeletons. ◆ M-Sa; closed at midday. Paseo Kukulcán, Km 9 (in Plaza El Parián). 830840

21 Centro de Convenciones (Convention Center) Cancún couldn't have made it as a world-class destination without a central convention center and facilities for major international events. The recently rebuilt center, containing meeting rooms and exhibition areas, is in the middle of Punta Cancún, the widest piece of land between the sea and lagoons, anchoring the intersecting lines of the hotel zone. Still to come is the 50-story **Cancún Tower** (pictured at right), designed by the Mexican architectural firm **Arqcan**; it will house shops and restaurants. When completed, the tower will be the tallest building in the Caribbean. ◆ Paseo Kukulcán (at Punta Cancún)

22 Camino Real $$$$ When it first opened, this was the most elegant of the Cancún hostelries, and it is still in a class of its own 20 years later. Located on the tip of Punta Cancún, the hotel is captivating, with bold unadorned white walls angled against equally striking walls of magenta, cobalt blue, and purple. Guests must be willing to cover significant territory on foot from the lobby, restaurants, pools, and beaches to their rooms. Accommodations are either in the original 291-room building made of staggered terraces facing the sea, or the 18-story, 87-room **Royal Beach Club,** where original folk art adorns the walls and corner suites have hot tubs. All the rooms are elegant, and have marble floors, tropical furnishings, and great toiletries; some have hammocks hanging on the terraces. A saltwater lagoon on the grounds enhances the tropical mood and gives snorkelers a chance to swim with turtles and tropical fish. Wind sailing is exceptionally good off the hotel's beach. ◆ Paseo Kukulcán (at Punta Cancún). 830100, 800/722.6466

23 Fiesta Americana Coral Beach $$$$ The 11-story, salmon-colored hotel is a palatial 602-suite affair that dominates the clutter on Punta Cancún. In the atrium lobby, potted palms and a stained-glass dome soar above sitting areas, and the energy level is reminiscent of Grand Central Station at rush hour. Still, when a string quartet plays during happy hour at the lobby bar, it all seems tranquil and sedate.

Designed to accommodate large meetings, small conventions, and the overflow from the main convention center, the hotel has a 660-foot-long swimming pool, a fully equipped health club, and an outdoor glass elevator that swoops from the beach to the 11th-floor penthouse suites. The standard suites have a spacious bedroom a few steps above a small seating area leading to a private balcony; master suites have private hot tubs. The decor is subdued Mediterranean/Art Deco with arches and pillars, and lounges, bars, and restaurants are tiered in a multitude of levels that break up the building's vastness. ♦ Paseo Kukulcán, Km 9.5 (at Punta Cancún). 832900, 800/FIESTA.1; fax 833076

Within the Coral Beach:

Coral Reef ★★★★$$$ A sumptuous feast at this romantic restaurant with a background of classical music, candlelight, well-dressed waiters, and plush decor begins with napoleon of salmon (thin slices of salmon layered with waffled potato chips, and topped with caviar). Move on to lobster or Caesar salad, followed by fresh yellowtail Grenoblese (sautéed with limes and white wine and topped with capers), and end with the incredible caramelized apples on puff pastry that is topped with vanilla ice cream. ♦ Seafood/Continental ♦ Daily dinner. Reservations advised. 832900

24 Plaza Caracol I and II Several shopping centers blend into each other in the crowded commercial zone on Paseo Kukulcán by the convention center. This one stands out from the others with its glass walls and twinkling lights, and is the only mall in this collection to be entirely enclosed and air-conditioned. Nearly 300 shops and restaurants create a confusing jumble of choices and decisions. Famous names such as **Gucci, Ralph Lauren, Guess,** and even **McDonalds** are represented, among the numerous jewelry, T-shirt, and handicrafts shops. It pays to tour the entire place once before buying anything, assuming you can find your way back to your first selection. ♦ Daily. Paseo Kukulcán (near Punta Cancún). 832805, 832450

Within Plaza Caracol:

Casa Rolandi ★★$$ The classiest of the plaza's restaurants has several dining rooms with vines hanging from copper pots, Spanish guitar music playing in the background, and a mesmerizing saltwater aquarium with a spectacular selection of fish. The Italian-Swiss owner has several restaurants in the Mexican Caribbean resorts, most specializing in pizza. Here, the wood-burning ovens are used to roast chicken, duck, and fresh fish, giving them a unique moistness and flavor. Appetizers include a melt-in-your-mouth salmon carpaccio and mussels in white wine. Pasta comes stuffed with shrimp, smothered in cream, and tossed with a decent pesto. The salad/antipasto bar provides a meal in itself. Try the mango mousse for dessert. ♦ Swiss/Italian ♦ Daily lunch and dinner. 831817

Amigo's Cuban cigars are the specialty at this tiny tobacco shop, and you can tell by the quantity being carted off by your fellow shoppers that they intend to bring some of Havana's best back home. Take heed, however: Cuban cigars are not allowed through **US Customs.** ♦ Daily. 832805

Galería Orbe Paintings and sculptures from Mexican artists are displayed in rotating exhibits. You can occasionally find distinctive serigraphs of the ruins and coastal scenes. ♦ Daily. 831333

Iguana Wana ★★$$ If you're determined to bypass all the US franchise restaurants but still have an inexpensive, quick meal, this may be your best bet. The menu selections should satisfy just about everyone in your group, with choices from Caesar salad to peel-and-eat shrimp to vegetarian dishes and prime sirloin steaks. There are also decent pastries, frozen yogurt, and strong espresso; the only drawback is the noise level, which can be deafening. ♦ International ♦ Daily lunch and dinner. 830829

25 100% Natural ★★★★$ What a find. This is absolutely the best place to go when you've had your fill of heavy meals and alcohol, and crave vitamins. *Licuados* (blended fruit drinks) are made with yogurt, milk, or orange juice in cleverly named combos such as "El Vampiro" (made of beet, celery, and carrot juices). Purists are delighted with the steamed vegetables over brown rice. And those desiring a heavy dose of protein and fat can go for the hamburger topped with a fried egg. Ravenous after a night of dancing and bar hopping? Stop in at 3AM for scrambled eggs with spinach and cheese or a broccoli omelette before crashing until noon. The waiters are consistently cheerful regardless of the time of day, and the clientele seems genuinely happy to be feasting on fresh, simple, satisfying meals. ♦ American/Mexican/Health food ♦ Daily 24 hours. Paseo Kukulcán (fronting the street in Plaza Terramar). 831180. Also at: Av Sunyaxchén 6. 843617; Plaza Kukulcán (between Punta Cancún and Punta Nizúc). 852200

26 La Mansión Costa Blanca Once a serene, classy shopping center, it has been painted a garish pink, which detracts from its Moorish arches and domes. The center is on the lagoon side of the maze of malls at Punta Cancún, and the shaded stairways and walkways are a peaceful escape from the neighboring noisy bars and restaurants. ♦ Daily. Paseo Kukulcán (between Punta Cancún and downtown, on the lagoon side). 841272

Within La Mansión Costa Blanca:

El Mexicano ★★★★$$$$ If you want a first-class floor show with dinner, a night here is a must. Step through the beveled-glass doors into a setting reminiscent of a New Orleans–style bordello. The large restaurant does a big business in groups, but singles and couples needn't feel out of place. The best seats for privacy and a view are on the raised section near the entrance by the windows, where you can enjoy the show without having to participate. Mariachi, folkloric dancing, and tropical Caribbean shows are interspersed with excellent dance music.

Appetizers, entrées, and desserts cover the spectrum of Mexico's cuisine, and, if you feel your food isn't spicy enough, you can always spoon on the green salsa made from the fiery *habañero* chili, onion, and lime. Save room for the *crepas cajeta* (thin crepes filled with caramel sauce, topped with chopped nuts, and flambéed with liqueurs) prepared tableside. Save this restaurant for your no-holds-barred, credit-card-busting night of dining and dancing. ♦ Mexican ♦ Daily dinner. 844873

La Galería Artist Gilberto Silva works at a small table carving reproductions of Maya stonework in sheets of limestone just like the original artists did thousands of years ago. Silva, who trained in Chiapas, where the Maya are studied religiously, travels to various archaeological sites and makes rubbings of the original carvings, using soft carbon crayons, as models for his work. Some of the rubbings, with detailed explanations of their meanings, are for sale along with the carvings. This place also has a good collection of fossils imbedded in limestone, opals in geodes, and pastel paintings of ocean scenes made by Sandra Ressler de Silva, Gilberto's wife. ♦ M-Sa; closed at midday. 833994

Mayart Artists of every persuasion and degree of talent attempt to replicate Maya carvings, drawing, and designs. This gallery brings together a gorgeous sampling of the best, with the gods of corn, birth, wisdom, and death carved in malachite, black obsidian, solarite, and quartz. The Aztec, Toltec, and Olmec cultures are represented in the art here, as well. ♦ M-Sa; closed at midday. 832113

27 Presidente Inter-Continental $$$$ Some Cancún regulars return here year after year for the friendly, accommodating attitude that has been the establishment's hallmark since it opened. The rectilinear hotel remains an architectural delight despite the addition of a 10-story tower overlooking the original building's pyramidal roof, inset with rectangles painted a vivid hot pink. All of the 298 rooms were recently renovated; if possible, splurge for one on the **Club** floors, where coffee and pastries accompany your wake-up call, and where complimentary continental breakfast, afternoon hors d'oeuvres, and after-dinner pastries and coffees are served in private lounges.

The grounds and beach are wonderfully secluded, since its neighbors are private residences rather than large hotels. The pool is one of Cancún's best, with a waterfall cascading by the swim-up bar (stand under the waterfall for a great shoulder massage). The restaurants are consistently good, especially for breakfast, which is served in **El Caribeño** by the pool. If you get to the beach early enough, claim one of the *palapas* with plastic lounge chairs for the right amount of sun and shade. The smaller swimming pool set near the tennis courts is a good place to sunbathe in relative solitude. ♦ Paseo Kukulcán, Km 7.5 (between Punta Cancún and downtown). 830200, 800/327.0200; fax 832515

28 Pok-Ta-Pok One of the few golf courses in the world with a Maya shrine on the green was designed by Robert Trent Jones Sr. Now, nearly two decades later, the course remains a beautiful greenbelt surrounded by private homes on an island in Laguna de Bojórquez, connected to the hotel zone by a bridge. The golf club has tennis courts, a swimming pool, marina, restaurant, and bar. Temporary memberships are available and can be arranged through most hotels. ♦ Daily (last tee-off at 4PM). Paseo Kukulcán, Km 6-Km 7 (at Laguna de Bojórquez). 830871

29 Plaza Nautilus A few gems lurk in this easily overlooked roadside mall. Parking is a bit of a hassle, and the best stores are hidden in out-of-the-way corners. ♦ Daily. Paseo Kukulcán, Km 3.5 (between Punta Cancún and downtown). 831903

Within Plaza Nautilus:

Super Deli ★★$ This combination deli/restaurant and gourmet market has a tantalizing array of frozen foods, cookies, crackers, and cheeses, and an excellent newsstand with English and Spanish periodicals and books on the region and Mexico. Specialties include reuben, pastrami, corned beef, and egg salad sandwiches, and they also serve decent pizzas. Seating looks out to the traffic on Paseo Kukulcán; another branch downtown has an outer patio. Both are good choices for a postdisco feast or an off-hours snack. ♦ Deli/Market ♦ Daily 24 hours. 841122. Also at: Av Cobá (at Av Tulum). 830846

Trattoria da Arturo ★★★$$$ More locals than tourists fill the dozen or so tables in this intimate eatery that is decorated in soft blue and white. The antipasto cart—with its impressive array of marinated seafood and vegetables—is reason enough to dine here. Though it's difficult to restrain yourself, save room for the red snapper en papillote or homemade cannelloni with spinach and cheese. The service, cuisine, and ambience make this the perfect spot for your romantic, last-night-of-vacation dinner. ◆ Italian ◆ Daily lunch and dinner. Reservations recommended. 832063, 832382

30 Los Almendros ★★★$$ Expertly prepared Yucatecan food draws the crowds at lunch, when locals settle in for lengthy meals of *pollo pibil* (chicken baked in banana leaves), *poc-chuc* (charcoal-broiled pork), and *pavo escabeche* (turkey marinated with garlic, oil, cinnamon, and vinegar). For the full effect, order the *combinado Yucateco,* that has all the above-mentioned dishes plus *longaniza* (sausage). All meals are served with spicy marinated red onions, a bowl of black beans, warm tortillas, and salsa. Portions are small, so order liberally, and accompany your meal with a bottle of León Negro or Negra Modelo beer. ◆ Yucatecan ◆ Daily lunch and dinner. Av Bonampak (at Av Sayil). 840807

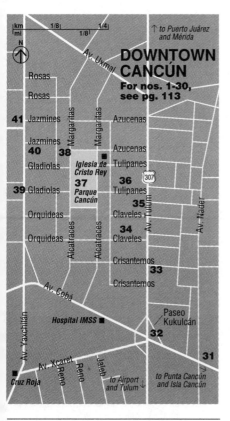

DOWNTOWN CANCÚN

For nos. 1-30, see pg. 113

↑ to Puerto Juárez and Mérida

Rosas
Rosas
41 Jazmines   Azucenas
Jazmines   Azucenas
40 38
Gladiolas   Tulipanes
Iglesia de Cristo Rey
37 Parque Cancún   **36** Tulipanes
39 Gladiolas   **35** Claveles
Orquideas   **34** Claveles
Orquideas
Crisantemos **33**
Crisantemos

Av Uxmal
Av Cobá
Hospital IMSS ■
Paseo Kukulcán
32
31
Av Yaxchilán
Av Xcaret
Reno
Jaleb
■ Cruz Roja
to Airport and Tulum ↓
to Punta Cancún and Isla Cancún

Restaurants/Clubs: Red   Hotels: Blue
Shops/ ♥ Outdoors: Green   Sights/Culture: Black

31 Ciao ★★$$ The fresh-ground, fresh-brewed coffee is served in pots big enough for two cups, while an array of sweets beg to be taken home. The prices are rather high, but the quality is unsurpassed. Although there are a few white plastic tables on the sidewalk, it's more pleasant inside, where air-conditioning and smooth jazz soothe a frazzled shopper's nerves. ◆ Desserts ◆ M-Sa. Av Cobá 30 (between Avs Bonampak and Nader). 841216

32 la dolce vita ★★★★$$$$ Simultaneously pretty and sophisticated, this place has a sidewalk patio area shaded by vine-covered trellises, candles flickering in hurricane lamps, and waiters gliding by unobtrusively in white uniforms with pink vests and bowties. The Northern Italian menu offers such innovative appetizers as liver pâté with gorgonzola cheese; carpaccio; and escargots with artichokes. Cannelloni stuffed with spinach and ricotta, veal ravioli, and pasta with lobster medallions and shrimp are but a few of the pasta temptations. The patio is a nice spot for an after-dinner espresso and pastry. ◆ Northern Italian ◆ Daily lunch and dinner. Reservations required in high season. Av Cobá 87 (between Avs Nader and Tulum). 841384

33 Ki Huic The main market for handicrafts spreads behind Avenida Tulum in a maze of stalls that can leave you bewildered and overwhelmed. If you're serious about searching for treasures and bargaining over prices, allow yourself at least two hours to make your way past hundreds of cotton blankets, polyester dresses, gaudy T-shirts, and bizarre displays of jeweled bugs. Examine your selections carefully; much of the junk sold here will fall apart the first time it's washed, worn, or used.

Don't start bartering until you're really sure you want that priceless pottery Chac Mool, then jump in with polite determination. Many vendors will try to make you name your price first, but you're better off getting an amount from them, then cutting it in half. It helps to walk away if you're getting nowhere, and remember to never pay more than 70 percent of the quoted price. It also helps if you gang up with other shoppers and purchase several items from the same seller, requesting a discount for your mass purchase. ◆ Daily. Av Tulum (between Avs Cobá and Uxmal). No phone

Cancún After Dark

Cancún is a night town, with clubs and discos hitting their stride around midnight. The dress codes at discos include no shorts or sandals; the better you dress, the easier it is to get in. Cover charges can run over $20 per person, and drinks are extraordinarily expensive. High-tech light and laser shows, fog machines, and fireworks are typical special effects, with each disco striving to outdo the other.

The more casual and less expensive spots normally have a US slant, specializing in rock and roll, and burgers and beer. More and more reggae and salsa clubs are opening, and jazz fans can find a few small clubs with top-notch musicians.

Here's a rundown on the current hot spots (all are open daily and have a cover charge unless otherwise noted):

Azúcar (Paseo Kulkucán, at Punta Cancún; 830100). A tropical decor, upscale clientele, and live bands make this a popular club for devotees of the salsa, rumba, and lambada. The dancers are as fun to watch as the band.

Batacha (Mission Park Hotel, Paseo Kukulcán; 831755). This small local club offers Cuban and Caribbean bands under a *palapa*.

Christine's (Krystal Hotel, Paseo Kukulcán; 831133). High on elegance, this is an enduring favorite of the well-dressed, glamorous disco set.

DadyO (Paseo Kukulcán, Km 9.5, near Punta Cancún; 833333). High-tech laser and light shows here attract a young, lycra-clad crowd.

Fat Tuesday (Paseo Kukulcán, between Punta Cancún and downtown; no phone). Dress is extremely casual at this beachside bar favored by the young sandals-and-shorts set who dance enthusiastically, fueled by shots of tequila. The large dance floor is emceed by a DJ.

La Boom (Paseo Kukulcán, between Punta Cancún and downtown; 831372). The light shows and special effects are updated frequently, making this one of the trendiest and most crowded nightspots. Another plus is an all-you-can-drink special price.

Planet Hollywood (Plaza Flamingo, between Punta Cancún and Punta Nizúc; 850723). **Arnold Schwarzenegger** is a partner at this club, with a restaurant, movie memorabilia (including the motorcycle from *The Terminator*), music videos, and one of Cancún's best DJs.

Señor Frog's (Paseo Kukulcán, between Punta Cancún and downtown; 832931). Nearly everyone comes here at least once, drawn by its legendary hipness. The noise level is astounding, the DJs and waiters absolutely hyper, the food in the restaurant consistently good, and there's no cover.

Hurricane Gilbert hit the Mexican Caribbean with raging 250- to 300-mile-per-hour winds in 1988, devastating parts of all the resort areas, including Cancún, Cozumel, and the mainland coast.

34 Rosa Mexicano ★★★$$ The menu in this hacienda-style restaurant is refreshingly different from the taco/fajita fare served in most of Cancún's "Mexican" establishments. Instead of serving nachos as appetizers, the restaurant offers *nopalitos,* the traditional salad made from the small buds of the nopal cactus combined with onion, pepper, cilantro, vinaigrette, and crumbled white cheese. Another salad has chunks of jicama and orange slices sprinkled with lime juice, salt, and ground chilies. The red snapper is smothered in cilantro, while the chicken is served in a ground-almond sauce or covered with mole *poblano,* a blend of spices with an incomparable taste. Desserts include tamales *dulces* (a steamed corn paste wrapped around raisins and cinnamon), papayas baked with honey and cheese, and a nut cake drenched with rum. If you're beginning to wonder if Cancún really is in Mexico, come here for a gratifying immersion in the country's flavors and smells. ◆ Mexican ◆ Daily dinner. Reservations required for patio seating. Claveles 4 (between Avs Tulum and Yaxchilán). 846313

35 Fama A general department store with a bit of everything, this place has racks and racks of magazines and paperbacks in English and Spanish, including a good selection of books and guides on the Yucatán Peninsula. Postcards, film, and sundries cost less here than in the hotels, and there's a good exchange rate for those cashing US traveler's checks or dollars. ◆ Daily. Av Tulum 105 (between Tulipanes and Claveles). 841839

36 El Pescador

★★★★$$ For more than a decade, this restaurant has proven that you don't need fancy gimmicks and frenetic activity to be a success in a highly competitive market. Good food, well prepared and reasonably and reasonably priced, is what keeps customers coming back again and again. Though the tables are placed as close as can be in the two dining rooms and on the sidewalk patio, there still isn't nearly enough seating for all the locals and visitors willing to wait indefinitely for what many consider to be the best fish dinners in town. The portions are far more generous than at most tourist restaurants. For a treat, have the lobster ceviche appetizer (which costs about the same as an entrée). The menu and prices are the same for lunch and dinner, but you'll have a better chance of beating the crowd if you show up around noon. The owners have opened a second restaurant, **La Mesa del Pescador,** at Plaza Kukulcán, which follows the same successful formula. ♦ Seafood/Meat ♦ Daily lunch and dinner. Tulipanes 28 (between Alcatraces and Av Tulum). 842673. Also at: Plaza Kukulcán (between Punta Cancún and Punta Nizúc). 852200

37 Parque Cancún Since Cancún is a new city without history and social traditions, its main plaza lacks a sense of soul, and seems to have been more of an afterthought on the part of city planners. Consisting of block-long concrete slabs and a statue of Francisco Madero, the first publicly elected President of Mexico, the plaza is at its best on Friday and Saturday nights, when free concerts are presented and local families turn out to socialize. ♦ Margaritas (between Tulipanes and Gladiolas)

38 La Habichuela ★★★★$$$ Peacock-style, white wrought-iron chairs and spacious tables are set in a romantic, tranquil garden that's watched over by a statue of Pacal, the Maya ruler of Palenque. The tables are covered with white and pink linen, tiny white lights sparkle in the trees, and soft, contemporary jazz plays almost imperceptibly in the background. Lobster, prepared nearly any way you can imagine, comes in three sizes—regular, jumbo, and bestial—but the dish that made this restaurant famous is the *cocobichuela* (lobster and shrimp in a light curry sauce served in a coconut shell). The waiters call it *el plato de los reyes Mayas* (the dish of the Maya kings). For complete decadence, end your meal with *crepas Brazil* (a combo of feather-light crepes, cognac, nuts, butter, and caramelized sugar), flambéed tableside, of course. The pseudo-Maya theme is continued with symbolic bas-reliefs and excellent reproductions of Maya personages in small arched niches in the walls. Service is impeccable, the food is sublime, and the location—just two blocks off the dreaded, noisy Avenida Tulum—is both convenient and peaceful. If you're going to go all out for a special night, do it here. ♦ Seafood/Nouvelle Mexican ♦ Daily lunch and dinner. Reservations required in high season. Margaritas 25 (between Jazmines and Gladiolas). 843158

39 Pericos ★★★★$ Wacky, weird, and wild, this is the ultimate let-loose-and-play saloon/restaurant. Dressed-up skeletons dangle from ceilings and walls, patrons perch on leather saddles at the bar, waiters hurry about with trays of drinks on their heads and gun belts slung across their chests à la Pancho Villa, and marimbas reverberate with a joyful sound. Unlike many such spots, it carries off the gaiety quite genuinely and entertainingly, amusing a wide cross section of Cancún tourists and residents. From the front, the building is deceptively covered with palm fronds, while inside it looks like a hacienda, with a fountain, a formal staircase, and a balcony from which to view the bizarre panoply below. Flaming entrées such as shish kebabs and coffee drinks loaded with liqueurs are served by waiters in firefighters' uniforms for some added drama. ♦ Mexican/American ♦ Daily lunch and dinner. Av Yaxchilán 71 (between Chiabal and Marañon). 843152

40 Plaza del Sol $ One of the nicest hotels in downtown, it's much quieter than the hotels closer to Avenida Tulum, yet within steps of some great restaurants and the park. The 87 rooms are carpeted and simply furnished with double beds, desks, and TVs. The courtyard swimming pool and patio is a peaceful spot for relaxing in the sun. Definite pluses are the sidewalk cafe and gated parking. ♦ Av Yaxchilán 31 (between Gladiolas and Jazmines). 843888, 800/221.0555; fax 718/692.1543

41 Pipo ★★★$ The owner is from Acapulco, which means the cuisine has a Pacific coast flair. The ceviche, *Acapulqueño* style, is thicker and more like cocktail sauce than the local lime-based version, and the seafood is as fresh as you can possibly get. On Thursdays, the owner follows his hometown custom, serving *pozole* (a pork and hominy stew). This is a good spot for authentic—unadulterated for tourists' taste buds—Mexican food. ♦ Mexican ♦ Daily lunch and dinner. Avs Yaxchilán and Sunyaxchén. 874831

Bests

Pia Brennan
Entrepreneur

Go to **La Prosperidad Internacional** (on López Portillo on the outskirts of Cancún, along the highway to Mérida) on a Sunday afternoon for a taste of the local life (you pay for the drinks and get free Mexican snacks and live music).

Make a side trip to **Akumal** (60 miles/96 kilometers south of Cancún) where life is tranquil, the beach is beautiful, and the snorkeling is great.

Ride horses at the ranch south of the airport (the stables are run by an American woman).

Visit the **Botanical Gardens** on the way to **Tulúm.**

Cancún accounts for 19 percent of Mexico's total tourism income.

Cozumel

It takes barely 30 minutes to fly from **Cancún** over the multicolored, mesmerizing **Caribbean Sea** to Cozumel. Behind you, hotel towers glisten in the light of the sun. Ahead, waters wash over shimmering white sands, and slender palms reach toward the cloudless blue sky. Millions of exotic fluorescent fish gracefully float with the currents near jagged, milky-white reefs through fertile feeding grounds.

Nature is Cozumel's calling card, and she presents it unpretentiously. No flash, no glitter, no glitz. No race to see how many hotel rooms can fit on a parcel of land. No need to embrace fast-food emporiums and hermetically sealed shopping malls. Cozumel's protectors have set a limit of 7,000 hotel rooms for the island, only half of which have been constructed thus far. Most of the businesses and some 60,000 inhabitants are concentrated in the village of **San Miguel** on the west side of the island; resorts and private villas line the soft white sand beaches to the north and south. A chain of coral reefs runs 16 miles along the southwestern shore, creating a windbreak that allows the Caribbean to flow peacefully in glittering turquoise bays.

Cozumel is 32 miles long, nine miles wide, and is Mexico's largest island. Only three percent of the island is developed; the rest is wild jungle covering a base of gray limestone populated by iguanas, foxes, deer, and other animals. The windward side is pounded by the open sea foaming above rocky cliffs. To the north, marshes, swamps, and lagoons shelter snow-white herons and terns. At least 60 Maya temples lie crumbling imperceptibly under a veil of ancient vines.

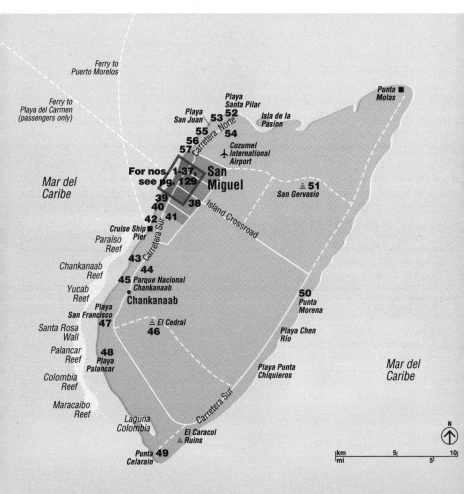

More than 100,000 visitors fly into Cozumel's airport each year, many bearing scuba gear. Since the early 1960s, when Jacques Cousteau called it a diving mecca when filming the nearby **Palancar Reef**, divers have swarmed here, making the island one of the top five scuba destinations in the world. Another 400,000 tourists arrive on cruise ships, filling San Miguel's restaurants and shops with a crush of eager spenders. Hotels are booked far in advance for Thanksgiving, Christmas, and Easter, when the temperature averages a comfortable 82 degrees, and the sun is almost guaranteed to shine daily.

The crowds are far smaller in the summer, when the rain, humidity, and mosquitoes hit their peak. However, visitors willing to withstand these minor incoveniences are treated to reduced hotel rates, uncrowded beaches, water temperatures over 80 degrees, and the unforgettable sight of mother sea turtles lumbering to shore to lay their eggs. Hurricanes are a concern in September and October; Hurricane Gilbert hit the island with a vengeance in 1988, though you'd hardly believe the tales of destruction now. Cozumel recovered with amazing speed, and even the fragile coral reefs that felt the storm's wrath are growing back.

The island is laid out logically, and it's difficult to get lost or confused. Hotels along the northwest shore are favored by families and recluses who want to relax in the sun on uncrowded beaches and are willing to travel to town for bar hopping, shopping, and people watching. The majority of Cozumel's most popular restaurants and shops line **Avenida Rafael Melgar**, also known as the *malecón*, in the town of San Miguel. Dedicated shoppers will likely return several times to browse and buy; those looking for rowdy watering holes will find them here. Culture seekers should visit the excellent **Museo de la Isla de Cozumel**, and spend time in the **Plaza Juárez**, where local families congregate to visit and watch their children play.

South of town are resorts that cater to divers who want to be close to the reefs. The snorkeling is better here than off the north shore, and the main road is lined with restaurants, hotels, and bars. The action is lively, youthful, and somewhat frenetic, except at the **Presidente Inter-Continental**, the ultimate self-contained retreat, where peaceful pampering is the norm. Drives along the windward side of the island are the most popular day trips. Many visitors soon weary of looking for excitement and stimulation, however, and settle into the island life-style, taking advantage of Cozumel's simple, relaxed, laid-back attitude, as the sun, sea, and tropical heat work their magic ever so subtly.

Area code 987 unless otherwise noted.

Getting to Cozumel

Airport

Cozumel International Airport is three kilometers (two miles) north of San Miguel.

Aero Transportes minibuses run from the airport into town and to the hotels for a low fare. Taxis cost a bit more but are a good choice if you are in a hurry or don't want to stop several times before reaching your destination.

Airlines

AeroCozumel and **AeroCaribe**	20928, 20877
Continental	50576, 20487
Mexicana	20157, 20263
Taesa	24210

Getting around Cozumel

Car Rental

Volkswagen Beetles are common rental cars; air-conditioned sedans are not readily available. If you want air-conditioning, it's best to reserve a car in advance through one of the following companies:

Avis	20322
Budget	20903
Fiesta Cozumel	20725
National	23263
Pay Less	20002
Rentadora Cozumel	21120

Ferries

The passenger ferry to Playa del Carmen on the mainland departs daily from the ferry pier (Av Rafael

Melgar at Benito Juárez). The schedule changes frequently and is posted at the pier, or you can call 21588. Trips last 30-45 minutes, depending on the boat. Independent boat operators also offer trips from Cozumel to the mainland departing from the pier. Look at the boat before you pay; the seas can be rough and a journey in a small boat will likely leave you and your luggage drenched.

The car ferry leaves from the international pier (Carretera Sur at the Island Crossroad) to Puerto Morelos on the mainland several times during the week. The trip takes three to four hours. For more information, call 20950.

Mopeds
Mopeds are a common mode of transportation for both locals and visitors, and it seems as if there is a moped rental booth on every street corner. Many of these small bikes are in dreadful, unsafe condition, and they usually break down at the most inopportune times. Check the vehicle carefully before you take off and make sure the tires have sufficient air and tread. Always wear a helmet (it's illegal to drive without one) and obey the traffic laws and right-of-way rules as if you were driving a car.

Taxis
Cab fares are regulated and are surprisingly inexpensive. Meters are not used, however, so agree on the fare with the driver before the taxi starts moving.

FYI

Emergencies
Ambulance 20639
Hospital, Calle 11S between Avs 15 and 16..............
....20140
Medical Specialties Center (24-hour emergency care), Av 20N, No 425 (at Calle 10)...............21419
Police 20092
Scuba Emergencies, Calle 5S, No 21B (at Av 5)........
....22387

American Consultation (Calle 13S, at Av 15S; 20654) provides a liaison with the consulates in Mérida and Mexico City, and can assist travelers with legal problems and translations.

Money
You can change money at the airport, hotels, and banks, with the latter giving you the best rate. Banks are open Mondays through Fridays from 9AM to 1:30PM, and you can change money from 10:30AM to noon. *Casas de cambio* (exchange houses) are scattered around downtown and open throughout the day and evening. International credit cards and US dollars are accepted in most restaurants, hotels, and shops. Try not to be short of cash on Sundays, because it can be difficult to change money on that day, except in some hotels. Always keep bills of small denominations on hand, since it can be difficult to change larger bills (except at banks).

Tours
Most hotels have tour desks offering trips to **Tulum** and **Chichén Itzá** on the mainland, either in small chartered planes or via ferry and bus. The plane trips are a much better option in terms of time and scenic value—few sights are as spectacular as the gray limestone temples of **Tulum** rising above the aquamarine sea. Tours on Cozumel include journeys to the windward side of the island and party boats that cruise the coast with a stop at **Parque Nacional Chankanaab** (Chankanaab National Park) for swimming and snorkeling. The following companies also offer tours:

American Express Av Rafael Melgar 27 20725
Aviomar Calle 6 Norte (Avs 10-15) 20477, 20588
Fiesta Cozumel Av 11 (at Av 30).........20725, 21389

Cozumel Central Reservations represents more than 30 hotel, condo, and villa properties and frequently offers packages including airfare, accommodations, and scuba diving. For more information, call 800/327.2254.

Visitors Information
There is a tourist information booth at the ferry pier (Av Rafael Melgar at Benito Juárez; no phone); open daily.

Area code 987 unless otherwise noted.

1 Avenida Rafael Melgar Better known as the *malecón,* this waterfront walkway is Cozumel's busiest street. Mopeds, VW Beetles, and jeeps angle into every available parking space and cruise the avenue in a slow procession. Police officers halt the parade as pedestrians stream across the four-lane street, often oblivious to the traffic.

This is Cozumel's version of downtown, where everyone sooner or later ends up to eat, shop, and eye their fellow revelers. It is the main paved road around the island, but is called Rafael Melgar only in the town of San Miguel. Outside of town it becomes Carretera Sur or Carretera a Chankanaab to the south, and Carretera Norte to the north. You can't get too confused by the names, since it is the only four-lane road running parallel to the waterfront.

1 Ferry Pier Tourists and workers arrive from the mainland at a long concrete pier that intersects Avenida Rafael Melgar. The ferry for Playa del Carmen departs daily from 4AM-8PM. ◆ Av Rafael Melgar (at Benito Juárez). 21588

Pirates Jean Lafitte and Henry Morgan used Cozumel as a base to attack cargo ships headed toward the mainland from Spain.

Restaurants/Clubs: Red   Hotels: Blue
Shops/ 🌳 Outdoors: Green   **Sights/Culture:** Black

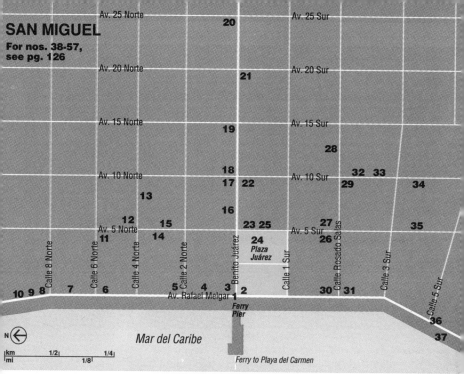

Av. 25 Norte | 20 | Av. 25 Sur

Av. 20 Norte | 21 | Av. 20 Sur

Av. 15 Norte | 19 | Av. 15 Sur

28

Av. 10 Norte | 18 | Av. 10 Sur | 32 33
17 | 22 | 29 | 34

13 | 16

12 | 15 | 23 25 | 27 | 35
Av. 5 Norte | 24 | Av. 5 Sur | 26
11 | 14 | Plaza | Juárez

Calle 8 Norte
Calle 6 Norte
Calle 4 Norte
Calle 2 Norte
Benito Juárez
Calle 1 Sur
Calle Rosado Salas
Calle 3 Sur
Calle 5 Sur

10 9 8 | 7 | 6 | 5 4 3 2 | 30 31 | 36
Av. Rafael Melgar 1 | 37

Ferry
Pier

N ←

km 1/2 1/4
mi 1/8

Mar del Caribe

Ferry to Playa del Carmen

2 Las Palmeras ★★$ The best seats on the waterfront are at this bustling open-air cafe looking across to the ferry pier. The view is better than the food, so stick to simple, inexpensive fare. Bottles of Tehuacan purified water sit on each table, but be aware that you'll be charged for the whole bottle if you open it. The nachos are unlike any others you'll ever find, and consist of two whole corn tortillas covered with a thin layer of refried beans, melted cheese, and salsa that tastes suspiciously like tomato soup. Breakfast of simple scrambled eggs and white toast is a better choice.
♦ Mexican/American ♦ Daily breakfast, lunch, and dinner. Av Rafael Melgar (between Benito Juárez and Calle 1S). 20532

3 Explora Sportswear with a safari theme fills this small store, which gets impossibly crowded when more than 10 customers squeeze in. The T-shirt designs are strikingly different from most, with gorgeous silkscreen paintings of lobsters, angelfish, and crabs under the store's slogan: "Nature at its best." The shop also has practical, sturdy hiking shorts and pants. ♦ Daily. Av Rafael Melgar (between Benito Juárez and Calle 2N). No phone

4 Casablanca Jewelery shops abound on Cozumel, and this place is one of the most impressive, with a staggering array of emeralds, diamonds, and sapphires in the raw or set in gold. The jewelry is arranged elegantly by type of gemstone in freestanding and wall-mounted display cases. The salespeople are knowledgeable about gems and extremely courteous. ♦ Daily; closed at midday. Av Rafael Melgar (between Benito Juárez and Calle 2N). 20982

5 La Concha A fine selection of folk art from throughout Central America is creatively displayed at this spacious shop. One section holds a fine collection of nativity sets and hand-painted Talavera pottery; another has purses from Guatemala. The display of skeleton figurines and altars for Día de los Muertos in early November is particularly impressive. ♦ M-Sa. Av Rafael Melgar (at Calle 2N). 21270

6 Museo de la Isla de Cozumel (Cozumel Museum) The former **La Playa** hotel, which housed guests in relative luxury at the turn of the century, has been remodeled, painted a

pale, seashell pink, and transformed into an excellent museum worth visiting for an hour or two. The first floor has sea and reef exhibits (including wonderful specimens of coral), and an island ecology display. A large map highlights the areas reserved as parklands. One of the most fascinating exhibits is on the second floor, where photographs, dioramas, and old newspaper clippings show Cozumel's history. In the courtyard, an exhibit on the Maya includes a typical Maya house, with rounded walls, thatch roof, and hammocks as the main furnishings. The museum has a mediocre cafe (★$$) on the second floor overlooking the *malecón,* and a small gift shop. ♦ Admission. M-F, Su. Av Rafael Melgar (between Calles 4 and 6N). 21545

7 Pizza Rolandi ★★★$ The courtyard of this Swiss-Italian pizzeria is the most enjoyable spot in town for a leisurely lunch or dinner. Locals and visitors alike congregate here day after day, unable to get enough of the distinctive cuisine. These pizzas are highly unusual, made on a crust that resembles light and airy pita bread. Toppings are as typical as olive oil, tomatoes, basil, and cheese, or as outlandish as a combo of mushrooms, asparagus, and ham. The homemade coconut ice cream topped with amaretto or cassis is the perfect sweet treat any time of day or night. For a total blowout, have the banana supreme, a full-scale banana split flamed with Cointreau. ♦ Swiss/Italian ♦ M-Sa lunch and dinner. Av Rafael Melgar 23 (between Calles 6 and 8N). 20946

8 Los Cinco Soles Allow yourself plenty of time to browse through the many rooms in this folk art shop with an excellent selection of crafts from all over Mexico. One room is devoted to Maya carvings, rubbings, and batiks, with a variety of designs; another is filled with resortwear, including a large selection of gauze dresses, blouses, and skirts made by Maria of Guadalajara. Fanciful carved wood animals, *nacimientos* (nativity sets), and gleaming black Oaxacan pottery are sold at prices far lower than in Cancún. ♦ Daily; closed at midday. Av Rafael Melgar 27 (between Calles 8 and 10N). 22040

Cozumel's non-numbered streets, Rafael Melgar and Rosado Sales, are named after doctors.

9 Pancho's Backyard ★★★★$$ Owner Pancho Morelos has created a tranquil courtyard restaurant behind his shop, **Los Cinco Soles,** with water burbling in stone fountains, and flowering vines wrapping around white archways and pillars. Enhancing the traditional Mexican setting are *equipale* tables and chairs, made of leather surfaces in bases of wooden slats. The hand-painted pottery dishes and blown-glass goblets are samples of the wares sold in the store, as are the candleholders and statues. His health-conscious menu emphasizes Mexican dishes prepared with a minimum of oil and a deft sprinkling of spices. Mexican wines from the **Calafia** and **Santa Tomás** wineries in Baja are featured and accompany the fragrant *chiles rellenos* wonderfully. ♦ Mexican ♦ M-F breakfast, lunch, and dinner; Sa dinner. Av Rafael Melgar (between Calles 8 and 10N). 22141

GALERIA DEL SOL
ISLA DE COZUMEL

10 Galería Del Sol Watercolors, oil paintings, and sculptures depicting island themes are artfully arranged in this serene gallery. Featured are local artists, including Gordon Gilchrist, whose etchings of Maya temples and pyramids are coveted by collectors. ♦ M-Sa; closed at midday. Av Rafael Melgar (between Calles 8 and 10N). 20170

11 Manuel's Hammocks During the day, you can usually find retired police officer Manuel Azueta on the front porch of his brightly colored house, weaving thin strands of cotton and nylon into hammocks. They may cost more than those found at the flea market, but the quality is well worth the price, and you're likely to get a lesson in weaving, along with some memorable snapshots. ♦ Most mornings and late afternoons. Av 5N (between Calles 4 and 6N). No phone

12 Bakery Zermatt Fresh crusty *bolillos* (rolls), cheese danish, chocolate croissants, thick pizza by the slice, and two walls of shelves filled with other sweet selections make it tempting to visit this aromatic place at least once a day. No preservatives are used, so buy only what you can eat immediately, then come back for more. ♦ Bakery ♦ Daily. Calle 4N (at Av 5N). No phone

13 d'Pub ★★★$$ A classic Caribbean-style wooden cottage, unusual for Cozumel, sits behind a landscaped garden on a quiet side street. The comfortable indoor dining room has a large bar and soft music playing in the background. Though it's cooler inside, romantics prefer the tables in the back garden amid flickering candlelight. Fish-and-chips is their hallmark dish, with a crisp, slightly greasy coating on fresh dorado or whatever the catch of the day may be. Grilled fish dishes are also good, and there is a wide selection of beers. ◆ Seafood ◆ Daily lunch and dinner. Calle 4N (between Avs 5N and 10N). 24132

14 Batik Factory Batik artist Carlos Texlo left his store on Isla Mujeres after Hurricane Gilbert nearly destroyed that island in 1988, and set up shop here. His batiks of underwater coral and fish scenes are gorgeous, especially when lit from behind. A back-room gallery displays his more erotic creations. ◆ Daily; closed at midday. Av 5N (between Calles 2 and 4N). 21960

15 Sports Page ★$ If you can't take a vacation without watching football, baseball, basketball, or other professional athletics on TV, you're sure to find what you want at this noisy, rowdy sports bar. T-shirts from every imaginable US team are tacked to the ceiling and walls. Tables are covered in red, white, and blue, and TVs blare sports events from around the world. The grill serves up a decent burger and fries. ◆ American ◆ Daily breakfast, lunch, and dinner. Av 5N (between Calles 2 and 4N). 21199

16 Morgan's ★★★$$$

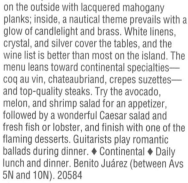

Locals and tourists alike consistently return here for a special night out. This former customs house has been paneled on the outside with lacquered mahogany planks; inside, a nautical theme prevails with a glow of candlelight and brass. White linens, crystal, and silver cover the tables, and the wine list is better than most on the island. The menu leans toward continental specialties—coq au vin, chateaubriand, crepes suzettes—and top-quality steaks. Try the avocado, melon, and shrimp salad for an appetizer, followed by a wonderful Caesar salad and fresh fish or lobster, and finish with one of the flaming desserts. Guitarists play romantic ballads during dinner. ◆ Continental ◆ Daily lunch and dinner. Benito Juárez (between Avs 5N and 10N). 20584

17 Alexpa Chances are the $9,000 black-coral lobster displayed in a glass case in the center of this tiny shop will still be here by the time you arrive. Have the clerk show you how the three-foot-long giant was made from 15,000 tiny sections of coral—a remarkable work of art. There's also plenty of moderately priced coral jewelry, and, if you must have a lobster, smaller and less expensive ones are available. ◆ M-Su. Av 10N (between Benito Juárez and Calle 2N). 23723

18 Miss Italia ★$ Yes, Cozumel has become so hip it even has gelato, in exotic flavors such as kiwi and *plátano* (plantain), as well as a deep dark chocolate, tangy lemon and lime, and cool, refreshing mint. Sold by the cup or cone, the gelato hits the spot after a grueling shopping spree. ◆ Ice cream ◆ Daily. Benito Juárez (between Avs 10 and 15N). 21077

19 Sonora Grill ★★★$$$ If you go fishing and catch something, bring your prize here for a dinner you won't forget. The chef in the open kitchen can turn your catch into a veritable fish feast—a heaping platter of grilled and fried fillets, along with bread, tortillas, rice, salad, baked potatoes, and vegetables. Of course, you don't have to provide the main course, and you don't even have to eat fish. They also serve a hefty dish of fajitas, decent *carne asada* (marinated and grilled meat), and grilled lobster. The second-story restaurant gets a nice breeze through the windows, and is quieter and more relaxing than those along the sidewalk below. ◆ Seafood/Mexican ◆ Dinner. Benito Juárez (at Av 15N). No phone

Nightlife

Cozumel isn't nearly as much of a party town as Cancún, especially since divers are supposed to have maximum rest and minimum alcoholic intake before heading for the reefs in the early morning. Some options if you don't need to curb your night owl tendencies:

Scaramouche (Av Rafael Melgar at Calle Rosada Salas; 21213) is the most glamorous disco (shorts and sandals are frowned upon), and attracts an adult crowd. Expect to dance alone if you arrive before 10PM. Open nightly, there's a cover charge in high season.

Neptuno (Av Rafael Melgar at Av Circunlavación; 21537) is more casual than **Scaramouche,** and has music videos. It caters nightly to an early-twenties crowd. Hungry dancers crowd the late-night taco stand around the corner. Be prepared to pay a cover in high season.

Quetzalez (Av Rafael Melgar at Calle 2N; no phone) offers live South American flute and drum music, as well as dinner. Part of a cafe (open daily for dinner), this casual place is popular among people of all ages. There's also a lovely view of the *malecón.*

Hours-long Mexican fiestas that include lavish buffets, an endless stream of tequila, and folkloric dance performances are held at the **Plaza las Glorias** (Av Rafael Melgar, Km 1.5, between Calles 5 and 7S; 22000) and **Fiesta Americana Sol Caribe** (Carretera Sur, between San Miguel and Chankanaab; 20700) hotels. Possible added attractions are contests of the bikini, muscle man, or wet T-shirt type, and fireworks.

Restaurants/Clubs: Red   **Hotels:** Blue
Shops/ 🌿 Outdoors: Green   **Sights/Culture:** Black

20 The Waffle House ★★★$ Jeanie DeLille (the island's best pastry chef) has her own cafe in a little wood house a few blocks from Plaza Juárez. Offering the best desserts in town, her chocolate tortes, nut pies, and cakes tempt diners whatever the time of day. At breakfast, however, the aroma of fresh-baked waffles is alluring enough to lead you away from the pastries to a table by the front door, where you can watch passersby as you devour waffles topped with chopped nuts, strawberries, even chocolate syrup. Omelettes, eggs, and French toast are also available. ◆ Breakfast/pastries ◆ Daily breakfast and dessert. Benito Juárez (at Av 25N). 23373

21 La Mission ★★$$ This place has developed a faithful following among the scuba set, who know they'll be fed generously for a reasonable price. Watch the cooks at the open grill to get an idea of the sizable portions and decide which tempting entrée will best satisfy your appetite. Lobster is a popular choice, along with Mexican combination plates heaped with tacos, enchiladas, refried beans, and rice. The dining room is open to the street and is festively decorated with stained-glass lamps, red-and-white-checkered tablecloths, and Mexican pottery. You won't leave here hungry. ◆ Mexican/Seafood ◆ Dinner. Benito Juárez 23 (between Avs 15 and 20S). 21641

22 Iglesia Inmaculada Concepción (Immaculate Conception Church) Cozumel's main Catholic church is just a block off Plaza Juárez. Religious processions and concerts by the church choir are held in the pedestrian walkway on Avenida Juárez. The church has a gorgeous stained-glass mural of the Archangel Michael standing on a devil engulfed in flames. ◆ Benito Juárez (between Avs 5 and 10S)

23 Flea Market To find the best array of tawdry souvenirs, browse this collection of stalls near the plaza—you can easily find it from the sound of blaring disco music. Amid the trinkets are old Spanish coins, Cuban cigars, bizarre stone reproductions of Maya carvings, and amber jewelry imbedded with fossils. ◆ M-Sa; closed at midday. Av 5 (between Benito Juárez and Calle 1S). No phone

24 Plaza Juárez Graceful flamboyant trees frame the central plaza with feathery leaves and brilliant orange blossoms. Children race up and down the stairs of the white wrought-iron gazebo, where local bands perform on Sundays. It seems the whole town turns out for these weekly concerts, which sometimes include impromptu dances. Hot dogs, french fries, and sodas are sold from stands around the edge of the concrete plaza, while balloon and cotton candy vendors entice children. Don't miss this display of small-town life, a reminder that that although Cozumel seems to be filled with foreigners, it is classically Mexican at heart. ◆ Benito Juárez (between Avs Rafael Melgar and 5S)

25 Agencia de Publicaciones English-language magazines, newspapers, and books are available at this small shop on the plaza. There's a good selection of books on Mexico and the Maya as well. ◆ Daily. Av 5S (between Benito Juárez and Calle 1S). 20031

26 Cocos Cozumel ★★★$ You may well end up having breakfast here nearly every morning—owners Daniel and Terri Ocejo's coffee alone is worth a visit. Some may opt for typical US breakfasts of eggs and hash browns, but you shouldn't miss their eggs scrambled with chilies and served with cheese sauce atop a fried tortilla, or the enormous cream cheese muffins. Lunch selections include burgers, bountiful salads, and the best milk shakes on the island. Another plus: The Ocejos run a library of sorts. Bring along the book you just finished reading and trade it for another. ◆ Mexican/American ◆ Daily breakfast and lunch; closed last two weeks of September and first week of October. Av 5S (at Calle Rosado Salas). 20241

27 Roberto's Of the many black-coral shops on Cozumel, this one stands out for its gorgeous carvings of hammerhead sharks, angelfish, and marlin by artist Roberto Franco. Branches of the fragile and precious coral—which look like dead brown ferns—hang in the back workshop. There is some dispute over the sale of this endangered species; expert divers say the supply from local reefs has all but disappeared, and those searching for it must go down 300 feet or more to find it, risking their lives in the process. Still, the demand is high, Cozumel's divers and jewelers make a handsome living dealing in black coral, and their work is impressive. Be aware, however, that you may have some problems bringing a purchase back into the US. ◆ M-Sa; Su evenings. Av 5S (between Calles 1S and Rosado Salas). No phone

28 Santiago's Grill ★★$$$ While this restaurant still packs them in, the place is earning fewer rave reviews than it used to (maybe the kitchen can't handle the success). The portions seem to have decreased, so it's best to stick to lower-priced items until the kitchen proves itself again. The conch (both ceviche and chowder) and the flaky white grouper smothered with garlic are good choices. ♦ Mexican/Seafood ♦ Daily dinner. Calle Rosado Salas 299 (between Avs 10 and 15S). 20175

29 La Choza ★★★$ Often cited by locals as the best Mexican restaurant in town, the menu offers *chiles rellenos* stuffed with shrimp, Veracruz-style jumbo shrimp (sautéed with tomatoes, onions, and peppers), chicken grilled with *achiote* sauce (a mix of spices unique to the Yucatán), and a highly unusual frozen avocado pie (which actually tastes great). Daily specials include *cochinita pibil* (a savory Yucatecan dish of pork chunks marinated with sour orange juice and slowly baked in banana leaves). Finish your meal with a fragrant cup of *cafe de olla* (rich Mexican coffee simmered with cinnamon and sugar). The *palapa* (palm-roof) restaurant is casual yet stylish—meals are served on pretty blue-and-white pottery, and giant tasty margaritas come in hand-blown glasses that are edged in sapphire blue. ♦ Mexican/Yucatecan/Seafood ♦ Daily breakfast, lunch, and dinner. Calle Rosado Salas 198 (between Avs 5 and 10S). 20958

Donatello RISTORANTE

30 Donatello ★★★$$ Elegance par excellence reigns here, in an ambience of pink linens and gray marble. Formally attired waiters greet customers and lead them past flowing fountains to candlelit tables. For a sublime meal, start with *le cozze gratinate nel forno* (baked mussels smothered with mozzarella and tomatoes). Next, have fresh snapper with garlic, tomatoes, capers, and oregano, or a thick New York steak. Finish with a heady, sweet cafe Donatello, a blend of strong coffee with *sambucca,* brandy, amaretto, and cream. ♦ Italian ♦ Dinner. Reservations recommended. Av Rafael Melgar 131 (between Calles 1S and Rosado Salas). 20090, 22586

31 Pepe's Grill ★★★$$ The best tables in the house are in the upstairs dining room looking out to the *malecón,* where you can feast on shrimp, steaks, and pasta in a romantic, nautical setting. The shrimp brochette has nine large shrimp grilled with chunks of green pepper, tomatoes, and onion, and is served with a baked potato and vegetables. *Spaghetti portofino* is prepared tableside in a copper chafing dish with bacon, white wine, and shrimp. There's also a decent salad bar. It's said to have the best prime ribs on Cozumel, but be prepared to pay dearly.

Save room for the tangy lime pie, one of the best versions of this ubiquitous island dessert. ♦ Seafood/Steaks ♦ Daily dinner. Reservations recommended. Av Rafael Melgar (between Calles Rosado Salas and 3S). 20213

31 Mi Casa This gallery of Mexican housewares has a select collection of hand-painted pottery, tableware, and vases, pewter and silver frames, brass hurricane lamps, and bas-relief plaques of Pacal, the Maya ruler of the ancient city of Palenque. It also has an excellent selection of books on the Maya and their culture, many in English. ♦ Daily. Av Rafael Melgar 271 (between Calles Rosado Salas and 3S). 21472

32 Cafe Caribe ★★★$ Coffee beans roasted under this label are appearing in restaurants around town (and on market shelves to take home as a souvenir). Sip an espresso, a cappuccino, or select from among nearly a dozen specialty drinks while indulging in a dense chocolate cake, flaky pecan pie, or whatever other desserts the baker comes up with each day. This small cafe is a good place to swap stories with fellow travelers while waiting for the sugar and caffeine to kick in. ♦ Coffeehouse ♦ Daily; closed at midday. Av 10S (between Calles Rosado Salas and 3S). 23621

33 Joe's ★★$$ Billed as a lobster pub, this is better known for the salsa and reggae bands that play here late nearly every night. Dining tables are set in a back patio, while the small stage and dance floor are inside by the bar, where it gets incredibly hot once the music gets the crowd moving. ♦ Seafood ♦ Daily dinner. Av 10S, No 229 (between Calles Rosado Salas and 3S). 23275

34 El Capi Navegante ★★$$ Once one of the top restaurants in town, it seems to be slipping a bit, with less quality for more money. Blue-and-white nautical decor gives a spanking-clean appearance to the open dining room. A large seafood platter is the house specialty; order it with conch ceviche, stuffed squid, and oyster appetizers and you easily have a meal for four. The restaurant is four blocks south of Juárez Plaza on a dimly lit street, an easy walk to help build up an appetite for a grand meal. ♦ Seafood ♦ Daily dinner. Av 10S (between Calles 3 and 5S). 21730

35 Villa Las Anclas $$ This is an excellent option for those wishing to set up house while on vacation. Seven apartments—each complete with a kitchen, living room, and two bedrooms (up a spiral staircase) with writing desks and bookshelves, and plenty of room to spread out—are offered at this small inn. Though not near the water and lacking a pool, it is cooled by lots of shade trees and has a pretty garden. There are several nice, small restaurants in the neighborhood, which is close to the *malecón*, yet quiet. ♦ Av 5S, No 325 (between Calles 3 and 5S). 21403; fax 21955

36 Safari Inn $$ Divers looking for basic, no-frills accommodations at below-budget prices will find a friend in owner Bill Horn, who also owns the **Aqua Safari** dive shop in the same building (there's also a branch at the **Plaza Las Glorias**; see below). The 12-room, three-story hotel has comfortable mattresses, big showers with plenty of hot water, high-powered air-conditioning, and good screens on the windows. One of the rooms has bunk beds and enough room for five close friends. Overall, this is a good choice for those who prefer to spend their money on dive trips rather than hotel amenities. There is no restaurant. ♦ Av Rafael Melgar 40 (between Calles 5 and 7S). 20101

37 Plaza Las Glorias $$$$ This has the best location of any hotel on the island, since it's right on the beach but also within easy walking distance to downtown. The pool (with a popular swim-up bar) sits right above the water and two small beaches. The 160 rooms include 148 junior suites with separate sleeping and living areas, a queen-size foldout couch, bathtubs, hair dryers, and terraces with ocean views. A dozen deluxe suites feature hot tubs on the terrace. All rooms have satellite TV and mini-bars. A lavish brunch with made-to-order omelettes is served daily in the poolside *palapa* restaurant, and complimentary snacks are provided in the lobby bar in the early evening. Guests, who tend to be young, athletic, and feisty, compete with the youthful, energetic staff members at beach and pool volleyball, limbo contests, and other fun-filled activities. ♦ Av Rafael Melgar, Km 1.5 (between Calles 5 and 7S). 22000, 800/342.AMIGO; fax 21937

Within Plaza Las Glorias:

Aqua Safari

Aqua Safari With the ultimate in underwater gear, this branch of one of Cozumel's best dive shops offers a full range of services to divers, from equipment sales and rentals to customized dive trips. Owner Bill Horn is known for running a safe shop, and his dive masters make a point of lecturing on safety and ways to protect the sea's fragile environment. His boats also pick up divers at other hotels south of town. ♦ Daily. 20101; fax 20661. Also at: Safari Inn, Av Rafael Melgar 40 (between Calles 5 and 7S). 20101

38 Parque Arqueológico de Cozumel (Cozumel Archaeological Park) A new attraction far from downtown and the beaches, this park seems to have been built as a diversion for the cruise ship passengers who arrive here by the busload. Lushly landscaped, it has exact replicas of 65 of Mexico's most famous archaeological finds, including the five-foot-high stone head attributed to the Olmec civilization, and replicas of Maya relics. If you haven't visited any archaeological sites on the mainland, you may find the park interesting. Be sure to wear bug repellent if you visit in the rainy season (June through September). ♦ Admission. Daily. Bounded by Avs 40S and 50S, and Calles 3S and 5S (inland from the cruise ship pier). No phone

Sportfishing

The sportfishing off Cozumel is spectacular, with tuna, dorado, wahoo, marlin, and sailfish in plentiful numbers from March through July, and record catches of billfish peaking in April and May. Fishing is not allowed inside the reefs along the western shores, but there is a channel between the reef and Playa del Carmen where sailfish abound. Cozumel hosts a **Billfish Release Tournament** and a **Marlin Tournament** in May, attracting top names in sportfishing circles. Boats can be chartered at **Club Náutico de Cozumel** marina and the **La Caleta** marina behind the **Presidente Cozumel** hotel. To choose a sportfishing charter, wander the marinas as the boats come in, and ask how other customers enjoyed their outings. Check the fishing gear provided, and keep in mind that a bathroom and a shaded area make the trip far more comfortable. Tour agencies and hotel desks can arrange sportfishing charters, or contact the following companies and captains:

Capt. Felipe Quinones	21817
Capt. Leonides Quiam	20481
Cozumel Angler's Fleet	20118; fax 21135
The Sharp Hook	24349; fax 23282

The highest point in Cozumel is 45 feet above sea level.

Restaurants/Clubs: Red   **Hotels:** Blue
Shops/ ♣ Outdoors: Green   **Sights/Culture:** Black

39 Hotel Barracuda $$ One of the least expensive hotels near the reefs, this pink 50-room property sits on a ledge above the sea. The no-frills rooms have small refrigerators, televisions, and seafront balconies; dive boats pick up clients at the hotel's small cement dock. There's nothing fancy about the place, but it's within walking distance of town, has good snorkeling just offshore, and is usually frequented by friendly dive groups. ♦ Av Rafael Melgar 628 (at Av Circunvalación). 20002; fax 20884

40 Galápago Inn $$$ This dedicated divers' hotel has several packages that include room, meals, and diving at reasonable rates, and is often filled with groups from US dive shops. The small white stucco inn has 58 rooms facing the inner courtyard and others in a two-story building looking out to sea. Rooms 36 through 41 have particularly nice views. One wonderful feature is the beachfront *palapa* with 12 hammocks hanging underneath—a perfect spot for relaxing and fantasizing about the creatures you've seen on your dives. There's a small pool above the beach. The dive shop, run by **Del Mar Divers,** is well equipped for shuttling boatloads of divers back and forth to the reefs. ♦ Carretera Sur (between San Miguel and Chankanaab). 20663, 800/847.5708

Within the Galápago Inn:

Galápago Inn Restaurant ★★★$$ A casual yet excellent second-story eatery overlooking the beach, it offers huge sandwiches and burgers, great french fries, and bountiful Mexican specialties. ♦ Mexican/American ♦ Daily lunch and dinner. 20663

41 Sol Caribe Cozumel $$$$ Many of Cozumel's best package deals include reduced rates at this gigantic 321-room hotel designed to capture and captivate its guests with lavish amenities. This pseudo-Maya, pyramid-shaped, 10-story building wraps around a lavish lagoonlike swimming pool. The hotel is one of the oldest on the island, but the guest rooms have been refurbished with bent-cane headboards and chairs, mini-bars, bathtubs, and satellite TVs. A glass elevator rises above the pool to the top floor, a great vantage point for snapshots of the grounds. An underground path leads to the hotel's beach across the road, where water sports equipment is available. The jungle swamp behind the hotel is one of the best in the area for bird watching. There is a restaurant on the premises. ♦ Carretera Sur, Playa Paraíso (between San Miguel and Chankanaab). 20700, 800/554.7605; fax 21301

42 La Ceiba $$$ Most guests choose this hotel for the sunken airplane located a hundred yards offshore, which serves as an artificial reef and attracts swarms of tropical fish. The hotel is named after the ceiba tree (there's an old one growing by the pool), which was sacred to the Maya. The majority of the 115 rooms are in an 11-story tower; many are in need of refurbishing, and you may need to check out a few before settling in. The rooms in an adjacent two-story section are in better shape, and have tiled baths, bizarre orange, yellow, and brown wall hangings, and king-size beds. This hotel is also close to the most popular reefs and next door to the international cruise ship pier. There is a restuarant in the hotel. ♦ Carretera Sur (between San Miguel and Chankanaab). 20812, 800/777.5873; fax 20065

43 Presidente Inter-Continental Cozumel $$$ Of all the hotels on the island, this one does the best job of seducing guests into never leaving the grounds. Set beside the jungle on a gorgeous sheltered cove, there are several levels of accommodations: modern rooms in a high-rise tower; relatively inexpensive rooms buried in gardens by the marina and a lagoon; and the best in the house, with private terraces hidden behind palms just steps from the sand. Go all the way if you can, and reserve one of these spacious rooms with sleek, light-pine furnishings, bright purple, pink, and blue touches in the decor, a dining table by the window overlooking the sea, and a large terrace with lounge chairs and private pathways leading to the beach.

The snorkeling is excellent along this stretch of rocky shore, especially at the southern end, where stone stairways lead down into the water filled with sergeant majors and angelfish, and at another rocky ledge by the *palapa* restaurant. A dive shop on the premises runs trips to nearby reefs. Though the hotel has 259 rooms and is often full, you never feel crowded, since there is a long beach north of the central swimming pool and cove, and private sunbathing areas are set apart under small *palapas*. The hotel has always excelled at personalized, gracious service, and returnees are greeted like old friends by staff, many of whom have been around for years. ♦ Carretera Sur (between San Miguel and Chankanaab). 20322, 800/327.0200; fax 21360

Within the Presidente Inter-Continental Cozumel:

El Caribeño ★★★★$ A fabulous breakfast buffet is served under an enormous *palapa* by the beach. The cheese danish and croissants are addictive, the array of tropical fruits beautiful and delicious, and the made-to-order waffles so crisp and light you'll be tempted to return for more. The lunch menu has a healthy, exotic flare, and includes a fragrant lemon-pepper pasta salad topped with grilled prawns, a grilled chicken breast with chili mayonnaise, and green *chiles rellenos* stuffed with shrimp. It's hard to resist the fresh onion-filled popovers served at lunch (if you smile sweetly, your waiter will bring more). Even if you're not staying at the hotel, consider stopping here for a leisurely breakfast or lunch, followed by a nap on the beach. ◆ Mexican/American ◆ Daily breakfast, lunch, and dinner. 20322

44 Fiesta Americana The Reef $$$$
Formerly the **Holiday Inn**, this hotel is ideal for those who want seculsion—it is located at the edge of the jungle across from a pristine white beach. All 160 rooms look toward the sea, but the view from the rear corridors is spectacular as well, especially in the early morning, when birds flock to the mangrove trees. Though totally devoid of character, the modern rooms pamper guests with firm, king-size mattresses, satellite TVs, big bathtubs, and a calming pink-and-gray color scheme. The **Reef Beach Club** is an elaborate affair, with mini-*palapas* lined up along the sand, a shaded restaurant and bar, and Windsurfer and jet-ski rentals. A tall *palapa* covers another restaurant by the pool. There's a blue metal bridge running over the road so guests needn't dodge the traffic. Scuba divers, take note—if you arrange to have a dive boat pick you up here, you'll be the last passengers on and the first ones off, and will have to ride only a few minutes to reach the most popular reefs. ◆ Carretera Sur (between San Miguel and Chankanaab). 22622, 800/FIESTA1; fax 22666

45 Parque Nacional Chankanaab
(Chankanaab National Park) Snorkelers, swimmers, and landlubbers can take part in the reef action without strapping on scuba gear. The Mexican government has created a wildlife sanctuary at this saltwater lagoon, where green-and-blue parrot fish, neon-orange starfish, and fragile pastel-pink anemones are visible from paths around the water. The bay is also full of colorful critters, who swim right up to shore. Snorkelers find an ideal spot in the cove, where the fish have been protected so long they don't fear humans. Rusted cannons, anchors, and statues of Christ and the Virgin Mary encrusted with coral litter the white sand floor.

The park is also a botanical garden, with more than 350 species of flowers, vines, and trees from 22 countries (along with 417 species of plant life found on Cozumel) lining the pathways. There is a small museum with relics from shipwrecks, and a mock Maya village with replicas of Maya carvings painted in bright yellows and blues, as they might have been originally. Facilities include four dive shops with snorkeling, scuba, and camera equipment rentals, a restaurant, several gift shops, lockers, rest rooms, and showers. Try to avoid going to the park when the cruise ships are in port, as the place fills up. ◆ Admission. Daily. Carretera Sur (between San Miguel and Playa San Francisco). No phone

46 El Cedral This temple was the first Maya ruin sighted by the Spanish exploring Cozumel in 1518, and is supposedly the site of the island's first Catholic mass. Apparently the Spaniards destroyed most of the site, and it is believed that the US Army Corps of Engineers finished the damage during WWII while building the island's airstrip. All that remains is a crumbling, gray limestone building with a stubborn tree growing out its middle. The temple is the island's agricultural center, and hosts an annual fiesta on 1-3 May. ◆ At Carretera Sur, Km 17.5; take the dirt-road turnoff inland and drive about three kilometers (two miles)

Mecca of the Maternal Maya

Ixchel, the Maya goddess of fertility, childbirth, medicine, and the moon, was believed to have resided on Cozumel, which the Maya called *Ah-Cuzamil-Peten* (Island of the Swallows). Women from throughout Maya lands were expected to make the pilgrimage to the island at least once in their lives, an arduous and sometimes dangerous trip that took them from their homes to the mainland coast, and then across the water in dugout

THE YUCATAN

Ixchel

canoes. Those wishing to become pregnant were especially devoted to Ixchel; they would bring her offerings of jade, and some even pierced their tongues to drip blood on her feet in tribute. Though Ixchel represented life and renewal, she appears in Maya drawings as a forbidding crone with a headdress of slithering snakes, a necklace of bones, and fingernails made of jaguar claws.

47 Playa San Francisco This three-mile-long white sand beach is one of the most popular weekend hangouts for locals. Plans to build luxury accommodations were halted in a wise move by Cozumel's civic and business leaders, who want to maintain the island's natural attributes and prevent its shores from becoming cluttered with hotel towers. For now, it will remain a beach lover's playground, with lounge chairs and *palapas* lining the sand, snorkelers and divers exploring the fringes of the reefs, and local bands performing in the *palapa* restaurant (★$$). This is a standard pit stop for cruise ship passengers; if you see the parking lot full of buses, you might want to save this beach for another day. ♦ Carretera Sur (between Chankanaab and Playa Palancar)

48 Playa Palancar Quieter than Playa San Francisco, this pretty white sand beach is a perfect hideaway. The Palancar Reef, a dramatic coral formation and one of the most popular diving spots off Cozumel, begins offshore from here, too far away to reach by swimming, however. Still, the snorkeling is terrific, and the setting is idyllic, especially if you're lucky enough to have the beach to yourself. ♦ Carretera Sur (between Chankanaab and Punta Celarain)

49 Punta Celarain The five-kilometer (three-mile) drive down the rutted dirt road to this solitary lighthouse can be a rough and deserted one, and should not be attempted during the rainy season. On the way you'll pass a tiny Maya ruin, so small it appears to have been built to house the *aluxes* (tiny Maya fairies). It's believed that the ruin's shell-shaped design, with holes at the top, served to warn of imminent storms, as the high winds passing through the holes would emit a sound resembling a foghorn. You will also drive by a forested lagoon; if you see a break in the foliage, hike through to the water for a glimpse of graceful white herons and terns gliding by peacefully.

The lighthouse sits at the end of a rocky point. Offer Primo, the keeper, a tip and he'll allow you to climb the winding staircase to the top, where the 360-degree view of the scruffy green jungle, languid ocher lagoons, and endless cerulean sea will take whatever breath you have left away. Primo's family sometimes prepares fried fish dinners on Sunday afternoons, and locals and tourists partake in a memorable impromptu feast. ♦ Carretera Sur (between Playa Palancar and Colombia de Sentos)

The striking brown-and-white-striped Splendid Toadfish, which exists only in the reefs off Cozumel, can suck down another fish in six milliseconds, making it one of the fastest eaters in the world.

50 Punta Morena A deserted hotel on an isolated beach serves as the base camp for a group of biologists striving to protect the endangered sea turtles who visit Cozumel every summer to lay their eggs. The Mexican government has placed the turtles under its protection and enacted a heavy fine for the capture or sale of the creature or its eggs. Still, turtle meat is considered both a delicacy and a staple of the islanders' diets, and the eggs are valued for their alleged aphrodisiacal properties. The biologists and the **Museo de la Isla de Cozumel** have run educational programs to enlighten the locals to the turtles' plight and enlisted them in guarding the eggs against poachers. Several years ago, tourists were able to watch the mother turtles laying their eggs at night, and were even allowed to bring the unhatched eggs to a hatchery, where baby turtles were released into the sea 60 days later. Though that practice has since been stopped by government officials, you may catch a glimpse of a mother turtle digging her nest if you're in Cozumel between May and August. Drive along the windward side of this beach late at night, and look for the glow of flashlights. If the guards let you pass by, you'll see a sight you'll never forget. ♦ Carretera Sur (off Island Crossroad)

51 San Gervasio This collection of small temples and columns can be a disappointment if you've seen the Maya sites on the mainland, but the trip into the isolated jungle is a worthwhile adventure. The rutted dirt road leading to the site cuts through dense vegetation. The short, stepped structures topped by small rooms are believed to have been the ceremonial center of Maya life on Cozumel from AD 300 to 1500. There is a soft-drink stand at the ruins, but bring a bottle of water for the ride. Try to visit the site just as it opens or closes, when the birds and iguanas are active. ♦ Admission. Daily. Take Benito Juárez east past Avenida 30, then turn left on a dirt road signposted "San Gervasio" and drive 10 kilometers (six miles)

52 Meliá Maya Cozumel $$$$ When designers revamped the property after Meliá took over, they included the chain's trademark entrance—a spacious, cool lobby filled with plants and ceiling-to-floor windows looking out to the pool and sea. A soaring pyramid-shaped *palapa* shades the pool's swim-up bar, and *palapa* beach umbrellas line a private stretch of sand that runs north into wild jungle.

The 200 rooms have tan marble floors, blond cane furnishings, floral pastel linens, mini-bars, and vanities with sinks separate from the bathrooms. Deluxe rooms have large balconies with tables and chairs. Spring for a room overlooking the ocean; those facing inland have a rather drab view of the road and swampy jungle. The hotel is the northernmost property on Cozumel, removed from traffic and peripheral noise. Its sense of privacy and seclusion pleases visiting dignitaries as well as vacationers. When Mexico's president Carlos Salinas de Gortari hosted secret meetings with Fidel Castro and South American presidents after the collapse of the Soviet Union, he chose this as his headquarters. The hotel has a restaurant on the premises. ♦ Carretera Norte (at Playa Santa Pilar). 20411, 800/336.3542; fax 21599, 305/854.0660

53 Club Cozumel Caribe $$$$ The ultimate diver's hangout, this somewhat rundown all-inclusive resort compound has 260 rooms, a long beach, two swimming pools, a disco, and group activities scheduled throughout the day and night. Rooms in the nine-floor tower section have seen better days, but have balconies looking out to the water or the jungle. Those in a newer two-story section have tiled baths, double beds, and terraces. Lockers are provided at the dive shop for your scuba gear so you don't have to lug it around. Meals are served in an open-air dining room or around the pool, and consist of generous, if somewhat boring, buffets. Nightly entertainment includes tropical dance shows, while days can be filled with aerobics, volleyball, Spanish lessons, and windsurfing classes (the club provides a day-care center that allows parents time for all this). Excursions to ruins on the mainland cost extra. While this is a good deal for divers and often has special package rates that include reduced airfare, it's a long boat ride to reach the reefs. The hotel also has an overnight dive trip that gets you in the water first thing in the morning, before the other dive boats arrive. ♦ Carretera Norte, Playa San Juan (between San Miguel and Punta Molas). 20100, 20055, 800/327.2284

54 La Cabaña del Pescador ★★$$$$ The chefs at this restaurant wisely apply their talents to one simple and sumptuous meal—steamed lobster (its name means "Lobster House") drowned in melted butter and served with rice, vegetables, and bread. The restaurant is set back from the road in a tropical garden where geese and ducks wander by a small stream. The simple dining room is made from lacquered poles topped with a *palapa*. Lightbulbs inside baskets hanging from the ceiling and oil lamps on the tables provide dim light, while ceiling fans stir the tropical air. Guests choose their lobster from a tray on the front counter, and the price is determined by the lobster's weight. ♦ Lobster ♦ Daily dinner. Carretera Norte (between San Miguel and Punta Molas). No phone

55 Sol Cabañas del Caribe $$$ Nine tiny cottages line a small cove shaded by palms and hibiscus. Named after flowers, the stucco cabanas were among Cozumel's original lodgings, built in the 1960s to serve the few lucky trailblazers who had the wherewithal to make it to an island barely discovered by the outside world. The cabanas have seen better days; the brown-and-white tiled baths could use refurbishing, and the foldout couches are lumpy and worn. Still, they are perfect for families, with kitchenettes and furnishings that can stand abuse from the kids. A small wading pool is a safe spot for the little ones to play, and the water in the cove is shallow and calm. A pair of tan-and-white, two-story buildings house 48 more modern rooms, also in a brown-and-tan color scheme. The resort is well hidden from the road and lacks both TV and telephones—a plus for those seeking a true escape. ♦ Carretera Norte, Km 6, Playa San Juan (between San Miguel and Punta Molas). 20161, 800/336.3542; fax 21599, 305/854.0660

Within Sol Cabañas del Caribe:

Windsurfing School Windsurfing champion Raul De Lille represented Mexico in the 1991 Pan-American Games in Cuba. When not practicing with the pros, he teaches windsurfing in the calm waters off Sol Cabañas's beach. According to him, Cozumel is ideal for beginners, who spend more time prone in the warm water than upright on their boards. The rates for instruction are very reasonable, and the equipment top-notch. Kayaks and other water sports gear are available for rent. ♦ Daily. 20017; fax 21942

Restaurante Sol Cabañas del Caribe ★★$$ Artificial lights illuminate a natural saltwater pool under the restaurant's deck, where sleek silvery fish (with the ungainly name of Bermuda grunts) swim. It is one of the prettiest restaurant settings on the island, and the nightly specials are a good choice—particularly the *sopa maya* (black bean soup) and the *pollo pibil* (chicken baked in banana leaves). There's a mountain-lodge feel, and locals tend to congregate at the bar, which is far more peaceful than most of those in town. ♦ Mexican ♦ Daily breakfast, lunch, and dinner. 20161

In the Driver's Seat

If you want to rent a car for a journey into the hinterlands, drive during the daylight hours, lest you wind up hitting a stray cow or horse or a truck driver whose headlights have burned out (a more common occurrence than you might think). Always fill up the gas tank whenever you see a station; although modern facilities are popping up all over the land, you can't always be guaranteed there will be anything in those gleaming new tanks. And do your best to avoid driving in overly congested Mexico City—it could end up creating the biggest headache of the trip.

As for the rules of the road, forget nearly everything you practice at home. Cars, buses, and trucks will pass you on the right or left, whichever is easiest. Bus drivers are particularly fond of passing three or four cars in a row while rounding a blind curve on a mountain pass; it adds a certain machismo to their style. Don't try to match their bravado.

Signals from other driver's headlights and taillights can be quite confounding at first. If the left blinker starts flashing on the slow-moving truck ahead of you, the driver may be signaling that it's safe for you to pass him on the left. Or he may be passing an even slower truck ahead of him, turning onto a well-hidden side road, or just greeting a fellow trucker headed toward you.

The increased number of tourists driving on country roads has created a rash of accidents, most involving confusion over the use of the left blinker. If turning left off a country road, use your right blinker, pull onto the right shoulder, watch for traffic, and cross both lanes when clear. If you use your left signal, the drivers behind you may assume they are clear to pass you, and would broadside your car as you turn.

Many of the highways between coastal resorts, archaeological sites, and other tourist attractions pass through small towns and villages where children, roosters, pigs, and dogs often roam the streets. To discourage speeding, most towns have *topes* (speed bumps) designed to obliterate the suspension system of any vehicle traveling faster than three miles per hour. Highway *topes* generally are paved ridges or bumps in the road, but in remote areas you may run into a row of large rocks or a length of thick rope lying in the sand. Keep an eye out for signs that say *"Disminuya su velocidad"* (Lower your speed), or those with drawings of a row of bumps. And remember, not all *topes* come with warning signs. Fortunately, the highways are patrolled by the *Angeles Verdes* (Green Angels), a fleet of vehicle-assistance

trucks bearing gasoline, tools, and uniformed drivers who usually speak some English and greet each new breakdown as a challenge to their resourcefulness.

If you have any spirit of adventure, you will eventually turn down a rutted dirt road that just might lead to a spectacular hidden cove or buried temple. Since the temptation to do so is irresistible, always carry a bottle of drinking water, mosquito repellent, a dependable spare tire, and an infinite measure of patience. If you break down, someone is bound to come along eventually and help, unless you're on the proverbial road to nowhere. Use common sense on these hypnotic back roads, especially in the rainy season.

TRAFFIC CIRCLE

In the cities, the *gloriettas* (traffic circles) are the driver's greatest challenge. Your best bet is to wrangle your way between two cars headed in roughly the same direction as you, and move when they do. Don't fret about which way to go; just stay on the circle until you figure your way out. Nearly everyone you ask will give you directions, regardless of whether they know the way. They're simply being polite. Ask two or three people and maybe you'll get a logical consensus and a vague sense of direction. In many areas directional signs and street names are rare and wondrous surprises. Again, just keep going around in circles or squares, asking *"dondé está. . . ?"* (where is. . . ?).

STOP

Signs with international symbols for common road conditions and warnings are starting to appear along major thorough-fares, but it helps to know a few Spanish words such as *alto* (stop), *peligroso* (dangerous), *cuidado* (watch out), and *despacio* (slow). A *derrumbe* is a rockslide or earthquake zone; a *vado* is a gully or arroyo; a *puente* is a bridge. Most rental car companies will give you a copy of the road signs and their translations, as well as maps for the areas you plan to visit.

CONSERVE SU DERECHA

USE RIGHT LANE

NO REBASE

NO PASSING

LIMITE

PARKING LIMIT

NO

NO PARKING

56 Condumel $$ Built of local limestone embedded with seashell fossils, this 10-unit condo complex is embellished with Maya touches in a refreshing departure from the usual unremarkable architecture. The building has reproductions of the Maya gods Ixchel and Chac on the walls and a mock corbeled arch at the entrance. Hammocks are provided for sleeping, or you can use the firm king-size mattresses instead. The kitchens are decorated with tiles hand-painted with flowers and vegetables, and have refrigerators stocked with the basics, plus stoves, toaster ovens, microwaves, and coffeemakers.

Air-conditioning is available, but the combination of ceiling fans and sea breezes is normally enough to keep you cool. Another plus are the bathrooms, with bidets and large bathtubs. Outside, tables and chairs perch on rocky points, and a ladder hangs from the limestone shelf on the beach into the water. The rates for the condos, which can sleep up to five people, are about the same as for one double room at the beachfront hotels. Maid service is available, and you can also have a cook prepare your meals. ♦ Carretera Norte (between San Miguel and Punta Molas). 20892; fax 20661. For reservations: Box 142, Cozumel, Quintana Roo 77600, Mexico

57 Club Náutico de Cozumel Grandiose yachts sporting satellite dishes dwarf dive and tour boats berthed for the night in the island's largest marina. If you're at all interested in fishing or cruising, take a walk along the docks in the late afternoon, when the boats are all coming in for the night. ♦ Puerto de Abrigo (between San Miguel and Punta Molas). 21024

The Undersea World of Cozumel

The greatest attractions on Cozumel are underwater, along the southwest side of the island where a 16-mile-long series of coral reefs harbors more than 230 species of tropical fish. Yellow, purple, orange, and white sponges and corals grow in fantastic formations, creating canyons, mountains, and plateaus in a striking backdrop for electric-blue queen angelfish, violet-and-jade-striped parrot fish, and thousands of neon-pink and yellow wrasses.

Scuba divers drift effortlessly with the current in the 70- to 80-degree water past brain-shaped coral the size of small buildings. Visibility is usually good to about a hundred feet, and can reach twice that in some areas.

Brown-and-white spotted moray eels slither in the reefs, while silvery barracuda glide by just out of reach. And the schools of divers in their fluorescent gear, bubbles streaming above them in the sky-blue water, are often joined by giant bronze Nassau groupers.

More than 30 dive shops on Cozumel offer trips to about 40 dive sites with a range in depth that should please both seasoned divers and neophytes. Many of the shops have joined together to form the **Cozumel Association of Dive Operators (CADO),** a much-needed organization that strives to improve safety conditions for divers and to protect oceanic ecology. Divers are instructed repeatedly to stay off the fragile coral, which is easily destroyed when struck by a diver's fins or even stroked by a careless admirer. (It's illegal to remove anything from the reefs, which are a national underwater preserve; thus, watchful divers can find incredibly large lobsters and crabs scuttling about fearlessly, and even a loggerhead turtle or two.) **CADO** offers classes for dive masters on emergency procedures, and supports the island's emergency clinic and decompression chamber by contributing $1 from every diver's fee. Operated by **D. Mario Abarca,** the clinic is open 24 hours daily (Calle 5 Sur 210; 22387, 21430).

With so many dive shops competing for clients here, you can afford the luxury of comparison shopping. Find out how many people go out on the shop's boats, and whether you have a choice of dive sites. Herding a dozen or more divers over reefs crowded with other groups is quite common during the peak seasons. Several shops offer six-pack boats, carrying a half-dozen divers to the sites of their choice; individual trips are also available. Certification courses are offered, or you can take a resort course, a shorter lesson that includes a shallow dive. The following operators are respected members of **CADO:**

Aqua Safari	20101
Caribbean Divers	21080
Del Mar Aquatics	21833
Deportes Acuáticos	20640
Dive House	21953
Dive Paradise	21007; fax 21061
Fantasía Divers	22840
Pro Dive	20221

During World War II the United States military had a submarine base off Cozumel.

S A F E T Y · B E A U T Y · E C O L O G Y · D I V I N G

Bests

Gaston Cantarell
Cozumel Hotel Association

On Cozumel:

There are scores of great restaurants with familiar Mexican fare—enchiladas, burritos, tamales, and the like. But don't miss some of the more adventurous and tasty regional dishes that are specialties of the Caribbean coast, the Maya community, and the Yucatán.

Among the best: tangy ceviche (cold marinated fish); chicken with *mole* (a savory sauce prepared with chocolate, cinnamon, tomatoes, and ground nuts); and pork or chicken *pibil* (barbecued and served with a sauce of oranges, garlic, cumin, and other spices). Also good are fresh snapper and spiny Caribbean lobsters.

One of my favorite places to spend an afternoon relaxing and contemplating the natural wonders of Mexico's Caribbean coast is Cozumel's **Chankanaab National Park,** with its beautiful natural lagoon, underwater preserve, and botanical gardens. The snorkeling is superb in the shallow, clear waters, and the gardens alongside the coast have an astonishing array of native plants, flowers, and trees.

It's difficult to select the best diving site around Cozumel, since the island is virtually surrounded by amazing reefs in sparkling clear water. But I can't imagine a diver coming here without spending time exploring **Palancar Reef**, one of the most famous underwater sites in the world. Towers of coral rise from the ocean floor, and the variety of sea life is astounding.

The **Museo de la Isla de Cozumel**, facing the waterfront, is a great place to spend the late-afternoon hours learning about the island and its people. The museum contains exhibits on history and ecology, including depictions of ancient and modern-day life on Cozumel.

Profesora Rosalinda Jinich Domingo
General Director, Museo de la Isla de Cozumel

Bicycling, motoring, or driving around the island to see the beaches, sites, and beautiful countryside. It's approximately a 60-kilometer (40-mile) trek.

Visit **Chankanaab National Park,** with its hundreds of rare and exotic tropical plants. There's sun-bathing, a natural lagoon, shops, a restaurant, and amazing snorkeling and diving in shallow water.

Take a boat trip to **Palancar,** the most magnificent reef formation, where you'll discover outstanding opportunities for fishing.

A sightseeing tour to the mainland will take you to amazing sea inlets, gorgeous beaches, and the famous Mayan ruins of **Tulúm** and **Cobá.**

Cozumel has many splendid restaurants offering a variety of cuisines and atmospheres, plus endless dancing throughout the night.

Bill Horn
Owner, Aqua Safari Dive Shop, Cozumel

Leisurely scuba diving off the coast.

Skinny-dipping on the windward side of the island.

A dinner date at **Pizza Rolandi.**

Dressing up for Carnival.

An overnight trip to Cobá.

Sharon Morales
Owner, Los Cinco Soles, Cozumel

The drive around the windward side of the island stopping at the southern lighthouse, **Punta Celarain,** where the lightkeeper's wife makes the best fresh conch ceviche. Afterward, climbing to the top of the lighthouse—fantastic view.

Listening to the shrieks of the parrot flocks in the early morning as they circle before flying to the mainland to feed for the day.

Savoring the *sopa de frijol* (black bean soup) at the very romantic **Pancho's Backyard** restaurant.

The fresh smell of soap on the Maya people as they head to the market in the morning.

Buying freshly roasted coffee beans from **Claus** at **Villa Las Anclas.**

Just-baked sweet rolls at **Los Portales.**

Snorkeling at **Yucab Reef,** one of a chain of reefs on the leeward (west) coast—an incredible variety of tropical fish.

March 21, watching the children's Spring Parade.

The Sunday night fiesta in the plaza or main square.

Carolyn Files
Executive Director, Mexico West Travel Club

In **Zihuatanejo,** the new **Villa del Sol** resort hotel is a small luxury beachfront hotel built on the side of a cliff with beautifully designed suites built around tropical gardens with paths that meander down to the sea. It is the ultimate in relaxation to laze on the private porch with a cold margarita.

Just forty-five miles from **Cabo San Lucas** on the Pacific side of **Baja California** is the **Cafe Santa Fe** in **Todos Santos.** The homemade pasta and organically grown fresh produce, make for the best Italian food anywhere. The old adobe building has a wonderful garden where you can enjoy your meal and soak in the sun.

After a rocking good time at **Planet Hollywood** (owned by Bruce and Arnold) in Cancún, I catch a boat to **Contoy Island** for a day of scuba diving and bird watching at this island paradise.

Restaurants/Clubs: Red	Hotels: Blue
Shops/ 🌳 Outdoors: Green	**Sights/Culture:** Black

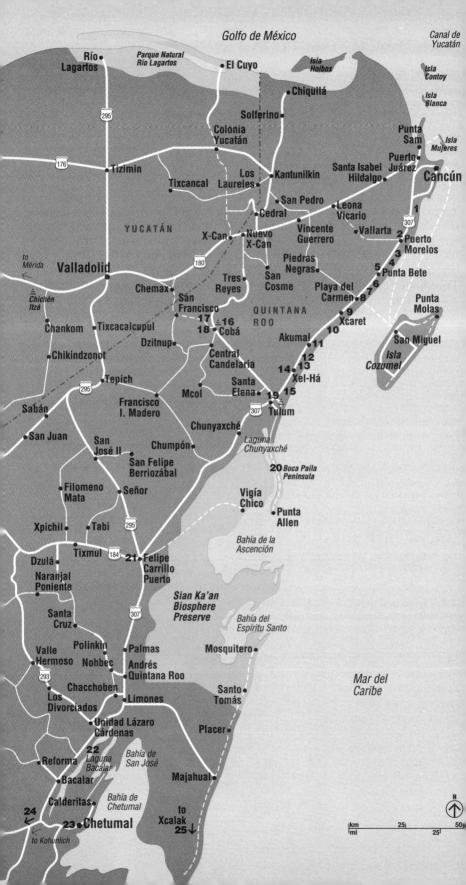

The Quintana Roo Coast

The Caribbean coast of Quintana Roo was once a secret Eden, cherished by a fanatical cult of adventurers eager to explore the 451 kilometers (282 miles) of virgin beaches and coral reefs stretching from **Cancún** to **Chetumal** at the **Belize** border. But Cancún's success has filtered south, and the white, sandy beaches lined with swaying palms have been discovered by developers, travel agents, and tour guides. Highway 307, a two-lane ribbon of asphalt rippling through a jungle that harbors parrots, monkeys, and crumbling Maya ruins just yards from the sea, has become a thoroughfare for taxis, trucks, and jeeps—a freeway to paradise.

The first hundred miles south of Cancún has been dubbed the **Cancún-Tulum Corridor.** It was an area targeted by the government and investors as the logical extension of Cancún, and it's now packed with marinas, golf courses, condo villages, and one-of-a-kind resorts. The corridor's attributes have long been familiar escapes for Cancún regulars and travelers wandering off the beaten path. Archaeology buffs flock to the Maya ruins of **Cobá** and **Tulum;** divers and snorkelers covet the hidden coves at **Akumal** and **Xcaret;** and explorers delight in the series of unmarked dirt roads leading from the highway to secluded hotels. Now mainstream travelers ply the corridor as well, buying time-shares in state-of-the-art vacation communities such as **Puerto Aventuras,** a 900-acre development with a marina, golf course, and condos galore. The port town of **Playa del Carmen** has become a destination unto itself, with ferries to **Cozumel,** dozens of budget hostelries, and **Playacar,** another full-scale resort development.

Sensing the potential endangerment of the **Yucatán Peninsula**'s wildlife and ecology, the Mexican government teamed up with **UNESCO** (United Nations Educational, Scientific, and Cultural Organization) in 1987 to create the **Sian Ka'an Biosphere Preserve,** which protects 10 percent of Quintana Roo's jungle and coastline from development. Starting just south of the Cancún-Tulum Corridor, **Sian Ka'an** incorporates the 35-kilometer-long (22-mile-long) **Boca Paila Peninsula,** a magnet for explorers addicted to Quintana Roo's isolationist character. Several small resorts and fishing camps are in the preserve, attracting nature lovers and escapists willing to drive down long, bumpy dirt roads to reach their versions of heaven.

The southern half of Mexico's Caribbean coast is beginning to feel the overflow from the north, as the pioneers who created resort hideaways near Cancún 20 years ago flee to less crowded shores. The **Xcalak Peninsula,** at the far southern tip of the state, has caught the attention of those seeking endless swaths of sand, plots of reasonably priced land, and the chance to create or re-create a tropical retreat. Forecasters figure Xcalak (pronounced *Eesh*-ca-lak) has about five to 10 years before paved roads, electricity, and brand-name hotels tear up this last stretch of wilderness. If you're interested in seeing what the Quintana Roo coastline looked like pre-Cancún, visit Xcalak—before the turn of the century.

Roseate Spoonbill, from Sian Ka'an Biosphere Preserve

Getting around the Coast of Quintana Roo

Airport
The nearest airport to the Quintana Roo coast is in Cancún; see page 113 for airline information.

Buses
It's easy to travel by bus down the coast of Cancún to Chetumal. The drawback comes when you reach your bus stop, as many of the coastal attractions are 1.5 kilometers (one mile) or more off the highway, a difficult walk if you're lugging heavy bags. Enterprising taxi drivers cruise the bus stops along Highway 307 and can take you to your ultimate destination. (Be sure to settle on the fare before you hop in.)

Cancún's bus terminal is at the intersection of Avenidas Tulum and Uxmal in downtown. Buses run frequently to Playa del Carmen and **Tulum.**

Playa del Carmen's station is on Avenida Juárez. Connections can be made to **Felipe Carrillo Puerto, Laguna Bacalar,** and Chetumal.

Car Rental
The best way to tour the Caribbean coast is by auto. Most rental cars in the area are VW Bugs or jeeps. Four-wheel drive is not necessary except during the rainy season, but comes in handy if you want to get off the beaten track. You can sometimes get better rates if you make arrangements in advance. If you want air-conditioning or a four-door sedan, reserve well ahead of your arrival. The following agencies have desks at the Cancún airport:

Avis	842328, 830828
Budget	840730, 840204
Econo-Rent	841826, 841435
National	860152, 851000

Ferry
A passenger ferry to Cozumel departs from the pier in Playa del Carmen about a dozen times a day. The trip takes 30 to 45 minutes, depending on the boat and weather conditions.

A car ferry to Cozumel leaves from Puerto Morelos about six times a week. For the latest schedule, call 987/20827.

FYI

Emergencies
Centro de Salud (Health Center) Av Juárez (at Calle 15), Playa del Carmen 987/21230

Hospital General, Av Andres, Chetumal ... 983/21932

Police (Chetumal) 981/62329

Police (Playa del Carmen) 938/20205

Money
Banks are open Mondays through Fridays from 9AM to 1:30PM. It's best to bank at the Cancún airport, in Playa del Carmen, and in Chetumal. You can usually pay hotel bills with traveler's checks (it's best to get them in small amounts, as otherwise it may be difficult to get change); credit cards are somewhat less useful, since smaller establishments may not be linked with the credit card companies. Carry a good amount of small-denomination pesos—many businesses do not have a lot of change. Cash larger bills at gas stations and busy restaurants.

Visitors Information
There is a visitors' information booth on the Plaza Principal in Playa del Carmen, but the hours are erratic. The phone number is 938/20856.

1 Croco Cun Don't let the hokey name fool you. This is actually a respectable zoological park that specializes in breeding morolette crocodiles and releasing them in areas where they have nearly become extinct. Guides are eager to give you an in-depth lesson in the reptile's lifestyle and habitats, and will let you hold a baby croc if you so desire. Interspersed among the crocodile ponds are exhibits of nearly all the species of animals that once inhabited the peninsula—spider monkeys, badgers, deer, wild pigs, pheasants, peccaries, plus a scarlet macaw from Chiapas.

The snake exhibit is enough to keep you out of the jungle forever, and the indigenous tarantulas are appallingly large. The zoo also has a family of hairless dogs called *xoloscuintli*, ancestors of those that lived with the ancient Aztecs. Allow a couple of hours for your tour and wear plenty of insect repellent. There is a small restaurant serving meals and snacks, and a gift shop. ♦ Admission. T-Su. Hwy 307, Km 33 (between Cancún and Puerto Morelos). 98/842822

2 Puerto Morelos The car ferry to Cozumel leaves from this small village of 3,000 residents (5,000 if you count part-timers with vacation homes and condos). When the ferry arrives and departs, the town's sandy streets are filled with cars and trucks waiting in line. Once they're gone, it returns to its natural somnolent state. Neighbors gather at the concrete main plaza to gossip and watch their children play, and fishers beach their boats on the sand near the plaza.

The town has remained remarkably unscathed by the rampant development taking place along the corridor around it. However, if you walk down the streets to the north and south of the town, you'll see neighborhoods of new homes and condos. There are precious few hotels and restaurants, and no tourist attractions, except for a spectacular coral reef just 500 yards offshore that's renowned for its fishing and an abundance of shipwrecks, making it a big lure for divers. If you're interested in diving at the reef, there is an unnamed scuba shop on the beach by the main plaza; ask for the manager, Nieto, who has a compressor and air for filling tanks, and takes divers to his favorite spots for a very reasonable price. ♦ Hwy 307, Km 36 (between Cancún and Playa del Carmen)

In Puerto Morelos:

The Caribbean Reef Club $$ Talk about hideaways. There's nothing in sight but long stretches of empty beach and the endless sea. Just a three- and four-story Mediterranean villa with 21 rooms and suites, all facing a deep blue swimming pool and the beach. The rooms have marble floors, satellite TV, fireplaces (in some suites), kitchens with microwaves, air-conditioning, ceiling fans, and cane-backed chairs and glass-topped tables. A boat is available for snorkeling and fishing trips, but you may just want to wander on the long secluded beaches, take an occasional dip in the pool, or while the hours away swinging in a hammock on your terrace. ♦ South of the ferry dock. 98/742932. For reservations: Apdo 1526, Cancún, Quintana Roo 77500, Mexico. 98/832636, 800/3.CANCUN; fax 98/832244

Within the Caribbean Reef Club:

The Caribbean Reef Club Restaurant ★★★★$$ Set away from the villa on a pathway bordered with red hibiscus and fuchsia bougainvillea, this white, open-air restaurant has a wooden patio overlooking the beach, and an indoor dining room with arched windows and seating nooks facing the sea. Guests and locals congregate in the restaurant's bar. Texas-style fajitas, chicken-fried steak, barbecued pork ribs, and curly french fries are some of its unusual offerings, considering the locale. ♦ American/Mexican ♦ Daily lunch and dinner. No phone

Ojo de Agua $ Hurricane Gilbert virtually destroyed this established divers' hotel (with its own dive shop), and it took the owners more than three years to build 12 replacement rooms and a small pool. The rooms, in a two-story motel-like building are immaculate, with kitchenettes complete with hot plates and refrigerators. It's set just off the beach north of town, where the snorkeling and windsurfing are excellent. ♦ Av Javier Rojo Gómez (turn north off the road into town and follow the signs). No phone. For reservations: Calle 12, No 96, Mérida, Yucatán 97050, Mexico. 99/250292; fax 99/283405

Posada Amor $ Just one block from the beach, this two-story, green-and-white building houses the oldest hotel and restaurant in Puerto Morelos. The 20 rooms have simple cement-slab beds covered with thin mattresses, dark drapes to keep sunlight away from late sleepers, and ceiling fans. Half the rooms come with private baths, but only six have hot water. ♦ Turn south at the end of the road into town. No phone

Within Posada Amor:

Posada Amor Restaurant ★★$ This is the town's gathering spot. Stick to the Mexican meals such as *huevos rancheros* (fried eggs served over a corn tortilla with spicy tomato sauce) and *carne asada* (grilled marinated beef) if you want to sample their best offerings; if you're hungry for something new, try the lasagna or fried chicken—certainly different from the kind you would have at home. ♦ Mexican ♦ Daily breakfast, lunch, and dinner. No phone

3 Jardín Botánico Dr. Alfredo Barrera Marin (Botanical Garden) Bug repellent is a must for a tour through this miniature jungle composed of many of the peninsula's indigenous trees, most labeled in Spanish. Try to visit early in the day, when the birds are chipper and the humidity is low. ♦ Admission. Daily (hours vary in the low season). Hwy 307, Km 38 (between Puerto Morelos and Playa del Carmen). No phone

4 Rancho Loma Bonita Horse lovers will find great spots here for riding through the jungle and coastline, though there are precious few mounts for hire. This small ranch, out of sight from the road, has the sole riding concession. The horses are in good condition, and it's a joy to ride along the edge of the sea with no other humans in sight. Call in advance for reservations to ensure that horses are available for all the members of your party. Most Cancún hotels and tour companies can arrange your equestrian excursion as well. ♦ Daily. Hwy 307, Km 42 (between Puerto Morelos and Playa del Carmen). 98/840907

5 Punta Bete One of the prettiest stretches of beach in this area is home to two of the most beloved hideaways on the coast, plus a couple of small campgrounds. Rumors of impending development along this part of the coast have drifted about since 1990, but thus far, the peace and beauty remain intact. A large concrete archway on the east side of the highway marks the entrance to the resorts, which sit by the beach about two kilometers (1.25 miles) east at the end of a dirt road. ♦ Hwy 307, Km 52 (between Puerto Morelos and Playa del Carmen)

At Punta Bete:

La Posada del Capitán Lafitte $$ Stucco bungalows with window fans and oceanfront porches line a wild beach where ocean breezes negate any need for air-conditioning. No wonder guests return annually for their dose of tranquillity. One of the first resorts along this coast, it remains one of the area's best. Offering the complete antithesis to Cancún's glitz, the resort is laid back and unpretentious. The 23 bungalows have electricity and hot running water, and the game room has satellite TV. Five buildings—each housing four rooms—were recently added, but old-timers still prefer the bungalows. The full-service dive shop runs trips to the nearby reefs. Breakfast and dinner are included in the room rate. ♦ Closed September-October. On a dirt road (follow the signs), about two kilometers (1.25 miles) off Hwy 307. No phone. For reservations: Turquoise Reef Group, Box 2664, Evergreen, CO 80439. 303/674.9615, 800/538.6802; fax 303/674.8735

Within La Posada del Capitán Lafitte:

Capitán Lafitte Restaurant ★★★$ This spot offers very varied fare, including chilled soups, curried chicken, and a weekly lobster night. Meals are served under a *palapa* (thatch-roofed hut) overlooking the water by waiters who instantly learn your name and memorize your preferences. ♦ Mexican ♦ Daily breakfast, lunch, and dinner, closed September-October. No phone

Kai Luum Camptel $$ The concept of luxury camping was the brainchild of Arnold Bilgore and his family, who have been creating their version of a tropical paradise for more than two decades. The 40 campsites are set in a palm grove by the beach; each tent has a *palapa* over it, with hammocks hanging from the supports. Rest rooms and showers are located down sand paths close to the tents. Gourmet meals are served family style at wooden picnic tables under a *palapa*. There is no electricity, and in the evening Maya workers bear torches as they walk along the paths, lighting oil lamps stuck in the sand. Meals, taxes, and tips are included in the room rates. It shares a dive shop with **Lafitte**.

The resort was completely destroyed by Hurricane Gilbert in 1988. After the storm, Bilgore and his son Mino sat amid the rubble, wondering if they should start over. Out of nowhere, truckloads of Maya workers appeared, hoping they would be able to rebuild their own homes with the wages earned in the reconstruction. Nine months later, the campsite was back in operation. Closed September-October. ♦ Hwy 307, Km 54 (between La Posada del Capitán Lafitte and Shangri-La Caribe). For reservations: Turquoise Reef Group, Box 2664, Evergreen, CO 80439. 303/674.9615, 800/538.6802; fax 303/674.8735

Shangri-La Caribe

6 **Shangri-La Caribe** $$$$ European groups seem particularly fond of this 70-unit beachside property. The accommodations are located in one- and two-story cabanas that resemble Maya huts, with whitewashed stucco walls and shaggy *palapas*, and hammocks hanging on the front porches. The dive shop is well equipped, and diving here, though not as spectacular as off Cozumel, is addictive. The freshwater pool is a refreshing gathering spot, and the restaurant serves excellent hamburgers and grilled seafood. Word has it that a 30-room beachfront expansion is in the offing. ♦ Hwy 307, Km 56 (at Punta Bete). No phone. For reservations: Turquoise Reef Group, Box 2664, Evergreen, CO 80439. 303/674.9615, 800/538.6802; fax 303/674.8735

7 **Las Palapas** $$$$ Similar to **Shangri-La** in architectural style, this hostelry has 55 spacious bungalows, each with thatch roofs, two double beds, a desk by the window, and two hammocks on the front porch. The property is a self-contained paradise, with two restaurants (breakfast and dinner are included in the rates), an absolutely gorgeous beach, a pool, a game room, and a dive shop. You can walk along the beach to Playa del Carmen, about 20 minutes south, or hire a cab or rent a car for trips to the ruins. Many of the European guests just stay put for days on end, which also isn't a half-bad idea. ♦ Hwy 307, Km 58 (between Punta Bete and Playa del Carmen). 987/22977. For reservations: Playa Travel, 7216 Columbine Dr, Carlsbad, CA 92008. 800/527.0022; fax 619/438.8201

8 **Playa del Carmen** The largest inhabited spot between Cancún and Chetumal, this beach town is going through a transformation from a backpacker's hangout to a full-scale resort destination. Development was inevitable here, given the location: Cancún is less than an hour's drive north; Cozumel is 30 minutes east on the ferry; and the ruins of **Tulum** and **Cobá** are less than an hour's drive south. This is the longest stretch of uninterrupted beach along the corridor; it also has the most tourist services, including banks, bus stations, a small airstrip, markets, pharmacies, and auto parts stores. Avenida Juárez is the main street leading from the highway to the ferry pier; it acts as a boundary between the town's past and future incarnations. South of the pier is the massive **Playacar** development, an 880-acre upscale resort. When completed (tentatively, within

---

Restaurants/Clubs: Red   **Hotels:** Blue
Shops/ 🌳 Outdoors: Green   **Sights/Culture:** Black

five years), it will include a golf course, marina, private homes, condos, and four hotels. The town's center is the waterfront plaza at the ferry dock, complete with a church, kiosk, playground, and sidewalk cafes.

Avenida 5, the first street parallel to the beach, has been paved with cement and made into a pedestrian walkway. Restaurants and shops are opening and closing at an astounding rate along this stretch, but the landmark inexpensive bungalow hotels are holding their ground quite successfully.

You're best off exploring on foot, as the narrow dirt roads run in a confusing one-way pattern and parking is nearly nonexistent. It will take considerable work to make this a pretty place—it's been funky and rundown far too long to become a paradise overnight. But if you're looking for gorgeous beaches, moderate prices, convenient bus service, and a youthful crowd, this is your best choice on the coast. ♦ Hwy 307, Km 68 (between Punta Bete and Akumal)

In Playa del Carmen:

Blue Parrot Inn $$ An old-timer by Playa standards, this hotel has been a cult favorite since it opened in 1984. The 30 guest rooms (at press time, there were plans to increase the number to 80) are housed in small cabanas and two-story, thatch-roofed stucco buildings right on the sand. The beachfront restaurant and bar is an enduring favorite of local expats, especially during Happy Hour in the early evening; movies and music videos are shown nightly in a second-story bar with a sand floor and beanbag chairs. The mood throughout is low-key, friendly, and comfortable, sans TV and phone, though air-conditioning may be coming to a few rooms soon. Reservations must be made through the US office, though if you're in the area, call the hotel directly to check on availability. ♦ Calle 12 (at Av 5). 987/30083; fax 987/30046. For reservations: 655 W Wisconsin Ave, Orange City, FL 32763. 904/775.6660, 800/634.3547

Plaza Rincon del Sol This bright-pink shopping center is an architectural delight, with Colonial arches, landscaped terraces, and the best folk art shops along the coast. ♦ M-Sa. Av 5N (at Calle 8). 987/30110

Within Plaza Rincon del Sol:

Xop Every item in this gallery is made by a truly talented Mexican artist; it's worth a stop here just for the selection of hand-crafted jewelry. The gorgeous amber found locally is set in earrings with porcupine quills, wild boar tusks, and even boa constrictor ribs; huge amber pendants embedded with fossilized insects hang from intricate silver necklaces; Maya gods with opal eyes are cast in silver pins. There is also an outstanding selection of masks from Guerrero and carved wooden *santos* (saints). All items can be packed for shipping. ♦ M-Sa 5-10PM. 987/30110

Albatros Royale $$ This is one of the prettiest hotels along the beach, with 31 basic—yet comfortable—rooms in two-story buildings. All have pine tables and plastic white chairs, two double or one king-size bed, large bathrooms with hot showers, cool tiled floors, thatch roofs, and balconies, complete with an orange-and-yellow hammock. Sea breezes and ceiling fans cool the white rooms, though at press time, there were plans to put air-conditioning in some. The beach is at the edge of the property, and there are plenty of restaurants and shops within a few blocks. ♦ Calle 6 (at Av 5). 987/30001, 800/527.0022; fax 987/30002

Limones ★★★$$ Stairs lead down from the sidewalk under an A-frame *palapa* to a sunken dining room that seems to be buried in trees and vines. If lobster is your desire, the chef grills a hefty portion and surrounds it with white rice and steamed vegetables, accompanied by a side dish of pasta and hot garlic bread. Garlic lovers take note—the fresh fish with *mojo y ajo* (oil and garlic) is smothered with crisp chunks of browned garlic and is absolutely superb. The nightly special (with appetizer, entrée, and dessert) is a bountiful bargain. ♦ Italian/Mexican ♦ Daily dinner. Av 10 (at Calle 2). No phone

Sabor ★★★$ Melinda Burns, pastry chef extraordinaire, spoils her fans with an irresistible display of desserts in her tiny cafe. The few small tables are almost always filled with loyal patrons sampling dense chocolate cake, flaky pecan pie, creamy cheesecake, coconut flan, or whatever other treat appears on the shelves that day. Full breakfasts, fruit salads, and sandwiches are also available. ♦ Health food/Desserts ♦ Daily breakfast, lunch, and dinner. Av 5 (between Calles 4 and 2). No phone

Máscaras ★★★$ The best vantage point for watching the plaza and the bustle of local life is from the outside tables at the most popular cafe in town. It's well loved by locals and visitors alike for the gourmet pizzas made in wood-burning ovens, marinated calamari, and bohemian ambience. ♦ Italian ♦ Daily lunch and dinner. Av Juárez (north side of the plaza). 987/30194

147

Ferry Pier Two ferry companies operate boats to Cozumel from Playa del Carmen. **Cruceros Maritimos del Caribe** (987/21942) runs the *Mexico* and *Mexico III,* both fast, air-conditioned boats that make the 30-minute trip 10 times daily. **Naviera Turistica** (987/21824, 21913) pilot the traditional ferries—the *Xel-Há* and *Cozumeleño*—which depart eight times a day. They have open-air decks, and are less expensive (the trip is 15 minutes longer). Several stands by the pier sell tickets. ♦ The street to the ferry is closed to traffic; there's a parking lot at Av Juárez and Av 10 that is open daily 24 hours. At the foot of Av 5 (one block south of Av Juárez)

Continental Plaza Playacar $$$ Built on the scale and style of a Cancún hostelry, this is the first hotel in the massive Playacar development. The 188 large rooms have woven cotton spreads covering the king-size and double beds, and pastel-colored, tropical-flower prints on the couches and chairs; the suites have kitchenettes. There are two good restaurants, noteworthy for their buffet breakfasts and dinners. The pool flows around islands and under bridges leading to one of the eateries (under a *palapa*), and the beach stretches uninterrupted for miles to the south. The hotel has a water sports center on the beach, a travel agency, a gift shop, a tennis court, and room service. The rooms are often filled with travelers on package deals and group tours; reservations are strongly advised. ♦ Hwy 307, Km 68, Calle 10 (off Av Juárez). 987/21583, 800/882.6684; fax 988/51403

Diamond Resort $$$$ Another property popular with groups, this all-inclusive resort is far nicer than most—it has attractive two-story *palapas* spread down a slight hill toward the beach. The 296 rooms are quite nice, with air-conditioning and ceiling fans, TVs and phones, big bathtubs and showers, and small balconies. The dining room is in the second story of an enormous thatch-roofed building where all meals are bountiful buffets; hot dogs and hamburgers are served in a smaller snack shop by the beach. Recreational pastimes include all water sports, tennis, volleyball, bicycling, and basketball, as well as other scheduled activities—such as aerobics and stretch classes—throughout the day. Tours to the ruins are available at an additional cost. The main drawback is the location, at least a 15-minute walk from downtown Playa. ♦ Playacar (between Punta Bete and Akumal). 800/858.2258

9 Xcaret Those who respect nature in the raw and the sanctity of Maya sites have a hard time accepting what this has become, but if you've never been here before, it's gorgeous. The hidden cove (the name, pronounced *Eesh*-ca-ret, means "little cove" or "inlet" in Maya) with temples, underground caves, and

secret snorkeling spots, has been transformed into a waterfront amusement park. Artificial beaches and lagoons are etched into the limestone, lush tropical flowers and trees grow along landscaped paths, and *palapas* shade overpriced restaurants overlooking the Caribbean. The beaches are beautiful, with soft white sand bordering a shallow clear pool where fish have yet to return. The big attraction is the river ride through the caves, included in the park's exorbitant admission price. Lockers, showers, and rest rooms are available, along with a large gift shop. If you are serious about snorkeling or exploring Maya ruins, go farther south to **Xel-Há** and **Tulum.** ♦ Admission. Daily. Hwy 307, Km 72 (between Playa del Carmen and Akumal). No phone

From Princes to Paupers—Everyone Prefers the Palapa

The ubiquitous *palapa* (a large palm-frond hut) found along Mexico's coastline has existed since the days of ancient cultures. Maya drawings and carvings from the first century show *palapas* shading kings and peasants alike, both on land and in their dugout canoes. Two thousand years later, the *palapa* has become an integral architectural feature of the most glamorous hotels in Puerto Vallarta and Cancún, and is the requisite beach shelter along the Pacific, the Caribbean, and the Mar de Cortés.

A basic, traditional *palapa* is made from a tree trunk with a roof of palm fronds that is nailed or tied on an umbrella-shaped framework of poles. (Large *palapas* also have upright supports for the circumference of the roof, which are ideal for hanging hammocks.) Resort and restaurant designers have taken the *palapa* to new heights with soaring 30-foot-tall palm-frond roofs shaped like pyramids, A-frames, and arches. It can take months to cover these elaborate wood-beam frames with palm fronds. Many of the modern *palapa* artists shun palms in favor of *zacate,* a thin, long grass from the state of Campeche sewn into long strips that wrap easily around the most intricate designs. When constructed properly, a well-made *palapa* can last 20 years or more and many can even withstand tropical storms.

G. L. G.

10 Puerto Aventuras It was inevitable. The Quintana Roo coast couldn't stay wild and undeveloped forever, especially with Cancún overspilling its boundaries. This 900-acre resort development is only one in a number of proposed megaprojects. The most critical feature is a 250-slip marina, a needed addition to these shores. To build it, the developers carved and blasted their way through the limestone, leaving surface area for hotels and condos while creating bays and lagoons surrounding miniature islands. At press time, nine of 18 holes were ready for play in the golf course. Terra-cotta-colored, Santa Fe–style condominium and time-share units are the cornerstone of the residential market here, and salespeople are stationed on the highway and throughout the complex, ready to weave their webs. ♦ Moderate greens fee. Hwy 307, Km 98 (between Playa del Carmen and Akumal). 987/22211, 987/23376, 800/446.2747; fax 987/23332

In Puerto Aventuras:

Museo Pablo Bush Romero CEDAM, the Mexican Underwater Explorers' Club, was founded in 1958 largely through the efforts of Pablo Bush Romero, an explorer, adventurer, and diver with a strong love for his country's Caribbean coast. He played a major role in the funding and creation of this scuba museum, which was inaugurated in 1988; his likeness stands near the entrance. Divers will be fascinated by the early copper hyperbolic chamber with leather seals where divers underwent decompression. The museum's displays include artifacts found at the wreck of the *Mantanceros,* a Spanish merchant ship that sank off this coast in 1741 (no one knows for sure why the craft went down). The collection of glass beads, golden coins, rusted cannons, poker chips and dominoes, and religious statues from this and other shipwrecks (including the *Nicolosa,* which sank in 1527 and was discovered off Punta Cancún in 1959) gives an eerie sense of what life at sea must have been like in days gone by, when pirates and rival nations waged war against each other with cannonballs. This is a must-see for divers and history buffs. ♦ Admission. Daily; closed at midday. No phone

Mike Madden's CEDAM Dive Center This is one of the best areas in the world for cave and cenote (underground well) diving and the site of expert Mike Madden's **PADI (Professional Association of Dive**

Instructors)-approved facility with equipment rentals and sales. Spectacular dive sites abound within a 10-minute boat ride. Those who've spent considerable time under water here say you can dive twice a day for a week and always find something new. The fish are larger here than in the underwater preserves, and divers typically see giant rays and sea turtles, including the legendary turtle said to be as big as a Volkswagen Bug. ♦ Daily. PO Box 117, Playa del Carmen, Quintana Roo 77710, Mexico. 987/22211

11 Akumal Mediterranean villas, basic bungalows, and modern hotels line the shores of this natural bay, once the nesting ground for thousands of sea turtles. The name is Maya for "land of the turtles." The sea turtles still return for their annual migration and have simply moved to more isolated spots away from humanity.

This was a Maya community and a coconut plantation long before tourism hit these shores. Explorers discovered the wreck of the *Mantanceros* offshore in 1926, and it was here that Pablo Bush Romero headquartered **CEDAM** in the 1950s. All that is left of the original village is a settlement of Maya workers at the entrance to the area's first resort. Several side roads lead from the highway to the resorts. ♦ Hwy 307, Km 105 (between Playa del Carmen and Tulum)

At Akumal:

Club Akumal Caribe & Villas Maya $$ A two-story villa sits at the tip of a rocky point, marking the northern boundary of this sprawling resort complex that includes four villas, three condominiums, 40 bungalows, and a small hotel with 21 rooms. Cannon House, the main villa, is the most luxurious of the accommodations, followed by a line of suites set back from the beach behind lush landscaping. The bungalows, some of which housed the divers exploring shipwrecks for CEDAM back in the 1950s, are set right on the sand, their thatch roofs replaced by red tile. The hotel is at the south end of Playa Akumal and has a private pool. Two full-service dive shops, three restaurants, an ice-cream stand, gift shops, and a small market are also part of the complex. ♦ Hwy 307, Km 105 (between Playa del Carmen and Tulum). No phone. For reservations: Akutrame, Box 13326, El Paso, TX 79913. 915/584.3552, 800/351.1622

Within Club Akumal Caribe:

Lol-Ha ★★★$$ The best of the three restaurants here, this is a large, open-air, thatch-roofed dining room set up on stilts above the sand. Breakfast is a feast that can easily hold you until dinner, especially if you consume all the sweet rolls and cookies in the basket set on each table along with your omelette or *huevos Mexicana* (eggs scrambled with tomatoes, onion, and green peppers). Dinners include thick charcoal-grilled steaks, lobster, and seafood, all served in generous portions with vegetables, rice or potatoes, and bread. Flaming desserts are a specialty.
♦ Seafood/Mexican ♦ Daily breakfast and dinner. No phone

12 Villas de las Palmas $$$ Loners and those who enjoy setting up a home away from home can rent condos on the beach by contacting US expatriates Daniel Mincey and Karen Jenkins, who manage many of the area's private vacation properties. With about 20 options, guests can stipulate the number of bedrooms they'll need and their preferred level of luxury. Mincey offers boat trips to the reef for fishing and snorkeling, and beachside group barbecues are a regular affair among the residents and guests. Maid service is available, and you can arrange to have someone come in to prepare your meals. Daily or weekly passes for the pools and water sports facilities at **Club Aventuras,** just down the road from the condos, may be purchased. ♦ Hwy 307, Km 107 (between Akumal and Tulum). 987/41886. For reservations: PO Box 124, Playa del Carmen, Quintana Roo 77710, Mexico

13 Chemuyil Local families gather on the beach along this gorgeous cove on weekend afternoons for hours of frolicking and feasting on the simple meals prepared at the nearby *palapa* bar and restaurant (see below). The bay used to be a wonderful snorkeling spot but has become a bit murky. The south end of the beach is a campground where travelers can pitch tents, hang their hammocks, or camp out of their vehicles for weeks on end. Circular *palapas* at the center of the beach are available for rent to hang your hammock in the shade for the day or evening—but there are no locks. Facilities include indoor showers and rest rooms, which apparently explains the admission fee. Highway billboards proclaim this to be "the most beautiful beach in the world." That was true once upon a time, but it has lost some charm due to increasing popularity. Also, the yellowing blight that has destroyed most of the palms along this coast has been particularly destructive here. ♦ Admission. Hwy 307, Km 109 (between Akumal and Tulum). No phone

At Chemuyil:

Restaurant Chemuyil ★★★$ Known by some as **Marco Polo,** this simple bar and restaurant serves ice-cold sodas, beer, *limonada* (lemonade), potent rum and tequila drinks, and grilled fish dinners. Chicken roasted over a fire at the nearby stand is served with fresh tortillas for a messy, yet satisfying, meal. Locals gather on hammocks hung around the bar. ♦ Mexican ♦ Daily lunch and dinner. No phone

14 Xel-Há An underwater preserve famous for its excellent snorkeling, it is located in a natural *caleta* (cove), where limestone rocks and ridges submerged in the sea provide an ideal gathering spot for giant parrot fish and schools of other tropical fish who breed undisturbed. The waters have grown a bit murky of late, and bathers are asked to not wear suntan oils and lotions into the water. Nonsnorkelers can spot turtles and tropical fish on the landscaped paths around the lagoons. A small museum has some relics from ships wrecked offshore. The *palapa* restaurant (★$) serves decent sandwiches and fish dinners, and there are showers, changing rooms, and lockers. Snorkeling equipment and underwater cameras are available for rent, and there is a large gift shop. Usually part of tours from Cancún to **Tulum,** it gets ridiculously crowded here from noon until 3PM. ♦ Admission. Daily. Hwy 307, Km 122 (between Akumal and Tulum). No phone

15 Casa Cenote ★★★★$ Worth searching for, this restaurant is perched beside **Tankah,** one of the largest cenotes (underground wells) on the Yucatán Peninsula. Lark and Gary Phillips have created the most popular restaurant along the coast for fellow US expatriates and travelers. The couple manages to prepare excellent meals without the aid of refrigeration or electricity. The menu includes casual fare such as great chicken fajitas, nachos topped with chicken or pork, and juicy hamburgers; all the beef, chicken, and cheese is imported from the US. On Sunday, the Phillips prepare a multicourse barbecue feast that lasts through the afternoon.

After (or better yet, before) a meal, take a dip in the cenote. It begins in a lagoon and runs out to sea, creating a fish trap of sorts just off shore, where the snorkeling is superb. Three manatees are said to live in the sinkhole, but they tend to be extremely shy and stay out of sight when humans are around. ♦ American/Mexican ♦ Daily lunch and dinner until sunset. Hwy 307, Km 127 (between Akumal and Tulum). No phone

Restaurants/Clubs: Red   **Hotels:** Blue
Shops/ ♠ Outdoors: Green   **Sights/Culture:** Black

16 Cobá Literally buried in the jungle, the site covers 81 square miles with five lakes (the name means "rippling waters" in Maya), and was possibly the largest Maya city-state on the Yucatán Peninsula during the post-classical period. Archaeologists estimate that 6,000 structures are spread throughout an area that held close to 50,000 residents during its peak, from AD 400 to 1100. Less than five percent of the buildings have been excavated, and the sites worth visiting are spread along unmarked trails that seem to disappear in the vegetation.

The maps available at the entrance station are very difficult to follow. To ensure a safe tour, it is well worth hiring a guide. Bring water and bug repellent, wear sturdy shoes, and try to avoid exploring during midday, when the sun's heat turns the jungle into a steam bath.

All those precautions aside, this place is worth more than a quick run-through. It's one of the few spots where you can wander relatively safely through the jungle and possibly run across a spider monkey or peccary. Once you're away from the entrance, the sounds of buzzing bugs and chortling birds seem almost deafening, then a ghostly silence falls. The sun filters through enormous ferns and palms, and the earth has a pungent aroma that seems almost primeval. The view from atop any of the pyramids is breathtaking, and from the highest, **Nohuch Mul,** you can begin to grasp the immensity of the ancient city. Though it's hard to detect, the site once had a network of *sacbes* (white limestone roads) connecting it with **Tulum** and other cities in the region. There is a small refreshment stand at the entrance to the ruins, but if you're planning to spend considerable time walking around you might want to carry some snacks.
♦ Admission. Daily. 56 kilometers (35 miles) northeast of Tulum on an unnamed paved road; traveling south on Hwy 307, turn right at the signs for Cobá just before the turnoff to Tulum. No phone

At Cobá:

Grupo Cobá The first set of ruins inside the entrance includes the 79-foot-high Iglesia (Church), so named by the Spanish because the Maya placed offerings at the top and lit candles to their gods. Archaeologists have yet to discover what the Maya called this shrine. The group includes several smaller buildings around a patio.

Grupo Nohuch Mul No matter what else you see at Cobá, you must make it to the tallest pyramid discovered on the Yucatán Peninsula, rising 12 stories above the jungle floor. It takes a hardy climber to make it up the pyramid's 120 narrow limestone steps to the temple on top, and whatever breath you have left from the climb will be taken away by the panorama before you. From the top of the

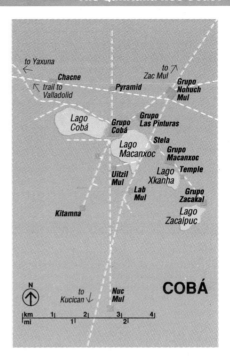

pyramid (also called El Castillo, The Castle), you can see other ruins poking through the dense vegetation, as well as the lakes from which the city got its name.

The pyramid is often compared to one in Tikal in Guatemala, which is similar in height and shape, but more ornate in decoration. There is a carving of the Descending God (the trademark of Tulum) on the temple. The longest *sacbe* in the known Maya world begins at its base and runs southwest for 99 kilometers (62 miles) to Yaxuná, near Chichén Itzá. Archaeologists and anthropologists are unsure whether these *sacbes* were used as commerce routes or ceremonial pathways. It is believed that the Maya did not use the wheel, yet these roads would seem ideal for transporting the heavy limestone blocks used in construction, as well as items for trade.

Grupo Las Pinturas Polychromatic murals from the postclassical era are still visible on the walls of the largest pyramid in this group. There is also a large carved stela—a tall limestone pillar carved with the important dates and events from that area. Stelae are found at nearly all Maya sites, and many are scattered along the pathways here; most, like this one, depict a Maya warrior standing atop his captives.

17 El Bocadito ★★$ If you're trying to keep expenses down, your best dining option near the ruins is this small indoor/outdoor restaurant. Home-style Mexican and Yucatecan cooking is the specialty here, and the portions are generous. The buses going inland and to the coast stop here, so it's a good place to rest while you wait for your ride. There are also eight basic rooms for rent, with double beds, ceiling fans, and cold showers (which provide some relief from the oppressive heat). The hotel fills up quickly, and has no phone, so check about a room before you head for the ruins. On the road to the ruins. For reservations: Apdo 56, Valladolid, Yucatán 97780, Mexico. No phone

18 Villa Arqueológica Cobá $$$ There are many good reasons for spending the night at **Cobá**, one being the opportunity to partake of the gracious hospitality at this small inn nearly buried in vegetation on the shores of Laguna Cobá. This is one of a chain of hotels built by the Mexican government and operated by Club Med at major archaeological sites. Forty small, air-conditioned rooms are arranged in a two-story white stucco building framing a pool and courtyard where bougainvillea and ferns seem to grow wild. Authentic Maya carvings and Mexican folk art make the hotel's corridors and dining room resemble a museum. Deer grazing in a side yard add to the feeling that you're far from civilization.

There is an excellent library with most of the classic texts on the Maya; some are in English. Reservations are strongly advised, as the hotel often fills up with tour groups from Cancún. ◆ Less than a kilometer (a quarter of a mile) northwest of the ruins. No phone. For reservations: 5/2033086, 800/CLUB.MED

Within Villa Arqueológica Cobá:

Restaurant Villa Arqueológica Cobá

★★$$$ This is by far the best place to eat at the ruins, supplementing the usual fresh seafood and Yucatecan specialties with pâtés and quiche. The tables by the pool are a pleasant spot for breakfast. ◆ Mexican/French ◆ Daily breakfast, lunch, and dinner. No phone

19 Tulum The setting is absolutely gorgeous. Crumbling alabaster limestone temples rise from a grass-covered cliff above the Caribbean. Fuchsia bougainvillea and purple Wandering Jews twist around cracks and along stone stairs. Mountainous clouds the color of new-fallen snow float in the dark blue sky, and if you're lucky, you might see a rainbow or two.

The city is the only Maya site built right by the sea. Though it lacks the pomposity and grandeur of **Chichén Itzá** or **Uxmal,** it is the prettiest archaeological setting you're likely to see. The cluster of some 60 small structures is surrounded by a 3,000-foot-long wall more than 20 feet thick in parts (*tulum* means "wall" in Maya) that dates from the postclassic period, circa AD 900 to 1500. Explorer Juan Grijalva and his crew were the first Spaniards to sight it as they sailed down the Caribbean coast in 1518, and Spaniard Gonzalo Guerrero

lived here and married a Maya princess. Their children were the first mestizos in the Yucatán. Bishop Diego de Landa, who singlehandedly destroyed most of the recorded Maya history during the Spanish conquest, wrote that **Tulum** had 600 inhabitants in the mid-1500s; by the end of the century it was completely deserted. The architecture shows the influence of the Toltecs, a tribe from central Mexico that dominated the Maya during the postclassical period. Few of the buildings spread over the 16-acre grassy plateau have significant carvings or architectural aspects, and the most distinctive buildings have been roped off as the stairs and carvings have deteriorated.

Unfortunately, tourists have left their mark here. Fumes from rows of tour buses from Cancún have left gray dust on the plants and buildings, and the sound of these engines running all day so the air-conditioning can stay on tends to spoil the ambience. If at all possible, come here early or late in the day to avoid the hordes. The road to the ruins is lined with tin-roofed souvenir stands and luncheonettes. Most of the stuff sold here is junk, but if you're staying in Cancún and won't make it back down the coast, this is a good place to pick up some cheap replicas of Maya carvings and T-shirts with Maya designs. You can easily tour the site in an hour; however, those interested in studying the buildings closely and soaking up the scenery should plan on staying at least two hours. Guides with varying degrees of expertise sit near the booth where you pay the entrance fee. ◆ Admission; free Sundays and holidays. Daily. Hwy 307, Km 131 (between Playa del Carmen and Felipe Carrillo Puerto). 988/31505

At Tulum:

El Castillo (The Castle) Rising three stories above a steep cliff overlooking the sea, this place in its prime must have been an incredible sight, painted in vivid blues, reds, and whites. The Maya frescoes that once covered the building are long gone, but the crumbling edifice is still astounding. At press time, the stairs to the top were roped off, which is unfortunate since the view inland over the city is spectacular. Two windows on the seaward side of the third story reportedly housed some kind of beacons that guided mariners safely through the reef to shore. An experiment by Mexico's Instituto Nacional de Antropología y Historia (INAH; Institute of Anthropology and History) in 1985 proved that lights shone from the two windows create a beam that points straight to a natural opening in the reef. Two serpent columns run up the stairway to the top of the structure, where there are carvings of the Descending God.

THE YUCATAN

Templo del Dios Descendente (Temple of the Descending God) A distinctive deity primarily found here, the Descending God sits upside down, looking outward with his head pointed to the ground. His wings suggest that he may represent the Bee God (an important deity in this honey-producing region). Those who believe the Maya either came from another planet or had contact with extraterrestrial beings say the god is proof that some creatures descended from space. One of the best carvings of this god is over the doorway of this temple, just north of El Castillo. Walk farther north to the edge of the cliff on a small point for a good overview of the site. A natural bay sits at the bottom of this cliff and is accessible from a pathway at the bay's west end. This is a nice spot for a cooling swim, though there are no showers or rest rooms.

Templo de los Frescos (Temple of the Frescoes) Palm-thatch awnings shade a series of faded paintings on the inner and outer walls. Depicting the major Maya gods of rain and the moon, the frescoes are difficult to make out, but the flecks of red paint give you an idea of how the buildings looked when the city was in its prime.

20 Boca Paila Peninsula The paved road south of the parking lot on this peninsula runs past small sandy paths leading to campgrounds, fishing cooperatives, and a few private homes. After four kilometers (three miles), a narrow spit of land splits from the mainland, and a dirt road leads to the small settlement of Punta Allen at the southern tip of the 40-mile-long peninsula. In 1987, UNESCO and the Mexican government designated the peninsula a World Heritage Site, part of the International Man and the Biosphere program. The entire peninsula and 10 percent of Quintana Roo's wildlands have been incorporated into the 1.3-million-acre **Sian Ka'an Biosphere Preserve.** The fish camps and existing resorts along the peninsula are included in the preserve, and their ecological impact is closely monitored.

An assortment of small campgrounds and hotels lines the first 16 kilometers (10 miles) south of **Tulum,** after which the road becomes rutted, bumpy, and eerily remote; don't venture on unless you've brought water, a

Section of a mural from the Templo de los Frescos in Tulum.

MAYA DESIGNS

jack, a good spare tire, and plenty of patience. It takes about three hours to travel the length of the peninsula, longer if you stop to appreciate the innumerable idyllic beaches. A wooden bridge crosses a channel between the sea and the lagoons on the mainland side of the peninsula. This is a good place to stop for a rest and look for some of the hundred-odd species of birds who inhabit this area. Punta Allen is a fishing village with a few unnamed restaurants and a handful of exclusive fishing resorts, where guests are often flown in by private plane from Cancún or Cozumel.

On the Boca Paila Peninsula:

Osho Oasis $ A standout among the resorts south of Tulum, this cluster of 22 cabanas provides a New-Age, holistic approach to vacationing, along with the best (and only) vegetarian restaurant on the coast. Like all the hotels along this road, it uses a generator for electricity; unlike the rest, it has hot water in the communal showers. The cabanas have wood platform beds hanging from chains suspended from the thatch roofs (it feels like a flat hammock with a mattress). The windows don't have screens, which isn't a problem when the sea breezes are blowing and the bugs are at bay; protective netting is provided when mosquitoes and sand fleas are out of control (normally around the rainy season, from June through October). Trips to the reefs and nearby cenotes can be arranged at the fully equipped dive shop. The *palapa* restaurant serves excellent vegetarian meals with grains and vegetables not normally found in these parts, plus fresh fish and lobster. ◆ Boca Paila Rd (between Tulum and the Sian Ka'an Biosphere Preserve). 987/42772. For reservations: PO Box 99, Tulum, Quintana Roo 77780, Mexico. 415/381.9861

 Sian Ka'an Biosphere Preserve It's hard to experience the real magnitude of the preserve, as little of it is accessible by road. The name means "where the sky is born" in Maya; the geography leads one to think of the preserve as the last true wilderness on the North American coast. The preserve

encompasses 62 miles of beach, two large Caribbean bays, freshwater and saltwater lagoons, mangrove swamps, unexplored jungle, and a system of canals built by the Maya, possibly in the postclassical period almost a century after the birth of Christ. At least 20 Maya temples have been discovered here, and about a thousand residents, primarily Maya, live in the preserve. The biosphere project aims to keep the people on the land, supporting themselves by fishing, farming, and working at the low-environmental-impact tourist centers along the peninsula.

Travelers are expected to stay on the road and not wander indiscriminately into the jungle. **Amigos de Sian Ka'an,** a volunteer organization based in Cancún, offers tours of the preserve. Thus far, tours are only presented in Spanish. ◆ The preserve begins about 16 kilometers (10 miles) south of Tulum. For information and tours: **Amigos de Sian Ka'an,** Plaza América, Av Cobá 5, Cancún, Quintana Roo 77500, Mexico. 98/845629

Caphé-Ha $$$ Located near the lagoons at the Boca Paila Bridge, this property has two solar-powered one-bedroom cottages, each with its own bath, and a main guest house with two rooms (which share a bath) on a five-acre palm grove with long, isolated beaches. The fishing on both the lagoon and sea sides of the peninsula is terrific (the resort's name means "between waters" in Maya), and tackle is provided. Guests can also go birding, snorkeling, and boating through the lagoon. Room rates include family-style breakfast and dinner. This is the ultimate hideaway. ◆ Boca Paila Rd, about 26 kilometers (16 miles) south of Tulum. No phone. For reservations: 99/213404, 212/219.2198

Sol Pez Maya $$$$ This all-inclusive fishing lodge offers seven cabanas set in a palm grove on the beach, a *palapa* restaurant, and electricity from a generator that runs cooling fans during meals. Fly-fishing and deep-sea fishing are available, or you can just alternate between sunning on the beach and taking leisurely swims in the sea. At least 320 species of birds have been spotted along this part of the peninsula, and in early morning they appear to rise simultaneously, ready to greet the day with a chorus of chirps and squawks. ◆ Boca Paila Rd, about 27 kilometers (17 miles) south of Tulum. No phone. For reservations: Box 9, Cozumel, Quintana Roo 77600, Mexico. 987/20072, 800/336.3542; fax 987/21599

Restaurants/Clubs: Red	**Hotels:** Blue
Shops/ ◆ Outdoors: Green	**Sights/Culture:** Black

21 Felipe Carrillo Puerto Located at the intersection of highways going north to Cancún and west to Mérida, this is a town of about 15,000 residents, with a large public market, a gas station, stores, and a fascinating history. Known as Chan Santa Cruz during the War of the Castes (1847-1901), this town was the central meeting place for Maya rebels and refugees fleeing oppression by the hacienda owners around Mérida who treated the Indians as slaves. The Maya revolted against the governments of Mexico and Yucatán, using guerrilla tactics that nearly won them the war, though half the Indian population of the peninsula died in the struggle. Chan Santa Cruz was the site of the *Talking Cross,* which had been carved into a mahogany tree and appeared to speak prophecies. Actually, the Indian priest Manuel Nahuat provided the voice from behind a curtain, and was believed to be translating messages from the gods. Mexican soldiers destroyed the cross, but the Maya simply carved other crosses and secreted them in their villages, continuing to hold that the gods spoke through these symbols of Christianity. The town's name was changed to honor the socialist Governor of Yucatán who instituted significant social reforms in land distribution, Indian rights, and education in the 1920s, and who was assassinated by a rival political party. ♦ Hwy 307, Km 226 (between Tulum and Chetumal)

22 Laguna Bacalar The second-largest lake in Mexico (after Laguna Chapala near Guadalajara), this 35-mile-long body of water is often called the "Lake of Seven Colors." Fresh and salt waters mix, creating varying shades of turquoise and blue that contrast vividly with the deep-green jungle growth along the shores. The lake is a popular vacation spot for Mexicans, but hasn't really caught on with foreign travelers. If you're exploring the southern part of the peninsula, however, this is the perfect base camp. The setting and accommodations are far more attractive than those in Chetumal, and you can tour the Xcalak Peninsula or the ruins of **Kohunlich** from here in a day trip. ♦ Hwy 307, Km 344 (between Tulum and Chetumal)

At Laguna Bacalar:

Rancho Encantado $$$ Lush tropical gardens and lawns border the shores of Laguna Bacalar at this luxurious, hidden retreat. Six thatch-roofed casitas are scattered far enough apart for privacy, and each has its own tiled kitchenette, bath, sitting area, and front porch with the requisite hammocks. The casitas and the main dining room are decorated with handwoven wool rugs from Oaxaca, hand-carved hardwood furnishings, and excellent reproductions of Maya sculptures. Breakfast and dinner are included in the room rate. The cuisine emphasizes fresh vegetables and fruits grown on the grounds, homemade breads, and fresh fish (no red meat is served). There's an ice-cream maker for delicious fresh coconut ice cream, and the chef comes up with some impressive dishes, including gumbo and lasagna. ♦ Hwy 307, Km 340 (just north of the town of Bacalar). 800/221.6509

23 Chetumal There's little reason to come here unless you're traveling on to Belize and Central America. It seems strange that the capital of Quintana Roo is at the southern end of the state, 300 miles (480 kilometers) from Cancún, but the city was a seat of power nearly a century ago and was by far the most populated part of the eastern peninsula until Cancún came along. Today the population stands at about 50,000, whereas Cancún's is approximately 250,000.

On the border between Mexico and Belize, near the Bahía de Chetumal and the mouth of the Río Hondo, Chetumal has a rundown Caribbean flavor, with an underlying rhythm of danger and mystique (a holdover from its smuggler days, when guns and ammunition frequently passed back and forth across the border). Businesspeople from throughout the state journey here to visit government offices reluctantly, since the accommodations and ambience are less than ideal.

If you feel the need to visit Chetumal, spend some time along Boulevard Bahía, which runs along the bay, with its pleasant restaurants and bars and pretty waterfront park. The downtown area looks dilapidated and unsavory, despite the fact that it was rebuilt after Hurricane Janet nearly destroyed it in 1955. Salsa, reggae, and marimba music blares from boom boxes in shops and restaurants, and the crowds on the street are a mix of Mexicans, Caribbean islanders, Middle Easterners, and Belizeans. Take some precautions when roaming the streets and don't bumble around like a tourist waiting to be taken for a ride. ♦ Hwy 307, Km 344 (south of Felipe Carrillo Puerto)

In Chetumal:

Del Prado Hotel $ Once part of the government-owned Presidente chain, this traditional salesperson's hotel manages to charge higher rates than would be expected since it caters to business travelers. The central courtyard and pool area are wonderful escapes from the noise and heat in the street, but the 80 rooms are serviceable at best. There are three restaurants—a coffee shop, a somewhat formal dining room, and a 24-hour cafe. ♦ Héroes 138 (at Chapultepec). 983/20544

Hotel Continental Caribe $$ Newer than the Del Prado, it has an atrium lobby with a fountain, a courtyard swimming pool, a serviceable restaurant, and 64 modern rooms with good air-conditioning. ♦ Héroes 171 (at Zaragoza). 983/21100

Sergio's ★★$ For those who live along the coast and have little access to exotic fare such as pizza and thick grilled steaks, this is a necessary stop. It's also the place to come for catching up on the local gossip. ♦ American ♦ M-Sa lunch and dinner. Alvaro Obregón 182 (at 5 de Mayo). 983/22355

Stucco bas-relief carving recently discovered at Kohunlich, near Chetumal.

24 Kohunlich A relatively recent discovery 56 kilometers (35 miles) west of Chetumal, this Maya site is particularly interesting for its portrayals of the Sun God on the **Pirámide de los Máscarones** (Pyramid of the Masks). The largest of these stucco bas-reliefs is 10 feet tall, with bulging round eyes, a prominent flared nose, and an extended tongue. The 10-square-mile site is still under excavation, and it is estimated that there are some 200 buildings in the area, though only five have been uncovered. Usually deserted except for the watchman, the site is overgrown with jungle foliage. Bring water and bug repellent, and don't wander far from the entrance.
♦ Admission. Daily. Hwy 186, 67 kilometers (42 miles) west of Chetumal. No phone

25 Xcalak Other than the **Sian Ka'an Biosphere Preserve** (see page 154), the last remaining undeveloped portion of the Quintana Roo coastline is this thin, 40-mile-long peninsula that ends near the border of Belize. Remarkably enough, the peninsula's main community is at the south end of a 30-mile-long rutted dirt road (rumors say it may someday be paved), with a few private homes, campgrounds, and fishing co-ops scattered

along the way. The Chinchorro Banks, 29 kilometers (18 miles) east of the peninsula, is virgin territory for scuba divers. Fishers in the towns of Majahual and Xcalak take divers to Chinchorro in their small boats. Dive resorts in the area have transportation as well. Hardy scuba enthusiasts camp on the small islands at the banks, and spend their days exploring the shipwrecks littering the ocean floor. When visiting the peninsula, start out early in the day, bring water and a good spare tire, and plan on stopping often to take in the idyllic scenery. It's best to make reservations in advance if you plan on spending the night, since Xcalak's popularity is growing. If you don't have reservations, give yourself time to return to Bacalar, Chetumal, or Felipe Carrillo Puerto before dark if the coastal resorts are full. ♦ Take the Majahual exit from Hwy 307 and drive until the road ends at the sea; turn right onto a graded dirt road to reach the town.

On the Xcalak Peninsula:

Costa de Cocos
$$ Literally at the end of the road on the peninsula, this tiny resort provides one of the last true hideaways on the Quintana Roo coast. Owners María and Dave Randall worked four years to build a clean, comfortable  haven near the fishing co-op, where running water, flush toilets, and electric lights are still rarities. The six palm-roofed cabanas have all those modern niceties, plus comfortable mattresses, bookshelves stocked with an eclectic assortment of paperbacks and magazines, screens, and hammocks hanging both indoors and out, as well as tiled bathrooms.

There is a restaurant on the grounds, or you can arrange to dine in one of the village's two restaurants by telling them early in the day what you'll want for dinner. The resident dive master takes divers and snorkelers to dozens of spectacular sites along the reef just a 10-minute ride from shore; tanks, air, weights, and some dive gear are available at the resort. Local skiff captains offer longer trips (about two hours each way) to the village of San Pedro on Belize's Ambergris Cay. ♦ Take the dirt road from Majahual and drive 56 kilometers (35 miles) south; it's about a 1.5-hour trip to the resort. For reservations: Turquoise Reef Group, Box 2664, Evergreen, CO 80439. 303/674.9615, 800/538.6802; fax 303/674.8735

During the war against Spain, the Virgin of Guadalupe was awarded the rank of general.

Bests

Alfonso Escobedo
Founder and Director, Ecoturismo Yucatán

Alberto's Continental in **Mérida** makes the best Lebanese food, their *tajine* being a delight to enjoy with some crunchy *kak* sesame bread. A chat with Don Alberto is almost as good as the food he serves.

Spending a night at the **Hacienda Chichén** in **Chichén Itzá** and waking up to the singing of the melodious blackbirds.

Dzitnup Cenote near **Valladolid** (east of Mérida) makes for a refreshing break as you dip into the crystal clear underground pool surrounded by impressive stalactites and stalagmites.

The **Rancho Encantado** on the shores of **Laguna Bacalar** (on the Quintana Roo coast south of **Tulúm**) is truly an enchanted ranch, off the beaten track and as yet not visited by the Cancún crowd...thank heavens!

Climbing the **Nohoch Mul Pyramid** in **Cobá** is rewarded with an unforgetable view of two lagoons and the Maya's rainforest world.

A walk on **Mérida**'s elegant **Paseo de Montejo**—a trip back in time to the turn of the century, with its elegant mansions and lovely old trees.

No visit to Mérida is complete without a ride in a *calesa,* horsedrawn carriages dating back to the French influence on Yucatán's culture.

What more fascinating way to pass an evening than to watch people in the **Plaza Grande,** old men having their shoes shined, children dashing around the flower gardens, young lovers sharing a common bench, even a "bag lady" or two.

One of the reasons Mérida is considered a romantic town is the regular Thursday evening concert, or *serenata,* held at the **Santa Lucia** park, offering Yucatecan dancing, poetry and guitar trios in a colonial setting under the laurel trees.

Stopping outside one of the many colonial churches at a Saturday night will most often yield a peek into a wedding in process.

"Mérida en Domingo" when the downtown square and nearby streets are closed off to vehicles, offers a wonderful opportunity for visitors and local families alike to stroll and enjoy the free public concerts and stands of local food and crafts which are there for the browsing every Sunday of the year.

Time spent driving between Mérida and the famous resort of Cancún has been greatly reduced with the opening of the new toll road (no speed bumps to ruin the suspension of your car!)

Don't forget your snorkle equipment if you stay at beautiful **Akumal Beach** south of Cancún.

Can you imagine sitting on a park bench but not being able to put your arms around your lover? The *confidentes* (benches) of Mérida are designed in an "S" shape so you end up looking into the eyes of your bench partner instead of sitting side by side. Quite an innovation.

Gardens and birds are the hallmark of the **Hacienda Uxmal** in **Uxmal,** within walking distance to the Uxmal ruins. A favorite spot to relax and forget the pressures of the city.

Los Almendros restaurant in Mérida is the best place in town to savor the world famous Yucatecan cuisine—especially yummy is the stuffed cheese and the turkey oriental style.

Gunter Spath Haaf
General Manager, Las Palapas, Playa del Carmen

Playa del Carmen—a quaint and charming little town, with some of Mexico's most beautiful turquoise beaches, and the most convenient spot from which you can explore the whole area.

Cozumel—this tropical island is a wonderful place to go diving, with the world's second-largest barrier reef. Or go snorkeling, especially in **Chankanaab National Park,** just a hop from **Playa del Carmen,** with frequent ferry boat service.

Tulúm—one of the best Maya sites in the whole **Yucatán Peninsula,** with an unbelievable setting and the Caribbean Sea in the background. It's a place you will always remember.

Cancún—a world-renowned island resort, with the Caribbean Sea on one side and the **Laguna de Nichupté** on the other. There are many fine restaurants and entertainment places here as well.

Cobá—this huge archaeological site, with grounds that extend at least 50 square kilometers, offers the chance to explore the jungle and its wonderful wildlife, including tropical birds, butterflies, insects, and reptiles. Only five percent of the site has been unearthed.

Xcaret—just five kilometers south of **Playa del Carmen** you can snorkel in either an underground river or in the magnificent water inlet full of colorful tropical fish.

"Solitude—the feeling and knowledge that one is alone, alienated from the world and oneself—is not an exclusively Mexican characteristic. All men, at some moment in their lives, feel themselves to be alone. And they are. . . . Solitude is the profoundest fact of the human condition."

Octavio Paz, *The Labyrinth of Solitude*

La Malinche was the Indian mistress, adviser, and interpreter who aided Hernán Cortés in his conquest of Mexico. Today, the pejorative term malinchismo refers to a person's preference for all things foreign.

The 30 years José de la Cruz Porfirio Díaz was in power (1877-80; 1884-1911) are called the Porfiriato.

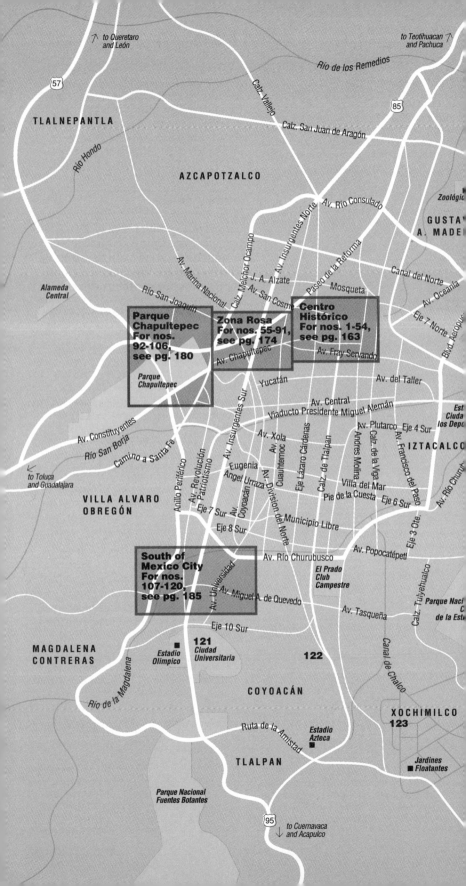

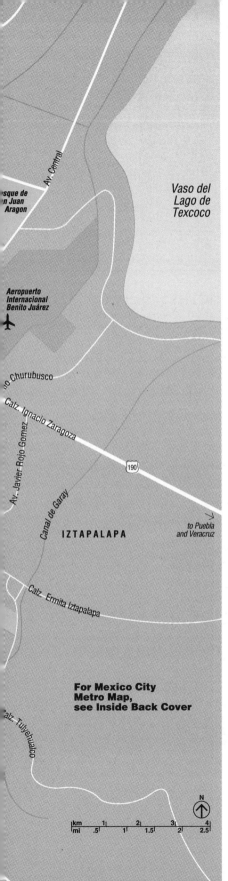

Vaso del
Lago de
Texcoco

Aeropuerto
Internacional
Benito Juárez

Av. Central

'sque de
n Juan
Aragon

o Churubusco

Calz. Ignacio Zaragoza

Av. Javier Rojo Gomez

Canal de Garay

190

IZTAPALAPA

to Puebla
and Veracruz

Calz. Ermita Iztapalapa

**For Mexico City
Metro Map,
see Inside Back Cover**

alz. Tulyehualco

N

| km | 1 | 2 | 3 | 4 |
| mi | .5 | 1 | 1.5 | 2 | 2.5 |

Mexico City

The nearly 700-year-old capital of Mexico is one of the world's great cities. Never mind the newspaper headlines that declare it a contaminated, corrupt, overcrowded, mad, bad, and dangerous place. Mexico City is all of these things to some degree, just like any big city, but it's also one of the most intriguing, vibrant, and stimulating metropolises in the world.

This metropolitan area of 20 million people (one-fourth of Mexico's entire population) grew from the ruins of **Tenochtitlán**, the religious, political, and economic center of Aztec civilization, founded in 1325. The Aztecs, who were in search of a home base, were told by their gods to look for an eagle eating a snake atop a nopal cactus; they found what they were seeking on a snake-infested island in the middle of **Lake Texcoco** and named the area "the place of the cactus fruit" (the eagle and snake later became the official emblem for the country). Within two centuries the Aztec Empire had flourished and grown so powerful its influence stretched across much of what is today Mexico and Central America.

Word of the Aztec city's wealth spread to Hernán Cortés, and in 1519 the Spanish conquistador arrived, troops in tow, to find 300,000 inhabitants and magnificent temples, avenues, and marketplaces—a city so splendid it conjured up images of Venice for Bernal Díaz del Castillo, whose journals are a record of the conquest. Emperor Moctezuma and his people welcomed the Spanish with gifts of gold, but Cortés wanted much more, and within two years he was destroying palaces and massacring the indigenous people, wiping out much of the Indian city. Mexico City was literally constructed from the rubble of Tenochtitlán—its churches and municipal buildings are made with stones from the Aztec's sacred temples, and many traces of the ancient people can still be found in sites throughout the area.

159

The foundation of present-day Mexico City was laid during the three centuries of Spanish rule; sanitation reforms were instituted, and a spectacular European-style city arose, including the very Parisian **Paseo de la Reforma.** This blending of Spanish and Indian styles has resulted in an architectural collage: Bold, avant-garde structures rub shoulders with Moorish and Baroque colonial buildings, and both stand atop remnants of Tenochtitlán that are occasionally unearthed. Such contrasts are the nature of Mexico City, where children beg for pesos in the same streets on which wheelers and dealers meet to shape the country's future, and where fascinating murals and green plazas are often lost in a haze of pollution, noise, and traffic snarls. This chaotic and discordant mélange has been a lure for some: John Dos Passos, Evelyn Waugh, Ernest Hemingway, D.H. Lawrence, Langston Hughes, and Jack Kerouac all spent time here, finding plenty of grist for their musings.

To discover the soul of the city, you have to browse through the markets that spill onto the streets, offering a rich cornucopia of sights, sounds, and smells. These *mercados* are the bustling social hub of life here, and the people who congregate daily are as colorful as the fresh fruits, vegetables, and flowers they come to buy. You must also sample the bars and cantinas of **Plaza Garibaldi,** where mariachi music and shots of tequila are the order of the day. And no matter how little time you have to explore Mexico City, don't miss the **Museo de Antropología** (Museum of Anthropology) or a boat ride on the canals of **Xochimilco.** Also try to venture beyond the cornflower-blue walls of Frida Kahlo's abode and wander around the **Palacio Nacional,** the home of Diego Rivera's unusually poignant murals. To get to know Mexico City requires patience, determination, and a bit of inquisitiveness. One must sift through the chaff of crime and grime to find its essence—a city with a history as rich as that of any Maya ruin.

Area code 5 unless otherwise noted.

Getting to Mexico City

Airport

Several major airlines have offices at **Benito Juárez Airport** and on or around Paseo de la Reforma. Most travel agents can reserve, book, or confirm flights and hotel reservations. The two main national airlines, **Mexicana** and **Aeroméxico,** have offices throughout the city. For general airport information, call 7627944.

The airport is only 30 minutes from Mexico City's major hotels. A well-organized taxi service with an official rate will get you into the city if you buy a prepaid ticket from the booths at the national and international arrival gates. Pay no more than the price of the ticket, which is good for up to four passengers going to the same destination with luggage weighing no more than 25 kilos (55 pounds) each. Count your change, as there have been reports of cashiers shortchanging arrivals who are unfamiliar with the monetary system.

To get to the airport from the city, hail a taxi on the street, make sure the meter is working, and ask for the *aeropuerto.*

Airlines

Aeroméxico	2078233, 2076311
American	2031837, 2086396
Canadian	2081837, 2081883
Continental	2803434
Delta	2073411
Mexicana	3250990
United	6270222

Getting around Mexico City

Buses

Buses run throughout Mexico City and are a great way to get around cheaply during non-rush hours. The **Oficina del Turismo** (Tourism Office) in the Zona Rosa (see **Visitors Information,** below) has bus maps. Maps are also posted at stops, which are marked with a green and white sign with a picture of a bus and the route number. The most important route for tourists runs along the Paseo de la Reforma from the Zócalo to Parque Chapultepec.

About 80 percent of Mexico City's population is less than 44 years old.

Bus Stations

Central del Oriente (East Terminal)
Ignacio Zaragoza 200
(at Av Ing. Eduardo Molina) 5427192

Central del Norte (North Terminal)
Av de los 100 Metros 1907
(at Av Instituto Politecnico)......................5871552

Central del Sur (South Terminal)
Av Taxquina 1320 (at Canal de Miramontes) 6890500

Central del Poniente (West Terminal)
Av Sur 122 (at Av Río Tacubaya) 2710342

Car Rental

Driving within Mexico City is a horror best left to bus and cab drivers. There's absolutely no need to rent a car if you're staying in the city and visiting attractions in the metropolitan area. If you plan on touring farther, ask the car rental company for the office closest to the highway leading to your destination and depart from there. Rental cars are included in the smog-reduction program that prohibits vehicles from being used one day per week (as designated by the numbers on your license plate). Be sure to ask the rental company which day your automobile will be prohibited from the city streets. The following companies have offices in the city and at the airport, as well as contacts at the large hotels:

Avis..5888888, 7621166
Budget 5330452
Dollar...2074060
Hertz..2552309

Metro

Mexico City's metro system is cheap, quick, clean, and efficient, though intimidating at first. Despite the seeming chaos, it is easy to use the metro. Buy a ticket (or a book of 10 if you plan to use the metro extensively) and pop it into the slot to open the barrier. The metro runs the length and breadth of the city; to change lines, follow the signs that read *correspondencia*. Trains run from early morning until after midnight, and tickets, maps, and information booths are available at all stations. See the inside of the back cover of this book for the metro map.

To cut down on crimes against women, the system now has cars designated for female travelers during weekday rush hours, 6-10AM and 5-8PM.

Taxis

Mexico City's cabs come in two shapes and sizes: the cheap street taxis (usually VW Beetles that are being painted a bright, ecological green as they switch to unleaded gas), and the large, black sedans that wait outside the tourist hotels. In general, the sedan taxis charge by the hour and have drivers who speak English, know the city well, and have room for four or five passengers, making them expensive. Street taxis charge by a reliable meter *(taximetro),* but can only hold a maximum of three passengers. If the meter is broken, confirm the fare before taking off. Not all taxi drivers know the city well; if the address you want is off the beaten track, try to find out what some of the major landmarks are near your destination.

Trains

There are modern, refurbished trains with daily departures to many of the major tourist cities. Don't even think of taking anything but a first-class train—the rest are murderously slow, unclean, and sometimes dangerous. The train station is located on Insurgentes Norte at Buenavista. For more information, call 5474114 or 5471084.

FYI

Emergencies

Canadian Embassy Schiller 259 2543288

Hospitals
American British Cowdray Hospital (ABC)
Observatorio Sur 136 (at Calle 132 Sur) ....
....2775000, 5158359

Hospital Angeles de Pedregal Camino Santa Teresa 1055 (in Colonia Héroes de Padierna)....................
....6526987

LOCATEL (6581111) offers bilingual information on lost people, possessions, or vehicles, as well as help with emergencies and emotional and physical crises.

Police Emergency 08

Police 6258008

Tourist Help—Procuraduria General de Justicia del Distrito Federal Open 24 hours a day year-round, the office's English-speaking public prosecutors can help you report crimes and fill out forms you will need to make insurance claims. It's located at Florencia 20 (at Hamburgo), in the Zona Rosa. 6258761. Also at: Argentina and San Ildefonso, in the Centro Histórico. 7890833.

US Embassy Paseo de la Reforma 305.........2110042

Money

Well-known international credit cards and US dollars are accepted at most first-class establishments. Traveler's checks can be exchanged at hotels, banks, and money-changing booths in most tourist zones. Try not to be short of cash on Sundays, and try to keep small change on hand at all times. Unlike many third-world countries, there are no advantages to finding a black-market exchange rate because the rates are standard—they're usually a little better in banks, and a little worse in hotels. If you're changing a large amount of money, ask for small denominations since it's often difficult to get change for notes larger than 20 pesos.

Banks are open Mondays through Fridays from 9AM to 1PM. A few banks in the major tourism areas now have 24-hour automated teller machines (ATMs) using the international Cirrus network, which may allow you to get cash advances with your credit cards or bank ATM card. Check with your bank or credit card carrier before leaving home to see if they allow international withdrawals.

Tours

Most large hotels have their own travel agents who can provide you with up-to-date information on tours of the area. You can also contact the following organizations:

American Express is great for members; you can buy or change transportation tickets, exchange or receive money, and get mail. The office is open daily and is located at Paseo de la Reforma 234 (in the Zona Rosa). Call 5330380 for more information.

Grey Line Tours is a good company if you're planning a tour anywhere within or outside of Mexico City. This reliable operation has years of experience and will pick up and drop off clients at their hotels. Open daily, the office is at Londres 166 (at Florencia). Call 2081163, 2081304, or 5331666 to speak to an English-language representative.

Visitors Information

The **Oficina de Turismo** (Tourism Office) is open daily. Many members of the helpful staff speak English, and can provide information on hotels, restaurants, and events. It is located at Amberes 54 (at Londres), in the Zona Rosa. 5259380, 5259384; fax 5259387.

LOCATEL (6581111) is the tourist office's 24-hour information line. In addition to emergency assistance (see above), it provides current details on shows, museums, and other attractions.

Area code 5 unless otherwise noted.

Centro Histórico (Historic Center)

There is no better way to plunge into the heart of Mexico City than by heading to the Zócalo, the vast main square in the center of downtown that has been the hub of life since the Aztec founded their capital here in 1325. When the Spanish conquerors arrived in 1519, led by Hernán Cortés and his native-born mistress, La Malinche, they smashed down the Aztec temples and palaces and built the public square and beautiful colonial palaces you see today. Aztec ruins are still being discovered here. When the subway system was being built in the 1970s, construction had to be constantly halted because of the hundreds of archaeological artifacts—from skulls and jewels to huge sculpted stones and religious offerings—that were found daily. The **Museo y Ruinas Templo Mayor** (Great Temple Museum and Ruins), on the northeastern edge of the Zócalo, houses the most important artifacts.

Although this part of the city is called the Centro Histórico, it isn't just about history and museums; it's the liveliest and most colorful part of Mexico City, with a flurry of activity in every corner. Huge wall-to-wall murals painted after the 1910 Revolution, popular bohemian theaters, and restaurants offering everything from savory tacos and enchiladas to exotic grasshoppers and iguana steaks are found throughout the area. There are also palaces, museums, churches, and eclectic shops, not to mention the largest pawnshop in the Americas. This neighborhood is no longer much of a residential district—earthquakes, subsidence (the city was built on a lake bed), and congestion have persuaded many people to move away. What is most remarkable, however, is the bustling street life: Stalls offer everything you might want to buy, from mariachi tapes to skimpy underwear. Organ-grinders also play for the crowds, lottery vendors all claim to have the winning tickets for sale, and vats of corn on the cob are peddled on street corners, smothered with mayonnaise, chili powder, lime juice, and salt. The city is making a concerted effort to move these roving street vendors into organized markets, but they are not going willingly.

1 Zócalo With each side measuring 792 feet, this is the largest square in the Americas and the second largest in the world after Moscow's Red Square. Formerly planted with gardens and trees, the plaza was the meeting place of viceroys and presidents; today the trees are gone and the square is an enormous gray cement slab with few seats and a rather inhospitable aura. Government ministries are now scattered throughout the city, but the president still has his official headquarters here in the **Palacio Nacional**. The section of the plaza facing the palace sometimes becomes a temporary home to protestors of various persuasions who set up tent cities and congregate for rallies protesting homelessness and other social inequities. Every morning and evening, the

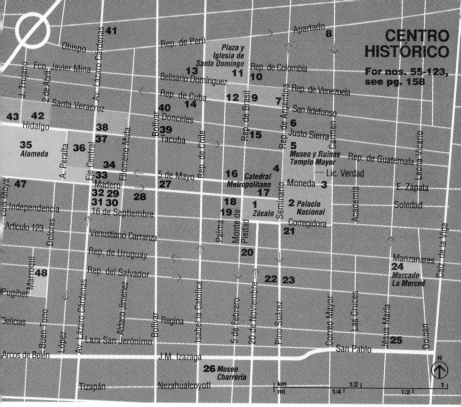

Map labels (Centro Histórico):

Obispo · 41 · Rep. de Perú · Apartado · 8 · Fco. Javier Mina · J. Trujano · 2 de Abril · Av. Lázaro Cárdenas · Plaza y Iglesia de Santo Domingo · Rep. de Colombia · Santa Veracruz · Belisario Domínguez · 13 · 11 · 10 · Rep. de Cuba · 12 · 9 · Rep. de Venezuela · 14 · 7 · Rep. de Argentina · San Ildefonso · 43 · 42 · Hidalgo · 40 · Donceles · Rep. de Brasil · 6 · Justo Sierra · Bolívar · 38 · 39 · Tacuba · 15 · 5 · Museo y Ruinas Templo Mayor · Rep. de Guatemala · 37 · Filomeno Mata · Rep. de Chile · 35 · Alameda · 36 · 34 · A. Peralta · Eje Central · 5 de Mayo · 4 · Lic. Verdad · Leona Vicario · 33 · Madero · 16 · Catedral Metropolitana · Moneda · 3 · E. Zapata · 47 · 32 29 · 27 · 17 · 31 30 · 28 · 18 · 1 · 2 · Palacio Nacional · Soledad · Independencia · 16 de Septiembre · 19 · Zócalo · Seminario · Academia · Carmen · Artículo 123 · Dolores · Venustiano Carranza · Corregidora · 21 · Rep. de Uruguay · 20 · Manzanares · Marroquí · 48 · Rep. del Salvador · 24 · Mercado La Merced · Pugibet · Buen Tono · López · Aldaco Jiménez · Isabel la Católica · Bolívar · Regina · 22 · 23 · Las Cruces · Jesús María · Delicias · Av. Lázaro Cárdenas · Palma · Monte de Piedad · Pino Suárez · Correo Mayor · 25 · Dolcan · Laza San Jerónimo · 5 de Febrero · 20 de Noviembre · San Pablo · Arcos de Belén · J.M. Izazaga · 26 · Museo Charrería · Tizapán · Nezahualcoyotl · Calz. de la Viga

km / mi · 1/4 · 1/2 · 1

N

Mexican flag is raised in the middle of the square, accompanied by a full military salute and the blast of horns and drums. For the ultimate taste of Zócalo life, visit on the weekend or during the Independence Day festivities on 15 and 16 September, when thousands of people pour into the square and make merry. ♦ Bounded by Monte de Piedad and Pino Suárez, and Corregidora and Madero

At the Zócalo:

Metro Zócalo The best subway station for visiting the Centro Histórico is in the middle of the plaza and gives a mole's-eye view of Mexican life. Its walls are lined with architectural drawings of the capital, and kiosks are staffed by potbellied men selling tickets and grudgingly handing out free maps. Vendors have recently been moved from the corridors to a market at the entrance in an attempt to reduce congestion. This is one place in the city where you should absolutely keep a tight hold on your wallet and your wits.

2 Palacio Nacional (National Palace) The palace was founded almost 600 years ago by the conquistador Hernán Cortés on the ruins of Emperor Moctezuma's palace and aviaries. Architecturally, the building dominates the whole east face of the Zócalo, although it has been chopped and changed many times, and was seriously damaged in 1692 by an enraged mob that wanted the Spanish to leave Mexico. The building has always been at the forefront of revolutions and coups. In fact, the very bell that started the War of Independence against the Spanish in 1810 is hanging above the central doorway; it is rung in commemoration every 15 September by the president. ♦ East side of the Zócalo

Palacio Nacional

Within the Palacio Nacional:

Diego Rivera Murals The 1910 Revolution against the dictatorship of Porfirio Díaz ushered in a new era of art for the people, inspired by the Russian revolutionary Mayakovsky. Public buildings became easels for young painters, and Diego Rivera painted 550 square yards of murals here between 1929 and 1951. He covered the first-floor corridor with vast, instructive panels showing the lives of each of the indigenous cultures before the Spanish conquest. There are scenes from the great Aztec market in nearby Tlatelolco, some showing Tarascan fishermen with their voluminous butterfly nets on Lake Patzcuaro, and still others detailing the preparation of cocoa and tequila. In the last of the corridor panels, Rivera delighted in shocking his public by depicting Hernán Cortés as a syphilitic hunchback suppressing the natives and getting rich off the pickings of the New World.

The three walls of the main staircase are a history lesson covering the last 500 years, from the conquerors brutally subjugating the glorified Aztec to life in the 1950s. There are myriad details,.and it takes a true history buff or a knowledgeable guide to pick out all the characters. To get an idea, concentrate on the south wall and the *Struggle of the Classes,* in which Rivera included his wife, the painter Frida Kahlo, her sister Cristina, and a large portrait of Karl Marx pointing the way to a glowing future. Rivera was a card-carrying Communist for many years, although he was often thrown out of the party for being too disruptive. ♦ Free. Daily.

Salas de Juárez (Juárez Rooms) On the left side of the first floor is the apartment where President Benito Juárez died in 1872. At press time, the rooms were closed for remodeling. ♦ Free. M-F. North wing. No phone

3 Calle Moneda One of the oldest streets in the city, it was host to a series of firsts: In 1536 it was home to the first printing press in the Americas (where it intersects Lic Verdad), the first university, and the first mint (for which the street was named). The mint is now the **Museo de Culturas** (Museum of Cultures), with exhibits from around the world and a 1938 mural in the entrance hall painted by Rufino Tamayo (1899-1991) to celebrate the

1910 Revolution. ♦ Free. Museum: Tu-Su. Moneda 13 (at Lic Verdad). 5127452

4 Fuente Modelo de la Ciudad de Mexico (Fountain Model of Ancient Mexico City) Here stands an impressive outdoor model of Mexico City (then called Tenochtitlán) as it was before the Spanish arrived in 1519. This is an awe-inspiring reminder of Aztec civilization at its best, with temples, canals, lakes, and palaces in miniature, contrasting with the ruins of the great temple directly in front of it. It is hard to imagine the city could ever have been so small and even harder to imagine that it was constructed in the middle of a lake, linked to the mainland by a series of causeways. ♦ Seminario (at Moneda)

5 Museo y Ruinas Templo Mayor (Great Temple Museum and Ruins) The Spaniards built their New World capital on top of razed Aztec temples, and over the centuries Aztec artifacts appeared whenever anyone stuck a spade into the ground. However, it wasn't until 1978 that the site of the most important twin temples to the gods of rain and war, Tlaloc and Huitzilopochtli, respectively, was properly excavated. The museum is the only one in the world dedicated solely to the Aztec. Designed by Pedro Ramírez Vásquez (who was also responsible for the Museo de Antropología and the Basilica of Guadalupe outside the city), it is a treasure trove of more than 3,000 Aztec splendors, ranging from the monolithic sculpted stone of the moon goddess Coyolxauhqui (on the second floor) to the *tzompantli,* or skull rack, where warriors displayed the decapitated heads of their prisoners. There are exhibits of the obsidian knives used to tear out the hearts of sacrificial victims, and of the tributes, such as shells, chocolate, and cochineal dye, that they demanded from subjugated vassals. ♦ Admission; free Sundays. Tu-Su. Seminario 8 (at the Zócalo). 5424785

Within the Museo y Ruinas Templo Mayor:

Bookshop Although small, this store has a very wide range of reference books on Mexico and its pre-Hispanic civilizations and art; many are in English. There are also posters, tapes, postcards, magazines, and gifts. ♦ Tu-Su. 5424785

6 Ex-Colegio de San Ildefonso (Ex-College of San Ildefonso) Founded in 1588 as a school for Jesuit novitiates, this college is famous for the murals painted around its patio. In the late 1920s, the enlightened minister of education, José Vasconcelos, commissioned young painters to cover the walls of public buildings with their own interpretations of Mexico and its revolution. For a population that was largely illiterate, murals were the equivalent of today's billboards, and this was the hatching ground for what would become one of Mexico's greatest cultural products.

The result was as surprising for the painters as for the government. Wealthy students who were vehemently opposed to the left-wing politics of the muralists did everything they could to sabotage their art, including defacing the works in progress at night. Nor did the new revolutionary government get what it expected; José Clemente Orozco (1883-1949) was always skeptical about the success of the revolution, and his murals *Justice and the Law* (1923) and *The Church and Reaction* (1924) implied that the golden age was still a long way off. At press time, the building was closed for much-needed renovations. Check with the tourist office (5259380) to find out when it will reopen. ♦ Justo Sierra 16 (at Rep. de Argentina)

Within the Ex-Collegio de San Ildefonso:

Anfiteatro Bolívar (Bolívar Amphitheater) Diego Rivera painted his first mural, *The Creation,* here in 1922. He managed to protect himself from the students' jeering catcalls by locking himself and his assistants into the building. In what was originally the church's cupola and organ loft, now the stage backdrop, he painted a mural that is far from his best. However, it is important because it marks not only the beginning of his career as a muralist but also the birth of the art form (murals differ from frescoes, which have been around since the Renaissance, in that they are painted on dry walls rather than wet plaster). In the lobby, Fernando Leal (1896-1964), a much-overlooked 20th-century muralist, painted Simón Bolívar (1933) as an exemplary revolutionary astride his white horse. ♦ Justo Sierra 14 (at Rep. de Argentina)

7 Secretaría de Educación Pública (SEP Ministry of Education); The painting of murals on public buildings reached its greatest glory with Rivera's massive work in the education minister's headquarters. Although lesser-known artists such as Jean Charlot and Amado de la Cueva had a hand in the work, it is Rivera's gargantuan effort in covering the majority of the 18,000 square feet and 250 panels that stands out. All three floors, the staircases, and elevators are painted with frescoes that span the spectrum of Mexican culture. The first floor presents visions of daily country and industrial life; the second concentrates on the Mexican states; and the third represents Mexico's heroes, arts, and trade. ♦ Free. M-F. Rep. de Argentina 28 (at San Ildefonso). 5219574

8 El Taquito ★★$$ This traditional restaurant for bullfighters has seen such luminaries as Pope John VI and Marilyn Monroe (on separate occasions) pass through its doors, as well as every bullfighter worth his salt. Beef, tequila, and bonhomie are the main ingredients. Come with an appetite and try the *botanas* (appetizers) such as *tostaditas con guacamole* (chips with guacamole) and *chicharrón* (deep-fried pork skin), before moving on to the huge beef dish, *carne a la tampiqueña,* which comes with beans, rice, avocado, and enchiladas. Live music is played from 2 to 10PM. ♦ Mexican ♦ M-Sa breakfast, lunch, and dinner; Su lunch and dinner. Carmen 69 (between Rep. de Bolivia and Apartado). 5267699, 5267885

9 Casa de Aduana (Customs House) Stop by this former customs house (now part of the Education Ministry) on the southeast corner of the attractive Plaza Santo Domingo to see David Alfaro Siqueiros's mural *Patricians and Patricides* on the walls of the Baroque staircase. He painted it from 1945 to 1971, long after the revolutionary government had softened its political stance. An arch-Stalinist, Alfaro Siqueiros continued to take a hard line with his uncompromisingly dynamic colors and postures, making him the last of the revolutionary muralists to keep up the tradition. ♦ M-F. Rep. de Brasil (between San Ildefonso and Rep. de Venezuela). No phone

10 Palacio de la Inquisición (Inquisition Palace) The much-feared Inquisition court was set up in Mexico between 1571 and 1820 by the Catholic church to keep dissenting citizens in line with the crown. They built this beautiful Italianate palace in the early 18th century for their public offices, but turned it over to the **Universidad de Mexico**'s medical faculty in 1854. Today it houses the nine-room **Museo de Medicina** (Medicine Museum), with displays of everything from pre-Hispanic herbal cures to current anticholera vaccines, as well as a reconstruction of a 19th-century apothecary's shop. ♦ M-F. Rep. de Brasil 33 (at Rep. de Venezuela). 5647892

11 Plaza y Iglesia de Santo Domingo (Santo Domingo Plaza and Church) This charming rectangular square and its church evoke the best of Mexico City's Centro Histórico with its mixture of traditional and modern life. In 1520 the powerful Dominican order chose this land on which to build their first great monastery and church (the order gained strength when the Inquisition began in 1571, and even oversaw government public offices). The present church, finished in 1736, is a beautiful, Baroque replacement of the original, which was destroyed in a flood. It is all that remains of a large group of monastic buildings that were pulled down in the anti-Catholic purges of the mid-19th century. ♦ Bounded by Rep. de Brasil and Rep. de Chile, and Rep. de Perú and Belisario Domínguez

12 Portal de las Evangelistas (Portal of the Evangelists) Along the west side of the square runs an arcade of makeshift stalls where modern-day public scribes carry on the ancient tradition of assisting illiterates who want help with their love letters and legal documents. ♦ Plaza Santo Domingo (between Rep. de Brasil and Rep. de Chile)

13 Hostería de Santo Domingo ★★★$$
This very traditional lunchtime restaurant has been open for more than a century and is busiest on weekends, when extended families come to eat and listen to strolling musicians. The speciality here is *chile en nogada* (*poblano* chili peppers stuffed with dried fruits, nuts, and meat, and covered with a wicked cream sauce and pomegranate seeds). Traditionally eaten in season, from July through October, the dish is available here year-round. ♦ Mexican ♦ Daily lunch and dinner. Belisario Domínguez 72 (at Rep. de Chile). 5101434, 5265276

14 La Casa de Malinche A plaque marks the private home where La Malinche, Cortés's first Mexican lover and translator, set up house with her husband, Juan Jaramillo, after the conquistador had tired of her. ♦ Rep. de Cuba 95 (at Rep. de Chile)

15 Bar León For Latin-music fans there are few better places in the city to go dancing. From the nondescript entrance, head into the dance hall to sweat, drink, and dance the night away. ♦ Cover. Tu-Sa until 3AM. Rep. de Brasil (at Donceles). 5213490

16 Monte de Piedad (National Pawnshop) This jam-packed, four-story pawnshop was founded in 1775 as a charitable organization by Romero de Torres, one of the country's richest silver-mine owners. The site was formerly occupied by Aztec royal palaces but is now invaded by browsers and brokers looking through room after room of family junk and treasures. ♦ M-Sa; closed at midday. Monte de Piedad 7 (at 5 de Mayo). 5873455

17 Catedral Metropolitana (Metropolitan Cathedral) Mexico City's main cathedral took 250 years to complete—and it shows. It is the largest cathedral in Mexico, although certainly not its most beautiful, displaying a hodgepodge of styles from the many architects involved in the design. It was begun in 1573 as a Baroque copy of Salamanca's 16th-century cathedral. In the late 18th century, the Spanish architect **Manuel Tolsá** adorned the central doorway with a clock and sculptures representing faith, hope, and charity. There are three grand doorways leading into the dimly lit interior. The 390-foot-long vaultlike interior has 16 small chapels, including one dedicated to St. Isidro Labrador (the Black Christ) and one to the miraculous Virgin. The most marvelous of

Catedral Metropolitana

them all is the Baroque **Chapel of the Kings** at the end of the nave; this gilt altarpiece was completed in 1737 after seven years of work by Sevillian craftworker Jeronimo de Balbas, who was known throughout Spanish dominions as the master of his day. The choir is set in the middle of the nave and houses two 3,000-pipe organs constructed with metalwork from the city of Macao. Underneath it is a crypt that holds more than 3,000 bodies, including most of Mexico's archbishops. Although the cathedral is not officially open to the public, there are guides at the entrances who can arrange visits to the tombs; it is customary to pay them a couple of dollars for their efforts. ♦ North side of the Zócalo

Beside the Catedral Metropolitana:

El Sagrario (The Sacristy) This later addition to the eastern side of the cathedral shows the Andalusian influences of its architect, **Lorenzo Rodríguez,** who labored from 1749 to 1760 on the intricate Baroque facade. Both the cathedral and the sacristry were built on the marshy ground of former lake beds, and each has tilted as it sinks deeper and deeper into the bog; reinforcement efforts were underway at press time.

18 Majestic $$ Overlooking the square, this former Spanish palace is one of the most charming and well-placed hotels in the city, with a stone fountain in the lobby, a glass roof over the central courtyard, and heavy carved wood doors and decorative tiles throughout. The 85 guest rooms, however, are modern in style. ♦ Madero 73 (at Monte de Piedad). 5218600, 800/528.1234; fax 5183466

Within the Majestic:

Majestic Restaurant ★★$$ Even if you're not a guest at the hotel, don't miss the top-floor terrace restaurant, which has both a superb view of the Zócalo and the best Sunday brunch in Mexico. Eggs can be prepared in front of you, tortillas are hand-patted to order, and the jugs of fresh fruit juices are constantly refilled. Delicious *chilaquiles* (tortillas fried with eggs and chicken) and *machaca* (dried beef) are kept warm for you on hot plates. ♦ Mexican ♦ Daily breakfast, lunch, and dinner. Seventh floor. 5218600

19 El Gran Hotel de la Ciudad de México $$ One of only two hotels right on the Zócalo, this 125-room hostelry is a fun place to stay if you want to be in the center of the action. It's

hard to believe that the elegant Art Nouveau interior, complete with its stained-glass dome by Jacques Gruber, was originally built as a department store at the turn of the century; the wrought-iron elevators, sweeping terraced floors, and bird cages all seem more appropriate for a Parisian hotel. Be sure to visit the rooftop restaurant to sit for a spell gazing out over the square. ♦ 16 de Septiembre 82 (at Monte de Piedad, across from the Zócalo). 5104040, 800/654.2000; fax 5122085

20 Palacio de Hierro (Iron Palace) One of Mexico City's two oldest department stores, it has been competing with its rival **Liverpool** on the same intersection for more than a century. Both were established by Frenchmen and are still part-owned by the founding families, although the style is now more north-of-the border than European. It was constructed of iron (hence its name), and the central gallery, with its stained-glass roof, has a wrought-iron balcony, which was the craze in the 1870s. Selling a good range of US and Mexican brand names, it is considered expensive by local standards. There are other branches around town, which are all bigger, but not such architectural jewels. ♦ Daily. 20 de Noviembre 3 (at Venustiano Carranza). 7473108

21 **Corte Suprema de Justicia** (Supreme Court of Justice) President Cárdenas commissioned this structure as the court building in 1935, although it looks more like a colonial palace. Cárdenas offered the job of painting the murals to José Clemente Orozco, one of the three great post-revolutionary muralists. Orozco's highly ironic portrait, *Injustice of Justice* (1941), at the top of the stairs, proved too much even for Cárdenas's liberal government, and the rest of the commission was handed over to US artist George Biddle, who painted *War* (1945) at the library's entrance. ♦ M-F. Pino Suárez (at Corregidora). No phone

22 **Iglesia y Hospital de Jésus** (Church and Hospital of Jesus) A hospital and church mark the site where Moctezuma, an Aztec emperor, and Hernán Cortés, the Spanish conqueror, are said to have met for the first time. To commemorate the occasion, Cortés ordered that the first Mexican hospital be built here in 1524 and that his remains be interred in one of the church walls (to the left of the chancel). The choir loft was painted from 1942 to 1944, not with the usual religious allegory, but with José Clemente Orozco's *Apocalypse*, a bold artistic commentary on World War II. ♦ Rep. del Salvador (at Pino Suárez)

Restaurants/Clubs: Red	**Hotels:** Blue
Shops/ ♥ Outdoors: Green	**Sights/Culture:** Black

23 Museo de la Ciudad de Mexico (Mexico City Museum) The Counts of Calimaya, former owners of this elegant colonial palace borrowed from Aztec sculpture and incorporated a serpent's head into the building's cornerstone. Today, this beautiful structure is a stuffy, historical museum of the city, an important project conceived with a lack of imagination. One of the few highlights is the top-floor studio of landscape painter Joaquin Clausell (1886-1935). Here he cleaned his brushes on the walls, creating from the strokes a variation on his water-colors, which show the halcyon, smog-free days of Mexico City in all its glory. ♦ Free. Tu-Su. Pino Suárez 30 (at Rep. del Salvador). 5420487

24 Mercado La Merced This vast produce center covers several streets east of the Zócalo and is Mexico City's biggest market. If you don't see what you want here, most likely it can't be found anywhere. To get there, take the metro *(Line 1)* and hop off at the **Merced** station. Sunday is the busiest day. ♦ Daily. Bounded by Jésus María and Doloan, and Manzanares and Rep. de Uruguay

25 Fonda Don Chon ★★$$ Much acclaimed, yet utterly unpretentious, this cafe specializes in exotic pre-Hispanic dishes served on Formica-topped tables in shabby surroundings. The ingredients come from all over Mexico and, depending on availability, may include termites, *gusanos de maguey* (cactus worms), zucchini and chrysanthemum blossoms, nopal cactus, grasshoppers, armadillos, iguanas, and boar in mango sauce. Difficult to find for some and difficult to stomach for others, it has remained authentic and unfussy. ♦ Pre-Hispanic/Mexican ♦ Daily breakfast and lunch. Regina 159 (at Jésus María). 5222170

26 Museo Charrería The most Mexican of sports, *charrería* (much like a rodeo, but with more pomp and circumstance) is honored here in the former Montserrat Church, a Baroque 18th-century construction. Spurs, saddles, spangled bolero jackets, and tight trousers embroidered with gold and silver, as well as historical documents, pistols, and wide-brimmed sombreros are all on display. ♦ Free. M-F. Isabel la Catolica 108 (between Nezahualcoyotl and J.M. Izazaga). 7094838

27 Ritz $ Although in the heart of the city, this attractive Art Deco hotel with 125 remodeled rooms is quiet and peaceful, offering a pleasant restaurant and a family atmosphere. ♦ Madero 30 (between Bolívar and Rep. de Chile). 5181340, 800/528.1234; fax 5183466

28 Palacio de Iturbide (Iturbide's Palace) The first palace built on this spot belonged to one of the original Spanish conquerors. Then in 1779 the Mexican architect **Francisco Guerrero y Torres** (1727-1792) was commissioned to build the most sumptuous palace in Mexico City to remind the owner, Don Pedro de Moncada, of his family home in Palermo, Italy. A masterpiece of civil Baroque architecture, the facade is constructed of *tezontle* (a reddish volcanic stone) interspersed with the local gray stone; the two materials complement each other and provide a surface for the elaborate sculptured adornments. In 1821 the owner offered the palace to the short-lived and flamboyant hero of the Independence movement, Agustín Iturbide, who accepted the office of emperor from the palace's balcony. It now belongs to Banamex, which uses the fine interior patio to exhibit its superb art collection. Open to the public, there is also a small shop to the right of the main doorway selling art books (some are in English) and posters. ♦ Free. Daily. Madero 17 (off Bolívar). 5215797

Palacio de Iturbide

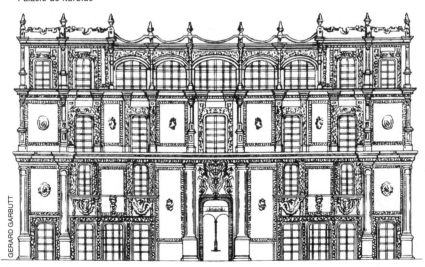

GERARD GARBUTT

29 Iglesia de San Francisco (Church of San Francisco) Construction of this important Franciscan church was begun in 1524, shortly after the conquest. Its monastery was demolished according to the anticlerical laws of the 19th century, and the addition of two wide streets cut swaths through the property, easing access to the congested downtown. Still, it is a good example of Churrigueresque, the exuberant architectural style, its facade studded with reliefs and sculptures. Set off the street in a courtyard, this is also one of the most peaceful places to escape from the street bustle into quiet tranquillity. ◆ Madero (off Eje Central)

30 Pastelería Ideal This immensely popular pastry shop takes up several floors and is an institution with a long history. In addition to the boggling array of mouth-watering concoctions, there are fabulous cakes for the much-feted *quinceañeras* (15th-birthday celebrations), street parties, first communions, and weddings. On the second floor you can see these towering creations with 12 or more tiers, a display of Mexican kitsch in its purest form. ◆ Bakery ◆ Daily. 16 de Septiembre 14 (between Eje Central and Bolívar). 5100052

31 Prendes ★★$$ Typical of the best of the Centro Histórico, this restaurant relies on nostalgia and a tradition that dates back to 1892, rather than the menu, to lure the crowds at lunchtime. The walls are lined with murals (by the important revolutionary painter Dr. Atl, and by Julio Castellanos, who is known for his metaphysical drawings) of celebrities and former patrons such as Pancho Villa and Walt Disney; the politicians and political watchers have all since moved on to other grazing pastures. However, it's still good for a Sunday lunch of *paella Valenciana*, coconut pie, and memories. ◆ Mexican ◆ Daily lunch and dinner. 16 de Septiembre 10 (between Eje Central and Bolívar). 5215404. Also at: Plaza la República 17 (at the Frontón Mexico Jai Alai). 5127517; Río Tiber 107 (in the Hotel San Marino). 5182624

32 La Torre Latinoamericana (Latin American Tower) A famous landmark since 1956, this tower is a glass needle—47 floors and 532 feet high—that was the first Mexican structure to be built on an earthquake-resistant foundation, and has survived all the subsequent tremors unscathed. There is a top-floor lookout and a passable international restaurant, **Muralto** ($$), but unfortunately, there is seldom a day clear enough to see the city without its cap of smog. The restaurant is busiest at night, when you get a good view of the city's lights. Music and dancing start at 9PM. ◆ Admission. Tower: Daily. Restaurant: M-Sa lunch and dinner. Eje Central (at Madero). 5217751

33 Sanborn's Casa de los Azulejos ★★$ Legend has it that the former home of the Counts of the Valley of Orizaba was constructed in the 1730s after a father bet his wild son that he would never earn enough money to build a house of tiles. How the son proved him wrong! Today the building is covered in Pueblan tiles and has been a drugstore with a restaurant and soda fountain since 1903. The dining room is a great place for heavy platefuls of Mexican staples, including the wonderful *chilaquiles*. In the restaurant's stairwell is a fine example of José Clemente Orozco's early work, the mural *Omniscience* (1925). ◆ Mexican ◆ Daily breakfast, lunch, and dinner. Madero 4 (at Eje Central). 5121331. Also at: Niza (at Hamburgo) in the Zona Rosa. 5253741; Jardín Centenario (between Francisco Sosa and Felipe Carillo Puerto), Coyoacán. 6582974

Ruinas de San Juan Teotihuacán

Mystery surrounds the massive pyramids and palaces of Teotihuacán, spread over an eight-square-mile site north of Mexico City. No one knows who built or inhabited this city, which housed over 100,000 residents in AD 500 and was completely deserted by 700. The site is overwhelming, especially when viewed the first time around, and is certainly worth a half-day's visit if you're a ruins buff.

Comfortable shoes, a hat, and drinking water are absolute necessities if you plan on climbing the ruins. The most impressive is the **Pirámide del Sol** (Pyramid of the Sun); with 248 steps to the top, it is the third-largest pyramid in the world (the ones in Cholula, Mexico, and Cheops, Egypt, are larger). The view from the summit is astounding and the climb breathtaking; take it slowly, especially if it's a smoggy day. The smaller **Pirámide de la Luna** (Pyramid of the Moon) is easier to climb, and provides a good overview of the ruins lining the **Avenida de los Muertos** (Avenue of the Dead), a broad boulevard lined with smaller temples. Some buildings along the avenue still have touches of paint remaining from the frescoes that covered the buildings when Teotihuacán was a living city. The avenue leads from the **Pirámide de la Luna** to **La Ciudadela** (The Citadel), a large sunken square surrounded by thick walls.

The **Unidad Cultural** (Visitors' Center) is opposite **La Ciudadela**, and contains a museum with some artifacts from the site (although most are on display in Mexico City's **Museo de Antropología**) and a scale model of the ruins useful in planning your tour. The center also has a restaurant, rest rooms, a bookshop (with many publications in English), and souvenir stores. The site is open daily; there is an admission charge except on Sundays. Travel agencies in Mexico City offer tours to the ruins, or you can get there on your own by taking a bus from the **Terminal Central de Autobuses del Norte** (Av de los 100 Metros 1907; 5871552); the trip takes about an hour each way.

34 Bar L'Opera ★★$$ For a taste of *belle époque* Mexico, spend an evening at this wonderful after-theater restaurant, where you can enjoy drinks at the splendid bar or have a full meal. The food isn't great (except for the pompano *à la Veracruzana*), but the atmosphere is, with street musicians and organ-grinders serenading diners in the midst of magnificent turn-of-the-century decor. Service is formal, and the old-fashioned waiters would never dream of giving the bill to a woman. Indeed, until several years ago, women were not allowed in unless accompanied by a man, and not long before that, they weren't admitted at all.♦ Mexican/French ♦ Daily lunch and dinner. 5 de Mayo 10 (at Filomeno Mata). 5128959

35 Alameda Named after the *alamos* (poplars) that once grew here, this place was built on drained marshes in the 16th century as an elegant park for Spanish nobles. Later it became the site of the Inquisition burnings. It's again a park and one of the most popular spots in the city on Sundays, especially for young lovers who meet here once a week for a chance to woo without parental supervision. On that day, it fills with families, buskers, popcorn vendors, cotton candy peddlers, and men who sell caged birds, carrying long poles that can hold up to 30 cages at a time. ♦ Bounded by Hidalgo and Juárez, and Dr. Mora and Angela Peralta

36 Palacio Nacional de Bellas Artes (National Palace of Fine Arts) Known by locals simply as **Bellas Artes,** this huge theater complex took 30 years to build, changing from Art Nouveau to Art Deco in the process. **Adam Boari**, the Italian architect, began work on the Carrara marble exterior at the turn of the century, but his plans were foundered by the 1910 Revolution. **Federico Mariscal** completed the interior in 1932. Many of Mexico's foremost muralists were invited to paint the walls of the upper floors: Rufino Tamayo worked on the second floor between 1952 and 1953 after the three giants—Diego Rivera, David Alfaro Siqueiros, and José Clemente Orozco—had completed their third-floor murals. Rivera was originally commissioned to paint *Man in Control of the Universe* for New York City's Rockefeller Center; horrified at the mural's socialist undercurrents, the sponsors destroyed it. Rivera, undaunted, made this copy from his drawings.

The Tiffany crystal stage curtain, designed by Dr. Atl, shows the local volcanoes Ixtaccíhuatl and Popocatépetl, and is normally displayed before appearances by the renowned **Ballet Folklórico.** ♦ Murals: Tu-Su. Shows: W, Su. Tickets to the shows are sold 48 hours in advance at the palace or at most hotels and travel agencies. Angela Peralta (off Juárez). 5101388

Within the Palacio Nacional de Bellas Artes:

Bookshop This extensive bookshop sells boxed sets of Frida Kahlo and Diego Rivera memorabilia, as well as the excellent Education Ministry publications (available in Spanish only, although some are worth buying for the pictures alone) at very low prices. With posters, piles of books, diaries, and a variety of gifts, it is a great place to find a memento of Mexico's rich artistic past. ♦ Daily. 5101388

Palacio Nacional de Bellas Artes

Café del Palacio ★★$$ The murals at the palace can be so overwhelming you may need a few moments to sit quietly over a cappuccino. This small cafe by the entrance to the bookstore is the perfect spot for a small salad or a sweet, and writing postcards (you can mail them right across the street). ◆ Cafe ◆ Tu-Sa lunch and dinner. 5120807

37 Dirección General de Correos (Post Office) In 1902 the main post office was built in Florentine style by its Italian-born architect, **Adam Boari**. Still the chief post office, there is also a small **Museo Postal y Biblioteca** (Postal Museum and Library) on the second floor. ◆ Free. M-Sa. Eje Central (at Tacuba). 5217760

38 Museo Nacional de Arte (National Museum of Art) Italian architectural tastes influenced much of the construction in turn-of-the-century Mexico City, and it was the Italian architect **Silvio Contri** who designed this building as the Palace of Communications and Public Works between 1904 and 1911. Today the museum exhibits the greatest of Mexican painting from throughout the country's history. The 20th-century collection is outstanding, chronicling the time when Mexicans began painting for themselves and not for European patrons. Styles range from the acid political critiques of Julio Ruelas and José Guadalupe Posada to the drawings and paintings of the muralists, the anguished self-portraits of Frida Kahlo, and the school of contemporary young artists. ◆ Admission. Tu-Su. Tacuba 8 (at Eje Central). 5536313

39 Café de Tacuba ★★★$$ Housed in an old convent, this long-standing cafe and restaurant was established in 1912 and has kept the original, attractive tiled walls. A favorite after-theater spot, it offers Mexican favorites such as tamales, *chilaquiles,* and enchiladas, plus coffee and cakes, which are great for capping off a busy day. The long dining room becomes noisy during lunch time, when businesspeople wait in line for a seat and everyone seems to be table hopping. It's best to arrive unfashionably early (before 2PM) for lunch. ◆ Mexican ◆ Daily breakfast, lunch, and dinner. Tacuba 28 (at Bolívar). 5184950

Restaurants/Clubs: Red   **Hotels:** Blue
Shops/ 🌳 Outdoors: Green   **Sights/Culture:** Black

40 Teatro de la Ciudad (City Theater) Founded in 1912, this popular theater presents everything from revue shows to international opera companies. The resident folk dance company, rivaling the popular Ballet Folklórico, often takes center stage. For performance listings, see the weekly magazine *Tiempo Libre,* which comes out on Thursdays and has an English-language section. ◆ Donceles 36 (at Bolívar). 5102197

41 Plaza Garibaldi This square is surrounded by several great bars and clubs, but the big attraction takes place every evening from 7PM to 2AM and all day Sunday, when mariachi bands congregate to play their wailing songs of love and treachery for anyone willing to pay. Often hired to serenade girlfriends or celebrate marriages and birthdays, mariachis are professionals and don't come cheap; they are an indispensable part of macho Mexican culture, in which the man is the victim of a faithless woman. The groups consist of violin, trumpet, and guitar players, and a heart-wrenching vocalist. Any lover worth his salt should know the songs so well that he will sing along (foreigners will be forgiven for their ignorance). The plaza is most fun late at night, but the neighborhood can be dangerous; take a cab back to your hotel. Several blocks south of the plaza, on busy Eje Central, young mariachis seek business from passing motorists by jumping into traffic in their tight, black bolero jackets and trousers to convince the drivers of their prowess. ◆ Av Lázaro Cárdenas (between Rep. de Andorras and Rep. de Perú)

At Plaza Garibaldi:

Plaza Santa Cecilia ★★$$ This restaurant and nightclub has great mariachi shows and a Mexican menu ranging from guacamole with corn chips to sea bass *à la Veracruzana.* ◆ Mexican ◆ Restaurant: daily dinner. Shows: daily. 5262455

42 Museo Nacional de la Estampa (National Museum of Printmaking) The art of printmaking, lithography, and etching reached its peak in Mexico during the last century with the advent of newspaper cartoons, caricatures, and spoofs. They quickly became the nation's most accurate and acerbic political commentaries, as can be seen in the work of José  Guadalupe Posada on the second floor of this museum. Printmaking has expanded to include silkscreens and engravings, also displayed here. There's hardly room to do the art form justice, since the building is small and dedicates half of its space to temporary exhibits of young printmakers and retrospectives on the masters, but it does provide a thought-provoking introduction. Set in a courtyard between two churches that sink visibly deeper into the subsoil every year, the museum has managed to stand its ground. ◆ Admission. Tu-Su. Hidalgo 39 (at 2 de Abril). 5104905

43 Museo Franz Mayer Formerly the Hospital of San Juan de Dios and later an orphanage, this elegant 16th-century mansion has been converted into one of the city's finest museums, housing the private collection bequeathed to Mexico by German art enthusiast Franz Mayer upon his death in 1975. Although cited as a collection of "applied art," in which all the pieces were practical and meant for everyday use, the exhibits are far from mundane. You'll get a glimpse into the life-style of the ruling classes of the colonial era who had the means to gather the best of the known world, including Talavera ceramics, silks and screens from China, solid-silver altarpieces, Philippine marquetry, English mahogany furniture, and a fine-arts collection. ◆ Admission; free Sundays. Tu-Su. Hidalgo 45 (at J. Trujano). 5182266

Within the Museo Franz Mayer:

Bookshop A small but well-supplied bookshop with a broad selection of art magazines, architectural tomes, elegant coffee-table books, postcards, and guides, some in English. ◆ Tu-Su. 5182266

El Patio ★★$ This lovely cafe sits on a beautiful and breezy colonial courtyard. It's a calm place to gently recover from museum fatigue while sipping a cappuccino, indulging in a sweet, or lunching on a salad and rolls, all to the strains of classical music. ◆ Cafe ◆ Tu-Su lunch. 5182266

44 Hotel de Cortés $$ This pleasant hotel has 29 rooms set around a charming Colonial-style patio. One of the nicest in the Alameda area, this hostelry has been modernized in ways that make it more comfortable without losing the original touches. The windows facing the busy street, for example, are double-glazed to seal out much of the noise, and the large bathrooms have marble sinks and powerful showers. The Baroque stone hotel was originally built as the Hospice de San Nicolás de Tolentino in the 18th century as a guest house for Augustinian monks; atop

the front gateway is a stone figure of San Tomás de Villanueva, patron saint of the needy. The government confiscated the building from the Catholic church after the Revolution of 1910, and it became a private hotel in 1943. A traditional Mexican fiesta is held on Saturdays at 3PM in the courtyard restaurant, a pleasant spot for a break from the city streets. ◆ Hidalgo 85 (at Paseo de la Reforma). 5221020, 800/528.1234; fax 5121863

45 Pinacoteca Virreinal de San Diego (Viceregal Art Gallery of San Diego) In front of the Inquisition burning stake and the Alameda, the former Convent of San Diego houses an impressive museum of 16th- and 17th-century viceregal ecclesiastical art. Its collection of colonial masters includes the Oaxacan-born Miguel Cabrera, who, between 1740 and 1765, painted some of the greatest religious art in Mexico's history. ◆ Admission; free on Sundays. Tu-Su. Dr. Mora 7 (at Paseo de la Reforma). 5102793

46 Museo Mural Diego Rivera (Diego Rivera Mural Museum) This museum was built in honor of Rivera's huge mural *A Sunday Afternoon in the Alameda,* formerly housed in the Hotel Prado, which was destroyed after the 1985 earthquake. Fortunately, the mural remained undamaged and was carefully moved across Avenida Juárez to a new home overlooking its subject—the Alameda. Among the many people depicted enjoying the Alameda are the young artist himself, between his wife, artist Frida Kahlo, and a skeletal nobleman. Behind and around the central figures are characters from Mexico's glorious and not-so-glorious past, including former presidents, emperors, enemies, and heroes. ◆ Admission; free Sundays. Tu-Su; closed at midday. Balderas (at Colón). 5102329

47 Museo Nacional de Artes e Industrias Populares (National Museum of Popular Arts) More a shop than a museum, this vast warehouse displays arts and crafts from all over the country. Everything is on sale at reasonable prices, and there's a far greater selection of unusual artwork than in the tourist shops of the Zona Rosa. In the entrance hall, the back wall is covered with a mural map of Mexico's folk art painted by Miguel Covarrubias, a former *Vanity Fair* cartoonist. ◆ Daily. Juárez 44 (between Luis Moya and Dolores). 5216679; fax 5103404

48 Mercado San Juan This market hawks not only unusual cure-alls, but the best and freshest produce around. In fact, chefs from

Mexico's top restaurants invariably come here to buy their ingredients, choosing from a selection that ranges from wild mushrooms and suckling pigs to exotic tropical fruits, such as the pink-fleshed *pithaya,* and *chihuahua* cheese made by Mennonites. All this, plus a mind-boggling array of chilies, herbs, and spices. ♦ Daily. Ayuntamiento (at Marroqui)

48 Florencia ★★★$ This tiny, bustling seafood cafe is a favorite with customers from the nearby market, who come for the high-quality, freshly caught fish. Many merchants who don't have time for a meal stop by the take-out window for oysters, octopus or crab tacos, and tostadas. People with time to spare wait in line for a table, where they linger over the excellent shellfish soup or the whole, grilled red snapper, either doused in garlic or *à la Veracruzana* (in a tomato and red pepper sauce). Shrimp cocktails and *calamar en su tinta* (squid cooked in its ink) are other wickedly good options. ♦ Seafood ♦ Daily lunch. Plaza San Juan (at Ayuntamiento). 5124048

49 Mercado La Ciudadela A nearby citadel that was built by the Spanish in 1807 to hold their enemies during the War of Independence now houses a library and has lent its name to this arts and crafts market. With more than 300 stalls selling ceramics, glassware, masks, and a hundred other choices, this market is a good choice when shopping for gifts. Overshadowed by the Zona Rosa's more accessible **Mercado Artesanía,** it tends to get overlooked, even though those in the know swear the prices here are lower. Some of the specialties include huge wooden masks from the state of Guerrero sculpted into sirens, mermaids, animals, dragons, devils, and skeletons. A few workshops have been set up in and around the open-air market so you can see the crafts being made. ♦ Daily. Bounded by Balderas and Bucareli, and E. Dondé and Ayuntamiento, (four blocks south of Paseo de la Reforma)

50 Fiesta Americana Reforma $$$ This former Holiday Inn has been taken over by the Fiesta Americana chain, known for its amenable service and dependable rooms. The location is ideal for those who enjoy walking, since you're about midway between the Zona Rosa and the Centro Histórico on the pleasant Paseo de la Reforma. The 610-room hotel has a fully equipped health club and sauna (but no swimming pool) and four restaurants. ♦ Paseo de la Reforma 80 (at Ramirez). 7051515, 800/FIESTA1; fax 5660391

51 Paseo de la Reforma The elegant, broad avenue commonly referred to as **Reforma** was designed in the 1860s by Carlota, wife of the short-lived Austrian Emperor of Mexico,

Maximilian. To the north and south there are many wonderful museums, shops, and markets that are often overlooked by tourists.

52 Monumento a la Revolución (Monument to the Revolution) At the turn of the century, an ambitious plan to build a new legislative palace (illustrated above) was set in motion by the dictator/president Porfirio Díaz, but his project was interrupted by the 1910 Revolution, which toppled him the following year. Construction ceased until 1930, when the design was altered by the architect **Carlos Obregon;** later it became a monument to the revolution. Today it houses a museum with a permanent exhibition on the building's history and the revolution that is so much a part of its past. ♦ Free. Tu-F. Plaza de la República (at Gómez Farías). 5661902

53 Frontón Mexico Jai Alai Jai alai, the offspring of an old Basque game brought across the Atlantic by the conquerors and merged with a similar ceremonial game played throughout pre-Hispanic America, is one of the great passions of Mexico. Similar to squash, it is a skillful competition in which teams of two or three players use *cestas* (long, basket-shaped racquets) to hit the ball off the narrow, high walls of the *frontón* (court). The ball travels faster than in any other game, and people flock to this spot to see the action. There are many opportunities for betting, both before and during play. The building housing the *fronton* mixes Art Deco detail into a functional sports stadium. ♦ Admission. Tu-Su. Buenavista (near Ramos Arizpe). 5465369

54 Museo de San Carlos The Neo-Classical Buenavista Palace was designed as a private home at the beginning of the 19th century by Spanish architect **Manuel Tolsá.** Emperor Maximilian handed it over to General Bazaine and his French troops in 1865. In 1968 the beautiful palace became a museum housing a large and impressive collection of European masters from the 14th to the 19th centuries, including works by Berruguete, Botticelli, Cranach the Elder, Rubens, Goya, and Reynolds. ♦ Free. Tu-Su. Puente de Alvarado 50 (at Ramos Arizpe). 5668522

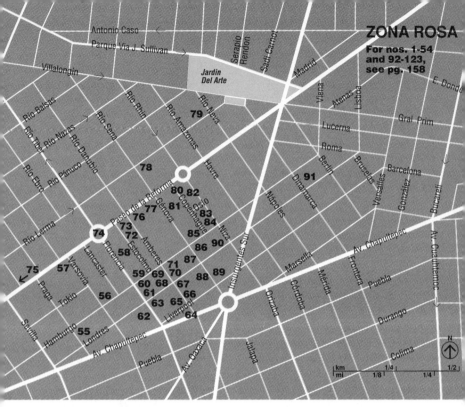

Zona Rosa

The Zona Rosa (Pink Zone) was once the city's high-class district with elegant town houses, smart shops, and exclusive restaurants. In the 1970s and 1980s, it degenerated into a shadow of its former self, but today it is undergoing a regeneration of interest and imagination: some streets are closed to traffic and filled with modern sculptures and trendy cafes, and trees have been planted everywhere. Only a few streets wide and a few deep, this tiny area boasts boutiques, antiques shops, and shopping malls linking one street to another. It's just a short journey along the Paseo de la Reforma to all the main sights, and the restaurants have more international offerings than in the rest of Mexico City. The area is at its best after 8PM, when the city's best-dressed denizens stroll the sidewalks and claim the best tables at world-class restaurants.

55 Ballet Teatro del Espacio Only open a few years, Zona Rosa's dance theater, under the direction of Gladiola Orozco and Michel Descombey, has quickly become one of the best companies in Mexico. Performances and contemporary dance classes are offered. ◆ Admission. Performances: Th-Sa. Hamburgo 218 (between Varsovia and Praga). 2073729

Restaurants/Clubs: Red   **Hotels:** Blue
Shops/ 🌳 Outdoors: Green   **Sights/Culture:** Black

56 Westin Galería Plaza $$$ This deluxe 439-room hotel provides comfort, quiet, and good management—rare qualities in the Zona Rosa—within a block of Reforma and the landmark **El Monumental a la Independencia "El Angel"** (Angel Monument). Other pluses include an executive section with fax machines in the rooms, three international restaurants, a breezy lobby, and a popular disco that is open to all. ◆ Hamburgo 195 (between Varsovia and Lancaster). 2110014, 800/228.3000; fax 2075867

57 Yug ★★★$ Don't let the name deter you from trying the granola and homemade yogurt with mango and papaya juices, or creamed spinach soup that soothes the shakiest stomach. The enormous, inexpensive menu includes whole-wheat sandwiches and superhealthful salads of alfalfa, carrots, watercress, and button mushrooms. Vegans be forewarned: Mayonnaise and creamy salad dressings go with everything. ◆ Vegetarian ◆ M-Sa breakfast, lunch, and dinner; Su lunch and dinner. Varsovia 3 (at Paseo de la Reforma). 5333296

58 Tourist Help—Procuraduria General de Justicia del Distrito Federal The narrow house built by **Rafael Quintanilla** in 1930 is the beleaguered tourist's refuge. Open 24 hours a day year-round, the office's English-speaking public prosecutors can help you report crimes, such as theft, and fill out forms you will need to make claims with insurance companies. ◆ Daily 24 hours. Florencia 20 (off Hamburgo). 6258761, 6258668. Also at:

Argentina and San Ildefonso in the Centro Histórico. 7890833

59 Auseba ★★$ This cafe draws weary shoppers who come to recuperate, and well-dressed women who share the latest gossip over pastries and coffee. ◆ Cafe ◆ Daily breakfast, lunch, and dinner. Hamburgo 159-B (at Florencia). 5113770

59 Coloniart There is a cluster of antiques shops on pretty and quiet Calle Estocolmo, and this is the best of them. The charming shop opens at the whim of its owner, but it's worth the wait to browse through the fascinating collection of crosses, crucifixes, altarpieces, Pueblan vases, and heavy Spanish furniture. ◆ M-Sa. Estocolmo 37 (between Paseo de la Reforma and Hamburgo). 5254389

60 Duca d'Este ★★★$ Situated at the intersection of two busy streets, with floor-to-ceiling windows, this is an elegant perch for people watching over a cup of Earl Grey and a slice of flaky apple strudel or strawberry cake any time of day. Pick up some rich butter cookies, berry tarts, and syrupy flan for an in-room treat. ◆ Cafe ◆ Daily breakfast, lunch, and dinner. Hamburgo 164-B (at Florencia). 5256374

61 Da Raffaello ★★$$ A loyal clientele packs this small Italian restaurant at lunchtime. Many come for the simple, yet perfectly done, linguini with clams. For a fine dinner, try the saltimbocca (veal medallions with ham, mozzarella, and red wine), followed by a dessert of zabaglione Marsala. It's wise to make reservations and ask for a highly coveted window seat. ◆ Italian ◆ Daily lunch and dinner. Reservations recommended. Londres 165 (at Florencia). 2077006

62 Casa de Prensa Yearning for the *Wall Street Journal* or the latest *GQ*? Peruse the excellent selection of international newspapers and magazines here, and pick up a few top-notch Mexican postcards as well. ◆ Daily. Florencia 57 (between Liverpool and Londres). 5257865

63 Mercado de Artesanías (Artisans' Market) This Aladdin's den of Mexican arts and crafts sells everything, including silver, serapes, pewter, ceramics, fabrics, and clothes. Spangled sombreros fight for space with multicolored hammocks. Locksmiths, butchers, grocers, and cobblers also have stalls, but the market is geared toward international tourism, and the prices and stock reflect this. A convenient place to begin and end a trip to Mexico, it gives an overview of the country's crafts, but is more expensive and less fun than buying direct from the artisans. Definitely bargain here. ◆ Daily. Bounded by Londres and Liverpool, and Florencia and Amberes (entrances at Londres 154 and on Liverpool)

64 Fonda El Refugio ★★★★$$ One of the best-recognized Mexican restaurants in the city, this place specializes in regional cuisine from throughout the country. English-speaking guests are presented a menu describing the dishes and their origins, which helps when you're faced with such offerings as *manchamanteles* (which loosely translates as "tablecloth spotter"). This dish, prepared only on Tuesdays, originated in Puebla and consists of fried chicken mixed with apples, sweet potatoes, bananas, pineapples, and a red pepper sauce. To counteract the spices, order a *jarra* (pitcher) of *aguas frescas* (drinks made from purified water, flowers, and fruits). Coffee is prepared in the traditional *cafe de olla* style—ground beans from Chiapas are simmered in a clay pot with brown sugar, cinnamon, and cloves. The restaurant is a delight from the moment you enter the pretty cornflower-blue building; be sure to tour the premises and take note of the intricate hand-painted tiles, hand-embroidered tablecloths, and typical pottery and glassware. ◆ Mexican ◆ Daily lunch and dinner. Reservations recommended. Liverpool 166 (at Amberes). 5258128

65 Krystal Zona Rosa $$$ A tall, modern, 330-room hotel with an ideal location and attentive staff, this is a great choice for business and pleasure travelers. Krystal Club guests are treated to complimentary breakfasts, newspapers, and evening hors d'oeuvres, but even those in the regular rooms feel pampered by powerful showers, firm mattresses, and evening turndown service. The outdoor pool isn't very conducive to lounging, but does come in handy for workouts. The hotel has become overwhelmingly popular with business travelers, who find suites with fax machines and large desks perfect for setting up their temporary offices. ◆ Liverpool 155 (at Amberes). 2289928, 800/231.9860; fax 2113490

Within the Krystal Zona Rosa:

Kamakura ★★★$$$ A small stream runs past the front door into this Japanese garden restaurant and sushi bar filled with bamboo, polished pebbles, and brooding Buddhas. For the full experience, take a seat at one of the *teppan yaki* tables, where Spanish-speaking

Japanese chefs display refined artistry in slicing and grilling vegetables, meats, and seafood on the tabletop grill, or at the long bar where sushi is prepared. Show restraint when ordering, as the portions are quite large. For the total experience, visit with a group of friends and plan to spend several hours savoring your meal, from the *cassis* and champagne aperitif to the warm sake finish. ♦ Japanese. ♦ Daily lunch and dinner. 2289928

66 Tané Probably the best silver shop in the country, it has a well-deserved reputation for carefully crafted and beautifully designed jewelry and silver sculptures. With an exclusive storefront backed up by metal doors and a gun-toting guard at the gate, it exudes opulence. ♦ M-Sa. Amberes 70 (between Londres and Liverpool). 5251522

67 FONART (Fundacion Nacional de Artesanías National Foundation for Mexican Artisans) A narrow, two-story treasure trove of folk art treasures from around the country, this shop always seems to have something on sale, and many things you can't live without, at a special price. There are five branch stores in Mexico City; the store near the **Alameda** also has an excellent selection. ♦ M-Sa. Londres 136 (between Amberes and Génova). 5252026. Also at: Juárez 89 (between Baldera and Humbolt). 5210171

67 Calinda Geneve Quality Inn $$ Opened in 1907, this hotel is filled with character and antiques, from the manual Underwood typewriters and oil paintings on display in the lobby to the heavy wood furnishings in the rooms. Depending on your point of view, the 347 rooms are charmingly old-fashioned or simply out of date. Street noise can be a problem; ask to see a few rooms before you choose. At press time, **El Jardin,** the hotel's original restaurant, was being restored, but be sure to stop by for a look. The iron-and-glass ceiling, brick floors, and stained-glass windows are classic remnants of the Zona Rosa's era of grandeur. ♦ Londres 130 (between Génova and Amberes). 2110071, 800/228.5151; fax 2087422

68 Los Castillos The Castillo brothers, famous silversmiths of Taxco, have a shop in the heart of the Zona Rosa. Although they have no workshop on site, there is a fine display of the family's work, ranging from full chess sets to moderately priced earrings and necklaces. Often using pre-Hispanic designs and semiprecious stones, they combine silver and turquoise into earrings modeled after Aztec headdresses. ♦ M-Sa. Amberes 41 (between Hamburgo and Londres). 5116198

69 Plaza del Angel Stone archways frame the entrance to this hacienda-style plaza linking Hamburgo to Londres (a favorite shortcut in the rainy season). Antiques shops are the main attraction, along with a few small cafes. ♦ Daily. Entrances on Hamburgo and Londres (between Florencia and Amberes)

Within Plaza del Angel:

Mercado de Antiguos (Antiques Market) On weekends the interior plaza becomes an open-air antiques market where vendors from outside the city come and set up their stalls. Everything is sold on Saturday, from Persian rugs and Pueblan ceramics to children's books featuring the cartoon character Tintin and tin trays from the 1950s. Then on Sunday the focus turns to antiquarian books, maps, and documents. The many antiques shops surrounding the plaza and nearby streets are also open during the week, but the weekend is the best time to visit. ♦ Sa-Su

Colección de Felgueras Originally housed in a closet-size shop that could barely hold three customers, the collection has moved to a larger space that fits up to six people. Miniature nativity scenes, *calaveras* (skeletons), and whole armies of soldiers fill glass cabinets and shelves; buyers make their selections by number and order at the counter. The miniature tableaux of everything from barroom scenes to weddings are addictive; many customers return to see what's new every time they're in the city. ♦ M-Sa. 5141405

70 Oficina de Turismo de la Ciudad de Mexico (Mexico City Tourist Office) Well positioned in the heart of the Zona Rosa, the tourist office (which has many English-speaking staffers) is ready to help with all queries. They provide the free English-language newspaper *Daily Bulletin,* as well as up-to-date information on hotels, restaurants, and events. ♦ Daily. Amberes 54 (at Londres). 5259380, 5259384; fax 5259387

70 Plaza Rosa A shopping mall with the latest designer clothing, sporting goods, and gift shops, as well as a couple of restaurants, this is a good place to see what's in vogue in one of the most style-conscious cities in the world. ♦ M-Sa. Bounded by Hamburgo and Londres, and Amberes and Génova

71 VIPS ★$ Forgive the ugly orange decor of this bookshop/cafe and enjoy being cossetted by the maternal waitresses. The menu is basically Mexican with hearty breakfasts, steak sandwiches, enchiladas, and *chilaquiles,* plus hamburgers and salads. ♦ Mexican ♦ Daily breakfast, lunch, and dinner. Hamburgo 126 (between Amberes and Génova). 2077094

72 Galería Sergio Bustamante This bright, open gallery is the perfect setting for Bustamante's fanciful ceramic sculptures. His original idea—the ceramic eggs from which emerge fully plumed birds and beasts—has so often been pirated and cheaply imitated that he now concentrates instead on larger pieces, including full-length mirrors out of which surreal animals poke their heads. ♦ M-Sa. Amberes 13 (between Paseo de la Reforma and Hamburgo). 2079354

73 Champs-Elysées ★★★$$$$ This French restaurant knows what it is doing and does it consummately well. Reserve a table with a window seat at lunchtime, order the *filet de boeuf avec béarnaise* (beef fillet with a shallot, butter, and wine sauce) or the fresh salmon with flageolet beans, and then move on to a dessert of guava sorbet for a long afternoon of great dining. Mexico's politicians and movers and shakers eat here regularly, largely because of the superb menu, but also to see and be seen. ♦ French ♦ M-F lunch and dinner. Reservations recommended. Jacket and tie required. Amberes 1 (at Paseo de la Reforma). 5146464

73 Champs-Elysées Boutique This boutique is actually a gourmet take-out delicatessen selling the sybaritic pleasures of its sister restaurant, from extra-virgin, first-pressing olive oil and miniature quiches to baguettes filled with either foie gras, bacon, and avocado, Parma ham, or duck with chutney. It's all wildly expensive. ♦ M-F. Estocolmo 4 (at Paseo de la Reforma). 5140450

74 María Isabel Sheraton $$$$ This deluxe hotel undoubtedly has the best possible view of **El Angel.** Situated on the north side of Reforma next to the **US Embassy,** it is perfect for those who want to be near, but not in, the Zona Rosa. There are 751 rooms and three restaurants, two quite formal and the third more casual. Other amenities include special floors for business travelers and state-of-the-art business services. ♦ Paseo de la Reforma 325 (at Florencia). 2073933, 800/325.3535; fax 2070684

Mexico City's dining habits are reflected in restaurant hours, which may seem strange to travelers from the US. Some places don't open for breakfast until 9 or 10AM, when office workers typically take an expanded coffee break. Lunchtime starts at 1PM and lasts until 4 or 5PM, though some places stay open as late as 8PM to accommodate early diners. Many of the more exclusive restaurants don't even open for dinner until 8PM, and are busiest around 10PM.

Restaurants/Clubs: Red   Hotels: Blue
Shops/ 🌳 Outdoors: Green   Sights/Culture: Black

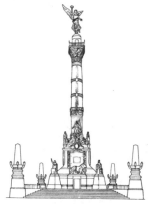

74 El Monumento a la Independencia "El Angel" (The Angel) A major landmark, this 118-foot-tall monument to Mexico's independence from Spain is a glorious golden-winged angel. Representing victory, it has been the unofficial symbol of the city since its inauguration by the architect **Rivas Mercado** in 1910. ♦ Paseo de la Reforma (at Florencia)

75 Marquis Reforma $$$$ A member of the Small Luxury Hotels of the World, this hostelry draws rave reviews from first-time guests who are never again satisfied with any other hotel. The pink stone and mirrored glass Art Deco facade stands out on the sedate Paseo de la Reforma, boldly proclaiming the hotel's departure from the norm. The 84 suites and 116 rooms follow through on the Art Deco theme, with precious wood and silk furnishings and gorgeous lamps. High tea and cocktails are served in the **Caviar Bar** to the accompaniment of a string quartet, and the spa specializes in luxurious pampering. ♦ Paseo de la Reforma 465 (at Río de la Plata). 2113600, 800/525.4800; fax 2115561

Within the Marquis Reforma:

La Jolla ★★★$$$ Sleek and minimal in style, this has become one of the trendiest restaurants in the city, attracting the glamour crowd. The Belgian chef has added Mexican touches to his native cuisine, creating nouvelle Mexican dishes with a Flemish twist. ♦ Mexican/Continental ♦ Daily breakfast, lunch, and dinner. Reservations recommended. Jacket and tie required. 2113600

76 Cine Latino Movie theaters in Mexico are cheap and popular, and this is a local favorite, showing art-house North American, European, and Mexican films. The selections are a step above the usual mainstream Hollywood flicks and range from the latest Mexican hit to Kurosawa. English-language films are screened in English with Spanish subtitles. ♦ Showtimes vary. Paseo de la Reforma 296 (between Amberes and Génova). 5258757

77 La Gondola ★$$ From its dark interior, this restaurant spills out into a sidewalk cafe along a pedestrians-only street. The tables are set up under a canvas roof with classical music (sometimes live) playing in the background. The pleasant atmosphere is reminiscent of a busy Italian trattoria, right down to the white-aproned waiters. The specialty is spaghetti Vivaldi, made with fresh vegetables. ♦ Italian ♦ Daily lunch and dinner. Génova 21 (at Paseo de la Reforma). 5140743

78 Les Moustaches ★★$$$$ Across Reforma between the British and US embassies sits a smart restaurant that lives up to its name—every single waiter, even the owner himself, sports a mustache. While over the top in both expense and ostentation, this dining spot does, nevertheless, serve excellent abalone and wonderful desserts. Formal in style and service, the restaurant is particularly popular with cognac-sipping businessmen bearing cellular phones; the waiters and clientele have little tolerance for casually dressed tourists. ♦ International ♦ M-F lunch and dinner. Jacket and tie required. Río Sena 88 (at Río Lerma). 5333390

79 María Cristina $ On the north side of Reforma, a 10-minute walk from the Zona Rosa, you'll find the most attractive medium-range hotel in the city, where loyal guests return time and again. The 150 rooms are comfortable and come with a private bathroom, telephone, and TV. Master suites have in-room hot tubs. Definitely a place for holiday-makers and families rather than expense-account business travelers—the pace is gentle, and the price is reasonable. The garden provides a relaxing spot to sit after a hard day of shopping and sight-seeing. The only negative is the inferior restaurant. ♦ Río Lerma 31 (at Río Neva). 5669688, 7031787; fax 5669194

80 Calle Copenhague (Copenhagen Street) This tiny, narrow street in the Zona Rosa has nothing but restaurants. In one block there are about a dozen, each with a distinct style and menu and nearly all with sidewalk patios. It is quite possible to move from one to the other enjoying a drink here, lunch there, and coffee somewhere else. ♦ Between Paseo de la Reforma and Hamburgo (pedestrian traffic only)

81 Piccadilly Pub ★★$$$ Hardly a replica of a typical British pub (although the inside dining room does have a portrait of Henry VIII), it belies its name by serving only Mexican beers. At least the menu is genuine, and the owner, Jane Pearson, is a British expatriate. Choose among Welsh rarebit, shepherd's pie, porterhouse steak, trifle, and strawberries and cream. With the nearby **British Embassy** providing a lot of business, the fare has to remain authentic. ♦ British ♦ M-Sa lunch and dinner; Su lunch. Copenhague 23 (off Paseo de la Reforma). 5143740

82 El Mesón del Perro Andaluz ★$$$ Directly opposite the **Piccadilly Pub** is a similarly nostalgic restaurant, but this one caters to the Spanish community. As popular for a drink or light lunch as it is for a full-blown feast, they take pride in their seafood and the light, refreshing gazpacho, a must in the hot weather. The outdoor cafe here has been a longtime favorite of locals and tourists but unfortunately the management appears to be overly confident in its continued success—prices have risen dramatically recently, and your check will reflect a charge for the bread served with your wine or soup. ♦ Spanish ♦ Daily lunch and dinner. Copenhague 26 (off Paseo de la Reforma). 5335306

83 Chez Pascal ★★$$$$ This elegant French restaurant is presided over by Chef Pascal Brunnereay, who hails from Ile du Rey. A busy man, he also suggests the daily specialties and takes each customer's order. It is an expensive place to see and be seen; those who come are seduced by fine wines and rich dishes ranging from mushrooms à la provençal to langoustine and lemon sole with salmon roe. ♦ French ♦ M-Sa lunch and dinner. Jacket and tie required. Oslo 10 (between Niza and Copenhague). 5250947

84 Focolare ★★$$$ Although this restaurant tries too hard to combine an excellent menu of regional food with a forced ambience of Mexican folklore, it is still a good place for those who want to broaden their palate. A few specialties are the 36-ingredient mole sauces from Puebla and Oaxaca, pork cooked in banana leaves from the Yucatán Peninsula, baby goat from the northern countryside, and corn tamales from Michoacán. The patio restaurant is a delight during the day, though it's a bit nippy at night. A leisurely tour of the breakfast buffet should keep you satisfied for hours. ♦ Mexican ♦ Daily breakfast, lunch, and dinner. Hamburgo 87 (between Copenhague and Niza). 2078850

85 Jugos Miami $ This tiny, one-room cafe opens onto the street and serves freshly made fruit juices of every imaginable combination, fruit salads, hamburgers, and bowls of granola. ♦ Fruit ♦ M-Sa breakfast and lunch until 8PM. Hamburgo 105 (at Génova). No phone

86 Daikoku ★★$$ This Japanese restaurant hidden off Génova in a tiny shopping mall is one of the most popular sushi bars in the city, offering grilled smoked salmon skins, *teppan yaki* (meats, shellfish, and vegetables are prepared on a grill at your table), and the dark meat of the *hamachi* (yellowtail tuna). Although tables are available, sitting at the sushi bar or in front of the grill makes gratification all the more immediate. ♦ Japanese ♦ M-Sa lunch and dinner. Génova 44 (at Hamburgo). 5334954

87 Café Konditori

★★★$$ In addition to the spacious dining room, this Danish-owned restaurant has tables set on the sidewalk, making it an excellent meeting place for any meal or occasion. The menu offers crepes, bagels with smoked salmon, and a variety of salads. ♦ International ♦ M-Sa breakfast, lunch, and dinner. Génova 61 (between Hamburgo and Londres). 5256621

88 Estoril

★★★$$$$ Although it's a little difficult to spot, this restaurant on the second story of a former private residence is worth tracking down. Small, elegant, and well decorated, it provides a relaxing and unhurried experience. From the aphrodisiacal fried parsley starter to the sea bass in coriander sauce to the homemade sorbets, the accent is on simplicity rather than lavishness. ♦ International ♦ Daily lunch and dinner. Jacket and tie required. Génova 75 (between Londres and Liverpool). 2076418. Also at: Alejandro Dumas 24 (in Polanco). 5314896

89 Mixup

For recordings of Latin dance music—*cumbias,* merengues, salsa, and *danzón*—this shop has it all. There's also a wide selection of music from all over the world. The owner is from the US, but has lived in Mexico all his life. The staff believes that there is no record, tape, or CD that can't be found either immediately or within a maximum of seven days. All this plus a good selection of international books and magazines, some in English. Tickets for all kinds of musical performances are also on sale. ♦ Daily. Génova 76 (between Londres and Liverpool). 5110033, ticket reservations 2070141

90 Bellinghausen

★★$$ Given a choice between lunch or dinner here, choose the former every time. Charming by day, when businesspeople and tourists make the most of the garden patio, in the evening it's much more somber. The menu is Mexican and ranges from the exotic *gusanos de maguey* (cactus worms) to the restaurant's specialty, *la chemita* (grilled steak with mashed potatoes). Mexican wines are served, as are draught beers, a rarity in this town. ♦ Mexican ♦ M-Sa lunch and dinner. Londres 95 (between Génova and Niza). 2076149

91 Don Vasco de Quiroga

$ Because this small, family-run hotel is a bit east of the Zona Rosa, both its pace and price are very desirable. After a day you become a well-known guest, and in a week you're one of the family. There is a large lobby on the first floor, a decent restaurant in the basement, and a variety of quirky rooms, 12 in all. While great for families and small groups, it's not ideal for businesspeople, as the telephones in the rooms don't have direct dialing. ♦ Londres 15 (between Dinamarca and Berlín). 5462614

Frida Fervor

Frida Kahlo (1907-1954) has become the best-selling Latin American painter of all time, outstripping even her husband, muralist Diego Rivera. Well known by artists, intellectuals, and collectors in her day, her work achieved public notoriety only in the 1980s. *Newsweek* dubbed her "a highbrow version of the Elvis phenomenon," and she has also been the subject of a Broadway musical. Her powerful, painful self-portraits are favorites with collectors, and one of her paintings (*Self Portrait with Loose Hair,* 1947) broke the auction record (more than $1 million) for Latin American art.

Part of the fascination with Kahlo's art is due to her persona, one of independence and outspokenness, and her passionate and fascinating life in post-revolutionary Mexico. She was the friend of many major artistic and political figures, including Tina Modotti, Edward Weston, André Breton, Leon Trotsky (with whom she had a brief affair), José Clemente Orozco, David Alfaro Siqueiros, and, of course, Rivera. However, it is her paintings that have inspired the cultlike admiration she has garnered. It was her honesty, strength, and anguish, and her ability to reveal her soul on canvas, that have turned her into a modern feminist icon.

Born in Coyoacán to a German-born photographer father and Mexican mother, she began painting in her teens, already vowing to marry Rivera, 20 years her senior. After surviving polio as a child, she later saw her dreams slip away when, at the age of 19, her backbone, pelvis, and leg were shattered in a bus crash. She slowly recovered, but was never able to have children (although she never stopped trying), and she spent many years bedridden. To strengthen her spine, she wore binding corsets, and the continual pain she suffered from her injuries is one of the subjects of her paintings, which feature such harrowing images as her own face studded with nails, circlets of thorns around her neck, and her spine depicted as a crumbling Greek column.

Although surprisingly few of Kahlo's works are on view in Mexico City, her enchanting house in Coyoacán is open to the public (Admission; Tu-Su; Londres 44, at Calle Allende; 5545999). Other places to see her work are in the studio she shared with Rivera, **Museo Estudio Diego Rivera** (Tu-Su; Calle Rivera, San Angel; 5483032) and the **Museo de Arte Moderno** (Tu-Su; Paseo de la Reforma , at Gandhi; 5536211). Her likeness appears in many of Rivera's murals (particularly those in the **Palacio Nacional**). To learn more about Kahlo's life, read *Frida,* by Hayden Herrera, or Marta Zamora's *Frida Kahlo: The Brush of Anguish.*

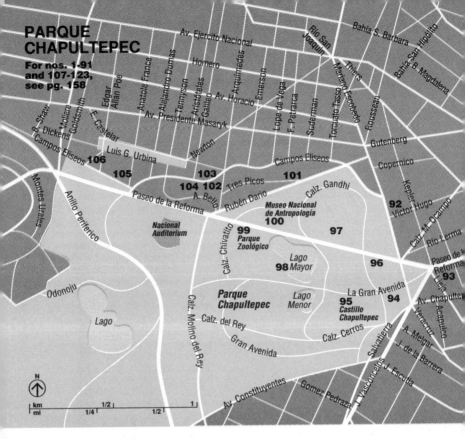

On the map:
Av. Ejercito Nacional
Rio San Joaquin
Bahía S. Barbara
Bahía San Hipólito
Homero
Arquimedes
Emerson
Thiers
Bahía B. Magdalena
Mariano Escobedo
Rousseau
Shaw
Moliere
Goldsmith
Edgar Allan Poe
E. Castelar
Anatole France
Alejandro Dumas
Tennyson
Aristoteles
Galileo
Av. Horacio
Lope de Vega
F. Petrarca
Suderman
Torcuato Tasso
Dickens
Campos Eliseos
Av. Presidente Masaryk
Newton
Gutenberg
Luis G. Urbina
Copernico
106
105
104 102
103
Tres Picos
Campos Eliseos
101
Kepler
Victor Hugo
Montes Urales
Anillo Periferico
Paseo de la Reforma
A. Bello
Rubén Darío
Calz. Gandhi
92
Calz. M. Ocampo
Rio Lerma
Nacional Auditorium
Calz. Chivatito
99
Parque Zoológico
Museo Nacional de Antropología
100
97
Paseo de la Reforma
Odonoju
Lago
98 Mayor
96
93
Lago
Parque Chapultepec
Lago Menor
La Gran Avenida
95
Castillo Chapultepec
94
Av. Chapultepec
Acapulco
Veracruz
Calz. Molino del Rey
Calz. del Rey
Gran Avenida
Calz. Cerros
Salvatierra
A. Melgar
J. de la Barrera
Gran Avenida
J. Escutia
N
Av. Constituyentes
Gomez Pedraza
J. Vasconcelos
km / mi   1/4   1/2   1/2   1

Parque Chapultepec (Chapultepec Park)

Commonly thought of as the lungs of polluted Mexico City, **Parque Chapultepec** runs alongside Paseo de la Reforma due west of the Zona Rosa and up into the *lomas* (hills) that mark the westernmost extension of the city. At the turn of the century former dictator/president Porfirio Díaz added fountains, lakes, picnic grounds, and access by street cars and trams to this vast stretch of green, making it the most popular, largest, and liveliest park in all of Mexico City.

Chapultepec—which recently underwent a $75-million renovation—is home to museums, zoos, lakes, and restaurants, and is frequented by schoolchildren, buskers, hawkers, and lovers. In the 15th century, when the area was still outside the city limits, Netzahualcoyotl, the king of the Texcoco region (and also a famous poet), established it as a park; it had already been used as a summer retreat and zoo by previous Aztec emperors. The zoo still exists, and is now filled with exotic species the Aztec never would have seen, such as giant pandas. Numerous trees and sculpted rocks dating back to the early 16th century are also featured at the zoo, but it's the park's modern additions that most interest visitors. This is where you'll find some of the city's most famous and best-run museums, ranging from the world-renowned **Museo de Antropología** (Museum of Anthropology) with its pre-Hispanic treasures, to several contemporary art museums, plus Mexico's first childrens' museum.

92 Camino Real $$$$ One of the most attractive hotels in the city, it was designed by one of Mexico's top modern architects, **Ricardo Legorreta**. Note his bold use of basic colors and sharp lines, and the fountain cascading in front of the main entrance—a stark contrast to the other nearby deluxe hotels with their anonymous, high-rise luxury towers. With 700 rooms, three swimming pools, four flood-lit tennis courts, and several restaurants, this is one of the most self-indulgent places to stay in Mexico City. The only drawbacks are the hotel's location—far from most tourist attractions and restaurants—and its layout, which makes you feel like you're hiking through a maze to reach your room (although it does give you a chance to examine the artwork by **Rufino Tamayo**, **Pedro Coronel**, and **Alexander Calder** scattered through the public spaces). Still, it a welcome escape from the noise of the city, and returning here after a hard day's touring absolute bliss. ♦ Mariano Escobedo 700 (at Victor Hugo). 2032121, 800/722.6466; fax 2506897

Within the Camino Real:

Fouquet's de Paris ★★★$$$$ Chef Philippe Barraut presides over this very high-class French restaurant, which serves the choicest and most elegant meals around. Specialties include salmon fillets with vanilla, quail à la provençal, and passion fruit sorbet. Imported wines are outrageously expensive. Reserve a window table overlooking the hotel's gardens. ♦ French ♦ M-F lunch and dinner; Sa dinner. Reservations recommended. Jacket and tie required. 2032121

93 **Four Seasons Hotel Mexico City** $$$$ Though this hostelry is newly built, it looks like it's always been a part of the historic Paseo de la Reforma. The Spanish Colonial facade hides an elaborate central courtyard surrounded by 240 luxurious guest rooms and suites. The best seats for dining are along the courtyard terrace of the hotel's gourmet restaurant; other options include an indoor cafe, lobby lounge, and a library-style bar. An outdoor pool and indoor health club sit atop the eight-story building, the perfect spot for relaxing after a session in the well-equipped business center. ♦ Paseo de la Reforma 500 (between Burdeos and Leija). 2301818, 800/332.3442; fax 2301817

94 **Monumento de los Niños Héroes** (Monument to the Child Heroes) The tall columns that mark the park's entrance are a monument to six young cadets known as the *niños héroes,* the oldest of whom was only 16. In a very patriotic nation, these young men are almost deified for protecting the Mexican flag during the US invasion of 1847. Instead of giving themselves up to the more powerful north-of-the-border troops, the last six cadets defending **Castillo Chapultepec** jumped to their deaths from the high terrace, wrapped in their country's flag to keep the pennant from being captured. ♦ Entrance near Paseo de la Reforma (at Calzado Chivatito)

95 **Castillo Chapultepec** The castle takes its name from the Aztec word *chapulin* (cater-pillar) and the hill on which the caterpillars congregated. Although now in the heart of the city, the hill was used as a summer retreat by the Aztec emperors and Spanish viceroys, and only became incorporated into the city in the middle of the last century. The Aztec emperors had their likenesses carved into the side of the hill, and although the Spaniards destroyed most of these, there are some remains on the east slope, most dating to the reign of Moctezuma II (1502-20). The castle was built on the top of the hill over-looking **Parque Chapultepec** in 1786 by the Catalonian architect **Agustín Mascaro** for the use of the viceroys. After the 1810 War of Independence, it passed into the hands of a military college and was home and school to the young cadets who died defending the flag.

The castle's next unfortunate lodgers were Maximilian of Hapsburg and his Belgian wife, Carlota, who were invited to rule the country by Napoléon III (for more on the couple, see page 186). It then passed from one ruler to another, occasionally serving as the **Presidential Palace**. In 1939 the left-wing president Lázaro Cárdenas bequeathed it to the nation as the **Museo de la Historia Nacional** (Museum of National History). ♦ Chapultepec Hill (near Calzado del Rey)

Within Castillo Chapultepec:

Museo de la Historia Nacional (Museum of National History) The history of Spanish influence on Mexico from the conquest to the eventual transformation into a distinct, bicultural nation unfolds in this museum. Covering two floors, there are examples of Spanish weapons, maps, and religious artifacts alongside portraits of Hernán Cortés and the viceroys, the Kings of Spain, heroes of the Independence, and the subsequent Presidents of the newly founded Republic of Mexico. Around the museum are murals by Siqueiros and Orozco, commemorating key acts in Mexican history. ♦ Admission. Tu-Su. 5536224

96 **Museo de Arte Moderno** (Museum of Modern Art) Set back from Reforma's traffic on the edge of Parque Chapultepec, this museum is set in an elliptical, two-story building. Alongside the temporary exhibits are two halls showcasing the permanent collection, including Frida Kahlo's famous work *The Two Fridas* (1939), in which she portrays twin representations of herself joined together by the heart. Along the walls hang paintings by Luis Nishizawa, Maria Izquierdo, and Abraham Angel, who died in 1924 of a broken heart at the age of 19. The upper floor's collection opens with Rufino Tamayo's *Hippy in White* (1972) and continues past the paintings of surrealists Remedios Varo from Spain and Leonora Carrington from England, both of whom spent many years in Mexico. The temporary exhibitions are always interesting, as are the large sculpture garden surrounding the museum and the small, well-stocked bookshop. ♦ Admission. Tu-Su. Paseo de la Reforma (at Calzado Gandhi). 5536211

The average worker in Mexico City is financially supporting five other people.

Restaurants/Clubs: Red   Hotels: Blue
Shops/ 🍂 Outdoors: Green   Sights/Culture: Black

97 Museo Rufino Tamayo (Rufino Tamayo Museum) The Oaxacan-born muralist, painter, and collector Rufino Tamayo died in 1991 at the age of 92. His private collection of modern art is housed in this museum designed by architects **Teodoro González de León** and **Abraham Zabludowsky.** In addition to Tamayo's own work, including the famous slices of ripe, red watermelons, there are paintings by Francis Bacon, Mark Rothko, Pablo Picasso, Willem de Kooning, and the Mexican masters Luis Nishizawa, Alberto Gironella, and fellow Oaxacan Francisco Toledo. ◆ Admission. Tu-Su. Paseo de la Reforma (at Calzado Gandhi). 2866519

98 Casa del Lago (Lake House) This pretty little building is often the setting for public events, political demonstrations, open-air performances, and buskers who use the adjacent amphitheater for every sort of activity. Inside are temporary art exhibits and a small cafe. ◆ Daily. La Gran Avenida (between Calzado Chivatito and Calzado Gandhi). No phone

98 Lago Chapultepec Restaurante
★★$$$$ **Lago Chapultepec** takes on an otherworldly appearance at night, when white lights illuminate streaming fountains and sparkle inside this lakeside restaurant. Formal to the point of pretentiousness, the restaurant is known more for its setting than its cuisine; stick to the lower-priced items on the menu. It's the most soothing place in the park for a leisurely lunch, though you may not wish to spend your day outdoors in clothing that will pass muster with the haughty maître d'. ◆ Continental ◆ Daily lunch and dinner. Reservations required. Jacket and tie required. La Gran Avenida (between Calzado Chivatito and Calzado Gandhi). 5159585

99 Parque Zoológico (Zoo) In the early 16th century, long before the current zoo came into operation, there was a menagerie of exotic animals from all over Mesoamerica in the **Parque Chapultepec** area. Today there are five giant pandas (the zoo was the first to breed them successfully in captivity), a white tiger, a pair of Mexican wolves (only 30 remain in the wild), and plenty of tamer animals, such as ponies, which children are allowed to ride. On Sundays it is one of the most visited spots in the city. Recently renovated, the zoo is now easier for visitors to walk through—the old-fashioned steel cages and cement floors have been replaced by landscaped areas designed to replicate the animals' native habitats as closely as possible, and a new bird section has been built, along with remodeled food stands and a gift shop. ◆ Free. Tu-Su. Paseo de la Reforma (at Calzado Chivatito). No phone

100 Museo Nacional de Antropología
(Museum of Anthropology) No journey to Mexico is complete without a visit to this outstanding anthropological museum. In this showstopper, delicate sculptures rub shoulders with sacrificial altars, and gods with tongue-twisting names—Huitzilopochtli (War), Coatlicue (Earth Mother), Tlaloc (Rain), Chalchiuhtlicue (Corn), Huehueteotl (Fire), and Mictlantecuhtli (Death)—appear again and again in many guises and under different names. However, the preoccupations throughout are always the same: corn, death, water, and sun. It is a fascinating overview of the cultures living in Mesoamerica before the arrival of the European conquerors, including an entire floor of ethnographical displays. The exhibits include murals, wall maps, sculptures, jewels, weapons, masks, and reconstructed temples, altars, and tombs. It is a beautiful museum, well deserving of its reputation as the best of its kind in the world.

The permanent collection is housed in 12 anthropological rooms on the ground floor and 11 ethnographical rooms on the upper floor. It covers every one of the great civilizations, from the Aztec in Mexico City to the Maya in the south, the Zapotec and Mixtec in Oaxaca, and the northernmost nomads. After the destruction of the pre-Hispanic civilizations—due to time, war, and diseases brought by the Spanish—their ruins were covered over, tombs were lost, languages were scrambled, and gods were incorporated into the Catholic canon. However, they were never forgotten, and artifacts turned up in city squares, fields, and deep in the jungle. European and north-of-the-border explorers rediscovered some of the pyramids and temples. Many other sites were well known by the locals, who continued to make offerings to their gods but refused to share their secrets with the Spanish.

Aztec Calendar

Many of the early discoveries were taken out of Mexico by collectors, explorers, and archaeologists who felt, perhaps rightly at the time, that their finds would only be lost again if they left them in Mexico. As the centuries passed, the Spanish also became curious about the civilizations they had conquered. It was Viceroy Antonio Maria de Bucareli who returned the first artifacts at the end of the 18th century. As the collection grew, Emperor Maximilian moved it in 1865 to the former Mint—the Museo de Culturas, behind the Palacio Nacional. After the 1910 Revolution, interest grew in re-creating the image of a preconquest Mexico. President Adolfo López Mateos inaugurated this museum in 1964 to honor Mexico's heritage.

Central column of the Museo Nacional de Antropología

Architect **Pedro Ramírez Vazquez** planned the building's construction; his design is remarkable, with a central patio onto which all the rooms open, allowing you to walk from the age of the Pyramids of the Sun and the Moon to the treasures of the Maya in their jungle kingdoms simply by crossing the patio. Alternatively, you can follow the chronological unfolding of the rooms and sense the development of the country in its different ages and geographical areas.

A few words of advice:

1) Leave time for several short visits rather than a long, exhausting one;

2) Join up with a guided tour (given in English every 30 minutes);

3) On Sunday admission is free, but the museum fills up with families and students;

4) When museum fatigue sets in, spend a few minutes in the cool courtyard or escape to the restaurant;

5) If possible, see the ruins at Teotihuacán (see feature on page 169) before your visit to put the grandeur and splendor of this great civilization into context;

6) If in a rush, skip the first three rooms on general world anthropology, which is of limited interest to non-Spanish-speakers, and begin with the exhibit on Teotihuacán;

7) Do not miss rooms IV (Teotihuacán), VII (Aztec), and X (Maya).

♦ Admission; Su free. Tu-Su. Paseo de la Reforma (at Calzado Gandhi). 5536226

Within the Museo Nacional de Antropología:

Bookshop One of the best in the city for books on history, art, architecture, and pre-Hispanic Mexico, it has the latest titles in Spanish, English, German, and French. There are also good official guides to the museum and other sites around the country, posters, videos, tapes, and postcards. ♦ Tu-Su. 5536226

Museum Restaurant $ Although the overpriced food isn't great, this is the only place to eat within acceptable walking distance of the exhibits. ♦ Mexican ♦ Tu-Su. 5536226

Outside the Museo Nacional de Antropología:

Tlaloc At the entrance to the museum is a huge stone sculpture to Tlaloc, the god of rain. It dates from the first century and was rediscovered 30 miles from here. The enormous 23-foot-high, 167-metric-ton statue had to be transported on a 72-wheel trailer that was specially designed for the two-day journey. ♦ Outside the main entrance (on Paseo de la Reforma)

101 Museo-Casa Siqueiros (Siqueiros House Museum) Muralist, Stalinist, and political activist David Alfaro Siqueiros lived and painted in this house during the last years of his life, and he donated it to Mexico a month before he died. It combines his living space with an art gallery and an exhibit on his life. There are occasional screenings of European films here. ♦ Admission. M-Sa. Tres Picos 29 (at Rubén Dario). 5313394

102 Hotel Nikko México $$$$ This is generally credited as one of the best business hotels in Mexico for its extremely high standards in everything from the comfort of the 750 rooms to the service. Japanese-style guest rooms with futon beds are available, and the regular accommodations are amazingly large. There are Japanese, French, and international restaurants, British and Mexican bars, and room-service cuisine is top-notch. Tourists who can afford to stay here prefer it above all others, because it overlooks **Parque Chapultepec** and is within easy walking distance of the museums. One less attractive feature is the view from the top-floor business/breakfast room, where you can witness thermal inversion putting its seal of gray smog over the city as the heat from cars and factories rises and is bottled up by the cold, early-morning air. The pollution is trapped for hours, sometimes weeks. ♦ Campos Eliseos 204 (between Tennyson and Arquimedes). 2801111, 800/645.5687; fax 2546980

103 Artesanías de Michoacán Devoted entirely to art and crafts from the state of Michoacán, a five-hour drive west of Mexico City, this boutique verges on the chichi.

For example, on display is elaborately painted furniture, made by two US expatriates in the tiny village of Erongaricuaro on the shores of Lake Patzcuaro, that is sold here at very inflated prices. Then there's the beautiful pottery of Tzintzuntzan (glazed emerald green), Patamban (tiny dotted art on a brown background), and fluted Aladdin pots. ♦ M-Sa. Campos Eliseos 189 (at Galileo). 2031503

103 La Galvía ★★★$$$$ There are as many fierce defenders as detractors for this restaurant. Those in favor praise the high quality of the menu, which ranges from a soup of baby cactus leaves and pinto beans to main courses such as the *pollo* (chicken) in phyllo. Critics find it overpriced, underspiced, and generally pretentious. Either way, it's always booked up. Try it and decide for yourself. ♦ Mexican ♦ M-Sa lunch and dinner. Reservations required. Campos Eliseos 247 (at Galileo). 2810560

104 Presidente Inter-Continental $$$$ Almost brushing shoulders with the **Nikko**, this is another excellent high-rise hotel overlooking the park. With tennis courts, a swimming pool, a huge lobby, and 659 rooms, many of which have been recently renovated and enlarged, it is a town within a town. To make the most of the views, smog permitting, get a room facing southwest, and as high up as possible. The club floors have a private lounge with complimentary breakfast and evening appetizers; all rooms are large and comfortable, and the service is superb. ♦ Campos Eliseos 218 (between Tennyson and Arquimedes). 3277700, 800/90444, 800/327.0200; fax 3277730

Within the Presidente Inter-Continental:

Maxim's de Paris ★★★$$$ Operated under the auspices of the Paris original, this elegant French restaurant is an enduring favorite of Mexico City's elite gourmands. The chef is at his best with classic French dishes, including escargots, a hearty cassoulet, and *coquilles St-Jacques* (scallops in a cream sauce). The menu changes frequently to constantly offer the loyal clientele new choices. The refined decor is enhanced by a stained-glass ceiling and Art Deco furnishings. ♦ French ♦ M-F lunch and dinner; Sa dinner. Reservations recommended. Jacket and tie required. 2540033

104 Centro Cultural Contemporáneo (Center for Contemporary Culture) The largest and most important private TV company in Mexico, Televisa, owns this four-story building in which they house their collection of art, sculpture, and photographs. In addition to the permanent collection, there are always thought-provoking international exhibitions. ♦ Nominal admission. Tu-Su. Campos Eliseos (between Tennyson and Arquimedes). 2820355

Within the Centro Cultural Contemporáneo:

Museum Shop A dangerously tempting store full of imaginative gift ideas, ranging from blue blown-glass vases to witty T-shirts, posters, books, and the miniature boxes of the great craftsperson Rafael Alvarez. ♦ Tu-Su. 2820355

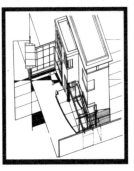

105 Galería Mexicana de Diseño (Gallery of Mexican Design) This gallery (pictured above) has a small but attractive space dedicated to innovations in contemporary Mexican design, from plans for buildings to light fittings, telephones, and pens. Many of the designs exhibited are on sale in the tiny shop downstairs, along with several other interesting creations. ♦ M-Sa. Anatole France 13 (at Paseo de la Reforma). 2020260

106 La Bottiglia ★★$$$ This pretty and popular Italian restaurant with a Bolognese chef is always bustling—bear with the occasional air of Italian anarchy in the service. The menu ranges from pasta in a pesto sauce to osso buco with white wine to the house specialty, carpaccio. The wine list is overpriced but does have some excellent Tuscan and Umbrian reds. ♦ Italian ♦ Daily breakfast, lunch, and dinner. Reservations required. Edgar Allan Poe (at Campos Eliseos). 5206033

106 Hotel Polanco $ In a delightful area right around the corner from **La Bottiglia**, this pleasant hotel is the only affordable option in the neighborhood. It's one-third the price of the more deluxe hotels overlooking the park and a very acceptable alternative, with 58 rooms and a coffee shop. ♦ Edgar Allan Poe 8 (at Campos Eliseos). 5206040

Restaurants/Clubs: Red
Shops/ 🌳 Outdoors: Green

Hotels: Blue
Sights/Culture: Black

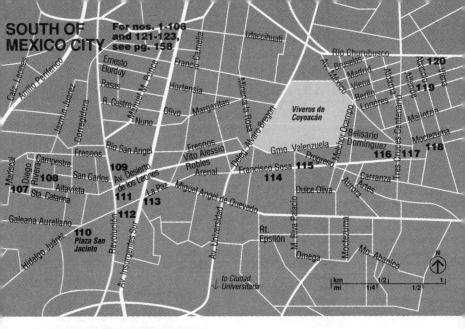

For nos. 1-106 and 121-123, see pg. 158

South of Mexico City

The city's southern portion stretches from the Paseo de la Reforma to the once-separate city of Xochimilco, Mexico City's last remnant of pre-Hispanic life, famous for its canals and nursery gardens. Avenida Insurgentes, the longest avenue in the world, is the central north-to-south street, running from the city's northern exit to the pyramids and from its southern exit to Cuernavaca. Some of Mexico City's loveliest neighborhoods are here: colonial San Angel, with its stalwart Spanish mansions and its famous Saturday-morning **Bazar Sábado** handicrafts market; and nearby Coyoacán, where such diverse figures as Hernán Cortés, Frida Kahlo, Diego Rivera, Leon Trotsky, and various ex-presidents have all lived. The south is a must for Rivera-Kahlo fans, since the couple spent most of their lives between Coyoacán and San Angel, and this is where their house and studios are located. It is best to visit this section of the city on the weekend, unless you want to get caught up in the hubbub of university life, as students congregate here to learn, dispute, and discuss. Make sure you have time to browse, since those exquisite wine goblets you'll see will tempt you to window shop; the south has plenty of finds for crafts lovers and people watchers. The restaurants, bars, and theaters are geared for locals, with no special effects for tourists—and they're the better for it.

107 **San Angel Inn** ★★★★$$$$ Certainly the most famous restaurant in the city, this is also one of the best. Many people come here just for its reputation and to enjoy the setting in an enchanting Spanish house with seating on the patio and inside. The menu is excellent, but with so much great dining in Mexico City, it can no longer claim superiority. Stick to what they do well (the duck in raspberry sauce, for instance), and dinner will be superb. Or you can just drop in for margaritas in the early evening and enjoy the fabulous gardens and the opulence of this former hacienda. Weekend lunches are particularly popular, and a meal at the inn is a great capper after a tour of San Angel. But be forewarned—the unspoken dress code is firmly enforced. Women wearing walking shoes such as canvas slip-ons or huaraches are not admitted, even if they only wish to tour the property. ♦ Mexican/International ♦ Daily lunch and dinner. Reservations recommended. Jacket required. Diego Rivera 50 (at Altavista). 5487568

108 **Museo Estudio Diego Rivera** (Diego Rivera Studio Museum) **Juan O'Gorman,** a painter and architect friend of Diego Rivera and Frida Kahlo, designed these double studios for the artists in 1930. Much of Rivera's easel work was done in his studio on the top floor. There are still more than 500 objects here from his life, including paintbrushes, empty paint tubes, and unusual objects of art, such as great papier-mâché Judas figures, photographs, press clippings, clothes, and the general clutter of genius. ♦ Free. Tu-Su. Diego Rivera (at Altavista). 5483032

109 **Museo Carrillo Gil** Méridan doctor Alvar Carrillo Gil (1899-1974) was a friend to many leading Mexican artists of the day. He started this fine collection when he was still a medical student and added to it throughout his life. Although it concentrates on national artists, there are also paintings from Japan, Europe, and other far-off places. Temporary exhibitions, special musical events, film screenings, and conferences also take place here. ♦ Admission. Tu-Su. Revolución 1608 (at San Carlos). 5303983, 5504018

Maximilian and Carlota: Mexico's Martyred Monarchs

Two of the most ill-fated characters in Mexico's history are the 19th-century Austrian archduke Maximilian and his Belgian wife, Charlotte, who changed her name to the Spanish equivalent, Carlota. His life ended at the age of 35 in front of a firing squad, while she went mad in the Vatican pleading for his release, and lived locked up in a Belgian castle until she was 87.

The young couple came to Mexico in 1863 at the bidding of both conservative Mexicans, who wanted to see a European-style monarchy replace the disorganized politicians who had run the country since 1820, and Napoléon III, who was trying to extend his empire overseas. Although Maximilian asked for a plebiscite to make sure the people wanted him for their emperor, it was soon obvious that it had been rigged and the Mexicans were not a bit interested in having a European ruler. No one met them upon their arrival, and Maximilian's liberal ideas (including restoring communal property to Indians and toughening child labor laws) and insistence on courtly manners and rigorous protocol were greeted with a surprised irritation.

Within a year, Napoléon had grown embarrassed by his puppet rulers, and, under international pressure, withdrew the French troops that were supporting them. As a result, Maximilian retreated for longer and longer periods to Cuernavaca, where he fathered his only child by a gardener's daughter, while Carlota sought solace with the remaining imperial guard officers. Oblivious to public opinion and common sense, they decided to stay in Mexico, and Carlota returned to Europe only to beg for support. Arriving in Rome, she burst into the Vatican on the verge of madness and refused to leave (making her the only woman to spend a night there). Meanwhile, Maximilian had retreated to the city of Queretaro, where he hoped to find loyalty, but instead was besieged, captured, and tried.

He was court-martialed as a traitor to Mexico, and was handed the death sentence by Benito Juárez, the former President of Mexico who had been deposed by the French troops. Maximilian was killed on 19 June 1867. Carlota lived for another sixty years, insane, and claiming to be Empress of Mexico.

Today, there is little trace of the doomed couple, except for the Paseo de la Reforma in Mexico City. Carlota had ordered this broad boulevard to be built as a reminder of Europe for her homesick husband.

---

110 Plaza San Jacinto This pretty plaza in the heart of the former village of San Angel is part of the great metropolis but still gives a strong flavor of small-town Spanish Mexico: cobblestone streets, an enchanting little church (one of the most sought-after in the city for weddings), and imposing Spanish mansions. The best day to visit is Saturday, particularly for the famous market which fills both the plaza and surrounding streets. ♦ Bounded by Hidalgo Juárez and Madero, and Dr. Galvez and Miramon

At Plaza San Jacinto:

Bazar del Sábado On Saturday mornings, artists and artisans set up their work in and around the square and the colonial house that housed the original bazaar. Soon the square is filled with people buying, bartering, haggling, selling, and browsing. There are fantastic wooden animals from Oaxaca, textiles from Guatemala, glass and ceramics from Guadalajara, Otomí embroideries, brightly colored wooden fish, a rainbow of beads, and every imaginable Mexican craft. Although prices are generally more expensive than in other markets, the choice is more refined, with little glitz and a great deal of artistry. ♦ Sa. East side of plaza

Bazar del Sábado Restaurant ★★★$ Flowers fill the central fountain in the market's courtyard restaurant, where exhausted shoppers refuel themselves at the all-day buffet-brunch with freshly squeezed fruit juices, eggs in spicy sauces, sweet breads, stuffed chilies, and tropical fruits. Marimbas play in the background, children frolic by the fountain, and the overall impression is one of a fanciful fiesta. ♦ Mexican ♦ Sa brunch. Plaza San Jacinto (between Dr. Galvez and Miramon)

La Casona del Elefante ★★$$ On Saturday morning get one of the outside tables at this northern Indian restaurant that overlooks the plaza, and while away the hours people watching. The menu includes hot curries and *lassi* (yogurt drinks), as well as an excellent vegetarian platter that has a little bit of everything and is more than enough for two people. ♦ Indian ♦ M-Sa lunch and dinner; Su lunch. Plaza San Jacinto 9 (between Dr. Galvez and Miramon). 5485238

Fonda San Angel ★★$$ More of an evening spot, this place offers chicken in pumpkin-seed sauce, shrimp stewed with roquefort, and chili peppers stuffed with Oaxacan cheese. ♦ Mexican ♦ M-Sa breakfast, lunch, and dinner; Su breakfast and lunch. Plaza San Jacinto 3 (between Dr. Galvez and Miramon). 5487568

FONDA SAN ANGEL

111 Le Petit Cluny ★★★$$ With not only the best baguettes and chocolate-filled croissants around, but the most delicious homemade pastas with pesto, carbonara, and *arrabiata* (spicy tomato) sauces, this small and busy restaurant is deservedly popular. The adjacent bakery keeps the same hours, so don't forget to buy the next morning's croissants after dinner. ♦ Italian ♦ Daily breakfast, lunch, and dinner. La Paz 58-14 (between Av Insurgentes Sur and Revolución). 5489135.

112 Los Irabien ★★★$$$ Supremely elegant, this is one of the most exclusive restaurants in the south of the city, catering to a yuppie crowd that gathers for power breakfasts, business lunches, or intimate dinners. The decor is seriously upmarket, with Mr. Irabien's superb art collection hanging on the dark blue walls. The menu itself ranges from prime rib to trout filled with salmon and served with a champagne sauce, as well as such Mexican innovations as red snapper topped with squash flowers. Between courses, servings of lemon sorbet keep the palate fresh. ♦ International ♦ M-Sa breakfast, lunch, and dinner; Su breakfast and lunch. Reservations recommended. Jacket and tie required. La Paz 45 (between Av Insurgentes Sur and Revolución). 6600876

113 La Carreta On one block, there are not only many great restaurants and a small branch of the state-run crafts shop, **FONART**, but also this cavernous shop. Alongside some junk, this pack rat's nest has many real jewels of Mexican work, including Pueblan ceramics, bark paintings, Oaxacan fantasy animals, and reproductions of pre-Hispanic sculptures in jade, onyx, and obsidian. ♦ M-Sa. Av Insurgentes Sur 1105 (at La Paz). 5482475

114 Nalanda Libros Classical music plays in the background in this serene bookshop, where crystals and tarot cards are displayed among texts on mysticism, astrology, and religion. The clerks and customers are good sources for referrals to everything from vegetarian restaurants to acupuncturists. ♦ Daily. Av Centenario 16 (at Francisco Sosa). 5547522

115 Francisco Sosa The most charming street in the city, it runs from Avenida Universidad, past several beautiful colonial houses, to Plaza Santa Catarina and on down to Coyoacán's two main squares. Walk its length for an evocative taste of past and present glories. The **Italian Consulate** is here, as are the *talleres* (workshops), where classes in dance, painting, and sculpture are taught all day. If it's open, stop in at **Viveros de Coyoacán,** a plant nursery and park—it's a pleasant place for a stroll. ♦ Universidad to the Jardín Centenario

On Francisco Sosa:

Las Lupitas ★★$ *The* traditional neighborhood place with good, cheap, homey food, particularly the excellent chili-and-cheese soup, plus the best breakfasts in Coyoacán. The setting may be low-key, but the atmosphere is fun and friendly; you'll stand out as a newcomer, but will be swiftly initiated. ♦ Mexican ♦ M-Sa breakfast, lunch, and dinner. Jardín Sta. Catarina. 5542875

 Plaza Santa Catarina A bust of writer Francisco Sosa, for whom the street is named, sits in this small square, one of the prettiest in the city. ♦ Melchor Ocampo

Los Geranios ★★$$ Ideally situated on Francisco Sosa as it meets the plaza, with tables both outdoors and in, this restaurant is perennially popular with the Coyoacán crowd of regulars. The owner spends his summers in Italy, and his menu ranges from fresh pastas or mozzarella and tomato salad to *carne à la tampiqueña* (a huge plate of thinly grilled meat with guacamole, beans, and rice). Steak lovers must taste the specialty, the superb *puntas de filete* (beef tips in gravy). While it's packed all day Saturday and Sunday, you never have to wait long for a table. The only major drawback is sitting on the most uncomfortable seats in town. ♦ Mexican/Italian ♦ Daily breakfast, lunch, and dinner. Francisco Sosa 19 (at Jardín Centenario). 5544745

116 Café El Parnaso ★★★$ For many people, this is the heart and soul of Coyoacán. It's right in the middle of the twin plazas of **Jardín Centenario** and Plaza Hidalgo in front of the church, and has ringside seats for the weekend mayhem. Both a bookshop and a cafe, it is a gathering place for polemical, political discussions, posturings, posings, and good plain gossip. Sipping a cappuccino while reading the left-of-center newspaper *La Jornada* is de rigueur.

The bookshop carries mostly Spanish-language titles by all the large and small Latin American and Spanish publishing houses, as well as art books in English and Spanish, small-press magazines, posters, postcards, and attractive diaries. With an enormous range of titles crammed into one small room, you need time and patience to find what you want. ♦ Cafe ♦ Daily breakfast, lunch, and dinner. Felipe Carrillo Puerto 2 and 6 (between Francisco Sosa and Belisario Domínguez, across from Jardín Centenario). 5542225

117 El Hijo del Cuervo ★★$$ In Mexico City it isn't often that you find a good drinking place that isn't a male-only cantina, is lively and good-humored every night of the week, and knows how to serve drinks properly. This spot is all those and more. Often full to overflowing with the cool, the hip, and the trendy, it's a great place to meet, chat, drink, and eat *botanas* (appetizers). ♦ Tu-Su. Jardín Centenario 17 (at Francisco Sosa). 6585306

Restaurants/Clubs: Red **Hotels:** Blue
Shops/ ♥ Outdoors: Green **Sights/Culture:** Black

118 Museo de Culturas Populares (Museum of Popular Culture) Close to Coyoacán's main square, this museum concentrates on popular culture, with exhibits ranging from soap operas to the cults of *maize* (corn) and the Day of the Dead, or from the Mexican fascination for *lucha libre* (masked wrestling) to the history of the radio in Mexico. The temporary exhibitions are always imaginative, well designed, fun, and thought-provoking, even though the museum itself is badly underfunded and constantly having to justify its existence to survive. ♦ Admission. Daily. Hidalgo 289 (between Allende and Abasolo). 5548968, 5548848

119 Casa de Frida Kahlo (Frida Kahlo's House) The cornflower-blue house where Frida Kahlo was born and lived most of her life is on the quiet, residential side of Coyoacán. Filled with memorabilia of her life as a child, a young woman, wife of Diego Rivera, and artist, it includes family photographs, her own self-portraits, fractions of her journals, and letters. There is a small collection of paintings by friends and the cubist group Rivera knew in Paris, as well as pre-Hispanic figurines and the round-bellied fertility goddesses that she was obsessed with (Frida was never able to have children and suffered several miscarriages trying). The couple's studio and library is on the upper floor, as is Frida's box bed, complete with a mirrored ceiling that helped her paint herself during the long months she spent bedridden. (For more on Kahlo, see "Frida Fervor" on page 179.) Be forewarned: Visitors are no longer allowed to take photographs inside the house, and the set admission hours are not always followed. ♦ Admission. Tu-Su. Londres 247 (at Allende). 5545999

120 Museo Leon Trotsky This biographical museum is in the house where the exiled Communist spent the last years of his life. He and his wife lived under constant fear of attack: Once the house was blasted with machine-gun bullets by the Stalinist painter David Alfaro Siqueiros (the holes still scar the walls of the bedroom), and Trotsky escaped only because he was feeding his pet rabbits in the garden. Then on 20 August 1945, a Catalan friend of his secretary asked for some help with a political piece, and, once in Trotsky's study, brutally stabbed him to death with an ice pick as he was reading.

The house, complete with gun turrets, high walls, thick metal-plated doors, and shuttered windows, has been kept much as it was (even the rabbit hutches are in place, but a tourist stole the infamous ice pick). There are photos and exhibits of every stage of his life, including the short Mexican chapter in which he was a friend of the surrealist André Breton and the Riveras (and supposedly a onetime lover of Frida). In every photo he appears as a shortsighted, bespectacled, kind-looking man, and certainly not the figure of terror he was to the Stalinists, who sent assassins all around the world to kill him and his political philosophies. The house is not always open during the hours posted outside; mornings seem to be the most opportune time to visit. ♦ Admission. Tu-F (closed at midday); Sa-Su. Río Churubusco 410 (at Viena). 6588732

121 Ciudad Universitaria (University City) This is the home of the 800-acre Universidad Nacional Autónoma de Mexico (UNAM). The original university, which dates back to 1551—making it the oldest in the Western Hemisphere—was previously located in the heart of the Centro Histórico until it was moved to this specially designed campus in the 1950s. Several architects and artists worked on the project, trying to integrate the surrounding volcanic rock with the needs of a vast student population, now numbering roughly 300,000. The result is a flamboyant, dynamic collection of modern architecture that incorporates lively mosaics and murals by some of Mexico's top artists. ♦ Bounded by Av Insurgentes Sur and Av Antonio Delfin Madrigal, and Av Universidad and Periférico; take metro *Line 3* to the Universidad stop. For information on university events, call 6581111, 5259380

At Ciudad Universitaria:

Centro Cultural Universitario (University Cultural Center) The campus's arts-and-performance complex provides culture-hungry students with inexpensive yet highly professional concert halls, art cinemas, exhibition spaces, a sculpture garden, and a cafe. To find out what's going on, check listings in the weekly magazine *Tiempo Libre,* which comes out each Thursday, and has listings in English. ♦ Circuito Escolar (the southeast edge of the campus)

Biblioteca (Library) Architect **Juan O'Gorman** used naturally colored tiles to create an amazing 10-story mosaic mural that wraps around the facade of the library, re-creating the course of Mexican history through depictions of many of its leading characters. ♦ Northwest side of the campus (between Circuito Escolar and Av Universidad)

Estadio Olimpico (Olympic Stadium) Artist Diego Rivera contributed to the construction of the university by fashioning a mosaic mural (unfinished) of polychromatic stones above the entrance to one of the world's largest stadiums, which was the venue for the 1968 Summer Olympics. ♦ Av Insurgentes Sur (at Av Ciudad Universitaria)

Rectoría (Rectory) Avant-garde artist David Alfaro Siqueiros played with colored glass on the exterior of this building and came up with an extraordinary collection of mosaic murals loosely dedicated to the importance of universities and education for the people of Mexico. ♦ Circuito Escolar (southeast side of campus)

122 Museo Anahuacalli As Diego Rivera's private gathering of pre-Hispanic pieces grew, he decided to build a special museum that he could bequeath to Mexico to keep his collection intact. The result is this extraordinary volcanic-stone pyramid, which provides a somber background for the lively and ingenious pieces, most of which originate from the western states of Colima, Jalisco, and Nayarit. He used part of the building as a studio, and his easel is still in place, holding the work that was in progress when he died. ♦ Admission. Tu-Su; closed at midday. Calle de Museo (at Moctezuma). 6772984

123 Xochimilco The name means "place of flowers" in the Nahuatl language, and today it's the nursery garden of Mexico City, with flower and plant markets abloom everywhere. At Christmastime, it fills with the blood-red *noche buena* (poinsettia), the traditional Christmas flower that is found in every home in the city. Save your visit for a Sunday, when the surrounding canals fill with families. Boats glide along the water and hook up with other watercraft offering mariachi music, food, and drink. Contamination of the waterways has been a great concern for the last decade or so, but the local council has introduced a massive clean-up scheme, and the canals are well on their way to recovery. It's the only place that the waterways and canals that once crisscrossed the ancient Aztec city of Tenochtitlán are still visible and in use. ♦ Difficult to get to, as it lies 24 kilometers (15 miles) southeast of the Centro Histórico, it is worth considering a tour (see **Grey Line Tours,** page 162) or take the metro south on *Line 2* to Taxquena and from there a bus southbound on Calzada Tlalpan.

Bests

Juan Diego Gallardo
Man-about-Town

Eating *gusanos de maguey* (cactus worms) and *filete chemita* (grilled steak) on the **Bellinghausen** restaurant patio.

Margaritas at **San Angel Inn.**

A late lunch at **Bar L'Opera.**

Shopping for silver wedding presents at **Tané.**

Strolling around **Plaza Santo Domingo** and the **Palace of the Inquisition.**

Going to **Plaza Garibaldi** at 3AM to drink tequila and listen to mariachis.

Walking through **Chapultepec Park** and the **Palace** buying goodies from vendors along the way.

A tour of the **Museo Franz Mayer,** followed by a restorative in **El Patio** restaurant.

The foie gras and the *confit de canard* at the **Champs-Elysées** on **Reforma.** Tables by the windows are best.

A jai-alai match followed by dinner at **Prendes** in the **Frónton México.**

Visiting the courtyard of **Iturbide's Palace** in the **Historic Center.**

Shelton Wiseman
Chef, La Place Cooking School

Take Flamenco classes at **Los Talleres** in **Coyoacán.**

Wander around the **Mercado San Juan,** talking with the vendors and tasting exotic fruits, then go to my favorite **Tacos al Pastor** stand (on Ayuntamiento next to **Europa**) for five tacos and an ice-cold Jamaica juice.

Walk through the maze of **Coyoacán** streets and alleyways that are barely wide enough for a car.

Stroll along **Avenida La Paz** and buy the best French bread and croissants in Mexico at **Le Petit Cluny.** Browse through **FONART** and **La Carreta** before hitting **Sanborn's** for a *Tiempo Libre* magazine that lists what's playing at the **Cineteca.**

Alain Giberstein
Photographer, Mexico City

Being present at **quinceñeras** (15th birthday parties) in the popular dance halls to see the girls come down the stairs in all their finery and waltz.

The **chiles en nogada** (chilies stuffed with meat, dressed in walnut sauce, and decorated with parsley and pomegranate seeds) between August and October in restaurants around the city.

A Sunday morning cappuccino on the **Museo Franz Mayer** patio.

Michael J. Zamba
Editor, *Insight,* Mexico City

Plaza Garibaldi—for a night of Mariachi music, excited tourists, and good cheer.

Coyoacán—great colonial charm and good restaurants. Many famous people have lived here, including Diego Rivera and Leon Trotsky.

Templo Mayor—this modern museum pays tribute to the temple of the once mighty Aztec empire.

Bazar Sábado—a Saturday in **San Angel's** main square. Start with breakfast, then spend the day shopping for arts and crafts.

Mexico City's **Alameda Park** on the weekend; there's cleaner air, less traffic and more room for fun.

In AD 600, Teotihuacán, near Mexico City, was the most highly urbanized center in the Western Hemisphere.

History

12,000 BC—Hunters track down the woolly mammoth and other large beasts in central Mexico.

7,000-2,000 BC—The nomadic hunters begin farming crops of corn, beans, and squash.

4,500 BC—Primitive corn is grown and becomes a major dietary staple.

1,500 BC—The Olmec civilization, the most advanced in Mesoamerica during this period, is considered the Mother of Mexican culture and begins to spread throughout the land.

1,200 BC—The Olmec civilization is at its peak.

800-400 BC— **La Venta,** a major Olmec worship center, is built near Veracruz on the gulf coast.

500 BC—After the decline of the Olmec, the Zapotec emerge and prosper. They are the most dominant culture at this time and build great ceremonial centers in Oaxaca.

100 BC—Teotihuacán, the first major city in the Americas, is established. It will reign as Mexico's most powerful settlement for the next six centuries.

AD 300—The Maya are at their cultural peak, as are other civilizations throughout Mexico; the Maya's work in art, astronomy, and architecture rivals similar projects around the world.

600—Teotihuacán is attacked by unknown tribes, and the city begins declining.

700—Teotihuacán is completely deserted.

900—The Toltec, a culture dominant in the region north of Mexico City, begin waging wars. They overtake other societies, leaving an imprint of their culture, which emphasizes military action and conquest. War becomes commonplace, as does human sacrifice.

1100—The Maya culture, portraying Toltec influences, spreads throughout the Yucatán Peninsula. Their civilization flourishes, and they make many advances in art and science.

1300-1400—The Aztec come to prominence and build Tenochtitlán, their grand capital city, on Lake Texcoco in the valley of Mexico.

1492—As Christopher Columbus enters the New World, the Aztec Empire continues to grow.

1519—On a quest for slaves, Hernán Cortés and 600 soldiers land on the coast of Veracruz. They begin exploring and conquering Mexico.

1521—Cortés defeats the Aztec. Emperor Cuauhtemoc is executed, and Tenochtitlán falls after three months of fighting.

1522—The Franciscans arrive in Mexico with papal sanction.

1535—Spain's first viceroy lands, establishing a basic form of government.

1541—The Yucatán Peninsula is settled by the Spaniards.

1547—Cortés dies.

1549—Friar Diego de Landa arrives. To rid the land of evil, he burned what he didn't understand, destroying the history of the Maya.

1563—Landa, charged with despotic mismanagement, is imprisoned in Spain and replaced with the humanitarian Bishop Toral.

1805—Mexico is home to one archbishop, eight bishops, 1,703 parishes, and 254 convents.

1810—Father Miguel Hidalgo y Costilla declares independence from Spain, initiating a war. Creoles, Indians, and mestizos rise up in revolt in response to Hidalgo's *Grito de Dolores* (cry for freedom), named after the town of Dolores, where he was a pastor.

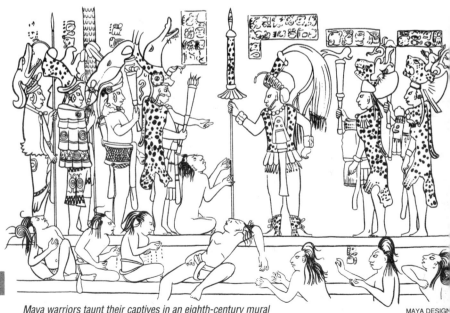

Maya warriors taunt their captives in an eighth-century mural discovered in Bonampak in the state of Chiapas.

MAYA DESIGN

1811—Hidalgo is executed. José Morelos y Pavón takes command of the revolution.

1815—Morelos is captured and executed by order of the Congress of Chilpancingo, the coalition he once sponsored to write a Declaration of Independence from Spain.

1821—Agustín de Iturbide, a colonel in the Spanish forces and a revolutionary leader, denounces the colonial government and formally pronounces independence. Spain recognizes the independence of Mexico with the Treaty of Córdoba.

1822—Iturbide manipulates the temporary Mexican Congress and public into proclaiming him Emperor Agustín I of Mexico, then abdicates nine months later after a short, chaotic period of misrule. A new constitution is drawn up and an elderly revolutionary general, who adopts the name Guadalupe Victoria, becomes Mexico's first president.

1828—Slavery of the various Indian groups, which began under the conquistadores, is abolished by Mexico's independent government.

1833—General Antonio López de Santa Anna, who had helped overthrow Emperor Augustín and had repelled Spanish attempts to reconquer Mexico, becomes the wily and unscrupulous president/dictator.

1835—In what is now Texas, a small group of North Americans intent on forming a slave state tries to gain independence from Mexico. Santa Anna fights back by leading an attack on the Alamo mission in San Antonio, Texas, where 150 Northerners are killed. In the following months, Mexican troops overrun Texas.

1836—Sam Houston's army defeats Santa Anna's troops at the Battle of San Jacinto, and Santa Anna signs the treaty making Texas a republic. However, the Mexican government refuses to recognize the treaty, and the issue is left unsettled.

1844—Santa Anna is driven into exile in Havana.

1845—The United States agrees to annex Texas, and the Mexican minister calls the action equivalent to a declaration of war. US troops under General Zachary Taylor enter disputed territory north of the Río Grande.

1846—The United States declares war on Mexico.

1847—US General Winfield Scott captures Veracruz with a force of 10,000 men, blocking Mexico's most important port.

1848—The Treaty of Hidalgo is ratified by the US Senate. Mexico cedes more than half of its territory, including Texas, California, and New Mexico, to the US for $15 million.

1853—Santa Anna returns from exile to become Mexico's dictator ("His Most Serene Highness").

1854—Santa Anna sells Arizona's Mesilla Valley to the United States for $10 million.

1855—During the War of Reform, Santa Anna is forced to leave Mexico. Moderate and liberal politicians control the government, passing a controversial law aimed at redistributing the vast landholdings of the church and another abolishing special privileges of the church and army. Benito Juárez, the former governor of his native state of Oaxaca, assumes the presidency and becomes Mexico's first Indian head of state.

1857—The new constitution promises a democratic representative government; freedom of speech, press, and religion; free education; and separation of church and state. A violent conservative reaction throws the country into civil war, unseating President Juárez and driving the liberal government from the capital.

1860—The last conservative armies are defeated in the War of Reform.

1861—Juárez returns to the capital and attempts to rebuild Mexico's devastated economy by declaring a moratorium on government debts; conservative reaction to this plan once again forces the leader into exile.

1862—After half a century of political chaos, during which time Mexican conservatives had lobbied in Europe for a puppet monarchy, the French land in Veracruz. Napoléon III's army marches inland to subjugate Mexico. The invading French army is repulsed in Puebla on 5 May by a poorly armed but inspired corps of about 5,000 (the event is commemorated annually with the Cinco de Mayo celebration). In September a renewed assault by the French succeeds in driving Juárez from the capital.

1864—Archduke Ferdinand Maximilian Joseph, of Hapsburg, is chosen to rule Mexico. He accepts the crown as Emperor Maximilian I, under the protection of Napoléon III, and arrives in Mexico with his wife, Carlota.

1867—Under international pressure to support an independent government in Mexico, Napoléon pulls his troops out of the country. Maximilian makes a stand at Querétaro; three months later he surrenders and is executed along with two officers. Juárez returns as president and lives in Mexico City, which is once again in liberal hands.

1872—After uniting the people of Mexico and successfully implementing reforms stated in the Constitution of 1857, Juárez dies of a heart attack.

1876—Porfirio Díaz, who had served as a guerilla fighter for liberals during the War of Reform and distinguished himself against the French, leads a rebellion and gains the presidency. He serves for 34 years (except for a four-year period beginning in 1880, when he allows a friend to take over). His term is essentially a dictatorship, since re-elections aren't permitted. This period is characterized by economic success and stability, but at the price of oppression and poverty for a large segment of the population.

1902—Quintana Roo adopts its present name after being segregated from the state of Yucatán and is now under the direct control of the President of the Republic.

1911—Porfirio Díaz retires to Paris. Francisco I. Madero, son of a wealthy landowner, becomes president in Mexico's first public election. Emiliano Zapata, Pascual Orozco, and Francisco "Pancho" Villa question Madero's ability to lead. A century after the war against Spain, a revolution breaks out again.

1913—Conservatives, with the assistance of the US ambassador to Mexico, plot to bring down the

Madero government and install Victoriano Huerta as president.

Madero and his vice president are shot. During Huerta's violent, 17-month dictatorship, many of his opponents are murdered or jailed. Revolutionary leaders garner armies and begin to raid and occupy properties.

1914—Huerta flees to the United States as revolutionary forces led by Alvaro Obregón and Venustiano Carranza enter Mexico City. Fighting breaks out amid the different liberal factions.

1917—A new constitution is written and reconstruction begins.

1920—The Carranza administration ends after three weak years. Carranza flees north with five million pesos in government funds, and is murdered in his sleep by one of his officers.

The presidency of Obregón marks the beginning of Mexico's stabilization. A series of handpicked successors to Obregón slowly implement dicta of the Constitution of 1917.

Great advances are made in education and culture. Politics blends with art in the murals of Diego Rivera, José Clemente Orozco, David Alfaro Siqueiros, and other artists commissioned by the education minister, José Vasconcelos.

1923—Pancho Villa is assassinated.

1926—Obregón's successor, Plutarco Elías Calles, closes all religious schools, which had been allowed despite being prohibited in the constitution. After a hundred priests and nuns are deported, the priesthood goes on strike for three years.

1934—President Lázaro Cárdenas, who was elected after Calles's term ended, begins a period of reform, including redistributing more land to peasants than had been apportioned in the preceding century. Many public works are constructed, government-sponsored farming operations are initiated, and the oil industry is nationalized. The administration gains the support of soldiers by raising their pay, thereby breaking down the traditional support that existed between the military and the conservative party.

1940—Conservative Manuel Avila Camacho, a Cárdenas protégé, becomes president and continues the policies initiated by his predecessor. An era of political stability continues with successive elections of presidents from the same political party, *Partido Revolucionario Institucional (PRI)*.

1946—Miguel Alemán becomes president. Among his many achievements is the construction of **University City.**

1952—Adolfo Ruiz Cortines becomes president.

1955—Women gain the right to vote.

1958—Adolfo López Mateos becomes president.

1964—Gustavo Díaz Ordaz becomes president.

1968—The **Summer Olympics** are held in Mexico City. Shortly before the games begin, 6,000 university students and their supporters assemble at the Plaza de las Tres Culturas near the **Estadio Olimpico** (Olympic Stadium) to protest social conditions that have led to an uneven distribution of wealth. More than 10,000 armed soldiers break up the demonstration; in the ensuing melee 50 people are killed, 500 wounded, and 1,500 arrested.

1970—Luis Echeverría Alvarez becomes president.

1974—Baja California Sur and Quintana Roo achieve statehood. The federal government establishes the **National Foundation for Tourism Development (FONATUR),** an agency devoted to expanding Mexico's tourism industry.

1976—José López Portillo becomes president.

1982—Miguel de la Madrid becomes president.

The peso is devalued and unemployment grows, creating an economic panic.

1985—On 19 and 20 September, an earthquake and several aftershocks destroy parts of Mexico City, killing thousands of people and causing an estimated $4 billion in property damage.

1988—In a bitterly debated election, Carlos Salinas de Gortari becomes president with the smallest margin of votes for the PRI (50.3 percent) ever recorded.

The systematic expansion of tourist facilities continues; *maquiladores* (foreign assembly plants) proliferate along the Mexico-US border; foreign investment is encouraged and solicited.

1991—The United States, Canada, and Mexico begin negotiations for a free-trade agreement, which would facilitate the exchange of goods and services among the three countries.

1991—A huge gas explosion in Guadalajara kills 190 people and injures hundreds of others.

1993—NAFTA (North American Free Trade Agreement) is ratified by the US Congress, creating a new economic partnership between Mexico, the United States, and Canada.

1994—The Zapatista Army for National Liberation invades the colonial city of San Cristóbal de las Casas in the southern state of Chiapas. Several towns within the state are briefly occupied by the rebel group protesting economic and social conditions in the state. The Mexican Army drives the rebels from San Cristóbal and negotiations begin between the Zapatistas and the federal government.

1994—Luis Donaldo Colosio, PRI presidential candidate, is assassinated at a political rally in Tijuana.

Moctezuma (1466-1520), Mexico's last Aztec emperor, must have believed that chilies pack a lot of power. He started each day by drinking a concoction of chocolate and hot chilies.

Spaniards who were born in Spain used to be called *gachupínes;* those born in New Spain were known as creoles; and people of mixed Spanish and Mexican heritage were called mestizos. By the 18th century, half of Mexico's population was mestizo and creole.

Index

Hotel Ratings

Each destination's hotels are listed alphabetically in the following chapter indexes. The hotels are also indexed according to their price ratings. The dollar signs reflect general price-range relationships between other hotels in the area; they do not represent specific rates.

$$$$	Big Bucks
$$$	Expensive
$$	Reasonable
$	The Price is Right

History **190**

Ixtapa/Zihuatanejo 60-73

Index

Mexico City Hotels

Mexico City Restaurants

Puerto Vallarta 42-53

Index

Puerto Vallarta Hotels

$$$$

$$$

$$

$

Puerto Vallarta Restaurants

★★★★

★★★

★★

★

The Quintana Roo Coast 142-157

The Quintana Roo Coast Hotels

The Quintana Roo Coast Restaurants

Uxmal 100-105

Uxmal Hotels

Yucatan Peninsula 86

Credits

Writer and Project Editor
Maribeth Mellin

Researcher
Deborah Ruiz

Writers (Previous Edition)
Chicki Mallan
Charlotte Thompson

ACCESS®PRESS

Editorial Director
Lois Spritzer

Managing Editor
Laura L. Brengelman

Senior Editor
Beth Schlau

Associate Editors
Kathryn Clark
Kathleen Kent

Contributing Editors
Susan Cutter Snyder
Joanna Wissinger

Map Editor
Karen Decker

Assistant Map Editor
Susan Charles

*Manager of Design
and Production*
Cherylonda Fitzgerald

Senior Designer
Claudia Goulette

Designers
Barbara J. Bahning Chin
Carrē Furukawa

Map Designer
Michael Blum

*Manager, Electronic
Publishing*
John Day

Printing and Otabind
WEBCOM Limited

*Acknowledgments
(Special Thanks)*
Jim Andrews
**Edwina Arnold,
Club Med**
Fernando Barbachano
Arnold Bilgore

**Cozumel Hotel
Association**
Isauro Cruz
Dover Press
**Edelman Worldwide
Public Relations**
Fiesta Americana Hotels
Gary L. Grimaud
Bill Horn
Hyatt Hotels
**Gilberto Limon de
la Rocha**
François Escutia Luca
Mayaland Tours
Teresa Borge Mazur
Julie Mendez
**Mexican Government
Tourism Office**
Laurence Mills
Cecilia Morfin
Javier Rivas
Linda Schramm
Pancho Shiell
Turquoise Reef Resorts
**Carlos Velaquez,
Mexico City Tourism
Department**
Ron Warren

Special thanks to the University
of Oklahoma Press for permission
to use drawings from their publi-
cation, *Maya Cities*, by George F.
Andrews (copyright 1975).

*In ancient Mexico, clay
stamps were often used
to create designs on pot-
tery, cloth, skin, and paper.
Animals were a common
motif, including those
pictured here.*

Printed in Canada